CROSS-BORDER CRIME INROADS ON INTEGRITY IN EUROPE

CROSS-BORDER CRIME INROADS ON INTEGRITY IN EUROPE

Petrus C. van Duyne
Georgios A. Antonopoulos
Jackie Harvey
Almir Maljevic
Tom Vander Beken
Klaus von Lampe
(eds.)

Cross-border crime inroads on integrity in Europe

Petrus C. van Duyne, Georgios A. Antonopoulos, Jackie Harvey, Almir Maljevic, Tom Vander Beken, Klaus von Lampe (eds.) Wolf Legal Publishers (WLP), 2010

ISBN: 978-90-5850-577-4

This volume is based on the presentations of the authors at the eleventh Crossborder Crime Colloquium, hosted 26-27 November 2009 by Gent University in Belgium.

This project was supported by:
Tilburg University (the Netherlands)
Heuni (Finland)
Gent University (Belgium)
Teesside University (UK)

The Cross-Border Crime Colloquium is an annual event since 1999. It brings together experts on international organised (economic) crime to discuss the latest developments in empirical research, legislation and law enforcement, with a special geographical focus on Western, Central, and Eastern Europe. The Colloquia aim at building bridges in three respects: between East and West Europe, between scholars and practitioners, and between old and young. The Cross-border Crime Colloquium, so far, has been organised eleven times:

2009 Gent, Belgium
2008 Belgrade, Serbia
2007 Prague, Czech Republic
2006 Tallinn, Estonia
2005 Sarajevo, Bosnia and Herzegovina
2004 Berlin, Germany
2003 Ainring, Germany
2002 Ljubljana, Slovenia
2001 Bratislava, Slovakia
2000 Budapest, Hungary
1999 Prague, Czech Republic

Copies can be ordered at
Wolf Legal Publishers (WLP)
P.O. Box 31051
6503 CB Nijmegen
The Netherlands
Tel: +31 24 355 19 04
www.wolfpublishers.com
E-Mail: sales@wolfpublishers.nl
www.wolfpublishers.nl

Cover design: Maarten van Dijck

Cross-border crime inroads on integrity in Europe

Petrus C. van Duyne

Introduction: crime-money, corruption and the state 1

Liliya Gelemerova

Fighting foreign bribery: the stick or the carrot? 17

Minna Viuhko, Martti Lehti, and Kauko Aromaa

Rules of the Game: A qualitative study of corruption on the Finnish-Russian border 41

Gudrun Vande Walle and Arne Dormaels

The first step to a tailor-made anti-corruption policy for public services: The case of the Flemish customs office 67

Petrus C. van Duyne, Elena Stocco, Miroslava Milenović, Milena Todorova

Searching for contours of the anti-corruption policy in Serbia 89

Brendan J. Quirke,

Croatia: Fighting EU Fraud: a case of work in progress? 123

Antoinette Verhage

The holy grail of money laundering statistics: Input and outcome of the Belgian AML system 143

Daniel Vesterhav

Measures against money laundering in Sweden: The role of the private sector 169

Johanna Skinnari

The financial management of drug crime in Sweden 189

Johanna Skinnari and Lars Korsell

Swedish international casinos: A nest of organised crime or just a place for ordinary tax cheaters? 217

Nicholas Dorn

Ponzi finance and state capture: The crisis of financial market regulation 235

Jon Spencer and Rose Broad
Lifting the veil on SOCA and the UKHTC: Policymaking responses to organised crime 261

Georgios Papanicolaou and Georgios A. Antonopoulos
'Organised crime' and productive illegal labour: The economic significance of human smuggling and trafficking in Greece 277

Stefano Caneppele and Francesco Calderoni
Extortion rackets in Europe: an exploratory comparative study 309

Klaus von Lampe
Situational Prevention of 'Organised Crime': Preventing phantom conceptions with phantom means? 337

Severin Glaser
Legal Protection against OLAF: The European fraud watch dog 361

List of contributors

Georgios Antanopoulos

Senior Lecturer in Criminology at Teesside University, UK

Kauko Aromaa

Kauko Aromaa is the director of Heuni, Helsinki

Rose Broad

Research Assistant, University of Manchester

Francesco Calderoni

Researcher at the Università Cattolica di Milano & TRANSCRIME

Stefano Caneppele

Researcher at the Università Cattolica di Milano & TRANSCRIME

Arne Dormaels

Assistant at University College Ghent, Faculty of Public & Business Administration

Nicholas Dorn

Professor of International Safety and Governance, Department of Criminology, Erasmus School of Law, Erasmus University, Rotterdam

Petrus C. van Duyne

Professor of Empirical Penal Law at Tilburg University, the Netherlands

Liliya Gelemerova

Doctoral (PhD) student at Tilburg University and Senior Investigator at Nardello & C0., London

Severin Glaser

Research assistant at the Institute for Austrian and European Economic Criminal Law, Vienna University of Economics and Business

Klaus von Lampe

Assistant Professor at John Jay College of Criminal Justice, New York, Department of Law, Police Science and Criminal Justice Administration

Martti Lehti

Researcher at the National Research Institute of Legl Policy, Finland

Miroslava Milenović

Certified fraud examiner and forensic accountant

Georgios Papanicolaou

Senior Lecturer in Criminology at Teesside University

Brendan J. Quirke

Senior Lecturer in Accounting & Finance at Liverpool John Moores University, UK

Johanna Skinnari

Researcher at the Swedish National Council of Crime Prevention

Jon Spencer

Director of the Anglo-Baltic Criminological Research Unit, University of Manchester

Elena Stocco

Senior researcher and Head Operations in Corruptio Research Project-Serbia

Milena Todorova

Consultant and researcher in the Corruption Research Project-Serbia

Minna Viuhko

Researcher at HEUNI, Helsinki

Antoinette Verhage

Assistant at Ghen University, Faculty of Law

Daniel Vesterhav

Researcher at the Swedish National Council for Crime Prevention

Gudrun Vande Walle

Assistant-professor at the University Colleg Ghent, Faculty of Public & Business Administration

(Crime-)money, corruption and the state

Petrus C. van Duyne

An intertwined or unholy trinity?

The 'state' and money have always bedevilled man's mind. Between the two there looms the evil interaction of corruption. Is this an unholy trinity? In history money or its equivalent, gold, has always been disputed just because of its potentially moral corrosion. The Spartans perceived it as threatening their pure life style. So they banned it and replaced it by iron bars, while culturally degrading their society by an autere life-style. The myth of king Midas who turned everything he touched into gold also serves as a warning against the barren nature of gold, while the adoration of the biblical Golden Calf is a symbol of the seductive attraction of material wealth in general, and money in particular, and the related loose morals.

Reflections on the state, its best form or its necessity, used to be critical too. From Plato onwards questions have been raised on what should be the best form of state, without tyranny, greed and corruption. Against a background of corrupt rulers and violent political upheavals, history shows a continuous striving for a virtuous state, with disappointing and often violent outcomes. The causes of such outcomes are inherent in the drive for virtue itself: it leads to totalitarianism. Why? In contrast to gold which has levels of carat and is easy to mix with less noble metals, virtuousness is 'non-dilutable'. One cannot have just half or three-quaters of virtuousness. As a Dutch minister of Internal Affairs once remarked about corruption: "It is like pregnancy: you cannot be a bit pregnant and you cannot be a bit corrupt" (Huberts, 1992). Therefore, this drive tends to be total.

Though there is a compelling logic in this statement, attempts to realise it have not brought much happiness. Zealots of whatever form of pure society more often than not saw dreams and lives end violently. Their list is long, cruel and wide indeed: from religious purists like Jan van Leyden (Anabaptist), ending in a cage of the bishop of Münster (1536) (Klötzer, 1992), to the 'incorruptable' Robespierre who could indulge for only 12 months in his political purist ideas, before he was beheaded himself (1794) (Soboul, 1994). Those who thought mankind should be liberated from the tyranny of the corrupt state and who unfolded the banner of anarchism ended at the gallows too, particularly in the 19th Century Russia (Sievers, 1980). The biggest 'real live experiment' to establish a pure (socialist) society by which the state would become superfluous, lasted almost seventy years and imploded two decades ago after a miserable record of covered failures. Indeed, history does not provide many positive examples to put much trust in moral fundamentalists turned into political purists. It rather proves the price to be paid: total virtue requires total control, which is only feasible in an absolute state. And how many absolute states were without corruption?

Though utopian schemes are considered as something of the past, the 'state' never abandoned its aim of keeping its citizens to the straight and narrow path. Not within a total utopian grand design, but piecemeal, topic by topic, whether it concerns safety or sex, health or property. It adapts pragmatically parts of its criminal law armamentarium to murky markets of 'vice' that are constantly springing up. Vice markets imply that criminal profits are being made. These crime-monies are considered to have an even greater potential to corrupt than is attributed to 'normal' money. Hence, a new control task developed: controlling criminal money management, which is supposed to affect the integrity of the financial system, unleashing a new drive for total control. This has been achieved through a global law enforcement regime (Stessens, 2000).

With this observation we are back at the triangle of (crime-)money, corruption and the state. To increase its control capacity the state invokes another moral principle: transparency. Upholding this principle is not just a concern of single, national jurisdictions: it must have a global effect. This applies not only to the (international) financial system, but to all corners of trade and industry where corruption is looming, whether at home or in transnational transactions.

One may wonder what aspects of society are left unguarded to prevent a sliding down towards moral desintegration. It is a process of encroaching moral control: all for the common good. But what about the state itself permeating and overarching society? Is the state a transparent, 'open book' as well? And if open, is it also readable? Or is the state the 'self-excepting fallacy'?

This volume deals with various sides of this triangle of (crime-)money, corruption and the state. Though one may think the order of the three arbitrary, I think it appropriate to start with discussing the chapters dealing with the subject where vice starts: corruption. Money may be clean, the state may be virtuous, but underneath corruption may eat into both sides.

Facing corruption: global and local

The history of corruption is characterised by bad conscience as well as connivance. Abuse of office and bribery has always been frowned upon, usually silently. This ambiguity allowed the launch of occasional accusations of corruption as a stick to beat a (political) dog. For example, the politician (and philosopher) Francis Bacon, ended his career in disgrace after being found guilty of bribery (1621) in a time when non-corrupt administrations did not exist. As a matter of fact, the nascent public administration was a market of coveted positions (Swart, 1990). Indeed, even in the most abject corrupt state, the concept of the immorality of corruption is not absent.

In the course of the 19th and 20th Centuries this connivance receded, but did not fully disappear. In the past decades exposure of corrupt dealings of politicians or high-level civil servants led to the end of their career if not a prosecution. In Europe, however, this was geographically an uneven development. Whether or not it is another cliché, in the protestant Northern Europe this development was more advanced than in the catholic Southern Europe. However, in the past decade, these Northern countries have witnessed a number of high-level corruption cases in Germany, the UK, the Netherlands and even Norway (Andvik, 1994). But the fact that these cases were exposed can be used to underline this cliché. In Italy exposure appears to have fewer consequences: MPs convicted of corruption (or other crimes) are allowed to retain their seats in Parliament (Stille, 2006).

Nonetheless, these uneasy feelings about corruption remained highly selective: while corruption at home was frowned upon, cross-border corruption by western corporations in other countries was condoned. These cases of bribery were considered necessary for obtaining foreign contracts; they were even tax deductable. In this way 'non-corrupt' western entrepreneurs declared themselves 'forced' to become 'a bit corrupt'. In the chapter of *Liliya Gelemerova* on the crusade against foreign corruption the author discusses this aspect of corruption as well as the way it was addressed forcefully by the USA.

What is the case? During the Cold War, the USA and other western countries supported any corrupt state as long as it was anti-communist. It kept kleptocrats like Mobutu in power for decades (Meredith, 2006). Bribery was also rife in foreign trade. But while a corruption condoning foreign policy continued, at least until the fall of the Wall, foreign trade relations did not escape so easily. In the sequel to the Watergate affair 1975, much evidence of foreign trade related corruption was found. Eventually this led to the Foreign Corrupt Practices Act (1977), which was a milestone of the American internationalisation of a domestic moral concern and policy. This internationalisation was preceded by the worldwide anti-drug policy (Van Duyne and Levi, 2005) and followed by the global anti-laundering policy (Stessens, 2000; Van Duyne *et al.*, 2005; Gelemerova, forthcoming), with which it shares many features.

Of course, there were sound national interests involved: if American companies wanted to avoid becoming outcompeted by foreign corporations the anti-corruption policy should be accepted universally. Ever since this the US government has endeavoured to make other countries accept the same policy, particularly through the US dominated OECD: in 1997 thirty three countries signed the 'OECD Anti-Bribery Convention' promising to make bribery an offence in domestic legislation.

The author describes how the US fight against international corruption turned into a crusade, comparable with the anti-laundering policy. Technically there is also much overlap between the two and a free field of fire for the prosecution: there is no corruption without laundering. In both fields the law has the immense dimension of a trawl net, drawing in whatever small it finds in its way: e.g. operating fully abroad but using a US server or bank account is sufficient for criminal liability in case of 'having attained an illegal advantage'. Another common element is the rule of due diligence, which is imposed in both fields. But they differ in clarity: concerning cross-border corruption the criteria of this rule lack proper precision and transparency. Surveying the case history the author concludes that the industry is left to itself to find out what criteria law enforcement will apply: it dodges its own transparency demands. What applies to potential offenders does not necessarily apply to the state.

As is usual, law in the books and law in action are different things, certainly with trading in remote corners, such as at the border between Russia and Finland. The chapter on corruption in this remote area by *Minna Viuhko, Martti Lehti,* and *Kauko Aromaa* makes clear that the OECD Anti Bribery Convention has little impact here, whether Finland has ratified it or not. At this point other rules prevail: no transport company is able to operate if it does not play along with the 'system' of the Russian Customs. And giving presents implies more than a bottle of vodka: it is a matter of being regularly 'milked' at the customs or interacting at a higher level with the corrupt predators. It is interesting to observe that cognitively there is no 'moral relativism' indeed between the Finns and Russians there appears to be little difference in understanding of the meaning of corruption. But there is a wide difference in acceptability. To the Finnish entrepreneurs bribery in whatever form is unacceptable, but they resign to playing along nevertheless. The Russian interviewees display more ambiguity which must be projected against a background of rampant corruption in the form of a top-down system which has its roots deep in the socialist era (Brovkin, 2003). In terms of own experience, the

Finns said to have to cope with it daily at the Russian border, while Russian interviewees referred in general terms to the widespread corruption in their country but said that they did not have experienced it themselves. Therefore the authors could not penetrate into the details of the corruption *system*. But if there is a system it can be anticipated, which was preferred by the Finish entrepreneurs, allowing them to pay a monthly instead of the unpredictable daily bribery. But who 'owns' the system when the owners deny ownership while those who are plausibly involved never happen to notice anything personally?

Obviously corruption is a troubled water phenomenon, not to be addressed by a one-causal or one-dimensional approach, as the authors *Gudrun Vande Walle* and *Arne Dormaels* elaborate in their chapter about the Belgian Customs Organisation. Besides other explanatory variables which the authors adopt from Gobert and Punch (2003), an important personal variable is the defence mechanism. This may take the form of rationalisations, neutralisation or flat denial, the concrete forms being determined by the surrounding landscape. A 'corruption tariff system' as is operated at the Finnish-Russian border gives little latitude for denial but the individual can evoke 'the system' as excuse. Whether this is the case within the Belgian Custom Organisation is less clear. Here another tension is created because of the intertwinement of two contrasting service attitudes: serving trade and industry by speeding up the handling of custom clearance and serving the public fund by levying the taxes due. This is a working environment which on the one hand, favours economic interests, furthered by pressure and the temptation of presents and favours. On the other hand, it gives cause to public scrutiny which at present is highly sensitive to profiteers. This has to be balanced against the organisational culture within the service itself: the management striving to reach commercially favourable targets, while the control units at ground level daily interact with transporters, balancing different interests. An organisational landscape in which it is not difficult to find self-serving rationalisations. Even if corruption is moderate (compared to the Finnish-Russian situation), there is a strong lid on the basket preventing much evidence coming out.

Knowing and talking about widespread corruption while finding so few actual cases or the 'owners' of the system is not restricted to Russia or Belgium. The researchers *Petrus C. van Duyne*, *Elena Stocco*, *Miroslava Milenović* and *Milena Todorova* report a similar outcome in their chapter on corruption in Serbia: allegedly a country with rampant corruption with an amazing shortage of facts, apart from a few scandals which were difficult to hide. On the other hand, unlike Russia, Serbia is forced to fight corruption if it wants to join the EU family. But this aim intersects with many established corruptive interests like jobs, positions and political power, which are 'owned' as Medieval fiefdoms. Again the question is: Who 'owns' the corrupt system, which in Serbia means: who owns the country? Before 1989 it was the Socialist Party. Now there are many owners: the state looks rather like a kind of old socialist apartment block after privatisation, being split up between a few powerful bidders with impoverished dependent tenants.

This turns the unfolding anti-corruption policy into an up-hill struggle of reformers with other interesting actors causing regular setbacks and delays. The authors capture this in the metaphor of Sisyphus, who had to push a stone up-hill but that rolled down again as soon when it got near the top. This counter reaction is not a matter of street-level bribery, but of strategic, higher level corruption, which has an interest in maintaining an opaque landscape.

Keeping things opaque does not only concern the actors' conduct. As a matter of fact, the authors found the whole situation, but particularly that concerning data management about corruption devoid of basic transparency. Databases which should match failed to do so. But whatever database the authors analysed, the number of convictions for bribery are dismally low. And even if ending in a conviction, the time taken to process the cases was very long: from reporting to sentencing it took on average 3,8 years, usually ending in mild sentencing (often on probation).

The state of corruption with an emphasis of fraud against the EU finances in the neighbouring state of Serbia is described in the chapter about Croatia by *Brendan J. Quirke*. In terms of corruption which accompanied the rise of a new Croatian elite, there are many similarities with Serbia. A combination of former war heroes, criminals and wily entrepreneurs connected to the authoritarian regime of Tudjman took over the best positions to serve their interests. Corruption did not end with the rule of Tudjman and his party. The corruptive stakes are too important and too much engrained in the tissue of the public administration to disappear with a regime change.

However, Croatia does not stand alone as it strives to be accepted in the EU family. This entails that another party, the EU Commission has come to the fore with strict demands concerning good governance, if only to protect its own financial interests. This produces an interesting picture of attempts to fulfil the demands and standards set by the EU, interacting with its 'fraud watch dog', OLAF (Office Européen de Lutte Anti-Fraude), and scandals which have come to light, which damaged European financial interests. As has been the case with other candidate countries, the process is far from flawless, which cannot be attributed to these countries only (Quirke, 2008; 2009). There were also defects at the EU side and OLAF demonstrates regularly that it is an organisation with a questionable learning capacity (Quirke, 2010). In many respects guidance and education is lacking and the Croatians are sometimes left to their own devices. However, in these cases the Croatian officials outdid OLAF: they took the initiative to organise things themselves, like educating and the establishment of an anti-fraud network (AFCOS).

Reviewing these chapters on corruption it becomes clear how difficult it is to penetrate the opaqueness surrounding the whole field: clarity is suspect. Obviously, the best informed actors are the most silent. However, this is not an unavoidable predestination. Quirke's chapter provides us with a spark of hope.

Crime-money: knowing and managing

While corruption research is difficult because so many do not want to know, and those who know do not want to be known, in the field of crime-money with so much emphasis on 'know your customer' and 'evidence based policy' the researcher should justifiably expect a knowledge oriented attitude. After all, together with transnational organised crime and corruption, crime-money undermines the integrity of the financial system and consequently our whole society.

This was the knowledge assumption of the researcher *Antoinette Verhage* when she set out to take stock of what is known of crime-money and laundering in Belgium. In her chapter she describes her search for the knowledge grail.

Having previously investigated the Anti-money Laundering Complex from the perspective of the compliance industry (Verhage, 2009, a&b), she had proper reasons to address the law enforcement agencies with the simple question: "What do *you* know?" Knowledge presupposes some system, so she set out to take stock of the objective signs of a knowledge production by the law enforcement agencies. And the primary token of knowledge production should consist of accessible and transparent data. This is not a too audacious assumption. Actually after twenty years of anti-laundering policy the EU-commission came to the same assumption and started to look around in the Member States. What did they find, the EU-commission in Europe as well as Antoinette Verhage in Belgium? Nothing but crude, rudimentary data, no transparency and no comparability. After two years the Financial Crime Subgroup or Eurostat had nothing to report: European anti-laundering policy is still a matter of *camera obscura*, as observed three years ago (Van Duyne, 2007).

Verhage pursued her search in Belgium and met as little cooperation as transparency of data. Most important: she did not find a unity of counting units between the responsible services. It was not possible to match the output from the reporting financial institutions to the input of the FIU or to the next processing link in the chain: the Public Prosecution Office. The latter office 'guaranteed' an additional database pollution by mixing the money-laundering cases with the offence of 'receiving stolen goods' making any effective measurement impossible. The Belgium Asset Recovery Office refused any cooperation.

Undaunted the author continued to look through the frosted glass of the Belgium law enforcement offices to distinguish the contours of the throughput and output of laundering cases. Combining whatever data were available she observed a dismissal rate of the laundering case input of almost 80% and a conviction rate of 12% (but with the cases of 'receiving' included). The author concluded to a Belgian *camera obscura*, which she contrasted with the financial expenses of the anti-laundering policy imposed on the financial institutions and society at large. A more appropriate conclusion would be: the authorities have put themselves in this field also in a state of self-exception concerning transparency standards, while at the same time imposing these standards on the private sector and letting them pay the expenses of compliance.

Given the EU-commission's admission of this state of affair, the Belgians do not stand alone. The image of an international lack of AML transparency is confirmed time and again. Also Sweden, orderly and in general high on the transparency valuation does not escape this judgement. However, from the chapter of *Vesterhav* about the situation in Sweden, one does not deduce law enforcement fear reactions about the phenomenon of crime-money. There is an awareness that many commercial sectors are obviously underreporting suspicious transactions. But the Swedish authorities are also aware of the vagueness of the laundering concept, its overlap with receiving stolen goods, the burdening obligations imposed on businesses and the very small part of all the suspicious transaction reports which eventually result in a conviction. It is remarkable that this did not lead Sweden to be rushed into a moral panic, resulting in more repression or broadening the already fuzzy laundering concept by also penalising self-laundering. This course of action appears to be favoured by many jurisdictions like the UK, the Netherlands or Belgium, though with equally meagre results. Instead, decentralised monitoring, persuasion and researching the unclear selection mechanisms (or hurdles) in the chain of case processing are chosen as the appropriate policy.

I think that this moderate policy is justified by what is empirically known about profit oriented law breakers and their revenues in Sweden. *Johanna Skinnari* provides us with an account of the financial management of drug crime in Sweden. Interestingly, she uses the phrase 'financial management' instead of 'money laundering'. And for good reason, as laundering is a legal construction, apart from the fact that *self*-laundering is not punishable in Sweden (and does that make the situation in Sweden worse?). The basic question of the research project concerned the threat posed by the drug money and the management thereof. The researchers collected a broad range of information: court files, interviews with drug dealers, and various registries, among them information from the Tax Office. While realising that each source has its own caveats, the findings fitted with observations from other research (Van Duyne and Levi, 2005; Levi, 2009).

Just like the proverbial saying that the truth of the pudding is in the eating, so the truth of the threat of the drug money laundering is in the way it is being used. What did the researcher find? Her most important observation is that there is little drug money left for laundering: the lower and middle layers of the drug trade have no or little money left after life-style and business expenses. As observed in other research (Van Duyne and De Miranda, 1999; Van Duyne and Soudijn, forthcoming), the distribution of income and savings is very skewed: few own much and many own little. And in the cases in which money is saved, criminals act economically the same as their fellow foreign criminal traders (Van Duyne, 2003): they buy a dwelling (abroad), some a legal enterprise such as a restaurant or a pub only to realise that legal business routines in the upperworld require other skills than the ones they use in the smuggling business. Against this background it is not surprising that the author does not find much evidence of sophisticated laundering techniques.

If that observation has a more general bearing, we are left with the unanswered question of the corruptive precipitation of the crime-money in society, also in Sweden. One of the outlets could be the four Swedish casinos. These are *state* casinos because gambling is considered a vice against which the authorities have a moral obligation.[1] Not being able to stop gambling, the state now controls this vice. This control is the more urgent as casinos are not only a place of sinful gambling, but may also be an outlet of crime-money and laundering, aggravating the immorality. In these institutions the threat of the crime-money from drugs and other serious crimes may therefore be acute. The researchers *Johanna Skinnari* and *Lars Korsell* investigated the Swedish casino situation to determine this threat. They could again make use of an extensive array of law enforcement registries (tax office, FIU, police, courts) to find out who was frequenting these facilities. Of course, the specific question was whether offenders of serious crime, like drug trafficking, placed their money in the casinos and if doing so would be posing a threat. To keep a long story short: they didn't. For professional risk avoiders/managers the casinos are too hot a place: from entrance to exit one is watched, photographed and monitored. Not attractive for a professional crime-entrepreneur. Did that mean that the Swedish casinos are 'clean' (except for the

1 Similar to the Netherlands: "Thy shall not tempt fate", which led first to the prohibition of gambling, then to a state monopoly (of sin). Now the European Commission is fumbling at this closed door, as monopolies are banned in the EU.

vicious gambling?). No, that would be almost surrealistic. Of course apart from the lion's share of normal visitors, people with an *economic* criminal back ground appear to be more often high-frequency visitors: in short the 'criminal upper-world'. Do they use the casinos to launder their crime-monies? The researchers could not find support for this threat-hypothesis. They concluded that casinos in Sweden are outlets for letting the money roll according to life style needs of normal citizens and affluent (economic) criminals alike: they just display the same economic conduct of letting money roll. Does that corrupt the closely watched Swedish casinos and through this institution the integrity of the financial system? Though puritans (and the FATF and FIUs) may still find reason for concern, the financial waters they have to protect were being troubled by pollution from a far more dangerous source.

What happened in the first decade of this century was far worse and had a deeper cause than the infiltration of crime-money into the financial system. The system destabilised and corroded itself with massive levels of debt, re-assembles into financial 'products', sold around the world and which nobody knew how to value. In the end they proved to be 'poisonous'. This occurred because ironically private interests regulated regulatory bodies: their thinking, models data and rules.

Was this a global 'Ponzi scheme'? *Nicholas Dorn* tries to project this dramatic financial episode against a broader background, steering us away from an easy criminal interpretative framework. Indeed, there were villains like Madoff and Stanford, but they operated in a climate of defective oversight which was created by many interested financial actors. They all were looking for financial 'innovations' few could (or pretended to) understand while passing the risks to participants outside their scheme.

The most plausible explanation of what happened was a 'state capture' by the financial sector: the confluence of private interests and governmental duties but in such a way that the regulatory bodies adapted their view to the interests of those they had to supervise. As if the history of defective collective decision making in 'group-think' situations had never been written (Janis, 1972; Janis and Mann, 1977), the supervisors and supervised adopted a similar way of (rosy) thinking. Is this a manifestation of collective incompetence rather than criminal intent? Following the French social theorist Pierre Bourdieu, Dorn re-interprets regulatory incompetence and failure in terms of a broader shift in the political and economic framing of knowledge, so displacing questions about criminality to the margins of his analysis.

That may be a bit naive: there was not only self-deception but also (criminal) negligence and deceit in knowingly (or 'should have known') passing overvalued bonds and other opaque financial instruments to third parties: a sliding towards 'Ponzi-finance'.

When we take these two sides of the threat to the financial system together, we observe strange interactions between the state, the financial institutions and money. In the interaction between the state and the financial sector there are two trends in almost two separate policy spaces. One may be called the '*laundering space*' in which the state demands full transparency and cooperation to keep crime-money out. The financial institutions grumble and resist a bit, then sigh and accept the burden, nevertheless complaining about the ineffectiveness (Harvey, 2005; 2008). The other side I call the '*financial instrument space*'. Here the state and the same financial institutions have inverted their roles. Now the financial sector sets the tune and demands a liberalisation of oversight, which is bound to lead to less transparency. In their turn the state and regulatory bodies give in and relinquish their grip by allowing themselves to be grasped, though now without any demur. And while the 'launderers' (are supposed to) bring at any rate money *into* the closely guarded banks, the bankers of the same banks managed to evaporate multi-trillion of assets. Not of criminals, as Van Duyne and Soudijn (forthcoming) argued elsewhere, but of ordinary savers who trusted their banks.

Clichés, tinkering at the organised crime 'altarpiece' and symbolism

Even if the governmental guards appear to be oblivious of many shady actors making inroads on the integrity of society, these guards are a fact of life representing a governmental protection task. Of course, this task is a too broad framework and it must be filled in with topics and budget: that is policy making. *Jon Spencer* and *Rose Broad* in the chapter on SOCA and human trafficking raised the question how such a policy making is connected to popular topics like 'organised crime' and human trafficking. The answer is surprisingly easy. Like a medieval carpenter, painter or other craftsman enrolled to work on the decoration of an altarpiece, policy makers take an existing mould which the public, parishioners, recognise immediately and without further reflection: be it crucifixion, the hell, resurrection or a few devils. In criminal policy making 'organised crime' is such a mould. Indeed, for the past twenty years criminal policy craftsmen have been working, updating old threat images with a few new devils, as long as these resembled the recognisable old ones.

If there have been any innovations put forward they concern the establishment of large and mainly ineffectual organisations, like Europol and in the UK the Serious Organised Crime Agency (SOCA) with its 'subtenant' the UK Human Trafficking Centre (UKHTC). Human trafficking could easily be taken on board because it could be fit into the frame of reference: illegal foreigners look and speak differently, live where nobody wants to live and some succeed in overcoming the hurdles of entry surrounding the country by relying on others to organise this aspect of their illegal mobility. All this does not require much craftsmanship to put this into the altarpiece of 'organised crime'.

Is this a correct update? Or was it merely a question of fitting in a few clichés which do not cover underlying reality but which must justify the organs involved. That would cast a shadow over their effectiveness. In line with my observations about governmental transparency, for researchers and Parliament alike, it proves to be virtually impossible to obtain insight into the functioning of these 'guardian bodies': with a staunch 'knowledge denied' policy, they succeed in fending off criticism of their 'invisible added value'. Apparently, transparency is good, but for 'the other'. Another token of self-exception.

The fitting of the illegal migrant problem into the 'organised crime altarpiece' could also be observed in Greece, as is elaborated in the chapter of *Georgios Papanicolaou* and *Georgios A. Antonopoulos*. In a detailed account they describe the development of Greece as a transit and destination country of asylum and economic luck seekers since the 1990s. Greece thrived on the influx of cheap labourers, advantageous to a broad range of entrepreneurs; from the construction industry to small farmers, as well as the middleclass housewife who could go shopping because she had a cheap nanny at home. However, as soon as economic advantage waned, the migrant workers' presences turned into an experience of nuisance followed by a process of criminalisation. From then on, a similar social-psychological process of policy making as in the UK (and elsewhere) emerged. It required little thinking to follow the international trend on subsuming illegal migration under the organised crime definition. The Greek authorities also follow a 'knowledge denied' policy, this time applied to themselves by neglecting the scarce empirical research there is. This negligence allows them to persist in casting the international illegal mobility within and through their country into the 'organised crime' mould, updated this time with the adjective 'transnational'.

This is not just a bit of tinkering with the police altarpiece. That would be little more than innocuous symbolism. This symbolism is very real in its consequences in terms of police powers, prosecution and sentencing, even if the majority of the human smugglers are not transnational organised criminals but are Greek operating in small networks with hardly any organisational features (which does not exclude the existence of more elaborate organisations).

Maybe we should learn to look at 'organised crime' from a more basic human perspective: if 'organised criminals' are rational and calculating offenders, we should keep in mind that they too are subjected to the general laws of psychology. One of these laws says that humans are (cognitively) rather simple than complicated, with a limited memory span of five plus-minus two elements (Miller, 1956). Above seven memory units mishaps become frequent. But humans are capable of creating and sustaining a lot of mental chaos, which is then called 'complex' because we eschew chaos. What does this mean for the 'organised crime' theory except confirming Reuter's (1983) disorganisation description?

Has this psychological angle relevance for understanding or preventing 'organised crime'? When it comes to the particular manifestation of what is strongly associated with 'organised crime', namely the protection racket, one may wonder how complex that really is. *Stefano Caneppele* and *Francesco Calderoni* provide a survey of what is known about criminal protection in Europe. Apart from definitional problems, this proved to be beset with methodological caveats, due to serious underreporting or low prevalence. That is difficult to determine, but higher prevalence regions like Southern Italy and Bulgaria (now declining), make clear that a situational combination of mal governance and sufficient 'strong men', provide a furtile breeding ground.

That brings us to the chapter of *Klaus von Lampe* on the situational prevention of 'organised crime'. This preventive approach is not a grand design to combat 'organised crime', but a detailed responding to the sequence of events, social and technical conditions which determine the organisation of operations and the facilitating surrounding landscape. It mirrors the thesis that the organisation of crime is draped around a core business, be it car theft, cigarette smuggling or VAT fraud. In its essence the commodity determines the operational conduct in bits and pieces. Learning these bits and pieces (also socially) or 'slicing up' the operations of the core business and environmental interactions allows a targeted approach to criminal organisations in preventing their operations. For correct reasons the author mentions a number of aspects of the organisation of crime for profit, which differentiate them from 'non-organised crime'. It is true, they are more resourceful, better embedded and with a broader grip on time and place. But, as in normal licit life, few possess all these traits. And if some of them do, it is more likely that we find them in the vicinity of Madoff and Stanford.

It is interesting to observe that by stepping down to the earthly level on which people do their daily work, the symbolism and the clichés of the altarpiece fade away. This applies to criminals as well as to the highest organs of state, including the Courts of Justice at the European level, encompassing the EU as well as the Council of Europe. But how does this apply and does the –symbolism – fades away likewise? Among the many aspects in this complicated field two stand out. First, these institutions must protect citizens' fundamental rights, in particular against (the organs) of the (EU) state. Secondly there is the legal symbolism or fiction that the EU cannot violate human rights. This amazing tension has been elaborated by Severin Glaser discussing the sensitive question of the protection against the European fraud watchdog OLAF. This is not a police organ, but it has nevertheless many investigative powers concerning corruption in the EU institutions and fraud against the EU funds. At EU level the subjects of this volume, 'state, money and corruption' come together in this body. In the execution of its watchdog task OLAF can make serious inroads on the human rights of citizens and entrepreneurs. However, there should be no right of intrusion without protection. Therefore the author raises the question: How to protect against this biting watchdog? Glaser's concern appears to be correct, because for years the highest European judicial instance, the European Court of Human Rights, has been wavering about the protection of human rights against acts of the EU, *i.e.*, OLAF. Apparently the highest European Court was most reluctant and withheld a robust and straightforward answer in favour of the European citizens. Instead, the legal fiction of an EU which is immune to human rights violation is maintained. A sublime display of 'statal' exception of wrong-doing.

Have we passed the three sides of the triangle 'money, corruption and state' or did we transform it into a spiral penetrating ever more complicated relationships between these three phenomena? In whatever metaphor we want to cast these relationships, and if it looks like a triangle, it is not a simple one if alone that no side of it is trustworthy. But the opening question of this introduction we can answer now: it is an unholy trinity.

Author's note
All numbers are in European normal continental annotation: the comma is for the decimals and dots for the thousands.

References

Andvig, J.C., Corruption in the North Sea oil industry: issues and assessments. *Crime, Law and Social Change*, 1995, *no. 4*, 269-313

Brovkin, V.N., Corruption in the 20th century Russia. *Crime, Law and Social Change*, 2003, *vol. 40*, 195-230

Duyne, P.C. van, Money laundering policy. Fears and facts. In: P.C. van Duyne, K. Von Lampe and J. Newell (eds.), *Criminal finances and organising crime in Europe.* Nijmegen, Wolf Legal Productions, 2003

Duyne, P.C. van and M. Levi, *Drugs and money. Managing the drug trad and crime-money in Europe.* Abingdon, Routledge, 2005

Duyne, P.C. van, M.S. Groenhuijsen and A.A.P. Schudelaro, Balancing financial threats and legal interests in money-laundering policy. *Crime, Law and Social Change*, 2005, *vol. 43*, 117-147

Duyne, P.C. van and H. De Miranda, The emperor's cloths of disclosure: hot money and suspect disclosures. *Crime, Law and Social Change*, 1999, *no. 3*, 245-271

Gelemerova, L., *The anti-laundering system in the context of globalization: a Panopticon built on quicksand?* PhD dissertation, forthcoming

Gobert J. and M. Punch, *Rethinking corporate crime.* London, Butterworths Lex-isnexis, 2003

Harvey, J., Just how effective is money laundering registration? *The Security Journal*, 2008, *vol. 21*, 189-211

Harvey, J., Controlling the flow of money-laundering or satisfying the regulators. In: P.C. van Duyne, K. von Lampe, M. van Dijck and J.L. Newell (eds.), *The organised crime economy. Managing crime markets in Europe.* Nijmegen, Wolf Legal Publishers, 2005

Huberts, L.W.J.C., Bestuurlijke corruptie en fraude in Nederland. Arnhem, Gouda Quint, 1992

Janis, I.L.J., *Victims of groupthink. A psychological study of foreign policy decisions and fiascos.* Bostson, Houghton Mefflin, 1972

Janis, I.L.J. and L. Mann, *Decision making: a psychological analysis of conflict choice and commitment.* New York, Free Press, 1977

Klötzer, R., *Die Täuferherrschaft von Münster.* Münster, Aschendorf, 1992

Levi, M., *Money laundering risks and e-gaming. A European overview and assessment. Final report.* Cardiff School of Social Sciences, 2009

Meredith, M., *The state of Africa. A history of fifty years of independence.* London, Free Press, 2006

Reuter, P., *Disorganised crime. Illegal markets and the Mafia.* Massachusetts, MIT, 1983

Sievert, L., *Deutsche und Russen. Tausend Jahre gemeinsame Geschichte.* Hamburg, Stern-Bücher im Verlag, 1980

Soboul, A., *The French Revolution, 1787 – 1799. 2: From the Jacobin Dictatorship to Napoleon.* London, Editions Sociales, 1974

Stessens, G., *Money laundering. A new international law enforcement model.* Cambridge, Cambridge University Press, 2000

Stille, A., *The sack of Rome. Media + money + celebrity = power = Silvio Berlusconi.* London, Penguin Books, 2007

Swart, K.W., The sale of public offices. In: A. Heidenheimer, M. Johnson and V. LeVine (eds.), *Political corruption: A Handbook.* New Brunswick, Transaction Publishers, 1990

Quirke, B.J., OLAF's role in the fight against fraud in the European Union: do too many cooks spoil the broth? *Crime, Law and Social Change*, 2010, *no. 1*, 97-108

Quirke, B.J., Romania and the fight against EU fraud: a Balkan success story? In: P.C. van Duyne, S. Donati, J. Harvey, A. Maljevic and K. von Lampe (eds.), *Crime, money and criminal mobility in Europe.* Nijmegen, Wolf Legal Publishers, 2009

Quirke, B.J., EU fraud and new Member States. In: P.C. van Duyne, J. Harvey, A. Maljević, K. von Lampe and M. Scheinost (eds.), *European crime-markets at cross-roads. Extended and extending criminal Europe.* Nijmegen, Wolf Legal Publishers, 2008

Verhage, A., Between the hammer and anvil? The anti-money laundering-complex and its interactions with the compliance industry. *Crime, Law and Social Change*, 2009, *no. 1*, 9-32

Verhage, A., The beauty of grey? AML as a risk factor for compliance officers. In: P.C. van Duyne, S. Donati, J. Harvey, A. Maljevic and K. von Lampe (eds.), *Crime, money and criminal mobility in Europe.* Nijmegen, Wolf Legal Publishers, 2009

Fighting foreign bribery: the stick or the carrot?

Liliya Gelemerova[1]

Introduction – the corrupt 'High Flyers'

The developed countries in the Western world like to point the finger at (a) countries east and south and (b) drug dealers with their corruptive crime-monies. However, alleged mega-fraud and corruption schemes (from Enron to Madoff and Stanford, from Elf Aquitaine to Siemens) abound in democratic states. During the past decade a series of such 'elite crime' cases shook the international community. They are best described as 'elite crimes' because these schemes did not concern the corruptive penetration of the legitimate world by 'underworld' figures and their crime-monies: the perpetrators were respected individuals and the companies involved worked with 'white' money and were established in economically advanced democratic states.

It is difficult to imagine how such fraudulent activities could have gone unnoticed for so long, in a highly-regulated environment which involves a range of banks, financial intermediaries, lawyers, notaries, administrative institutions and regulators, all of which have had to apply scrutiny and due diligence.[2] And all of them were under the oversight of a range of 'watchdog institutions'.

Such cases demonstrate the array of issues we face, *e.g.* efficiency of existing laws and their enforcement, and of due diligence practices, when tackling fraud,

1 Liliya Gelemerova is a doctoral (PhD) student at Tilburg University and Senior Investigator at Nardello & Co., London.

2 The term 'due diligence' denotes procedures applied to verify the identity and credentials of a potential customer or a partner, the authenticity of documents and material facts (*e.g.* assets and liabilities) pertaining to a potential investment or a prospective business relationship. It can focus on legal or financial aspects. Additionally, as a matter of sound risk management and as a result of anti-money laundering regulations, checks have developed into enhanced background/reputational due diligence, *e.g.* of sources of wealth, political exposure, indications of involvement in illegal or corrupt practices (especially in the context of the US Foreign Corrupt Practices Act discussed in this paper).

money laundering, unethical behaviour as well as 'elite crime'. One may think that the phrase 'elite crime' has become outmoded: something of the 1970s, the time of the Watergate scandal. Recent events, as we have seen, refute this idea. The concept of 'elite crime', else defined as corporate or white-collar crime, subspecies of which is the corruption of officials, still proves its relevance. It is, as sociologists define it, crimes perpetrated by individuals of high social status in the context of their occupation (see Sutherland and Cressey, 1978; Andersen and Taylor, 2005). Crimes for profit at such a high social and entrepreneurial level do not stand alone: they are usually embedded and furthered in a corrupt social landscape. This makes elite crime a conceptually many facetted subject involving a range of separately identifiable but ramified and interconnected offences.

The concept of corruption and the growing uneasiness

In the case of petty corruption things are less complicated. However, in the case of high-level fraud and corruption, it is difficult to differentiate between the various subsets of elite crime (especially with some manifestations being viewed as 'unlawful but not criminal'[3]). Usually corruption of officials or 'public corruption' goes hand in hand with private sector corruption. Public corruption, as Neild (2002) defines it, is "*the breaking by public persons, for the sake of private financial or political gain, of the rules of conduct in public affairs prevailing in a society in the period under consideration.*" Van Duyne defines corruption as:

> "*an improbity or decay in the decision-making process in which a decision-maker (in a private corporation or in a public service) consents or demands to deviate from the criterion, which should rule his decision making, in exchange for a reward, the promise or expectation of it.*" He further notes that "*[c]orruption is an exchange relationship [. . .], while fraud can in principle be committed as a solitary act. [. . .] [T]he decision maker [. . .] must pretend to have acted in accordance with the accepted criteria of decision making or – if there is a monetary trade-off, he will have to defraud, which is the reason why fraud is so often technically connected to corruption.*"

Corruption can have different forms, involving private individuals, corporations, public sector and political corruption, official-to-official relationships, and any of these in various combinations that suffer from bad or unethical governance (see

3 For instance, some anti-competitive transactions, such as participation in a cartel, may be illegal but not necessarily a criminal offence in some countries (see Van Duyne, 2007; see also Conklin, 1977).

Goudie and Stasavage, 1998; Van Duyne, 2001). It seems that the surge in anti-corruption investigations we have seen in the past ten years has drawn public attention mostly to the type of corruption that involves both private sector and public sector corruption. Examples of such investigations would include the UK BAE Systems, German Siemens and Norwegian Statoil, all firms from developed western democratic states. These cases demonstrate that democracy does not necessarily exclude corruption. Developed countries that claim to have a long history of democracy not only exhibit clear symptoms of corruption themselves but 'export' corruption to emerging and less developed markets. Powerful and highly regarded multinationals are prepared to bribe officials of governments in developing countries to ensure business advantages. For a long time and particularly since the Watergate scandal in the USA, there has been growing evidence of this phenomenon. Indeed, until recently, in many countries (foreign) corruption-related expenses were deductable from the corporate income tax. The growing uneasiness in the industrialised world about unethical and outright corrupt practices led to a strong counter reaction, particularly in the USA.

Whether private corruption drives public corruption, or vice versa, *i.e.* public corruption facilitates or even creates private corruption, is difficult to determine in general terms. Regardless of who initiates the bribery, both parties involved are of high social status and perpetrate the crime in the context of their occupation. Intertwined in complex business processes, this type of crime perpetrated by the elite tends to be more refined than other crimes and is often interwoven with political agendas.[4] Therefore, the counter reaction against it requires not only commitment and political will but also a clever multi-disciplinary approach, utilising a range of regulations and tools, including anti-money laundering intelligence gathering and integrity pacts[5] in procurement.

The US Foreign Corrupt Practices Act (FCPA) has become a key instrument for enforcing this counter reaction. But while it is being used by the US government as a wielding stick, it is a question whether and to what extent this counter reaction has been adequately thought through, in particular as far as the imposition of insufficiently clear rules and standards is concerned. This paper will exam-

4 In 2006 the investigation into alleged corruption at British arms firm BAE Systems in relation to the 'al-Yamamah' arms deal in Saudi Arabia was dropped by the UK authorities due to "*national security grounds*" and "*irresistible pressure*" (Verkaik, *The Independent*, 2008). The media reported that the UK Serious Fraud Office (SFO) had abandoned its inquiry after this had embarrassed the Saudi Royal Family and threatened a new £10 billion defence deal awarded to BAE by the Saudi kingdom (Robertson, *The Times*, 2009). Subsequently inquiries were resumed by the US Department of Justice and by the SFO (into deals in other jurisdictions) and BAE had to pay penalties (Leigh *et al.*, *Guardian*, 2010).

5 Transparency International has developed a tool called Integrity Pact aimed at preventing corruption in public contracting and procurement.

ine this issue and the inadequacies and problems relating to the enforcement of this counter reaction against the corruption of foreign officials. In particular the question will be addressed whether the FCPA, in the absence of clearer rules, is a sufficiently adequate instrument for countering the corrupt 'High Flyers'.

Bribery of foreign officials: legislative developments

Similar to anti-drug trafficking and anti-money laundering policies (see Gelemerova, 2008; Van Duyne and Levi, 2005), the US has also been the driving force behind legislative developments in the area of corruption of foreign officials. In early 1975 the US Securities and Exchange Commission (SEC) founded the Watergate Special Prosecution Force and in late 1976 the US Department of Justice (DoJ) established a task force to investigate allegations of foreign corporate payments (see Staggers, 1977). The Watergate scandal led to revelations about a considerable number of US companies maintaining 'slush funds' and paying bribes to foreign officials and political parties to gain business advantages. These corrupt payments were concealed from audit and public scrutiny (see SEC Report, 1976; Thomsen, 2008). At the proposal of Stanley Sporkin, then Director of the SEC's Division of Enforcement, the US authorities introduced the voluntary disclosure programme under which self-reporting and fully cooperating corporations were likely to avoid enforcement action by the SEC (Sporkin, 1998; Thomsen, 2008). Notably, it was reported that over 400 companies, including over 100 *Fortune 500* firms, voluntarily disclosed bribes and other questionable payments amounting to over $300 million (Staggers, 1977; *Newsweek*, 1979; Thomsen, 2008). The payments that had remained undiscovered may have exceeded this figure by far. Given this scale, it can reasonably be expected that such payments had been made on a routine basis and had likely become part of these companies' corporate culture. The disclosure programme was enabling these companies to 'wash their hands,' without being punished. After completing that 'ritual' they could continue as before.

On the basis of extensive testimony received during the 94th and 95th Congresses, the Subcommittee on Consumer Protection and Finance concluded that criminalisation would be a more effective deterrent than disclosure (Staggers, 1977). It was noted that the anticipated benefit of bribery, *e.g.* a highly profitable deal, would generally exceed the adverse effect, if any, of a disclosure. As result, in 1977, the first major piece of legislation in the USA (and in the world) that addressed bribery of foreign officials was adopted: the Foreign Corrupt Practices

Act.[6] Now it was important that similar legislation was passed in other countries to ensure that non-US firms did not have a competitive advantage over US firms. However, it took almost two decades for the rest of the world to follow suit. In 1988, the US Congress directed the Executive Branch to actively encourage other countries, principally US trading partners, to pass similar legislation. In 1997 US lobbying efforts finally bore fruit. In December that year, in Paris, thirty-three countries signed the Organisation for Economic Cooperation and Development Convention on Combating Bribery of Foreign Public Officials in International Business Transactions (the 'OECD Anti-Bribery Convention'). All parties to the OECD Anti-Bribery Convention had to make the bribery of foreign officials a criminal offence. Additionally, the convention calls on all parties to assert territorial jurisdiction broadly and, establish nationality jurisdiction in accordance with their national legal principles (the concept of 'functional equivalence,' see for commentary Pieth *et al.*, 2007).

In order to strengthen the FCPA and make it conform to the OECD Anti-Bribery Convention, in 1998, the US Congress introduced the International Anti-Bribery Act, which amended the FCPA. Essentially it expanded the FCPA's scope and reach.

- Firstly, the FCPA's scope was broadened to include payments made to secure "*any improper advantage*," in addition to criminalising payments made to influence a decision of a foreign official or to induce him to do or omit to do any act.
- Secondly, the FCPA's definition of public officials now included also officials of public international organisations.
- Thirdly, in addition to issuers[7] with securities registered under the 1934 Securities Exchange Act and "*domestic concerns*" the FCPA's coverage was expanded to include all foreign persons who commit an act in furtherance of a foreign bribe while in the USA.

6 Although domestic bribery has been illegal for a long time, it appears that transparency in party funding, unethical lobbying and other issues relating to domestic corruption have been addressed with less vigour, or mere lip service, than corruption of foreign officials (even though the FCPA is modelled on domestic corruption legislation). Among the more obvious reasons for targeting the latter, it has been argued that it affects the country's reputation. In addition, the US authorities have pointed out that the effects are often domestic, *i.e.* US firms seeking to 'outcompete' US rivals (see Staggers, 1977). Even a more obvious reason is to prevent unfair 'out-competing' of US firms by foreign rivals.

7 The term 'issuer' usually refers to companies issuing and selling securities on the stock-exchange. Under the FPCA, issuers are US or foreign entities which have a class of securities registered pursuant to the US Securities Exchange Act of 1934 or which are required to file reports under the same Act.

- Fourthly, the FCPA was expanded to assert jurisdiction over US businesses and nationals for acts in furtherance of unlawful payments that take place outside the United States.
- And fifthly, the FCPA was amended to eliminate the disparity in penalties applicable to US nationals and foreign nationals employed by or acting as agents of US companies (previously, foreign nationals were subject only to civil penalties).

The FCPA's wording, strengthened by the new amendments, was cast in such a way as to avoid any loopholes. The current FCPA's anti-bribery provisions prohibit US persons, issuers and domestic concerns to corruptly commit any act outside the USA in furtherance of a payment, or offer or promise of a bribe. It also prohibits any person or entity,[8] while in the territory of the USA, from making use of the mail services or any means or instrumentality of interstate commerce corruptly in furtherance of a payment, or an offer, promise or authorisation of a payment of money or anything of value, directly or indirectly (through a third party), to a foreign official or (an official of a) political party or a candidate for foreign political office, to induce them to do or omit to do any act in violation of their official duty or use their influence with a foreign government or instrumentality thereof, in order to assist in obtaining or retaining business or securing any improper advantage.

And if this net has not been woven tightly enough, the FCPA also contains important accounting provisions: US security issuers must maintain internal accounting controls and keep accurate records of all transactions.

The broad scope of the FCPA

FCPA's tight grip

As reviewed above, the language of the FCPA was cast in a way that broadens its scope and reach as far as possible. And while extending its reach, the FCPA overlaps remarkably with anti-money laundering laws. The overlap is that both ends of the corruption deal acquire an illegal advantage, or 'illegal proceeds', the possessing and disguising of which is money laundering, under the broad definition of international anti-money regulations.[9] The administrative processing of these

8 Including subsidiaries, officers, directors, employees, agents and stockholders.

9 See the 1990 Council of Europe Convention No 141 on Laundering, Search, Seizure and Confiscation of the Proceeds from Crime (known as the 'Strasbourg convention') and the

proceeds entails that any senior executive within a company, particularly its financial director and chief accountants, if not involved in corruption, can certainly be charged with money laundering.[10] This link between money laundering and corruption, as a predicate offence, enables prosecution on money laundering charges in cases of corruption.[11] But the FCPA also allows the opposite: to prosecute under the anti-corruption law in cases of laundering the proceeds of corruption. The accounting provisions of the FCPA (mentioned above) put the anti-corruption law in close proximity to anti-money laundering laws: *e.g.* concealing corruption-related illicit payments can become the subject both of FCPA prosecution and a money laundering investigation.

Furthermore, the language of the FCPA enables the US authorities to assert jurisdiction in a wide range of situations. Notably the FCPA does not simply say: *it prohibits the making of a bribe.* It reads: "*to make use of the mails or any means or instrumentality of interstate commerce corruptly in furtherance of [. . .]* ". With its 1998 amendments the FCPA enabled the assertion of territorial jurisdiction over any foreign person that acts in furtherance of corruption while in the territory of the USA. In order for this territorial principle to apply, there must be some (even if insignificant) connection to the territory of the USA: *e.g.* having a representative in the US, or making payments via US accounts, or using email communication transmitted via a US server.

The definition of a 'government official' is also quite broad and leaves scope for interpretation. Irrespective of what the term means in the countries of operation of a company, it is important how it is interpreted by the DoJ and the SEC. Their interpretation includes not only employees but also any person *acting* on behalf of a government or *instrumentality* thereof. This can have serious repercussions for business in countries such as China, Russia or anywhere in the Middle

---

subsequent Council of Europe Convention on Laundering, Search, Seizure and Confiscation of the Proceeds from Crime and on the Financing of Terrorism (the 'Warsaw convention') opened for signing in 2005 and signed by the European Union in 2009; the Council Directive of the European Communities of 10 June 1991 on Prevention of the Use of the Financial System for the Purpose of Money Laundering and the subsequent directives of 2001 and 2005.

10 Reportedly, in the cases of Siemens (SEC, 2008) and Statoil (SEC, 2006), as in other cases investigated under anti-corruption laws, the alleged illicit payments involved false contracts and accounts/firms registered in tax haven jurisdictions. Irrespective of the 'white' origin, the monies involved in such cases are tainted for three main reasons: (i) the revenues are earned through corrupt practices, (ii) the purpose of the payment is illicit (iii) for the money to reach its destination undetected, bookkeeping has to be often carried out fraudulently. The result can be considered crime-money: it leaves the main firm 'white', goes into the channel under a false disguise and leaves it again under another disguise.

11 The OECD Convention (Article 7) has also made the bribery of foreign officials, irrespective of where it has occurred, a predicate offence for the purpose of application of anti-money laundering laws.

East where business and politics are closely intertwined. In China many companies are still state-owned (or state-controlled) enterprises (SOEs). As Mike Koehler (2009) notes, the DoJ and the SEC view employees of these SOEs, regardless of rank or how they are classified under Chinese law, as being 'foreign officials' based on the theory that SOEs are 'instrumentalities' of the Chinese government. As Koehler points out, the DoJ clearly demonstrated this interpretation in the July 2009 Control Components, Inc. enforcement action which in relation to a list of specific Chinese SOEs concludes that:

> "*[t]he officers and employees of these entities, including but not limited to the Vice-Presidents, Engineering Managers, General Managers, Procurement Managers, and Purchasing Officers, were 'foreign officials' within the meaning of the FCPA . . .*". According to Koehler, "*this is the functional equivalent of someone telling you tomorrow that your neighbour who works for General Motors or the guy you play softball with on Thursday nights who works for AIG are both U.S. "officials" [. . .]*" (Koehler, 2009[12]).

In other words, this can mean that any employee of a company that has been bailed out, is also a 'government official' within the meaning of the FCPA.

Additionally, the act of bribery does not have to have taken place or to have produced results for the FCPA to be enforced. The word *corruptly* indicates an *intent* or *desire* wrongfully to influence the recipient wherever.

Loosening the grip . . .?

The wording of the FCPA, particularly the word *corruptly*, is designed in a way as to distinguish *corrupt* payments, aimed at influencing an official in exercising discretionary powers, from *facilitating* payments, or 'grease payments', that are only made to expedite a routine matter, *i.e.* a *routine governmental action*, that has to be performed in any event as part of the official's normal duties. The FCPA provides an exception for *routine governmental actions* encompassing purely clerical duties (papers and stamps) which may be speeded up with some grease money.[13]

Additionally, the law provides affirmative defences in cases of (prospective) payments that are lawful under local laws or constitute a reasonable and *bona fide* expenditure, such as travel, incurred by or on behalf of a foreign official in relation to the demonstration of products or services, or the execution of a contract.

---

12 Tenth paragraph of Koehler's post (as the article was posted online, no page number is available).

13 The UK Bribery Act 2010, the introduction of which was largely driven by the FCPA, does not envisage an exception for facilitation payments.

. . . but don't let your guard down

While the envisaged affirmative defences and the exception for *routine governmental action* show a great deal of understanding on the part of the authorities of the difficulties facing businesses in different cultural environments, businesses may be misled by this apparent amnesty and heave a sigh of relief where there are no grounds for one.

Indeed, it is difficult to define a commonly tolerable threshold for *facilitating* payments beyond which payments begin to border on bribery. This is especially problematic in environments such as the Middle East or China, as noted above. Koehler (2009) warns that if you are selling to SOEs in China, be aware that the "*wine and dine*" hospitality culture "*is no trivial matter*" in the context of the FCPA (Koehler, 2009). The US case law system enables the US authorities to continuously expand the scope of the FCPA, linking it to a range of other offences such as money laundering and tax evasion, and interpret its regulations as broadly as possible. Quite indicative in this respect is the case against *David Kay* and *Douglas Murphy*.

> In 2002, Kay and Murphy, executives of American Rice, Inc., were indicted for bribing Haitian customs officials in order to reduce duties and taxes in breach of the FCPA. After a first dismissal (US v. Kay, 2002), in 2004 the US Court of Appeals reversed the district court's verdict and confirmed the DoJ's broad interpretation of the FCPA by ruling that the bill also applies to payments made to obtain an undue advantage in gaining or retaining business, including favourable tax or customs treatment (see also OECD report, 2005). The court ruled that the conduct of the defendants fell within the scope of the FCPA because of their corrupt intent, *i.e.* to pay bribes for the undue advantage.[14] This ruling reinforced the broad reach of the FCPA beyond obtaining government contracts.

The question is how far we can interpret this ruling. Grease payments in the case of a *routine governmental action* can also help a business gain advantage over a competitor. Acquiring the necessary licence sooner than a competitor, ensures an advantage. Despite the exemption and possible affirmative defences envisaged by

---

14 Kay was sentenced to 37 months in prison and Murphy to 63 months. They appealed but in October 2007 the Fifth Circuit affirmed their convictions. They then filed a petition for rehearing *en banc* but on 10 January 2008, the US Court of Appeals for the Fifth Circuit denied their petition (for relevant comments see FCPA Blog, 2008).

the FCPA, cases in recent years, such as the US v Kay, have created uncertainty in interpretation.

In the following years after the 1998 amendments we saw a substantial increase in FCPA investigations. The impact on business was inevitable. The question is how clear the standards are with regard to FCPA compliance and how businesses can ensure a defence against FCPA prosecution. Issues related thereto will be reviewed in the next section.

Implications for business

The FCPA biting

As reviewed above, the reach of the FCPA is international and many companies headquartered outside the USA may not be aware of circumstances in the orbit of their activity that can make them the subject of the FCPA. Furthermore, when in 1997 the US' major trading partners agreed to sign the OECD Anti-Bribery Convention, the US efforts in the crusade against corruption of foreign officials received a major boost.

The implementation of the anti-corruption laws, most of all the FCPA, now means that businesses can be held liable for any questionable payment to a foreign official, even where such questionable payments had previously been a norm. In the past ten years FCPA enforcement by the DoJ and the SEC has become increasingly aggressive, both in terms of frequency and severity. The following table illustrates the increase in actions launched by the DoJ and SEC since 2004:

Table 1

FCPA enforcement actions by DoJ and SEC: 2004 - 2009

2004		2005		2006		2007		2008		2009	
DoJ	SEC	DoJ	SEC	DoJ	SEC	DoJ	SEC	DoJ	SEC	DoJ	SEC
2	3	7	5	7	8	18[15]	20	20	13[16]	26	14

Source: Gibson Dunn, 2010

In 2007, US public companies disclosed over 50 pending FCPA investigations (Norton Rose Group, 2008). In assessing its financial results for 2008 the SEC concluded that FCPA enforcement was certainly a "*growth area*" (SEC, 2008a).

15 According to DoJ's report, in 2007 the DoJ filed 16 enforcement actions (DoJ, 2009).
16 According to SEC' statistics, in 2008 the SEC filed 15 cases (SEC, 2008a).

The DoJ assesses that from 2004 to 2009 it has launched more actions than in the previous 26 years (DoJ, 2009). According to further estimates, while several years ago there were only 20 to 30 open cases at any one time, 19 new cases were launched in the first half of 2009, adding to about 100 cases under way as of the end of 2008 (McCann, 2009).[17]

Additionally, while originally the majority of cases focused on US corporations, the number of investigations into foreign corporations has steadily increased. In 2004, four investigations focused on foreign corporations, whereas in 2005-2007 there were 12 investigations into foreign corporations (Newcomb, 2007). The number of FCPA actions against individual executives has also increased (McCann, 2009).

In addition to frequency, the fierceness of FCPA enforcement can distinctively be observed in the increasingly larger penalties. In 2007, oilfield service provider Baker Hughes agreed with the SEC and DoJ to pay $44 million – the highest penalty up until that point. The penalty included a criminal fine of $11 million and a civil penalty and disgorgement of approximately $33 million. The SEC is seeking, ever more, disgorgement of the profits, earned through the activity that had breached the FCPA, from settling companies (Newcomb, 2007; Norton Rose Group, 2008). The authorities have also started using non-prosecution (deferred prosecution) agreements, where defendants have effectively cooperated with the DoJ. Perhaps indicative of the extent of aggressiveness of FCPA enforcement, there has also been an increase in self-reporting in merger and acquisition situations (Newcomb, 2007).

As a consequence of this aggressiveness businesses have increasingly begun to apply due diligence procedures prior to acquisitions or mergers in order to establish and report to the authorities any evidence of FCPA violations associated with their takeover target.

Responsibility beyond compliance

It may well be that prior to mergers or acquisitions companies are now increasingly seeking to identify FCPA-related red-flags through due diligence checks. But does that mean that we have achieved a change in corporate behaviour for good and that corruption of foreign officials has been constrained?

Due diligence is indeed a key step to avoiding liability[18] and is a major element of the anti-corruption efforts of any company (for comments from industry

---

17 It should be noted that many are being pursued both civilly by the SEC and criminally by the DoJ and this counts as two cases in the government's statistics (see McCann, 2009).

18 Including successor liability in the event of mergers and acquisitions.

experts see McCann, 2009). Due diligence aims at identifying possible anti-corruption laws' violations and thus helps improve compliance programmes and discourage fraudulent behaviour. It also provides opportunities for self-reporting,[19] thus helping to avoid prosecution (or alleviate possible punishment) for FCPA offences committed by a company's acquisition target. But situations, where FCPA prosecution risks can occur, vary widely, and are not limited to mergers and acquisitions.

Regardless of the situation, companies have to ensure compliance with anti-corruption laws, not just the FCPA but also the OECD Anti-Bribery Convention and other relevant laws and regulations. All companies in the signatories to the convention have to ensure that they have an adequate compliance system, including due diligence measures, in order to prevent corruption.[20] But how does this exactly work? Due diligence measures, in the context of anti-corruption laws, are not an explicitly prescribed obligation,[21] but only recommended. Would the implementation of such measures exonerate companies?

The FCPA is indeed biting and its net is cast worldwide. German Siemens and Norwegian Statoil are just some of the examples. It can be argued that only those with a guilty conscience should be concerned. The ultimate message is: 'don't bribe'. But within foreign '*wine and dine*' cultures this may be just wishful thinking. The commercial and political realities are often different (see the chapter on corruption on the Finnish-Russian border in this volume). And what is morally ideal is often quite subjectively implying moral and social norms that are not quite clear-cut.

This lack of clarity is compounded by the huge liability due to the geographical spread of business operations. For example, how can a chemicals producing company ensure that 20.000 distribution agents spread across culturally different environments do not engage in corrupt practices on its behalf. Regulators require

19 Voluntary disclosure.

20 On 26 November 2009 the OECD adopted a Recommendation of the Council for Further Combating Bribery of Foreign Public Officials in International Business Transactions, amended on 18 February 2010 to reflect the inclusion of Annex II, "Good Practice Guidance on Internal Controls, Ethics and Compliance". It recommends that, among other measures, companies apply "*properly documented risk-based due diligence*" on partners (p. 2). Other recommendations have also been introduced, including the Recommendation of the Council on Tax Measures for Further Combating Bribery of Foreign Public Officials in International Business Transactions of 25 May 2009 [C(2009)64].

21 The 'ought to have known' principle can be interpreted as a requirement to take due care to gather sufficient information, *i.e.* to undertake due diligence. In U.S. v. Victor Kozeny, *et al.* and the related U.S. v. Frederic Bourke, Jr., which concerned a bribe-tainted deal (a failed attempt to take over Azerbaijan's state oil company), with regard to defendant Frederic Bourke, Jr., owner of the luxury handbag brand Dooney & Bourke, the court found that "*sticking one's head in the sand*" does not help. The court applied the theory of conscious avoidance and found that even if not directly involved, Bourke ought to have known that there was high probability that circumstances predisposing corruption existed.

compliance with the law but companies are left to their own devices as to how to ensure compliance. Leading business executives preach that corporate responsibility should go beyond compliance with the prescribed minimum but what is the prescribed minimum and how do you go beyond it? Businesses often struggle to find the right formula to ensure defence against prosecution and, ultimately, to fight corruption.

There are some minimal standards, as recommended by the OECD, *e.g.* due diligence, training, ethics programme and a clear corporate policy prohibiting bribery. But there is a lack of clear rules, and, as a result, a lack of consistent implementation of these existing minimal standards with regard to FCPA compliance and due diligence procedures.

The lack of standards leads to organisational diversity and sometimes strange outcomes. Executives of some large international firms shrug their shoulders saying they know their agents well enough and do not need FCPA due diligence. Other big corporations seem to believe that by demonstrating they have some basic due diligence procedures in place, they remain on the safe side. The latter feel satisfied that they have in place some simple vetting procedures,[22] a code of ethics and a policy concerning gifts, entertainment and political contributions, perhaps even a whistle-blowing 'hot line', although this may be little more than outward appearance. As Caulkin (2006) notes, in the late 1990s Enron was also highly rated by ethical investment funds. But history proved different: the company was hiding a weak checks-and-balances system.

If conducting due diligence *per se* is becoming a standard, there is a lack of clear standards as to what due diligence and compliance programmes should entail. The lack of clear standards allows a simplified 'tick-the-box' approach based on elements with unclear contents. This is particularly the case in situations of economic downturn when businesses are cutting back on costs. After all, compliance is a cost-generator.[23] This applies both to anti-corruption and anti-money laundering due diligence, which follow similar investigative steps.[24] However, it is more problematic with regard to anti-corruption due diligence.

---

22 Often companies believe that asking their potential joint-venture partner or agent to complete a questionnaire and running their name on the internet is sufficient to identify risks.

23 The principles of the free capitalist market make it a clear choice for profit-oriented organisations and we see this every day. Large businesses which enter into deals worth millions are not willing to spend a small fraction of the prospective earnings on quality due diligence. Once they get fined, their risk management procedures become focused on warding off regulatory scrutiny rather than minimising broader corporate risks including the risk of being defrauded by a partner or an employee.

24 With regard to anti-money laundering due diligence, generally companies are encouraged to use a risk-based approach and are largely allowed to decide at their own discretion whether they should limit their procedures to basic checks or should undertake enhanced due diligence (see Gelemerova, 2008). Regulations, however, do not indicate clearly to what level research should be taken within enhanced due diligence.

Anti-money laundering compliance procedures, at least in the form of know-your-customer checks, are an explicit obligation of the regulated financial services sector. Laws against the bribery of foreign officials can apply to any company seeking to do business abroad but anti-corruption due diligence, as previously noted, is not an explicit obligation. Those that realise the importance of due diligence, often struggle to understand whether their compliance procedures are adequate. They seek to take measures 'adequate to risk' in the spirit of high corporate responsibility but that is easier said than done. As Vogel notes, corporate social responsibility is a virtue the supply of which is mainly constrained by the capitalist market itself (Vogel, 2005). There is uncertainty as to what responsible attitude can achieve on its own (see Vogel, 2005; Caulkin, 2006) in the absence of explicit rules and clearer regulations.

It appears that companies learn through bitter experience, rather than based on clear rules, as to what is 'adequate'. We see a demonstration of this in cases not only in the US but also in other countries that have sought to adopt laws similar to the FCPA. For instance, on 8 January 2009 the UK Financial Services Authority (FSA) fined Aon Limited, a UK provider of insurance brokerage and risk management services,[25] £5,25 million for failure to take reasonable care regarding anti-bribery control, particularly in high-risk jurisdictions (FSA, 2009a). FSA's director of enforcement, Margaret Cole, said:

> "*This . . . sends a clear message to the UK financial services industry that it is completely unacceptable for firms to conduct business overseas without having in place appropriate anti-bribery and corruption systems and controls*" (FSA, 2009[26]). According to the FSA, the company's failures contributed to "*a weak control environment*" which led to "*an unacceptable risk that Aon Ltd could become involved in potentially corrupt payments to win or retain business*" (FSA, 2009a, pp. 2-3).

As a result of this weak control environment, Aon Ltd made 66 suspicious payments to overseas third parties amounting to approximately $2,5 million and €3,4 million. Certain payments were reported promptly to the Serious Organised Crime Agency (SOCA) and the FSA as suspicious. But the company failed to subsequently carry out assessment to determine whether there were weaknesses in its systems and controls.[27]

25 Although registered in the UK, the company is a unit of US insurance broker Aon Corporation.

26 Paragraph 4 of the text (online posted and, therefore, no page number available).

27 As Aon Ltd cooperated with the FSA and agreed to settle at an early stage of the FSA's investigation, it qualified for a 30% discount under the FSA's settlement discount scheme. Otherwise, the company would have paid £7,5 million. The FSA also notes that Aon Ltd's self-reporting of some of the suspicious payments served to mitigate the seriousness of Aon Ltd's failings.

Undoubtedly the FSA had a valid point that the main controllers at Aon Ltd should have had power to monitor all payments made to third parties, should have been aware and should have questioned the purpose of such payments.[28] Aon Ltd has since tightened up its control systems including by introducing strict policies regarding the use of third parties. The FSA explains that Aon Ltd's

> "*new policy (which has been fully implemented by Aon Ltd) generally prohibits the use of third parties whose only service to Aon is to assist in the obtaining and retaining of business solely through client introductions in countries where the risk of corrupt practices is anything other than low. These jurisdictions are defined by reference to an internationally accepted corruption perceptions index*" (FSA, 2009a, p. 5).

Unfortunately, that index is debated as well and companies often overlook risks in countries deemed to be of lower risk.

The message clearly is that, as under anti-money laundering regulations, under anti-corruption laws companies should take due care to learn more about their agents, customers and partners and should always conduct adequate due diligence. However, it remains a question what exactly "*adequate levels of due diligence*" means. In late 2008 the FSA began a review of the adequacy of anti-bribery and corruption control systems in commercial insurance broker firms and made some attempt to provide clearer guidance on this issue. The FSA stated that its review found due diligence and monitoring of third-party relationships and payments as generally weak. A particular concern, according to the FSA, is that the majority of firms rely heavily on basic checks (such as printing the third party websites) and only few firms conduct detailed checking of higher-risk third parties similar to anti-money laundering 'enhanced due diligence' (FSA, 2009b). Despite that we still hit the question, to what level research should be taken within 'enhanced due diligence' in order to make it adequate (see Gelemerova, 2008).

The caveats

Those companies, which claim to understand the standards in compliance practices, should bear in mind some intricacies of due diligence.

- *Lost in obfuscation on the risk-based approach*

Without doubt, the 'stick' approach works, to an extent, but in order to make it work better, rules should become clearer. What is '*reasonable care*' and what is '*effective systems and controls*' is not entirely clear in the absence of a clear stipulation what this due diligence should imply. As previously noted, companies often limit their anti-corruption due diligence to basic checks (such as checking the website

[28] It is not clear whether and at what point any of the suspicious payments had been reported by the banks or financial intermediaries, involved in the transactions, to the relevant Financial Intelligence Unit under anti-money laundering regulations.

of their prospective partner, as observed by the FSA), in order to keep cost minimal, but at the same time claim to have effective compliance systems. For a strong checks-and-balances system the 'box-ticking' approach may not be sufficient, unless it is based on clear and reasonably high prescribed standards. On the other hand, regulators' behaviour is contradictory: they do not have a prescribed benchmark to make it a target for companies and are not willing to prescribe clearer rules because they say the approach should be 'risk-based'. Yet, through sanctions and legal actions they set the benchmark quite high nonetheless.

What the authorities apparently mean is that companies should focus their compliance effort on jurisdictions deemed to be associated with higher risk such as emerging markets, *e.g.* the former socialist countries or countries in the Middle East. This neglects the risk of corrupt or unethical practices in advanced developed countries perceived as low-risk jurisdictions. As a result, in low-risk jurisdictions companies are simply less vigilant risking entanglement in the schemes of 'low-risk' persons like Madoff and Stanford. In high-risk jurisdictions they tend to demonstrate the alertness the regulators expect from them instead of being led by their common sense of sound risk management and corporate responsibility. Thus, ill-defined rules and concepts lead to unconstructive obfuscation.

- *Varying cultures*

Secondly, things are not made easier by the difference in corporate cultures and environments across the world. The attitude towards corruption may vary across countries. If in Japan a compromised politician or a businessman can go as far as to commit a suicide, in the former socialist countries he may be able to reinvent himself and come out of the scandal even stronger. Furthermore, the realities of doing business may vary and any due diligence research should take into account local customs and practices. However, that is not easy. In the Middle East, for instance, extended family ties are particularly important but to examine all family connections is quite difficult. In addition, successful businessmen often depend on ties to Royal Family members. How are companies to interpret this in the context of Western anti-corruption laws?

In emerging markets politics and business are closely intertwined. Successful businessmen often have ties to politicians. But this may not be straightforward to establish. Even where this is possible to establish, it is not clear to what level research should be taken. As a result, due diligence research is often limited. Furthermore, even if the US authorities seek to provide some guidance in this direction, it remains a question whether companies in other states that have adopted laws driven by the FCPA are provided with such practical guidance.

- *Practical difficulties in developing information*

Another caveat to remember is that, similar to anti-money laundering due diligence (see Gelemerova, 2008), the extent of fact-finding research is dependent not only on the assiduousness of the compliance officers but also on the availability of information in the public domain and the knowledge of a particular social and business environment. The availability of open sources and public records varies largely from jurisdiction to jurisdiction. Even within the European Union the disparity between countries is striking. For instance in Spain or Luxembourg considerably less information of relevance is available in the public domain (*e.g.* in terms of corporate records) compared to the UK, but even more so, compared to the majority of states in the USA. For companies, especially those that seek to spend minimum on compliance, verification of the ownership and credentials of a company or checks for links to politically exposed persons (PEPs) may soon be abandoned, if they try at all.[29] There is also the category of companies which take the due diligence exercise seriously and are willing to undertake informal enquiries, often through outside investigators, to assess whether their future partner has ever been associated with corruption or is related to PEPs. The caveat here is that they should distinguish fact from speculation and watch out for the various difficulties posed by privacy and data protection laws. The line between business security and personal privacy is indeed a fine one (see Wilson *et al.*, 2009). In relation to the series of corporate spying cases in Germany some argued that "*practices seen as reasonable elsewhere, such as background screening of employees, are tricky or illegal in Germany*" and "[*h*]*aving unreasonable limits* [. . .] *means some companies may feel it is not worth attempting to stay within them*" (Wilson *et al.*, 2009, quoting an unanimous European corporate investigator). In relation to the spying scandals, German officials commented that they did not want to stop companies from fighting corruption but believed that data protection rules should be strengthened even further (Wilson *et al.*, 2009). This would set a legal barrier to due diligence in Germany.

- *Finding the balance in interpretation*

Furthermore, those that are diligent enough and undertake in-depth research, to the extent possible, in accordance with data protection laws, often are at disarray as to how to proceed based on their findings. How do you treat information that indicates that the company you are planning to hire as an agent is a legitimate firm but is actually headed by the cousin of a high-ranking PEP in the Kingdom of Saudi Arabia or Kazakhstan? Perhaps this is what you need – a company with well-established links in an environment where connections provide credibility. However, it is important to establish how and, whether at all, a company has benefited from these connections. Yet, some businesses are unwilling to go that

29 In terms of anti-money laundering regulations, companies within the regulated sector are obliged to undertake such checks. With regard to anti-corruption laws, this is a matter of good practice and it is, therefore, often the case that businesses limit the checks to the minimum or, deviating from good practice, have no checks at all in order to keep the cost minimal, as previously noted.

extra mile in analysing their findings or conducting further research. And why should they, when there is no clear criteria as to what is appropriate and what is not. A primer on doing business abroad prepared for The George Washington University explains that "*in certain circumstances it may be a criminal offence to host a foreign government official or even to talk to him*" (The George Washington University, 2006, p. 1). Interpretations can go as far as that, when there is a lack of clear standards.

The results of a due diligence exercise and, more importantly, the contextual analysis and interpretation of findings, often depend not only on the level of experience and assiduousness of researchers, but also on the parameters of instruction. Companies decide at their own discretion what the scope and focus of the due diligence exercise should be. The question is: is it realistic to expect that a reputational due diligence investigation can determine a multitude of perhaps contradictory risks, *i.e.* whether a business is a profitable addition (as was the case with ELECTRI v. Kroll[30]) and, at the same time, provide an in-depth analysis of whether this business may be exposed to corruption and money laundering? It is often the case that businesses are profitable exactly because they do not steer away from corrupt and questionable practices. But left to their own devices companies have to balance commercial realities versus the morally required goals and decide what constitutes reputational (including corruption or money laundering-related) risk,[31] while seeking to achieve an 'ISO-stamped'[32] integrity recognition.

30 In 2009 ELECTRI International filed a lawsuit against investigative firm Kroll for alleged gross negligence and breach of contract. Kroll provided a due diligence report on Antigua-domiciled Stanford International Bank ('SIB') in 2007, about a year before SIB's owner, Allen Stanford, became the centre of a financial fraud scandal. The plaintiff claims that Kroll gave SIB a "*clean bill of health*" (ELECTRI v. Kroll complaint, 2009, p. 11) thus giving a "*green light to invest*" (*ibid*, p. 2). The complaint alleges that Kroll failed to indicate Stanford's political and financial influence in Antigua and the fact that the Antiguan government often relied on him for funding. The plaintiff also claims that Kroll had concealed a conflict of interest arising from the position of one of its senior executives as a paid consultant hired by Stanford.

31 Reputational due diligence aims at uncovering reputation-related risks, *i.e.* anything that can cause embarrassment by association and directly damage a company's reputation, including corruption and money laundering. In the absence of clear standards sometimes companies apply what became known as the 'The New York Times Test' which helps measure corporate conduct in ambiguous areas: do not do something if you do not wish this to appear on the front page of the New York Times (Paskoff, 2007).

32 The International Organization for Standardization, widely known as ISO, is an international non-governmental organisation which develops and sets international standards. The reference to ISO in this paper is metaphorical.

The ISO-stamped compliance and integrity

Similar to the elite crime cases such as the Enron, Worldcom, Madoff and Stanford cases, in a significant portion of the corruption cases, questionable transactions have gone unnoticed over long time. This implies that the financial intelligence gathering system (see Gelemerova, 2008), aimed at preventing the use of the financial system for illegal purposes, has failed to spot the signs of corruption and money laundering at an early stage (or early signs have simply been ignored). The investigation into Siemens, for instance, may well have started after a suspicious transaction report but the suspicious activities had apparently gone unnoticed for too long. As we have seen, a connection between the two phenomena, money laundering and bribery, exists but it remains a question whether this connection has been used in terms of prevention by the authorities.

The main purpose of due diligence is to improve corporate culture and governance and ensure integrity of business. However, the lack of clear standards means that implementation is dependent on risk perception as set by regulators. That risk perception will be variable, but with a plausible tendency of allowing firms to cut corners even where they are obliged to undertake enhanced due diligence checks. Against this background the value of an in-depth reputational due diligence is often underestimated. Due diligence providers often come under pressure to keep budgets low and to report what their clients want to hear because at the end of the day companies want to proceed with their deal and the due diligence provider does not want to lose a client. This clearly confirms that regardless of the high-minded pursuit of ethical corporate governance, the fight against corruption and elite crime, companies remain, first and most of all, profit-oriented enterprises. That is their '*raison d'être*'. Therefore, having a showcase of a range of components of a compliance programme, such as code of ethics, a whistle-blowing hotline and some very basic 'box-ticking' due diligence procedures, does not mean yet that the corporate culture within a company completely excludes the possibility of involvement in corrupt practices. Often the problem lies not with uneducated employees, corrupt intermediaries or agents but with the senior management of a company, the very same people who sign off expenses and approve of compliance decision processes. Therefore integrity and compliance certification,[33] that validates what a company has on paper, can be helpful to

33 Organisations such as TRACE International and ETHIC Intelligence have introduced in their range of services the concept of business integrity and compliance certificate. A company which wants to demonstrate its compliance system conforms to best international practices can apply for accreditation. For comments on this concept see report by Basel Institute on Governance (2006). On its website ETHIC Intelligence states that its "*certificates in no way guarantee that an act of corruption has not been and shall never be committed. They merely attest to the fact that a company has established a level of vigilance in corruption prevention in accordance with*

an extent, as it demonstrates that a company is making an effort. But it would have been of much more help if there were prescribed benchmarks and effective procedures in place that enable validating how a company puts in practice what it has on paper. Otherwise, it remains an issue how integrity and compliance, let alone responsibility beyond compliance, can be 'ISO-stamped'.[34]

Given the basic attitude of the business community, one may wonder why the regulators (in the US, the UK and elsewhere) have first set a legal framework without proper standards and then started to wield the stick against wrongdoers. And having hit and hurt a few times, the formulation of clearer standards is still not forthcoming. It is remarkable that corporations are under the threat of far-reaching liability if they obtain some corrupt advantage, while the authorities can dispense with better guidance and standards of transparency from their side. This gives them improper latitude which is at odds with the goal to fight corruption.

Another approach is to be recommended. Before punishing companies and making them learn a lesson the hard way, consideration should be given to the practical difficulties in the implementation of anti-corruption laws and whether the overlap between compliance with anti-corruption laws and compliance with anti-money laundering laws is effectively used by the authorities. Punish companies for something of which there is little understanding is not going to take us far in the fight against corruption, especially in a world where geopolitical interests, corporate greed, ignorance and indifference tend to dominate and further elite crime. Against grave breaches of law by the corrupt High Flyers the stick must be wielded, but always balanced against a smart use of the carrot.

References

Andersen M. L. and H. F. Taylor, *Sociology: understanding a diverse society*. Belmont, CA: Thomson Wadsworth, 2005 (fourth edition)

Basel Institute of Governance, *Business integrity certification: overall concept appraisal for ETHIC Intelligence*. September 2006,

international good practices" (http://www.ethic-intelligence.com/business/the-Certification-process-25.html).

34 Reputational due diligence is often described as 'integrity' due diligence. However, ensuring someone's integrity through due diligence may be just a wishful thinking. A report on someone's background and reputation may indicate that no adverse information has been found in the public domain. This does not mean yet that the subject of due diligence has integrity. Sometimes it is only possible to report things as they appear, not as they are in reality, especially when companies are not prepared to spend on in-depth checks.

http://www.baselgovernance.org/fileadmin/docs/pdfs/ETHIC/ETHIC_Intelligence_Homologation__step_1_.pdf (accessed 6 September 2009)

Caulkin, S., *The shaky marriage of capitalism and virtue.* The Observer, 29 October 2006, http://www.guardian.co.uk/business/2006/oct/29/theobserver.observerbusiness6 (accessed 13 March 2010)

Conklin, J.E., *Illegal but not criminal: business crime in America.* Englewood Cliffs (NJ), Prentice Hall, 1977

DoJ (U.S. Department of Justice), *The accomplishments of the U.S. Department of Justice, 2001 – 2009.* 2009, http://www.justice.gov/opa/documents/doj-accomplishments.pdf (accessed 27 June 2010)

Duyne, P.C. van, *Will Caligula go transparent? Corruption in acts & attitudes.* Forum on Crime and Society, 2001, vol. 1, nr. 2, pp. 73-98

Duyne, P.C. van, *All in the Dutch construction family: cartel building and organised crime.* In: L. Holmes (ed.), *Terrorism, organised crime and corruption: networks and linkages.* Cheltenham, Edward Elgar, 2007

Duyne, P.C. and M. Levi, *Drugs and money. Managing crime-money in Europe.* London, Routledge, 2005

ELECTRI International – The Foundation for Electrical Construction, Inc., Plaintiff, v. KROLL Inc. and Kroll Associates, Inc., Defendants, United States District Court Southern District of Florida, Civil Action N. 09-21385, filed on 21 May 2009

ETHIC Intelligence, *The certification process.* http://www.ethic-intelligence.com/business/the-Certification-process-25.html (accessed 1 March 2010)

FCPA Blog, *U.S. v. Kay: Once More To The Courts.* 28 February 2008, http://fcpablog.blogspot.com/2008/02/us-v-kay-once-more-to-courts.html (accessed 22 August 2009)

FSA, *FSA fines Aon Limited £5,25m for failings in its anti-bribery and corruption systems and controls.* Press Release (FSA/PN/004/2009), 8 January 2009, http://www.fsa.gov.uk/pages/Library/Communication/PR/2009/004.shtml (accessed 31 August 2009)

FSA, *Final notice to: Aon Limited.* 6 January 2009a, http://www.fsa.gov.uk/pubs/final/aon.pdf (accessed 13 March 2010)

FSA, *Interim findings: anti-bribery and corruption in commercial insurance brokers.* 11 September 2009b, http://www.fsa.gov.uk/pages/About/What/financial_crime/library/interim.shtml (accessed 14 March 2010).

Gelemerova, L., *On the frontline against money-laundering: the regulatory minefield.* Crime, Law and Social Change, 2009 (published online 3 December 2008), *no.* 1, pp. 33-55

Gibson Dunn Publications, *2009 Year-End FCPA Update.* 4 January 2010, http://www.gibsondunn.com/publications/pages/2009Year-EndFCPAUpdate.aspx (accessed 27 June 2010)

Goudie, A. W. and D. Stasavage, *A framework for the analysis of corruption.* Crime, Law and Social Change, 1998, vol. 29, *no 2-3,* pp. 113-159

Koehler, M., *Understanding the China FCPA risks. Who is a foreign official?* An article posted by Dan Harris on the China Law Blog of Dan Harris and Steve Dickinson, 22 September 2009, http://www.chinalawblog.com/2009/09/understanding_china_fcpa_risks.html (accessed on 1 March 2010)

Leigh, D., R. Evans and M. Tran, *BAE pays fines of £285m over arms deal corruption claims.* Guardian, 5 February 2010 http://www.guardian.co.uk/world/2010/feb/05/bae-admits-bribery-saudi-yamamah (accessed 1 March 2010)

McCann, D., *Feds oil up their anti-bribery machine.* CFO.com, 29 July 2009

Neild, R., *Public corruption: the dark side of social evolution.* Anthem Press, London, 2002

Newcomb, D., *FCPA digest of cases and review releases relating to bribes to foreign officials under the Foreign Corrupt Practices Act of 1977.* Shearman & Sterling LLP, 5 October 2007

Newsweek, *Business without bribes.* 19 February 1979, p. 63

Norton Rose Group, *FCPA developments.* 2008, http://www.nortonrose.com/expertise/businessethicsandanticorruption/default17466.aspx?lang=en-gb (accessed 15 August 2009)

OECD, Directorate for Financial and Enterprise Affairs, United States: Phase 2, *Follow-up report on the implementation of the phase 2 recommendations on the application of the Convention and the 1997 recommendation on combating bribery of foreign public officials in international business transactions.* 1 June 2005, http://www.oecd.org/dataoecd/7/35/35109576.pdf (accessed 15 August 2009)

Paskoff, S. M., *Ethics and The New York Times Test.* 18 October 2007, http://www.eliinc.com/insights/blog/Ethics-and-The-New-York-Times-Test (accessed 1 March 2010)

Pieth. M. (ed.), L. A. Low, P. J. Cullen, *The OECD convention on bribery: a commentary.* Cambridge University Press, New York, 2007

Robertson, D., *BAE Systems and SFO discuss compromise deal after epic investigation into arms sales.* The Times, 7 September 2009, http://business.timesonline.co.uk/tol/business/markets/africa/article6823980.ece (accessed 1 March 2010)

SEC (U.S. Securities and Exchange Commission), *Report of the Securities and Exchange Commission on Questionable and Illegal Corporate Payments and Practices Submitted to the S. Comm. on Banking, Housing and Urban Affairs*. 94th Cong. 2d Sess. 1976, reprinted in 353 SEC. REG. & L. REP. 36-41

SEC (U.S. Securities and Exchange Commission), *Order instituting cease-and-desist proceedings, making findings, and imposing a cease-and-desist order pursuant to Section 21C of the Securities Exchange Act of 1934, in the matter of Statoil, ASA, Respondent*. Administrative Proceeding, File No. 3-12453, Release No. 54599 / 13 October 2006, http://www.sec.gov/litigation/admin/2006/34-54599.pdf (accessed 26 June 2010)

SEC (U.S. Securities and Exchange Commission), *Complaint filed with the United States District Court for the District of Columbia in U.S. SEC, Plaintiff, v. Siemens Aktiengesellschaft, Defendant*. Case: 1:08-cv-02167 Assigned To: Leon, Richard J., 12 December 2008, http://www.sec.gov/litigation/complaints/2008/comp20829.pdf (accessed 26 June 2010)

SEC (U.S. Securities and Exchange Commission), *SEC announces fiscal 2008 enforcement results*. Washington, D.C., 22 October 2008a, http://www.sec.gov/news/press/2008/2008-254.htm (accessed 15 August 2009)

Sporkin, St., *The worldwide banking of Schmiergeld: A look at the Foreign Corrupt Practices Act on its twentieth birthday*. 18 NW. J. INT'L L. & BUS. 269, 1998

Staggers, H., *Unlawful corporate payments act of 1977*. US House of Representatives, 95th Congress, Report No. 95-640, 28 September 1977, http://www.usdoj.gov/criminal/fraud/fcpa/history/1977/houseprt-95-640.pdf (accessed 7 July 2009)

Sutherland, E.H. and D.R. Cressey, *Criminology*. Philadelphia: J.B. Lippincott Company, 1978

Telegraph.co.uk, *MPs' expenses: a flipping outrage. They have no one but themselves to blame for this mess*. Telegraph View, 08 May 2009, http://www.telegraph.co.uk/news/newstopics/mps-expenses/5297716/MPs-expenses-a-flipping-outrage.html (accessed 6 September 2009)

The George Washington University, *A brief primer on doing business abroad: U.S. laws that affect GW's International Activities*. Prepared by Patton Boggs LLP with the Office of the Vice President and General Counsel. Posting Date: April 2006, http://www.gwu.edu/~vpgc/pdf/Primer_on_Doing_Business_Abroad.pdf (accessed 1 September 2009)

Thomsen, L. Ch., *Speech by SEC Staff: Remarks before the Minority Corporate Counsel*. U.S. Securities and Exchange Commission, Division of Enforcement, Chicago, Illinois, 27 March 2008, http://www.sec.gov/news/speech/2008/spch032708lct.htm (accessed 24 July 2009)

United States v. Frederic Bourke, Jr., United States District Court for the Southern District of New York, S2 05-CR-518-SAS

United States v. David Kay, Douglas Murphy, 200 F. Supp. 2d 681, Southern District of Texas 2002

United States v. David Kay, Douglas Murphy, United States Court of Appeals, 359 F.3d. 738, 5th Cir. 2004

United States v. Victor Kozeny, *et al*., (United States District Court for the Southern District of New York, 05-CR-518-SAS)

Verkaik, R., *Blair used 'irresistible pressure' to halt investigation into BAE-Saudi arms deal*. The Independent, UK, 15 February 2008, http://www.independent.co.uk/news/uk/home-news/blair-used-irresistible-pressure-to-halt-investigation-into-baesaudi-arms-deal-782541.html (accessed 6 September 2009)

Vogel, D., *The market for virtue. The potential and limits of corporate social responsibility*. Brookings Institution Press, US, 2005

Viuhko, M., M. Lehti and K. Aromaa, *The rules of the game. A qualitative study of corruption on the Finnish-Russian border*. In: *Cross-border crime inroads on integrity in Europe*. Nijmegen, Wolf Legal Publishers, 2010

Wilson J., R. Milne and G. Wiesmann, *An enhanced vantage*. Financial Times, 17 August 2009

The Rules of the Game
A qualitative study of corruption on the Finnish-Russian border

Minna Viuhko, Martti Lehti, and Kauko Aromaa[1]

Introduction

In international corruption surveys, for example, in the Global Corruption Barometer and the Corruption Perception Index of Transparency International, of the last two decades Russia has regularly been among the most corrupted countries in the world, and Finland among the least corrupted (see Transparency International 2009a; 2009b). According to these surveys, the border between the two countries is one of the sharpest corruption borders in the world. There is, however, only fragmentary knowledge concerning corruption on the Finnish-Russian border, and even this is largely based on hearsay and informal narratives. There exists a general belief that corruption is rampant in, for example, the Russian customs and police authorities on the border, but this belief is not based on systematic research (e.g. Aamulehti, 2007).

The objective of our study (see Aromaa *et al.*, 2009; Viuhko and Lehti, 2009) was to consult Finnish and Russian civil servants and businessmen about their knowledge, attitudes and experiences concerning corruption on the Finnish-Russian border. The study was conducted in 2008 - 2009 in cooperation with the Finnish Ministry of Justice, the European Institute for Crime Prevention and Control (HEUNI), the National Research Institute of Legal Policy in Finland (hereafter "NRILP"), and the Northern Branch (Petrozavodsk) of the Russian Legal Academy of the Ministry of Justice of the Russian Federation (hereafter "NBRLA").

The chapter describes the main findings of the study. These include, in addition to empirical findings, also lessons learned about the problems of the applied methodology in corruption research.

---

1 Minna Viuhko is researcher at HEUNI, Martti Lehti is researcher at the National Research Institute of Legal Policy, Finland and Kauko Aromaa is the director of HEUNI.

Data and Method

The study was qualitative in its nature. In Finland, the data collection was carried out in the winter of 2008–2009 by HEUNI and NRILP, and in Russia by NBRLA. The original plan was to collect the data by using similar face-to-face interviews in both countries. In Finland, the study was carried out according to this plan: the data comprised interviews with five police officers, six customs officers, four border guard representatives and thirteen businessmen. The selection of the interviewees from police, customs and the border guard was made by identifying persons whose work was connected with cooperation with Russia; also expertise related to corruption issues was taken into account. These persons were contacted by telephone or e-mail, and almost all of those contacted were willing to be interviewed.

The interviews with the businesspersons were initiated by developing a list of potential targets representing Finnish or Finland-based businesses operating in North-western Russia. The list was drawn from the databases of the Finnish-Russian Chamber of Commerce, the Finnish enterprise authorities, and the Finnish chambers of commerce. Furthermore, the internet was searched for participants at business seminars related to trade with the area and for road transport companies engaged in transport to Russia. Suggestions for further potential contacts were also solicited from the interviewed persons. The majority of the business interviewees had at least ten years of experience of trade with Russia, and one-third had also lived in Russia for extensive periods of time. All respondents were Finnish nationals. The companies comprised both Finnish and foreign-owned businesses. However, none of them were Russian-owned.

Since the objective was to locate information about phenomena that the companies felt to be problematic, it was decided that companies and persons who were reluctant to participate should not be pushed to do so. In this respect, there were significant differences between different business sectors: the interviewed group consisted mainly of representatives of business sectors victimised by everyday small corruption, while companies from sectors most likely to be involved in predatory large scale corruption declined to take part. Two additional observations deserve attention in this context. First, we were able to recruit the participation of only one representative of export trade (from Finland to Russia). It is possible that export businesses felt that the topic was unfamiliar or irrelevant to them. However, it is also possible that the topic was more delicate for export businesses. In border corruption related to export trade, the role of the business is often active,[2] in contrast to, for example, corruption targeting import trade and the transport sector, where the businesses are more clearly in the role of passive victims. Also, financial interests are likely to be larger in corruption that is related to export trade. The second observation was that all Russian-owned companies which we contacted in Finland refused to participate in the study.

In Russia, it turned out that neither civil servants nor businesspersons were willing to be interviewed face-to-face (which was quite telling as such). Thus, the Russian data had to be collected mainly by anonymous e-mail questionnaires. For their questionnaires the Russian researchers used the Finnish interview outline which had not been designed for this purpose – a fact which complicated the interpretation of the Russian results. It was not always easy to find out afterwards how the Russian researchers and respondents had understood the questions, and whether their understanding was comparable to that of the Finnish researchers. Among the Russian respondents there were six customs officers, seven representatives of the Federal Veterinary and Plant Protection Administration, one representative of the Federal Service of Officers of Justice, and one representative of the Department of International Cross-border Cooperation and protocol of the Ministry of Economic Development, as well as fifteen businesspersons. The border guard administration refused to participate in the study. The selection of the civil servants was made by identifying relevant authorities engaged in border control activities on the Russian-Finnish border and in cooperation with Finland.

The selection of the businesspersons in Russia was made by approaching the Industrial Business and Trade Association of the Republic of Karelia. From this source, information was received from about thirty-four entrepreneurs and companies that had business with Finland. Many potential respondents refused to participate, referring to business and commercial secrets. Eventually, fifteen companies agreed to participate. They represented mainly small- and middle-size firms practicing timber trade or transport or offering travel services. Thus, the group included mainly representatives of Russian independent entrepreneurs. Because of this, it is probable that the Russian group of business respondents was similarly as biased as the Finnish one: most of the respondents represented business sectors mainly victimised by petty corruption while sectors potentially prone to active large-scale corruption were not included (see, for example, Laurén, 2009; Levin and Satarov, 2000; Luukkanen, 2009).

In both countries, the interviews were carried out following a semi-structured thematic interview outline developed by the Finnish researchers. One of the

---

2 I.e. although the businesses seldom act as the initiators of corruption even in these cases they usually take part actively in corruption by concrete acts (for example, by writing two sets of invoices) and exploit corruption systematically for their own profit.

starting points in preparing the thematic questions for the outline was the information needs of the Finnish Ministry of Justice; also earlier studies on the topic were used for orientation (Aromaa and Junninen, 2000; Aromaa and Lehti, 2001; Generalov, 2008; Larjavaara, 1999, 2004, 2007; Lohiniva, 2008; Marttila, 2007). Furthermore, we wanted to get first-hand information both on the views and the experiences of the parties involved in cross-border activities.

Separate question outlines were developed for the interviews with the representatives of the administration and with the businesspersons. They were partly overlapping, containing questions for both respondent categories, and questions designed for each respondent group separately. The questions were related to the following four main themes:

1. how the businesspersons and officials perceived corruption (in the beginning of each interview the interviewee was asked to explain what he/she meant when talking about corruption);
2. what kind of concrete corruptive phenomena existed on the border (in this case each interviewee was asked separately what phenomena he/she had personally encountered on the border and of what phenomena he/she had only second hand knowledge);
3. how the interviewees coped with corruption: did they accept corruptive practices and if so, to what extent, as well as what kind of methods they used to minimise the possible problems and costs that corruption caused to their activities; and
4. how the interviewees perceived corruption prevention, regulation of corruption and cooperation between authorities.

The interviews conducted in Finland were recorded and transcribed. The transcribed interviews were read carefully, and divided into different themes according to the focal themes defined in the project plan and interview outlines. In Russia, the interviews were not recorded because the interviewees did not allow this. The Russian data comprised mostly written questions. The replies to each question were summarised.

It is relevant to ask how good a research method is that consists of asking civil servants and business persons about corruption closely related to their everyday work and in their own administrative branch or business sector.

Corruption is a difficult phenomenon to study because of several reasons. The definition of corruption varies significantly not only across countries and cultures, but also within countries and cultures; for example, between different professional groups or subcultures (see e.g. Dobryninas et al., 2001; Dobryninas, 2005; Heine et al., 2003). The comparability of corruption data for different groups, countries or cultural areas is often poor; and it is also not always self evident that, for example, in multinational research projects on corruption the participants (even researchers) fully understand each other. On the other hand, both asking for a bribe and offering a bribe as well as other corruptive acts are criminalised in most countries - for example, bribery is criminalised in both Russia and Finland. In Finland, also bribing foreign civil servants is criminalised irrespective of the law of the country in question. Thus, it is usually in the interest of the respondents to conceal their participation in corruption or at least describe their role in more positive terms than it is in reality. Even in the cases where the respondent him/herself has not done anything illegal, it is possible that he/she does not want or dare to talk. With regard to one's own organisation, to talk about problems and unlawful behaviour may often be considered unacceptable; there may be fears of reprisals or other unpleasant consequences within the organisation even if the interview is anonymous. There may also be the feeling that it is not desirable to speak openly about problems in a neighbouring country either. The respondent may think that negative views may damage cross-border cooperation with colleagues or business operations on the other side.

One relevant factor in this respect is how painful, shameful or concealed corruption is as a topic in the countries where the study is carried out. From this point of view, Finland and Russia differ to some extent. Corruption is certainly rampant in Russia today, but it is also openly discussed, in general terms, in all sectors and on all levels of society. It is neither a concealed topic (when discussed in general terms), as it was twenty years ago; nor a very painful or shameful topic either (Grodeland, Koshechkina and Miller, 1998; Laurén, 2009; Levin and Satarov, 2000; Washington Times, 2009). Actually the loudest and sharpest critics of border corruption between Finland and Russia during the last two decades have been the Russians; authorities as well as businesspersons. However, when it comes to speaking about concrete cases and actual crimes, the attitudes towards the topic are not so tolerant, at least at the official level (e.g. Kansan Uutiset, 2010; Suomen Kuvalehti, 2009).

In Finland, the situation is to some extent the reverse: corruption, especially Russian corruption, is considered to be a delicate topic in public. For example, a few years ago the Finnish Ministry for Foreign Affairs caused a publication by the Russian-Finnish chamber of commerce[3] to be temporarily withdrawn from circulation as the results were seen unsuitable for the general public: the book gave, *inter alia*, advice on how to deal with bribe requests. On the other hand, privately the topic as well as concrete cases (Finnish and Russian) can and are discussed openly among both the Finnish authorities and businessmen without fear of repri-

3 The conflict was about Haapaniemi *et al.* (2005), currently in its fourth edition (Haapaniemi et al., 2010).

sals. (However, it should be noted that many of the interviewed Finnish businesspersons said that if their names and stories would come to the knowledge of the Russian authorities they would be in trouble in Russia.)

One important general question in qualitative research is how to identify the best or most suitable participants and, subsequently, how to get their consent to participate. In this study, in both countries, refusals occurred, and these were partly systematic. Both in Finland and Russia, among businesspersons representing sectors where active involvement in bribing Russian authorities is most likely or at least more potentially profitable than in other sectors, refusals were the rule. In Russia, in addition, also the entire border guard administration refused to participate. This no doubt decreased both the representativeness and the comparability of the data. It was likely that targeted respondents who had something to hide regarding corruption, and whose attitudes towards corruption were potentially more permissive, were more reluctant to participate than those who were mainly victimised by corruption and had the most uncompromising attitudes.

From a comparative perspective, it was also problematic that the two studies could not be carried out in an identical fashion. They were not identical in terms of the data collection methods, nor were they identical as to what sectors the respondents represented. Furthermore, the results have not been reported in a similar way for both countries. In addition, some of the interview questions seem to have been misunderstood by the Russian research team, or the translation of the questions from Finnish into Russian was inaccurate. The data collection was designed to be carried out by qualitative face-to-face interviews, but in practice, only a small part (five respondents) of the Russian data was constructed in this way. Instead, the majority of the Russian responses (and all Russian business responses) were received by using the Finnish interview outlines as an anonymous e-mail questionnaire. This was obviously not what the interview outlines were designed for, and contributed to the fact that the information content remained rather shallow. This also complicated the comparison of the results of the two countries. These problems would certainly have been alleviated if it had been possible to achieve a more systematic and intensive cooperation between the two research teams, including a common working language. In similar studies in the future, such issues would need more attention.

Since the samples were not random and the research approach was qualitative, the results cannot be generalised in a statistical sense to correspond to all relevant authorities and companies in Finland and Russia. The results provide, in the first place, information about the attitudes and experiences of the selected persons.

Against this, however, the selected data collection method does have its advantages. The qualitative approach is usually considered to be a fairly good tool for illuminating a phenomenon that has not been studied much and about which there are only rather vague ideas and subjective, often prejudice-based knowledge (see, e.g. Berger and Luckmann, 1966; Gubrium and Holstein, 1997; Silverman, 1997). It is also suitable for research that attempts to study how a given phenomenon is generally understood and what people mean by it (*ibid.*). In a successful thematic or in-depth interview, many issues are found that would not be captured in a standardised interview or by a standard questionnaire. The interviewer is often able to create a confidential atmosphere in which delicate issues may be discussed. Mutual misunderstandings can also be better avoided or cleared up in a face-to-face interview than in other modes of data collection.

We tried to avoid some of the above problems with the interview arrangements. For example, we used native researchers both in Russia and in Finland. This minimized interpretation problems and mutual misunderstanding between the interviewers and interviewees. We also asked at the beginning of each interview (at least in Finland) in detail, what the interviewees' understanding of corruption is and thus tried to find out what they actually meant when they discussed corruption. Also the refusals of some business sectors were not as problematic as they could have been, because at least in Finland it was possible to obtain reliable information about the practices of these sectors from the interviewed group. For example, the transport firms seemed to have fairly good knowledge of the dealings of the export firms using their services. (Actually, it was extremely important for them to have this knowledge because according to Russian law they were ultimately responsible for any wrongdoings of their customers.) It is even possible, that they were a better source of information concerning the practices of the exporters than the exporters themselves would have been, because they could probably speak more openly having less to hide.

It is also relevant to note, that many issues emerged from several of our interviews (some from almost all of them), and that both the Finnish and the Russian respondents had almost identical views on several of the discussed topics. It is likely that these views, commonly shared in the interviewed groups irrespectively of the professional background or the nationality of the respondents, were not merely one single person's opinion but were more generally representative of the groups from which the respondents were selected, perhaps even of Finnish and Russian societies as a whole. Last, but not least, the way the research had to be carried out, the obstacles we faced and the ways of solving them (or failing to do so), are in itself telling for the corruption situation in both countries.

Corruption in theory and in reality

In this section we focus on the main results of the study (Aromaa *et al.*, 2009; Viuhko and Lehti, 2009); especially on the definitions of and attitudes towards corruption of the interviewees, as well as their personal experiences of corruption.

Definition of corruption

Corruption was understood by the interviewees in a rather similar fashion irrespective of the professional background or the nationality of the interviewees. Both the Finnish and Russian participants, civil servants as well as businessmen, defined corruption as comprising a broad variety of phenomena in the grey economy, as well as abuse and malpractice by the authorities. The majority of the participants reported various types of bribery to be the most usual form of corruption encountered in the cross-border activities between the countries. The described cases generally corresponded to both the Finnish and the Russian criminal law definitions of corruption/bribery offences. In fact, at least in Finland the definitions given by the interviewees closely resembled the definitions of corruption crimes in the Finnish Penal Code.

According to most Finnish interviewees, the borderline between a gift and a bribe was unclear both in Russia and in Finland, and depended on the particulars of each situation. The formal position of the recipient (director general vs. lower official, or individual official vs. a delegation), the time when the gift is being offered (e.g. before or after negotiations), together with the motive for offering the gift were seen to be relevant when the limits of acceptability are assessed. A gift was understood to be an expression of politeness, friendship or good will, nothing more; a standard working lunch, a bag of coffee or a small souvenir were regarded as acceptable gifts. The basic requirement was that they must not be of a high value.[4]

The Finnish civil servants commented generally that it has become less common in Finland during the last decade to give any gifts at all to civil service representatives, and the Finnish authority practice has become increasingly strict and negative about accepting any kind of hospitality and benefits. However, they also recognised the fact that the limits of and the attitude towards gifts are internationally variable. Some respondents observed that in Russia, "*nothing works without presents*". The views of the Finnish businesspersons were similar to those of the civil servants. Several of them observed that in Russia, the borderline between

4 For an example of a more detailed distinction between bribe, gift and tip, see Miller et al. 2001, 149–156. In our data, such detail was not reflected directly.

acceptable and illegal influence in respect to the authorities is more fluid than in Finland. According to them, it was culturally more common in Russia than in Finland for businesspersons to offer gifts to the civil servants with whom they cooperate, while the gifts are also more valuable. Unlike in Finland, Russian authorities also expect gifts and active signs of cooperation. However, also the businessmen commented that in Russia, too, the distinction between a bribe and a gift is fairly clear, both for the one who offers and for the one who receives the gift. In the Finnish interviews, the difficulty in distinguishing the dividing line with corruption could be observed. When respondents spoke about gifts, presents and bribes, it was not always clear whether reference was being made to a bribe in the sense used in the Penal Code, to a morally questionable 'present' or to an acceptable gift. When a Finnish respondent said that a Russian does not see offering and receiving presents as being corruption, it was not always clear what size of gift he/she was referring to. Furthermore, it was also not always clear whether such a gift or bribe was considered to be acceptable if the respondent felt that there was no other alternative.

Several Finnish interviewees (especially the businesspersons) discussed the dilemma in cross-border activity that related to dissimilar cultural behavioural norms: should one apply the cultural norms of the person who is giving the benefit or the person who is receiving it? In cases where the action is unacceptable according to both sets of cultural norms there is no problem, but the grey area between clearly criminal and clearly legal behaviour was considered often to be broad in the Finnish-Russian case. Another question was of course how accurately the ideas of the interviewed Finns concerning the existing cultural norms on corruption in Russia corresponded to reality. Among the Finns and Russians participating in this study, corruption (for example, abuse of official position) was understood in a rather similar fashion. The results did not support the idea that there would be a great difference between the Finnish and Russian cultures in this respect: what is illegal and what again is legal seems to be more or less the same on both sides of the border. However, there seemed to be differences concerning the acceptability of illegal behaviour. It is possible that the interviewed Finns (also those who had lived for long periods of time in Russia) were thinking of this when speaking about cultural norm differences.

Acceptability of corruptive behaviour

From the above observations, it is fair to conclude that interviewed Finnish and Russian civil servants had a relatively similar understanding of what kind of practices were corruptive. However, there was a significant difference in their attitudes concerning the acceptability of abusing one's official position for personal benefit. All the interviewed Finnish civil servants stated that the use of one's official position for personal gain was not acceptable in any circumstances. In contrast, half of the Russian respondents said that asking for bribes or abusing otherwise one's position was acceptable in certain situations of personal distress.

The examples provided by the Russian respondents were primarily connected to the weak social protection of civil servants and their family members in Russia. For example, one situation when abuse was deemed to be acceptable was

> "*when a person is being influenced, blackmailed, threatened, or his family members are being threatened, then he may use his official position to pass infonnation to third persons*".
>
> Another example was when
>
> "*a close relative is seriously ill and money is needed for an expensive operation, in such a case [asking for bribes] can be understood on humane grounds*".
>
> A further example of a situation in which corruptive measures were acceptable was
>
> "*if a person cannot afford to feed his children, or a close relative is seriously ill, or all his property has been destroyed in a fire, and in such a situation a concerned party offers money*".

Thus, all of these examples referred to quite extreme situations of distress, not to everyday routine requests for bribes to be paid for standard services. Thereby one could conclude that everyday small-scale corruption in the border authorities (the most common type of cross-border corruption met by the Finnish interviewees) was seen by the interviewed Russian civil servants, either illegal and unacceptable in all situations, or also as a commonplace that it was not considered to be corruption at all. Unfortunately, the way the study was carried out in Russia made it impossible to interpret the answers in this respect. (On the attitudes of Russian police officers to corruption, see also Beck and Lee, 2002.)

There were also some attitudinal differences among the interviewees that were related to their professional backgrounds. In Finland, the interviewed businesspersons shared the civil servants' opinion that corruption in principle was never acceptable. However, their attitudes towards corruption in practice *in Russia* were less rigid than those of the Finnish civil servants. The interviewed Finnish businesspersons explained that when operating in Russia it was often practically unavoidable to yield to unlawful requests made by the Russian authorities. If you did not do so, your operations were made impossible (in one way or another) in the long run (see also Larjavaara, 1999 which supports this view). This attitude was not restricted to any particular business sector, but was shared by practically all of the Finnish business interviewees. The attitudes of the participating Russian businesspersons seemed to be more uncompromising towards corruption than those of their Finnish colleagues (and much more uncompromising than those of the Russian civil servants). However, in this case, too, the interpretation of the answers was complicated by the method by which the data were obtained. It was not fully clear how the participants had actually understood the questions sent to them by e-mail and how their answers should be interpreted. In spite of this, it seemed fairly obvious that their attitudes towards corruption in general and especially their attitudes towards large-scale corruption among state authorities were more negative than those of the Russian civil servants.

One corruption-related problem which emerged in several interviews of the Finnish businesspersons was the real or perceived difference in the corruption-related socio-cultural norms between the two countries: should one behave in Russia according to Finnish or Russian (corruption-related) behavioural patterns? Usually the interviewees seemed to follow the Russian pattern. However, it was not always clear whether the Russian norms they followed were actually the local norms or merely their own perceptions of the local norms. It is probable that in some cases it was a matter of the latter ones. Many of the Finns seemed to believe that all the abusive and corruptive practices they met and saw in Russia were seen by Russians as the custom of the country and thus acceptable (although not legal). However, the attitudes and definitions of the Russian respondents of the study did not support this opinion. Although corruption is rampant in the country (see, for example, Heinemann-Grüder, 2009; Luukkanen, 2009; Laurén, 2009; Transparency International, 2009a; 2009b), the majority of both Russian civil servants and businesspersons do not seem to think that corruption is morally right (this is also the opinion of Laurén, 2009).

Experiences with corruption

In practice, both the Finnish and Russian respondents had witnessed corruptive activities mainly on the Russian side of the border. All the interviewed Finns, both civil servants and businesspersons, told that they had never met corruptive practices or unlawful requests from the side of the Finnish authorities on the border.[5] It is unlikely that especially the businesspersons would have had any reason

5 This view is also supported by earlier Finnish research on corruption: petty corruption and bribery of individual civil servants is deemed to be almost non-existent in Finland. Finnish corruption is related mainly to large-scale deals between businesses and political parties or individual civil servants; or to funding of the activities of political parties and individual politicians. On corruption in Finland, see e.g. Isaksson, 1997; Juslén and Muttilainen, 2009; Korruptiotilannekuva 2008; Korruptiotilannekuva 2009; Laitinen, 2004; Lehtola and Pak-

to conceal possible malpractices of Finnish authorities or individual civil servants, thus, probably they told the truth. The cases of corruption in Finland experienced by the interviewees had been mainly linked to the activities of the Russian shadow economy in Finland (related to tax and duty frauds in exports to Russia – so called double invoicing – and different types of smuggling) and as a rule the perpetrators had been Russians.

The Russian respondents had a very similar opinion about the corruption situation on the border: corruption existed mainly on the Russian side, at the Russian border and among customs authorities (see also Karhunen *et al.*, 2008, 175-180; Venäjän-kaupan barometri, 2009). According to them, there was much less corruption in Finland, and the "mentality" of the Finnish civil servants was perceived to be radically different from that of their Russian colleagues. Many of the Russian respondents, especially the civil servants, perceived the government structures of their country to be "*thoroughly corrupted*", and thought that corruption in Russia was "*a mass phenomenon*". The interviewed Finns, irrespective of their professional background, seemed to share this view, although they were usually more diplomatic in their wording.

Although both the Finnish and Russian respondents agreed that corruption within the border authorities mainly manifested itself on the Russian side, there was a significant difference concerning the stories about their personal experiences of corruption. The examples of concrete corruption cases and problems related to corruption were mainly reported by the Finnish businesspersons. On the other hand (and in spite of their devastating assessments of the general corruption situation in their country and in the civil service of their country), almost all Russian respondents claimed that they did not have any first-hand experiences of corruption and that they did not know of any concrete cases of corruption associated with their colleagues or their administrative or business branch. Thus, there was a certain inconsistency between the descriptions of the general corruption situation and the personal corruption experiences of both the Russian civil servants and the businessmen – an inconsistency which could hardly be explained by any other way than that either the descriptions of the general situation or the stories of personal experiences were not altogether honest. This kind of inconsistency was not found in the Finnish data; the descriptions of the general situation and of the personal corruption experiences corresponded to each other fairly well.

---

sula, 1997; Salminen, Viinamäki and Ikola-Norrbacka, 2007; Salminen and Ikola-Norrbacka, 2009.

Table 1
Types of corruption met on the Finnish-Russian border.

Main category	Sub-category	Modus operandi	Description
Predatory	Big corruption	Fixed tenders, prearranged privatisation processes, "dear brother/old boy" networks.	Corruption related to the privatisation of public property, use and control of natural resources, tenders for public projects.
Predatory	Export-trade-related	Double invoicing, changing of tariff numbers, forging of clearance values, circumvention of insurance regulations, smuggling .	Activities related to customs and tax frauds in export and transit trade to Russia.
Predatory	Corruption related to administrative decisions	Direct or indirect bribes (worth hundreds or thousands of Euros or even more).	Bribing of officials with the purpose of obtaining a positive decision in an administrative or a court process
Predatory	Corruption related to official documents	Direct or indirect bribes (worth hundreds or thousands of Euros or even more).	Bribing of officials with the purpose of obtaining fraudulent documents.
Petty	'Milking-machines'	Consultation services by civil servants, money collection by conflicting regulations, money collection by documents, border-crossing fees, money collection in traffic control checks, money collection by excess weight fees, service fees, systems based on a special opportunity.	Various organised and relatively permanent systems of extorting small illegal fees from businesses on a regular basis by civil servants or administrative authorities; the systems are usually based on conflicting, unclear regulations or on arbitrary decisions of individual administrative authorities.
Petty	Corruption by random opportunity	Direct bribes (worth twenty to fifty Euros at the highest, usually less).	Random petty corruption by individual civil servants.

Likewise, the Finnish civil servants had very few concrete personal experiences of corruption in Finland to talk about, but this corresponded fairly well to the general picture of the corruption situation on the border provided by both the Finnish and the Russian respondents. The inconsistency between the general opinion and personal experiences of the Russian respondents was harder to explain. Because of all this, the description of the concrete corruption situation and existing forms of corruption on the border had to be based mainly on the interviews with the Finnish businesspersons.

In Table 1 we have classified the corruptive phenomena on the border as experienced by the Finnish businesspersons, primarily using their own concepts.

The Finnish businesspersons talked mainly about experiences of administrative corruption in Russia which they divided into two main categories: *predatory* corruption and *petty corruption*.

In predatory corruption, the company was an active initiator of the corruptive activity. The objective could be to reach a favourable result, for example, in a privatisation auction, in a public project tender or in an administrative process; or to obtain economic profit by various kinds of tax and customs frauds.

In petty corruption businesses[6] were mainly passive victims of an illegal collection of fees (or 'fund-raising') by administrative authorities or individual civil servants. Petty corruption was divided into two sub-categories: 'milking-machines' meaning organised collection of illegal fees on a more or less regular and permanent basis by administrative authorities or small groups of civil servants, and in 'corruption by random opportunity' meaning random petty corruption by individual civil servants.

Mostly, the described cases concerned petty corruption: organised small-scale corruption in which the businesspersons were in the role of a passive victim who had to consent to various extra illegal or pseudo-legal fees for permits, licences and services, or illegal or pseudo-legal fines for alleged misdemeanours. The individual amounts of money involved were usually small (ranging from ten Euros to a few hundred Euros per occasion) but over time they represented a considerable extra financial burden to the business. In addition to the direct costs, this form of criminality caused significant indirect expenses to the companies in the form of delays, obstacles to competition and business activity, various extra processing and court expenses, and the general insecurity of the business environment.

In the interviewed group, the greatest problems with border corruption were experienced by the road transport companies. At the time of the study, money was collected from road transport companies mainly at the border in the form of so-called excess weight fees (imposed when the total weight of the truck or one

6 According to contemporary sources, this extends also to individual travellers.

of the axle weights was alleged to exceed the norm[7]) and inside Russia in the form of various summary fines for alleged traffic violations, collected at traffic control checks. The reason why the Finnish respondents considered these fees and payments to be corruption was the fact that they usually had an unclear legal basis, and the companies always had to pay them in cash without any receipt or other documentation (for the long history of the corruptive practices of Russian militia organisations, see, for example, Shelley, 1996: 90–91). Some transport companies with regular daily traffic to Russia had made private arrangements with the employees of the Russian Transport Inspection Authority (RTI) at the border to pay on a monthly basis. Also these payments were made in cash and without any documentation. This protected them against random requests at the border and made their border procedures smooth. However, this did not protect them against requests inside Russia, for example, at various traffic control checks.

The relative extra expenditure burden caused by this 'milking' was approximately the same for all interviewed companies in proportion to their traffic volumes – the direct annual costs per company were estimated to be tens of thousands of Euros; the indirect costs were considerably higher. In a business sector subjected to heavy competition, the burden was considerable. Apart from the road transport companies, in the interviewed group it was mainly the Finnish timber import companies that had been directly subjected to border corruption. Their experiences mainly concerned corruption related to the numerous and varying documents required to bring timber from Russia across the border. According to the interviewees in this case, the systematic 'milking' of money was based on (legal) consultant firms owned by the same civil servants whose job it was to provide the documents. The *modus operandi* was to make obtaining the documents by official channels as complicated and time consuming as possible, and in this way to direct the businesses as paying clients to the consultancies.

In the interviewed group of businesses in Finland, businesses most likely to take part in predatory corruption in Russia were underrepresented – the business sectors, for example, export companies, declining to take part were usually those with the closest potential links to active corruption. Since the disintegration of the Soviet Union, one central topic concerning corruption in the Finnish-Russian trade has been double invoicing – the practice of Russian importers of using two sets of documents relating to the value of the imports, with the objective of avoiding import duties and taxes in Russia. This practice has been made possible by the cooperation of Finnish exporters. The opinions of the interviewees (who had mainly second-hand knowledge only of the current practices in the trade)

---

7 In part facilitated by the discrepancy between relevant EU and Russian norms.

diverged when asked about the scope of double invoicing today. Some were of the opinion that double invoicing was still the rule both in transit trade through Finland to Russia as well as in direct trade between the countries. Others thought that it had been replaced in the direct trade by new more subtle methods (what these methods were, was not discussed or not known). There were also differing opinions on whether double invoicing as such was corruption. However, all of the interviewees agreed that the practice would not be possible without large-scale corruption in the Russian customs and border authorities.

According to the interviewees, double invoicing and related fraud schemes were also the main reason for the very slow pace of freight traffic through the border at the moment (and for many years) which has created long lorry lines on the Finnish side with related problems for traffic safety and general public order. The interviewed businesspersons were of the opinion that the main reason for the lines was the fact that each Russian transport firm had its 'own man' in the customs; and had to wait on the Finnish side of the border until this man was at work and able to handle their papers. This system was called 'ticket window', or 'luukku' in Finnish.

Coping with corruption

A general policy followed by the interviewed Finnish companies in order to avoid corruption was to transfer those activities to Russian middlemen or local staff where the potential for corruption was known to exist (such general policy has been observed to be common among Finnish companies operating in Russia; see Heininen et al., 2008). The companies did not want to know how these middlemen or staff members dealt with these issues; the only thing that mattered was that the potential problems were taken care of.

This type of delegating produced its own problems, because corruption could be easily used by the Russian middlemen and local staff for their own purposes and profit. Some of the interviewees had experiences of cases when attempts to influence administrative decisions by middlemen had been unsuccessful; in some cases it was likely that the money given for this purpose had actually ended up in the middleman's own pockets, rather than with the intended targets of bribes.

If the possibility of delegating problematic tasks to the Russians was unavailable, then the general policy among the interviewees was to play along and hope for the best.

Consequences of corruption

The interviewed Finnish businesspersons saw the long-term consequences of corruption in Russia as being mainly harmful for Finnish businesses. Corruption caused extra costs, and impaired the working environment of both foreign and local businesses. It was also considered to be harmful for the economic development of Russia, for economic growth, and for the development of a stable rule-of-law state. Corruption was also considered to be an obstacle for Finnish companies trying to expand their trade with Russia, or to invest in the country, and was also in general terms thought to harm the business relationships between the two countries.

On the other hand, some Finnish respondents argued that corruption in Russia has also created economic advantages for Finland which were, nonetheless, assessed to be of a short-term nature. For instance the large volume of transit transport through Finland to Russia was thought to be significantly influenced by this circumstance – the organising of customs and import tax frauds was seen to be easier for the Russian importers in the transit trade than in the direct trade to Russia.

Cooperation between the Finnish and Russian authorities

One of the topics of the study was Finnish-Russian authority cooperation, regarding corruption and corruption prevention. Within this area, the cultural differences concerning talking about corruption were made clearly apparent. In general, the Finnish civil servants said that the cooperation was smooth and was not affected by corruption in any way. In contrast, three out of four Russian respondents thought that corruption influenced the cooperation, especially as it caused distrust. Their Finnish colleagues actually said the same, but with different words: although denying any influence of corruption in the cooperation, several of them said that there were situations where one had to be careful about what one said and what information it was safe to give to the Russian authorities. They also commented that the exchange of information was not balanced, since the Russian party preferred to receive rather than provide information, and it was also not possible to openly share all available information. Among the Finns, one particular problem was felt to be that Russia had in recent times refused several requests for operational assistance made by the Finnish police, in which cases Russian authorities were asked to interview crime suspects in Russia. Consequently, the volume of requests for operational assistance had decreased in both directions.[8]

The Finnish businesspersons were not asked about their assessment of the impact of corruption on cooperation between the Finnish and the Russian authorities. Instead, they were asked how the Finnish authorities had been able to promote and defend their interests in issues of border corruption. They were also asked how their information exchange with the Finnish authorities was working in relation to corruption and other problems at the border.

The representatives of transport companies were the largest sub-group among the businesses interviewed. For this sector, a representative of the national interest group was interviewed too. If we compare the comments of the company representatives with those of the representative of their interest group, one conclusion was that information about various problems on the border was being transmitted openly and fully from the businesses to the interest group. The interest group again had close contacts with the key bureaucrats in different administrative branches. Therefore, there is no reason to suspect that the information about the problems experienced by transport companies on the border is not reaching the authorities responsible for dealing with the problems. This indicates that the Finnish central authorities are well informed about the current forms of border corruption as well as of the problems that these are causing to the transport business (and very probably the same is also true for the corruption-related problems of the other Finnish business sectors in Russia).

How this information has been utilised in the everyday work of the authorities and in Finnish-Russian authority cooperation is another question. None of the Finnish business respondents said that the Finnish authorities had had much success in this regard. However, most of them did not blame them, because they considered the possibilities of the Finnish authorities to influence corruption in Russia to be non-existent. In individual specific problem situations, help had usually been received when needed. The Finnish embassy, the consulates and the other Finnish authorities operating in Russia were considered to be competent, pragmatic and well-informed about the local situation.

On the other hand, the representatives of the transport companies were of the opinion that although the Finnish authorities could not influence the corruption situation in Russia, they could have done more to protect Finnish companies against corruption related problems. Russian road transport companies were seen to enjoy general advantages in the traffic to Russia as a result of the corruption on

8 The majority of such requests come from Russia to Finland, not vice versa, and thus the respondents considered that the policy change on the part of the Russian authorities was self-destructive and not easy to understand rationally.

the border. According to the interviewees, Russian companies usually had close connections with Russian border authorities and participated actively in the customs and tax frauds committed on the border which gave them a significant advantage in the competition for freight contracts. The interviewed Finnish entrepreneurs were of the opinion that the Finnish authorities had deliberately left them at the mercy of the Russians. The existing bilateral agreements provided instruments that could have been applied to influence the situation, for example, by regulating the activities and traffic volumes of Russian companies to and in Finland. This had not been done, however, because, according to the interviewees, the Finnish authorities preferred their own comfort to the interests of the businesses, and did not want to jeopardise their friendly relationships with their Russian colleagues. On the other hand, the interviewees also said that the possibilities of controlling the traffic from Russia to Finland had collapsed over the last few years also as a result of decisions taken in Finland on the political level: the decisions to reduce the staff of police and customs. This staff reduction policy had achieved small savings in the state budget, at the same time as thousands of jobs in the transport sector and related business had been lost, and the state had lost significant tax revenue. A further factor influencing the inability of the Finnish authorities to control the situation was said to be the insufficient language skills of the Finnish authorities: because one was not able to communicate with the Russians, it was easiest to simply close one's eyes and pretend that everything was all right.

Summary and conclusions

The study was carried out simultaneously in Finland and in Russia, and provided an opportunity for comparing differences between Finnish and Russian perceptions and experiences concerning corruption. It also gave first-hand experience of the suitability of this kind of research approach for obtaining information about corruption in two societies with significant differences concerning, for example, the relations between administration, economic life, and civil society, not to mention the actual corruption situation.

Problems related to topic and methodology. The first problems emerged at an early stage, when it became apparent that both Russian civil servants and businesspersons were very reluctant to give face-to-face interviews on the topic. The Russian respondents were quite frank in their general assessments of the Russian corruption situation, but not willing to talk about their personal experiences. This was likely to be partly also a consequence of the survey mode (anonymous e-mail questionnaire). Written statements may have been seen as simply too much work, but also potentially dangerous (it is not clear how confident the respondents could be about the anonymity of their answers). It is clear that the Russian respondents were not willing to talk about corruption on a case level or from own experience.

On the whole, the topic should have been much easier for the Finnish interviewees: they were mainly discussing foreign corruption and usually from the point of view of a victim; in spite of this, the topic also seemed to be unpleasant to many of the interviewed Finnish civil servants. Their replies often remained brief and superficial. Discussion on a general level was possible, but when more concrete issues were addressed, the discussion faded. The reasons for this may have been various. As far as we could conclude, one concern probably was that they were reluctant to provide negative opinions about their Russian colleagues because they did not want to jeopardise their relationships with the colleagues on the other side of the border. There were problems also concerning the Finnish business interviews: the representatives of business sectors most probably involved in large scale predatory corruption in Russia usually declined to take part.

The data collection in Russia could possibly have been more successful if the interviewers had not been representatives of a government institution but of an independent research institute. With the benefit of hindsight, one could say that a government institute is perhaps not the best possible solution to carry out studies on corruption in a society where administrative corruption is rampant and where there exists a considerable lack of confidence between civil society, business sector and the government. Even though the professional standards and ethics of the actual researchers were high and blameless in this case, their work was significantly complicated and hampered by a lack of confidence on the part of the respondents.

The semi-official role of the Finnish parties (both HEUNI and NRILP operate under the Finnish Ministry of Justice) may also have influenced the interviews in Finland. In particular, the Finnish civil servants might have been more willing to talk openly if the interviewers had represented a totally independent research institute. In this respect, the interviewed Finnish businesspersons formed a group apart. They seemed to have no problems in describing their experiences, even those not favourable for themselves, in detail and with frankness. The main reason for this was probably that they saw themselves as victims, and had nothing to conceal. In this case the semi-official status of the interviewers may even have been a benefit. It is possible that the frankness of the interviews was partly due to the fact that many of the interviewees saw the interviewers as a direct link to the administration, as a possibility to create increased awareness about their concerns, which perhaps could even improve the situation on the border in the long run. It should also be noted that there exists a long tradition of confidential information exchange between the Finnish companies involved in trade to Russia and the Finnish administration. This type of study was not something totally new among the interviewed group. Some of the respondents had also earlier taken part in similar studies (not concerning corruption but business security in general in Russia) already in the 1990s (see e.g. Aromaa and Lehti, 2001; Aromaa, 1999; Aromaa and Lehti, 1998).

The problems mentioned above have certainly influenced the results to some extent. For example, in the business interviews in both countries the respondents who told about their problems were mostly victims of corruption. The opinions and attitudes of businesses using corruption actively for furthering their own interests are mostly missing. In spite of this, we think that the problems have not been fatal if one keeps them in mind when interpreting the results. Furthermore, at least in Finland, reliable information about the corruptive practices of missing business sectors, for example, of export firms could be obtained from the interviewed group.

Definition of corruption. According to the results, Finns and Russians understand and define corruption in a fairly similar way irrespective of their professional background. Their definition of corruption is based on two main sources: the stipulations of the national legislation, and personal first-hand experiences. Corruption was understood to comprise a broad variety of phenomena in the grey economy, as well as authority abuse and malpractice.

Acceptability of corruption. Although Russians and Finns seem to have similar views about what is right and wrong, their attitudes differed in regard of the acceptability of wrongdoings when corruption was concerned. Among all the interviewed Finns, corruption as such was not accepted irrespective of professional background. However, most of the interviewed Finnish businesspersons accepted corruption in practice when operating in Russia. They said that it was a necessary evil to take part in corruption in Russia, *i.e.* to yield to illegal requests made by Russian authorities, if one wanted to operate there at all. An even more significant difference could be observed regarding the attitudes to corruption of the Finnish and Russian civil servants. All interviewed Finnish civil servants were of the opinion that it was never acceptable to abuse one's office for corruption, while only half of the interviewed Russians shared this opinion. The other half maintained that asking for bribes and other corruptive activities was acceptable and understandable in certain situations of distress. The attitudes of the Russian businesspersons seemed to be the strictest among the interviewed groups: none of them accepted corruption. However, their responses seemed rather to refer to large-scale corruption than to everyday petty money collection.

Experiences of corruption. All interviewees, irrespective of nationality or profession, were more or less at ease when discussing corruption in abstract and general terms. However, personal experiences of corruption were a difficult topic for many of them, especially for the Russians but also for some of the Finnish civil servants. The only group willing to discuss the topic in detail were the Finnish businessmen. Thus, most of the information about current forms of corruption on the border was obtained from them only. Both the Finnish and Russian respondents had witnessed corruptive activities mainly on the Russian side of the border. The cases of corruption in Finland experienced by the interviewees were usually related to the activities of Russian shadow economy in Finland (related to tax and duty frauds in exports to Russia – so called double invoicing – and different types of smuggling).

Types of corruption. In Russia, the Finnish interviewees distinguished two main categories of corruption in the relations between businesses and authorities: predatory corruption and petty corruption. In predatory corruption, the company was an initiator of the corruptive activity. The objective could be to reach a favourable result, for example, in a privatisation auction, a public project tender or an administrative process, or obtaining economic profit by various kinds of tax and customs frauds. In petty corruption, businesses were mainly passive victims of an illegal collection of fees (or 'fund-raising') by administrative authorities or individual civil servants.

Practically all interviewed Finnish businessmen had first-hand experience of some form of corruption in Russia. Usually the examples were about systematic petty corruption, 'milking-machines', when the businesses had to pay to the authorities for every border-crossing a more or less fixed sum paid as penalty or service fees, and in exchange for various extra illegal or semi-illegal licences.

Overall, the problems that the interviewed Finnish businesses had experienced with regard to border corruption were primarily problems related to road transport. This was partly due to the composition of the interviewed group, but probably partly also mirrored the actual situation on the border[9]. According to the interviewed businesspersons, the main reason for the problems was that the Russian operational authorities on the border and in the border region (customs, RTI, traffic militia, licensing authorities) did not act in accordance with international and bilateral agreements ratified by Russia.

Coping with corruption. In business sectors where it was not absolutely necessary to deal with the border authorities, the Finnish companies were systematically avoiding and minimising their contacts with them. This would minimise the

9 This is because the study was about the border, and grand corruption and predatory corruption is usually not thought to occur there but elsewhere.

opportunities of being asked for bribes. Simultaneously, the strategy of 'externalising' critical functions in which problems might occur by having Russian middlemen to deal with them also minimised the risk of getting directly involved in corruptive practices. A common method of dealing with corruption was to delegate critical functions and potential problems to Russian middlemen or local staff, when this was possible. It was irrelevant whether problems actually occurred or how they were solved. What was important was that they were solved. Thereby potential involvement in criminal conduct became out-sourced.

Discussion. If the results differ from expectations formulated on the basis of earlier work, they inform the researcher that the frame of reference needs to be adjusted and complemented with insights derived from the qualitative work. This was not the case: on the contrary, the results more or less corroborated the views based on earlier information (for example, Aromaa, 1999; Aromaa and Junninen, 2000; Aromaa and Lehti, 1998; Aromaa and Lehti, 2001; Generalov, 2008; Larjavaara, 1999; Larjavaara, 2004; Lohiniva, 2008; Marttila, 2007). They reinforce the perception about the institutionalised and persistent nature of corruption on the Finnish-Russian border and in the export trade from and over Finland to Russia (Heinemann-Grüder, 2009; Larjavaara, 1999; Larjavaara 2007). On the other hand, the corruption-related perceptions of the Finnish civil servants and businessmen are surprisingly close to the perceptions of their Russian colleagues. It was also positive to notice that the individual Russian civil servants discussed the phenomenon quite openly on a general level. Overall, both the Finnish and the Russian respondents had quite similar views concerning the actual corruption situation on the border, its causes and consequences.

In addition, their recommendations as to what should be done to achieve improvements in the situation were to a large extent the same. Thus, the problem seems not to be that Finns and Russians perceive corruption differently (although there seem to be some differences also in this respect), or that there are no effective means to eliminate corruption from the border. The main problem seems to be in the lack of political will, in Russia and in Finland, to put these means into practice.

References

Aamulehti,
http://www.aamulehti.fi/sunnuntai/teema/asiat_paajutut/5157383.shtml, 16.6.2007, accessed 8.2.2010

Aromaa, K. (ed.). Eastern Crime. A Selection of Reports on Crime in the St. Petersburg Region and the Baltic Countries, 1993-1999. National Research Institute of Legal Policy Publication, *no. 168*, 1999

Aromaa, K. and M. Junninen, *Corruption in road transports*. XIII Baltic Criminological Seminar, Tallinn, 24–27 June 2000. Conference paper

Aromaa, K. and M. Lehti, Foreign Companies and Crime in Estonia, Latvia and St. Petersburg in the 1990s. In Aromaa, K (ed.), The Baltic Region. Insights in Crime and Crime Control. *Scandinavian Studies in Criminology*, 1998, vol 15, 104–134

Aromaa, K. and M. Lehti, Pietari ja Baltia suomalaisyritysten turvallisuusympäristönä 1994–1999. Helsinki: Oikeuspoliittisen tutkimuslaitoksen julkaisuja 176, 2001

Aromaa, K. with M. Viuhko, M. Lehti, A. Taybakov, P. Klemetshov, P., Demin, R. Tumanov, *Corruption on the Finnish-Russian Border. Experiences and observations of Finnish and Russian civil servants and businesspersons on corruption on the border between Finland and Russia*. Helsinki: Heuni Publication Series No. 61, 2009

Beck, A. and R. Lee, Attitudes to corruption amongst Russian police officers and trainees. *Crime, Law and Social Change*, 2002, 38(4): 357–372

Berger, P., and T. Luckmann, *The social construction of reality*. Garden City, NY: Doubleday, 1966

Dobryninas, A., L. Zilinskiene and R. Alisauskiene, *Map of corruption in Lithuania: 2001*. Vilnius: Transparency International, Lithuanian Chapter, 2001

Dobryninas, A., Lithuania's anti-corruption policy: between the 'west' and the 'east'? *European Journal on Criminal Policy and Research*, 2005, 11: 77–95

Generalov, O.-E., *Kaksoislaskutus Venäjän kaupassa. Opinnäytetyö*. Jyväskylän ammattikorkeakoulu, 2008

Grodeland, Å., T. Koshechkina W. and Miller, Foolish to give and yet more foolish not to take – In-depth interviews with post-communist citizens on their everyday use of bribes and contacts. *Europe-Asia Studies*, 1998, 50(4): 651–677

Gubrium, J.F. and J.A. Holstein, *The new language of qualitative method*. New York, Oxford: Oxford University Press, 1997

Haapaniemi, M., M. Moijanen and K. Muradjan, *Kak ili kak? Venäläistä tapakulttuuria suomalaisille*. Helsinki: Suomalais-Venäläinen kauppakamari, 2005 (Fourth edition 2010)

Heine, G., B. Huber and T.O.Rose (eds.), *Private commercial bribery. A comparison of national and supranational legal structures*. Beiträge und Materialien aus dem

Max-Planck-Institut für ausländisches und internationales Strafrecht. Freiburg im Breisgau 2003

Heinemann-Grüder, A., Kontrollregime. Russland unter Putin & Medvedev. *Osteuropa*, 2009, 59 (9): 27–48

Heininen, P., O. Mashkina, P. Karhunen and R. Kosonen, *Leningradin lääni yritysten toimintaympäristönä. PK.sektorin näkökulma.* Helsingin kauppakorkeakoulun julkaisuja B-88, Helsinki 2008

Heusala, A-L., *The Transitions of local administration culture in Russia.* Helsinki: Kikimora Publications, Aleksanteri Institute Series A:12. University of Helsinki

Isaksson, P., Korruptio ja julkinen valta. Tampereen yliopiston yhteiskuntatieteiden tutkimuslaitoksen julkaisuja 15/1997. Tampere, 1997

Juslén, J. And V. Muttilainen, Vesa, Korruption ydinalueet 2000-luvun Suomessa. Havaintoja sääntelystä, piilorikollisuudesta ja poliisin tietoon tulleista rikoksista. Tampere: poliisiammattikorkeakoulun raportteja 84/2009

Kansan Uutiset, http://www.kansanuutiset.fi/uutiset/ulkomaat/2119591/miliisin-korruptio-raivostuttaa-venajalla, 30.1.2010, accessed 8.2.2010

Karhunen, P., R. Kosonen, J. Logrén and K. Ovaska, *Suomalaisyritysten strategiat Venäjän muuttuvassa liiketoimintaympäristössä.* Helsinki: Helsingin kauppakorkeakoulun julkaisuja B-84, 2008

Korruptiotilannekuva 2008. Vantaa: Keskusrikospoliisi, 2008

Korruptiotilannekuva 2009. Vantaa: Keskusrikospoliisi, 2009

Laitinen, A., Suomalainen poliisi ja korruptio. Oikeus 2004, (33):1, 80–87

Larjavaara, I., *The Russian administration: a study of Russian authorities encountering international road freight transport.* Helsinki: Finnish Institute for Russian and East European Studies, 1999

Larjavaara, I., *Public Procurement in Russia.* Helsinki: Kauppa- ja elinkeinoministeriö, 2004

Larjavaara, I., *Funktionaalinen transitioteoria: Hallinto, oikeusjärjestys ja instituutiot Venäjällä.* Helsinki: Kikimora publications, 2007

Laurén, A.-L., *De är inte kloka, de där ryssarna.* Stockholm: Bokförlaget Atlantis, 2009

Lehtola, M. and K. Paksula, *Talousrikosten tilannetorjunta.* Helsinki: Oikeuspoliittisen tutkimuslaitoksen julkaisuja 142, 1997

Levin, M. and G. Satarov, Corruption and institutions in Russia. *European Journal of Political Economy*, 2000, *vol 16*, 113–132

Lohiniva, A., "Mistä se oikea partneri löytyy?" Selvitys suomalais-venäläisestä viranomaisyhteistyötä talousrikosten torjunnassa ja tutkinnassa – Suomen keskusrikospoliisin näkökulma. Tampere: Poliisiammattikorkeakoulun raportteja 70/2008

Luukkanen, A., *Kuka omistaa Venäjän*. Porvoo: WSOY, 2009

Marttila, J., Venäjä Suomen puurakennusteollisuuden mahdollisuutena. Julkaisematon metsä- ja puuteknologian pro gradu -tutkielma. Joensuun yliopiston metsätieteellinen tiedekunta, 2007

Miller, W., Å, Grodeland and T. Koshechkina, *A culture of corruption. Coping with government in post-communist Europe*. Budapest: Central European University Press, 2001

Salminen, A., O-P. Viinamäki and R. Ikola-Norrbacka, R., The Control of Corruption in Finland. *Administration and Public Management Review* 9/2007, 81−96. Bucharest: Academy of Economic Studies

Salminen, A. and R. Ikola-Norrbacka, *Trust and integrity violations in Finnish public administration: The views of citizens*. Halduskultuur, 2009, (10):1, 74–93

Shelley, L., *Policing Soviet Society. The evolution of state control*. London: Routledge, 1996

Silverman, D. (ed.), *Qualitative research. Theory, method and practice*. London, Thousand Oaks, New Delhi: Sage, 1997

Suomen Kuvalehti, http://suomenkuvalehti.fi/jutut/ulkomaat/korruptio-venajalla-putinin-lahipiiri-kahmii-omaisuuksia, 11.10.2009, accessed 8.2.2010

Transparency International, Global Corruption Barometer, 2009a

Transparency International, Corruption Perception Index (see www.transparency.org), 2009b, accessed 29.1.2010.

Viuhko, M. and M. Lehti, *Korruptio Suomen ja Venäjän rajalla. Suomalaisten viranomaisten edustajien ja liikemiesten kokemuksia ja näkemyksiä korruptiosta itärajalla*. Helsinki: Oikeuspoliittisen tutkimuslaitoksen tutkimustiedonantoja 99. Heuni Publication Series No. 60, 2009

Venäjän-kaupan barometri. Kevät 2009. Helsinki: Suomalais-venäläinen kauppakamari, 2009

Washington Times, http://www.washingtontimes.com/news/2009/mar/26/-rampant-corruption-in-russia/, 26.3.2009, accessed 8.2.2010

Understanding the aetiology of corruption:
The first step to tailor-made anti-corruption for the Belgian Customs Office

Gudrun Vande Walle and *Arne Dormaels* [1]

Introduction

The Corruption Perception Index of 2009 of Transparency International was not flattering for Belgium. In comparison to the previous year Belgium went three places back and ended 21st as one of the worst students of the old Europe.[2] An explanation suggested in the newspapers was that other countries have taken some anti-corruption measures in the last year while Belgium has been leaning back doing nothing against corruption (De Standaard, 18 November 2009). But that may be too harsh a conclusion. Actually, at federal level, Belgium has a stringent anti-corruption legislation, while the Flemish government enacted a legal protection for whistle blowers. Further some public departments such as the federal police and also the Belgian Customs Office (BCO) organise training sessions in integrity and anti-corruption for their employees. The most obvious explanation for this low score for Belgium in the Corruption Perception Index is the series of corruption cases that have recently filled the newspapers. Public opinion, measured by the Corruption Perception Index may be sensitive to such recent media attention. Examples are the huge corruption case in the Direction of Public Buildings that is now subject of a judicial investigation; suspicions of corruption in the Brussels court of justice; and corruption in the customs office of the Antwerp harbour who favoured the surrounding companies.

Another explanation could be that the anti-corruption measures that have been taken are not the right instruments to remedy the irregularities that led to

---

1 Gudrun Vande Walle is assistant-professor at the University College Ghent, Faculty of Public & Business Administration. Arne Dormaels is assistant at the University College Ghent, Faculty of Public & Business Administration – working on a Phd. Both authors belong to the research unit 'Governing and Policing Security' (GaPS) and the associated research unit 'Governance of Security' (GofS) – Assocation University Ghent.

2 For the ranking of the corruption perception index, see: http://www.transparency.org/policy_research/surveys_indices/cpi/2009

violations of the rules of public integrity. This does not imply that the instruments are wrong, but rather that they are not applied to the situation for which they were designed. Therefore, we need to look for a more tailor-made instrument adapted to the specific context. But how can we arrive at such an instrument or policy? The principle prerequisite to set up a tailor-made anti-corruption policy is the knowledge of the aetiology of corruption for that specific organisation (Vogl, 2007, p 174; Passas, 2010, p 2).

In this chapter we will reflect on the first step in the two-steps-way of thinking about an anti-corruption policy: the aetiology of corruption (first step) in preparing the selection (second step) of the right remedy. For this aetiological exploration we selected a case-study of the Belgian customs office. This public service is vulnerable to corruption because it works at the heart of the global market also literally because customs are often situated at the nodes of trade such as the harbours and airports. The BCO is a unique case for the Belgian administration in the sense that it is an example of a public administration that has, as part of the production chain, the power to directly slow down economic activities by intensifying its control function or conversely to stimulate market activities by a limitation of control. Other administrations such as the environmental inspectorate or the labour inspection are more indirectly a potentially restraining factor depending on their stringency but they do not touch the core activities of private organisations.

Nature of the research project

This limited research is part of a larger research project "*the effectiveness of anti-corruption policy: a shared task of public and private actors*" in which we explore both main players of the market, the companies and the state, on their anti-corruption initiatives and more precisely on the interaction of anti-corruption policies. The leading hypothesis of this larger research project is that effectiveness depends on the interconnectedness of anti-corruption policies. We started the exploration at the public side of the 'corruption chain', taking the BCO as a case. The next stage is the exploration of anti-corruption policy in the private side being, in this case, the companies that work closely together with the BCO. An example might be the shipping agencies that are private companies providing the service of facilitating trade in charge of companies and that work together with the BCO on a daily basis.

The results of this first step are based on an exploration of the BCO in the period between autumn 2007 and spring 2010. The first method was an observation of the Dutch speaking BCO during a two year anti-corruption training project that our research unit was involved with. Secondly the authors presented the preliminary results to some experts in five additional interviews. We will describe the methodology in more detail in a later section.

This empirical research experience led us to specify the potential vulnerabilities of this organisation and allows us to make some suggestions for an efficient anti-corruption policy for the BCO. The tool for systematic analysis is the "key of variables" developed by the criminologists Gobert and Punch in order to explain crime phenomena without falling into a one-dimensional causal explanation and without prejudicing 'the authenticity' of every specific crime case (Gobert and Punch, 2003, p 14). In the first phase we provide information on this key and its importance. In the past criminologists have tried to squeeze cases into a theoretical straightjacket with the aim to confirm their theory rather than to explain the case. This new approach turns the exercise to a contextual exploration directed by a number of theoretical concepts that have proved their value. In a second phase we present the criminological aetiology of corruption in the case of the Dutch speaking BCO.

This model of analysis introduced by Gobert and Punch contains five key variables:

1. the social, economic and cultural factors;
2. the nature and structure of organisations;
3. the elements of intent, rationality and competence;
4. the defence mechanisms and mechanisms of dissociation; and
5. finally the consideration whether the industry is crime-facilitative or crime coercive.

We will elaborate the first four variables introduced by Gobert and Punch. In our contribution special attention is devoted to the mechanisms of neutralisation, a variable that should not be underestimated in the aetiology of corruption: corruption occurs and continues because people and organisations succeed in denying these illegal activities or the illegal nature of corruptive practices. Bandura calls it the art of moral disengagement (Bandura *et. al,* 1996). The observations and the interviews created the opportunity to explore the neutralisation techniques, respectively the techniques of moral disengagement. It should be understood as the ability to 'rationalise' deviant behaviour in such a way that it appears to be less harmful (Bandura *et. al*, 1996, p 365). It makes colleagues decide to keep silent and enables the offenders to continue in this case the corruptive activities. We did not deal with variable five – crime-facilitative and crime-coercive industries – because in this stage we only have information pertaining to the public side of corruption. The exploration of the private companies vulnerable for corruption is a next step in our research trajectory. We end this contribution with some suggestions for anti-corruption policy for public bodies based on the aetiological analysis.

The aetiology of corruption: a key to understanding

For a correct understanding of what we mean by corruption we can refer to the definition of Van Duyne who says: corruption is an

> "*improbity or decay in the decision-making process in which a decision-maker (in a private corporation or in a public service) consents or demands to deviate from the criterion, which should rule his decision making, in exchange for a reward, the promise or expectation of it*" (Van Duyne, 2001).

Corruption is an act of at least two individuals, the corrupter and the corruptee, which makes it different from fraud that may be committed on an individual basis. Also the idea of exchange is fundamental for corruption. One party must at least try to persuade or seduce the other party to collaborate in the corruptive construction. Since the reform of the anti-corruption legislation in 1999 the intention to offer or to accept is sufficient. In practice the exchange element is not always obvious to detect, for example, when the element of exchange is a promise or is a moral or emotional benefit. With this description in mind we continue with the aetiological elements.

In the first phases of research into corporate crime some people thought spontaneously of "greed" as the explanatory variable for corruption (Box, 1983, preface). If this was true an efficient measure to remedy this attitude of greed would probably be an intensive mental therapy. Most researchers however would agree that the answer is not that simple.

Researchers today have distanced themselves from such a one-sided classic aetiological model while the classic concepts of motivation, opportunity, and neutralisation are still considered valuable and have survived the storms of criticism on traditional aetiology. When concentrating on organisational criminology this is the case for Vaughan who worked originally on two levels, the meso and the macro-level (Vaughan, 1985, p 54-55) but enlarged later on the scope to the micro-level (Vaughan, 2002, p 122). She further selects three variables: motivation, opportunity, and control. It is a broad way of working that is often present in the vulnerability studies of Tom Vander Beken, e.a. (Vander Beken e.a., 2009) and in the work of Wim Huisman (Huisman, 2001) on corporate crime. A similar broad approach can be discerned in the study of police corruption by Punch who goes beyond the idea of the bad apple by broadening the explanation of police deviance and corruption to the nature of the police organisation, police culture and police work. He especially focuses on the organisational component with the aim to widen the bad apple metaphor to *the bad orchard if not the rotten fruit industry and its owners* (Punch, 2000; 2009, p 25). In this view maybe the individual cop has a personal responsibility in committing corruption but the organisational context and the kind of police work are just as much contributing factors. In "rethinking corporate crime" Gobert and Punch deny the sense of an all-embracing causal explanation for the misconduct of private companies. They also warn against quick generalisations over space and time (Gobert and Punch, 2003, p 16-17). *All sorts of companies break the law for all kinds of reasons while others who are seemingly similarly situated, do not.* Single variable explanations such as differential association (Sutherland, 1949) may be valid for some companies while totally going beyond the reality for others. Instead of trying to press all kinds of cases in a straightjacket Gobert and Punch selected, as mentioned before, five key variables that serve as a guideline for the study of corporate crime cases.

These variables made up the key elements for an aetiological analysis in respect of the specificity of every case. Gobert and Punch have had private companies in mind when they developed their aetiological toolbox. Being aware of the complexity of public corruption, also for the civil servant, we have checked the key variables of Gobert and Punch to specify the aetiology of corruption for public actors. First we start with a limited description of the social context that contributes to the content of the job, the workload, its complexity and the relationship to other actors. If collusion is a problem within the customs it is basically because of a changed relationship to other actors, such as a changed balance between state power and economic power. Second in accordance to Punch' analysis of police corruption we consider the organisational structure and culture as factors of opportunity. Third it is worth discussing the rationality of deviant decision making. Do people have enough knowledge to decide in a proper way; and are they free in taking the right decision? The last variable that we borrow is the defence mechanisms and techniques of dissociation. People try to distance themselves from their deviant behaviour, first to preserve self-image but also to avoid personal liability (Gobert and Punch, 2003, p 21-23). In Gobert and Punch's work the dissociation corresponds to passing on the responsibility to a colleague or to a subsidiary organisation. The facilitative role of moral disengagement responsible for blameworthy conducts has been verified in diverse contexts. Important is that Bandura's concept of moral disengagement *not only functions at the individual level but does so with even more profound and pervasive impact at the broader level of social systems* (Osofsky *et al.*, 2005, p 374). In our analysis dissociation can be more subtly hidden in expressions of neutralisation. Neutralisation helps at that very moment to take a distance from the liability and to preserve self-image. But it also supports the continuity of deviant behaviour which can end into what Box called a "*subculture of structural immorality*" or a subculture that institutionalises the neutralisation techniques into the order of the day (Box, 1983, p 54).

Gobert and Punch end their list of variables with the differentiation between crime-coercive and crime-facilitative industries. Some organisations, such as the pharmaceutical industry or the weapon industry, work in a favourable environment to commit crime. Because these industries are important for national wealth they enjoy a preferential treatment. Other organisations, such as the catering industry or retail trade may feel coerced to commit crime because of the steep competition and the difficult working conditions. We did not use this variable because it explicitly refers to the private sector. In a further stage of the research project after the exploration of the public sector, it will be interesting to explore whether BCO deals with crime-coercive or crime-facilitative industries.

A last remark is the interrelation and strong interaction between the variables. Rational decision making partly depends on the internal organisation that also depends on changes at the macro-level. We must be aware that making subdivisions is an artificial but opportunistic choice and that the tailor-made anti-corruption policy must in the end primarily be a reflection of the complete picture.

Methodology used to explore the BCO

In 2008-2009 the research group Governance of Security[3] participated as trainers in an anti-corruption training programme for the BCO. The aim of this training was to sensitise the customs officers for corruption they may encounter in their work environment and for the corruption vulnerabilities of their complex job. It was a one-day training containing a theoretical introduction to the legal framework and the social meaning of corruption, a short dilemma training and an afternoon of communication training in order to enable them to act correctly in

3 The GofS research group is an affiliation of three research-units: (1) the Research Unit Social Analysis of Security of the Department of Criminal Law & Criminology, Faculty of Law of Ghent University (SVA), (2) the Institute for International Research on Criminal Policy of the Department of Criminal Law & Criminology, Faculty of Law of Ghent University (IRCP) and (3) the Research Group 'Governing and Policing Security' (GaPS) of the Department of Business Sciences and Management of Ghent University College.

case of corruptive vulnerable situations on the job. The BCO is divided in four levels: level A, B, C and D basically related to the level of education. People belonging to the A-level hold an academic master degree. People hired in level B have a professional bachelor. Both levels are selected for their specific expertise or to work in a knowledge-oriented job. Only a small percentage of level A officers are hired in a manager's function. People of the C-level hold a degree of secondary education. These people give technical or administrative support. For the level D no specific educational degree is expected. In practice, officers working on the levels C and D have similar job contents.

We started the training project with the highest levels A and B. 30 days of interactive training for about 1000 Flemish customs officers gave a rather clear idea of their perception on corruption in the organisation and the corruption-related risks such as the legal complexity of the procedures, the internal organisation of the Belgian Customs Office and vulnerabilities external to the organisation. In autumn 2009 we started a second series of 38 training days for the customs officers of the lower levels C and D who work in the more executive functions. When comparing both series we can say that people of the C and D-level were more open in discussions whereas A and B played a waiting game.

The second source of information came from a round of five interviews with people that are considered as key persons in the field of BCO and in the field of integrity and corruption in order to further explore the hypotheses we formulated after the training. The two first interviewees were two level-A officers of the BCO who both initiated the anti-corruption training programme at the time. To have a broader scope on the federal administration, its vulnerabilities and its initiatives to reinforce integrity and anti-corruption we organised an interview with the Federal Bureau for Ethics and Deontology. Finally we had an interview with the director of Transparency International–Belgium (TI-Belgium). As an independent knowledge and pressure centre, TI-Belgium has an overview first of what happens in Belgium in the domain of anti-corruption but also of the vulnerabilities on all levels of politics and administration.

Based on the intensive training experience and the additional interviews we will formulate some hypotheses on the aetiology of corruption in the case of customs officers in order to make the anti-corruption policy more responsive to the specific context.

Gudrun Vande Walle, Anne Domaels

The aetiology of customs corruption

Introduction

The Belgian customs administration is part of the federal Department of Finances. Since the opening of the inner borders of the European Union the customs administration disappeared out of the scope of the ordinary citizen which used to slow down when crossing the borders to catch sight of the customs officer. It might surprise people that today more than 3.500 people are employed in the BCO of which half of them work in the harbour of Antwerp.[4] Recently the customs officers reached the newspapers, this time not for an extremely impressive drug bust but for the failure of the customs control system in the Antwerp harbour. A succession of failures such as the permanent technical defects of the electronic paperless registration system (PLDA) and a system of risk-analysis that is not yet functioning perfectly have led to a lot of frustration of company directors who are dependent on the customs services. Some of them call Belgium *a paradise for smuggling* (De Standaard, 6-7 February 2010). But frustration is also deeply rooted within the organisation itself. Failures of the PLDA-system are a well-known source of frustration today for the customs officers who are professionally depending on it and regularly see their work blocked. Feelings of frustration are, therefore, a first aetiological element for corruption in the Belgian customs administration. However, frustration does not appear out of nowhere: digitalisation and its consequences for job-satisfaction is one among a range of causes. In the next section the aetiology is disentangled by means of the key variables of Gobert and Punch.

Social, economic and cultural factors

An important principle of the *key variables* model of Gobert and Punch is the appreciation of the social, economic and cultural context, not simply as a background for the explanation but as a fundamental aetiological element. The last decennia are characterised in broad terms by a globalisation of the market to new economic players, new products and new traffic routes and a liberalisation of markets to more public-private co-regulation. In the case of customs, whose working domain is at the centre of the economic activities, the change of the political-economic power relationship does matter: they are confronted daily with

4 It is maybe important to mention that not all people participated to the training, and that for different reasons: some people were ill, some almost retired and were exempted of participation and we suppose that some refused to come even if the training was an obligation.

the import of new products; they discover the transport of protected natural resources. In addition, they have to work with continuously changing regulations. Next to these effects of globalisation that makes the job more complex they have an ambiguous position in the international economic market: the customs officers take care of public revenues for the national or international community by collecting taxes and import duties. They also have to protect an international free market against unfair competition and against harmful activities. Finally they have a role in the protection of the community, for example by inspecting dangerous materials. The priorities of their job change over time depending on the economic and political climate. The aim of security protection has gained priority since 9/11 events of terrorism.

It seems to be a general feeling among the customs officers that the fight against the trade in counterfeited products and against the trade of weapons has gained priority at the expense of the first task, the collection of taxes and duties. This feeling is not restricted to the customs administration. For a few years the Belgian Department of Finances has complained of a total amnesia concerning the financial control function of public administration (DS, 14/02/2009; Trends, 13/03/2008; Knack, 29/10/ 2008). "*It is as if the public authorities have forgotten what they are basically working for: the revenues of the state*". Civil servants working for the Department of Finances have the idea that the current Cabinet of Finances under the direction of a liberal minister Reynders minimizes the obstacles for a free economy (De Tijd, 19/05/2009). This attitude of protecting the free market against public intervention and public restriction of private gain is also something that determines the work of the customs officers. Customs officers have the impression they work in favour of the private sector and not for the well-being of the Belgian state. Controls are accepted to a certain limit and for a specific category of companies.

The idea of liberalisation and a limitation of public intervention seem to be fortified by the introduction of risk-analysis and self-regulation. Based on risk-analysis some companies will never be submitted to control while other companies who are considered to be a risk are ranked in the database of regular control.

If this feeling of an economically favourable climate corresponds to a political-economic reality one could ask to what extent a company still needs to commit corruption in order to protect its interests? Could it be that the amount of corruption in the sense of bribery is lower in a climate that favours free trade at the expense of state intervention? This is in agreement with the idea of Ponsaers and Hoogenboom in "the carrot and the stick" (*de wortel en de stok*) that collusion and corruption are two opposite kinds of behaviour. In normal situations the regular police officers are sensitive to corruption because of the personal distance from the citizens. However, inspection services work in a less distanced and more collusive relationship with the companies they have to control which means that corruption is less needed (Ponsaers and Hoogenboom, 2004). Or could we say that collusion is a facilitating factor for corruption and that the amount of corruption has increased? The close relationship between the customs officers and the private companies might also make it easier to bribe discreetly. Customs officers in responsible positions said they work closely together with the companies they have to control: they have regular business lunches, they go to receptions and parties, they accept invitations for exclusive restaurants and sometimes they go on business trips. If we go back to the definition of Van Duyne we could say that the close collusive relation gives more opportunities for bribery. In agreement with the definition of Van Duyne we could raise the question whether the liberalisation of the market has broadened the criminological spectrum to abuse of power and to the subtle collusive relations of exchange (see also: Vande Walle, 2010) More than anything else in the public administration the customs officer is a facilitator in the economy and market relationships of a country or region.

But increasingly, and certainly in the case of economic crisis, the facilitating function precedes, pushing the controlling factor aside. For an explanation we have to refer in the first place to a reduction of state power in economic affairs and an economic hegemony. In this climate customs are under pressure to commit 'corruption' with the aim to protect the interests of the private sector. Customs have to work also in a competitive climate. Companies threaten to leave the harbour for another one if the customs officers apply controls too strictly. Under these circumstances custom officers feel themselves forced into very ambiguous positions and pushed into 'corrupt' decision making. It is important to refer to the work of Anand, Ashforth, and Joshi (2005) who stated that "*denial of responsibility is a rationalization that is rather easily adopted when experiencing intensive pressure from top management to meet numeric targets*" (Anand, Ashforth, and Joshi, 2005, p 12). At the individual level officers might justify their decisions pretending that this is the only way to reach organisational objectives. Consequently, they minimise their personal responsibility in the process of corruption.

Gobert and Punch estimated the social, economic and cultural factor as 'contributing' to a tolerant climate for crime. In studying the aetiological elements of corruption in the customs administration, the macro-level seems to take a more prominent place than purely 'contributing'. The pressure for a more liberal market and the restriction of public control on international trade is central to the development of grand corruption in the customs administration: it puts people and the whole organisation under pressure and disturbs the relationship between controller and controlled.

The nature and structure of the organisation

The second step of our analysis concerns the nature of the organisation. Questions that arise when talking about the nature of the organisation are: Can we say something relevant about the culture? How is the organisation's formal structure presented? How does it work in practice? Do people communicate?

A first element that is striking is the heritage of a bad reputation. Saying you work for the customs administration still makes people smile: *customs are people who live of earned wages two times, one officially and one informally by the extras they are offered or take.* Customs still carry a bad name because of the activities of the past: 20 years ago corruption was a way of working. It was part of the organisational culture. The customs officers with a considerable number of years of service confirmed the habit of 20 years ago to put some money in the documents that had to be verified, even without any direct expectations. Other stories varied from customs officers who worked for crates of beer, excise controllers who get drunk during their trajectory of controlling bars, even bosses who had their office in the pub, senior officers who were overloaded with presents on New Year's Eve, custom officers who took samples of sport shoes or clothes for private use. Even though people still relate the profession of customs officer to corruption and even though some customs officers still abuse their job position, we dare say that this explicit culture of "doing nothing for nothing" belongs to the past. However during the frequent contacts with the customs administration it was obvious that the bad name has in the best case a negative influence on job satisfaction. This bad reputation may for some people lead to a kind of self-fulfilling prophecy which turns the heritage of a bad reputation into an aetiological factor for petty corruption or street corruption. As one of the customs said: "*when controlling the cargo of cigarettes and alcohol we are used to getting a bottle of whisky or something else tax free. So What? That's not corruption hey?*"

A second element of the organisation that may explain corruption of customs is the weak leadership of staff in leading positions. In "police corruption" Punch writes: "*as an emergency organisation with considerable powers one might expect that leadership would be forcefully present in policing. In practice the top layers of police organisations are, like other organisations, arenas for egos and power-plays, and inter-personal factionalism fosters divisiveness, infighting and paralysis at the top of the echelon*" (Punch, 2009, 35). The Federal Bureau of Ethics and Deontology considers the lack of leadership on all levels of the administration as one of the main furthering circumstances for corruption. The lack of leadership quickly filters through the layers of the organisation. The interviewees of the Bureau see a strong leadership as a guarantee for a corruption free organisation (interview-31/05/'10) Weak leadership is also experienced as a problem in the customs administration, not only at the top level but on every layer of the organisation. "*Customs in responsible positions see themselves as practising an independent profession without taking on the related accountability. The only thing they do is delegating*" (interview-11-06-10).

An element that makes leadership in the customs administration different from that of the police service is the relationship to the private companies and the expectations on the level of economic support we described regarding the first key element. When private companies try to keep a grip on the control activities of the customs officers it is at the level of those in responsible positions that are the first target to be influenced: they have the competence to adjust what are perceived as too severe procedures or decisions. These people have the difficult task of finding the balance between taking care of the continuity of the customs order and not restricting the economic activities too heavily. Some of them incline too much towards favouring the private companies and set a bad example to the lowers ranks of people who work for them. This was one of the reasons why it was a hard job to organise a compulsory anti-corruption training for the lower levels C and D of the organisation which see corruption "*as a problem of the top of the organisation!*"

Another aspect that makes organisations vulnerable to corruption is the commercial way of thinking that has gradually infiltrated into public organisations since the introduction of New Public Management. Civil servants are supposed to call the citizens and companies they have to control their "clients" and they are asked to work "client-oriented". Speaking in terms of clients and taking a client-related attitude places customs officers in an ambiguous position. It is as if they have to take care not to lose the company they have to control while in fact they only have to provide a correct and proper service. "The competition between the harbours of Antwerp and Rotterdam" has often been cited as a motivation for being "client oriented".

A last example of vulnerability in the nature of the organisation is the control side. Control in an organisation takes the same shape as control in society, top-down formal control and horizontal informal control.

To start with the top-down control the disciplinary regulation of civil servants forces staff to report irregularities to their superiors in the organisation. It was striking that the overwhelming majority of customs officers refuse to report irregularities and illegal activities to a superior. A first reason for keeping silence is the fear for reprisals of the superior or the colleague, such as being transferred to another service or being marginalised on the work floor. This fear was mainly illustrated with specific stories about people who were *banned* to the farthest check point of the customs because they reported irregularities. Further research is needed to know whether the fear of reprisal is well-founded or only a wrong perception. A second reason for not reporting was the feeling that it makes no sense: when they report a severe violation of a company, the complaint seems to be dropped or the proposed sanction is lightened; when they report improper behaviour of colleagues, they receive the advice to shut up. A third reason is the unmanageable disciplinary rules. A disciplinary procedure takes too long and is too complex to be a deterrent for the perpetrator and for his surroundings. "*It takes years before the definitive judgement can be pronounced and in most cases it means a warning*" (interview BCO – 11-6-10).

Also the informal social control of colleagues at the same level seems to be weak. As mentioned before some specific functions are considered to be independent jobs that do not need any consultation of the colleagues. In general most people did not see the value of informal control in their team. It is a culture of every man for himself. People see things and know very well who is correct in the job and whose integrity is doubtful but they keep quiet out of collegiality, because of little interest in the job, because of an organically growing kind of hierarchy based on age, gender or seniority or as already mentioned because of fear for reprisal. The trainers have felt this informal social control of talking to colleagues, warning colleagues against irregularities, supporting the integer behaviour of colleagues as one of the major conditions for an efficient preventive anti-corruption policy for the BCO and that particularly because the customs officers are not ready to report irregularities to the supervisor.

Rationality / intentionality

A third key variable for Gobert and Punch is the question of whether people deliberately commit corruption. That implies a rational decision making. However, some characteristics of the job make rational decision making difficult. A first element is the lack of distinct rules: the charter of the federal public officer (Statuut Camu of 1937) forbids for example to accept any favour or present. In practice there is an unwritten rule that customs officers must be reasonable in accepting presents within a context of being customer oriented. For the lowest levels of the organisation accepting a pen or a ca-lendar for Christmas is reasonable. However the definition of reasonability seems be extremely flexible the higher one comes in the organisation. Also the limit of what is acceptable is not clear. Most people have enough experience and self-control to know the limit of acceptability: a calendar for New Year or some sweets to share with the colleagues is acceptable but a present after dealing with a difficult file of a private company is not acceptable. Some people are not able to define the limit of what is acceptable because of a lack of experience or because of a blurring of ethics allowing the demarcation line of the unacceptable to become vague.

Some decisions are rational but based on limited information about the rules. Younger people who enter the job without a proper training in integrity are sometimes in doubt of what is acceptable or not when a client tries to persuade *that it is really a habit to accept and that the predecessors did always accept.* Some people have the chance to work together with experienced colleagues who know the rules and introduce new people to the tricks of the private companies. Others have to work independently without support and without training or receiving clear rules. In some cases customs officers confirmed to be victims of unintentional corruption because of a lack of professional support.

Communication and transparency is fundamental for rational decision making. Because of a strict hierarchic construction and a structural fragmentation in the organisation customs officers in the lower executive positions have the feeling that the top-down communication is totally blocked. For all kinds of technical support and practical questions people feel as if they have to find *a creative solution* that may be irregular and sometimes even illegal. "*But what can we do if a row of truck drivers are impatiently waiting at your counter because the electronic system has broken down again?*"

Because of the limited and vague information "bounded rationality" is a more appropriate expression of decision making in the organisation (Vaughan, 1996, p 37-38).

Neutralisation / moral disengagement

A fourth and last variable we explore is the neutralisation or moral disengagement of customs officers. During the anti-corruption training we ran into a constant opposition from the side of the participants. The origin and genuineness, the importance and the usefulness of this training were questioned within almost every group. Regarding the origin of the anti-corruption training for example, we received comments that this was "*only for the interest of the top-level managers who want to safeguard themselves against current scandals which will be uncovered soon*". Or: "*This is only for promoting our director-general candidature for a function within the World Customs Organization*". The importance of this prevention programme was also questioned in relation to more urgent and practical professional training e.g. dealing with aggression, language training courses, handling accounting programs etc. "*There is never money for courses and now they put so much money for this anti-corruption training!*". Last but not least we received comments referring to the usefulness of this training. "*I never experienced corruption on the job so why do I need this training?*" On the other hand some motivated that "*because we have never experienced corruption on the beat we have no idea how things go and how this can be prevented*". These comments might be expressions of job frustration within this organisation. Or even if we do not know the severity of the corruption problem in the organisation, it might be a technique to minimise the uneasy threat of corruption. This introduction brings us to the mechanisms of disengagement as a mechanism to deny corruptive practices.

This social cognitive theory of 'Moral Disengagement', introduced by Bandura, attempts to explain how individuals who are engaged in reprehensible behaviour justify their activities. This social-cognitive perspective conceptualises moral identity as an organised cognitive representation, or schema, of moral values, goals, traits, and behavioural scripts (Shao *et al.,* 2008). Within this context moral disengagement should be understood as a person's ability to 'rationalise' deviant behaviour in such a way that it appears to be less harmful (Bandura *et al,* 1996, p 365). These rationalisations might follow deviant behaviour as protecting the perpetrator from blame of others after the act while maintaining his self-esteem. Disengagement mechanisms however, may also morally facilitate non-compliance and pave the way to corruption (Huisman and Vande Walle, in review; Coleman, 1987; Topalli, 2005, p 825-826). The sociological neutralisation theory of Sykes and Matza also argued that there is reason to believe that neutralisation techniques precede deviant behaviour and make deviant behaviour possible (Sykes and Matza, 1957, p 666; Anand *et al.*, 2005). Bandura distinguished eight different cognitive mechanisms through which the moral disengagement process operates (Bandura *et al.*, 1996, p 365-366; Moore, 2008, p 130). In the first place, the mechanisms euphemistic labelling, moral justification and advantageous comparison with more reprehensible activities facilitate the cognitive restructuring of acts in such a way that they appear to be less harmful. Secondly, an individual may minimise his part in the caused harm using cognitions which allow for displacement of responsibility and diffusion of responsibility. Finally, one might reframe the impact of his actions by distorting the consequences, dehumanization or attribution of blame.

So far, scientific work on moral disengagement primarily focused on explaining large-scale inhumanities (Bandura *et al.*, 1996, p 366) and more recently Osofsky empirically observed the disengagement mechanism involving prison personnel engaged in executions (Osofsky *et al.*, 2005, p 371). More recently researchers started to address the question of rationalisation strategies and corruption in organisations (Moore, 2008; Rabl and Kühlmann 2009). In 2008 Celia Moore theoretically explored for the first time Bandura's concept of moral disengagement in the context of organisational corruption. She argues that the mechanisms of disengagement help to 'initiate', 'facilitate' and 'perpetuate' corruption in an organisation through their effect on morale awareness, unethical decision-making and organisational advancement (Moore, 200, p 129).

Figure 1
Scheme of disengagement

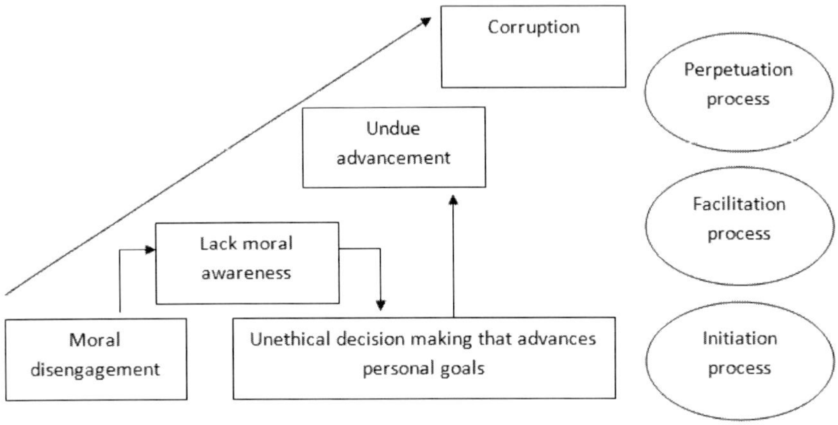

Based on the pictorial representation of the moral disengagement process within context of organizational corruption introduced by Celia Moore (2008).

During the course of the anti-corruption training we not only had the opportunity to discuss neutralisation techniques but also to observe in an indirect way the dynamics of disengagement mechanisms on the 'initiation', 'facilitation' and the 'perpetuation' process. Our observations intuitively support the theoretical framework introduced by Celia Moore. She hypothesises that moral disengagement 'initiates' corruption by easing and making individual decision making less strict. In doing so, some individuals set a tone by repeatedly making unethical decisions resulting in a tacit tendency towards corruption. This opens the door for the socialisation of other colleagues into corrupt actions (Moore, 2008, p 131). Take for example a bureau of customs agents having an espresso machine and receiving regularly very fine coffee for free. Striking is the interpretation they give to this situation: "*It is not our fault that we have a big importer of coffee in our district. What should this company give us otherwise . . . and besides the amount of coffee we receive has no value at all for such a big company.*"

This moral justification makes it very easy to restructure the context of the behaviour as less blameworthy. Another example is the case in which private companies pay for expensive private training for custom agents or give them a portable notebook. Private companies financing training courses of public servants might undermine the independent position of custom officers doing their job and result in a conflict of interest. However, this way of gift giving is not questioned at any time during the prevention training: "*Because this allows us to organise our controls in a more efficient way and not to avoid investigations*". . . "*the government does not give me a portable pc, but since I got one I'm able to finish my controls more quickly and efficiently*". In a very easy way persons seem to facilitate the cognitive restructuring of high risk situations to appear not corrupt at all: "*It is in the interest of my job, the government and the companies. This is no corruption . . .*"

Moral disengagement is also hypothesised to be involved in the 'facilitation' of corruption because it erodes the awareness of the moral content of decisions. Firstly, a frequently used euphemism to avoid speaking about corruption is that officers "*have to serve the economic interest, or have to re-orientate their position from a controlling to a more client-oriented service*". In doing so, individuals might have the impression to be less responsible for decline of morals within the organisation. Secondly, the mechanism of comparing advantages seems to play a significant role in the facilitation process: "*Do you call this corrupt? You should know how they did business in the past, that is what I call corrupt . . .*" Another mechanism that we observed on this level is persons stating that they have no other options than to go with the main stream: "*If all my colleagues accept this . . . it would be suspicious that I refuse to do so.*" It is surprising how easily people construct a moral justification for being engaged in blameworthy activities. Both examples illustrate the cognitive restructuring of corrupt acts to appear less harmful or blameworthy. Discussing the issue of smuggling waste to poorer countries evokes the mechanism of displacement of responsibility to minimise the actor's role in harm caused by corruption "*This is not our responsibility but the one of the African waste manager dumping toxic waste, he is responsible for the damage and not us*".

Finally, moral disengagement mechanisms further the 'perpetuation' of corruption. In some way this is an exceptional situation because corruption is a real fact. From a preventive point of view the following observations are very pertinent. A lot of participators raised the point that "*it is not any more to them to address corrupt colleagues. This is solely the responsibility of the directors*". Or: "*If our director doesn't take his responsibility, why should we do it instead of him or her?*" In some way this is the dissemination via the displacement of responsibility and diffusion of responsibility. Others stated that it is more important to cover for a colleague than to report alleged infringements to the management. "*We have been working together for years, we know each other and I don't want to be the cause of proceedings against him.*" This is a moral justification for not blowing the whistle. Striking is that also the nature and the structure of the organisation have influence on the mechanisms of moral disengagement. The already cited computer-controlled PLDA system selecting the verification of goods leads to situations in which diffusion of responsibility and attribution of blame pave the way for moral blurring and perpetuate corruption within an organisation:

> "*If the top managers think they know it better, they should do the verifications themselves. I have a premonition about suspicious transports, but if the system does not select it to be controlled it is not longer my responsibility.*" "*The system itself is corrupt because it is too liberal and only serves the interest of private companies. It is made to protect corrupt companies.*"

One might question the relevance of our attention to the mechanisms of moral disengagement. However, once the process of corruption starts it is very difficult to put a stop to corruption. According to Osse this can be explained by the social psychological concept '*cognitive dissonance reduction theory*' from Festinger (Osse, 1997, p 59). This theory stated that people desire to keep their cognitions in balance. Whenever there is a cognitive inconsistency – a state of mind with which one's his beliefs, attitude and behaviour are not compatible – people might display irrational and sometimes maladaptive behaviour or adapt their attitudes (Brehm and Kassin, 1996, p 399) to restore the imbalance. This can be illustrated by the following scenario: verifications are organised in a lax way to favour particular companies. This might produce a state of moral discomfort which has to be reduced. Note that since the behaviour already took place, the only way out to reduce these "bad feelings" is to change his cognitions. Take for example a custom officer who accepts gifts. He knows he is a good servant and knows that accepting gifts is not allowed (cognition 1). However, he accepts the gift which gives him a bad feeling (cognition 2). Seeing that the acceptance has already taken place he has to add a new cognition to end his bad feeling: "*This gift does not mean that I am no longer independent in doing my job and it will not affect my decisions*" (add a new cognition). It is at this point that we brought in dilemma discussions into the training in order to sharpen their insight in the mechanisms of moral disengagement and become less vulnerable. Secondly, we found that servants are experts in re- cognising signals that might indicate that other colleagues are also struggling with integrity. As it has been repeatedly observed, (Kamp and Brooks, 2005, p 447; Werner, 1983, p. 151) the influence of the attitudes of colleagues on the behaviour of employees should not be underestimated. Employee deviance is more constrained by informal social controls present in primary work-group relationships than by the more formal reactions to deviance by those in positions of authority within the formal organisation. At this point we brought in communication training in which communication skills are practiced within the frame of

'Systems Thinking'. The customs officers train the skills of naming the deviant behaviour of their colleague.

Conclusion and discussion

To gain a better understanding of the aetiology of corruption in the specific context of the BCO we utilised the key variables of Gobert and Punch. We consider this aetiological exploration as a first step into the establishment of a tailor-made anti-corruption policy. We must bear in mind, however, that the daily practice of the BCO is more complex than presented in our discussion and oversimplification must be avoided. Concepts such as leadership encompass much more elements than brought into our discussion. Besides, we are the first to admit that the presented variables do not interact independently and are related to each other. As a result of a too fragmented analysis one might conclude that one particular measure used to influence just one variable will lead to a corruption free organisation. That is too narrow an approach. Corruption is a slumbering process of blurring moral norms. Neither persons nor organisations turn out to become corrupt from one day to another. For that reason we are convinced that the best way to fight corruption is the prevention by awareness raising, especially because we have experienced during the prevention training that it is difficult to stop corrupt activities that have become embedded within daily routines.

An anti-corruption training is a possible preventive tool to make people aware of corruption. Some participants came to the training with a limited understanding of corruption: *corruption was something for crooks*. During the training we think we have succeeded in giving people a more comprehensive understanding of the phenomenon, its causes and consequences. Firstly, knowledge gives people the ability to take rational decisions and to recognise contexts and situations potential risks related to corruption. Secondly the communication training on specific corruptive situations forced people in saying *no* to corruption and to alert colleagues in a delicate position. Also the point of weak informal social control was something we worked hard on during the training: *how to condemn unethical behaviour of a colleague without destructing the relationship*. A reaction of colleagues at the first sign of corruption may protect the corrupter to slip further into a career of corruption. Thirdly the introduction of the concept of moral disengagement and the illustration of neutralisation techniques prepared people to be attentive for neutralisations. Finally and that is maybe the strongest argument for a day's training session was the chance to discuss a topic that otherwise never comes up for discussion and to exchange experiences and moral attitudes with colleagues.

Nevertheless we are convinced that an anti-corruption training should not be an isolated initiative. There is no doubt that on the organisational level some elementary preconditions must be respected. For example a code of conduct and a culture of integrity must be elaborated. But there are other conditions to be fulfilled. Most of the participants made it clear that they are in fact willing to support the prevention of corruption but not at any price. Once confronted with corruption the willingness to take action decreases. The positive informal social control is weak because people fear reprisals and harassments, which points at another, negative social control.

A central problem is the question of the status of the whistle-blower. It was a common feeling that rather than the offender, the one who reports a case of corruption will be the scapegoat. Most of the participants admitted also that they did not have a clue who they should address to report cases of corruption. We stress the importance of a clear channel for individuals to report information on corruption with attention to the position and protection of the whistle-blower. In the meantime the BCO has taken initiative to set up a kind of report desk at the top level of the organisation for not integer practices. The initiators are aware of the dependency-problem that pops up when people are invited to report to members of the organisation. Nonetheless, it is at least something awaiting a formal regulation of whistle blowing for the federal administration. Another weakness is leadership of people who are resistant to the economic pressure and support their employees in an integer exercise of their duties. Also the absence of top-down communication makes the organisation vulnerable for corruption when customs officers are forced to take creative solutions or when they are forced to work with new systems of control without any explanation why. The Flemish customs administration consists of too many frustrated people who started the job full of idealism but who gradually lost the motivation to do their job properly. This training experience provided evidence that an anti-corruption policy is than a discussion on the new paint colours. In order to be efficient we first need to scrape off the old layers of paint before choosing the new colour.

References

Anand, V., B. Ashforth and M. Joshi, Business as usual: the acceptance of perpetuations of corruption in organizations. *Academy of Management Executive*, 2005, *no. 4*, 9-23

Bandura, A., C. Barbaranelli, G.V. Caprara, C. Pastorelli, Mechanisms of moral disengagement in the exercise of moral agency, *Journal of Personality and Social Psychology*, 1996, 364–374

Box S., *Power, crime and mystification*, London, Tavistock Publications, 1983

Brehm, S. and S. Kassin, *Social Psychology*, Boston, Houghton Mifflin, 1996

Coleman, J.W., Toward an integrated theory of white-collar crime. *American Journal of Sociology*, 1987, *no. 2*, 406-439

Duyne P.C. van, Will Caligula go transparent? Corruption in acts and attitudes, *Forum on Crime and Society*, 2001, vol. 1, *no. 2*, 73-98

Gobert J. and M. Punch, *Rethinking corporate crime*. London, Butterworths Lexisnexis, 2003

Huisman W., *Tussen winst en moraal. Achtergronden van regelnaleving en regelovertreding door ondernemingen*. Den Haag, Boom, 2001.

Huisman W. and G. Vande Walle, The criminology of corruption. In: G. De Graaf G., P. von Maravić and P. Wagenaar, *The good cause. Theoretical perspectives on corruption*. Barbara Budrich, 2010

Kamp, J. and P. Brooks, Perceived organisational climate and employee counterproductivity, *Journal of Business and Psychology*, 2005, *no. 4*, 447-458

Moore, C., Moral disengagement in processes of organizational corruption, *Journal of Business, Ethics*, 2008, *no. 1*, 129-139

Osofsky, M., A. Bandura and Ph. Zimbardo, The role of moral disengagement in the execution process. *Law and Human Behaviour*, 2005, *no. 4*, 371-393

Osse, A., Corruption prevention: a course for police officers fighting organised crime, *Crime, Law & Social Change*, 1997, 53-71

Passas N., Anti-corruption agencies and the need for strategic approaches: a preface to this special issue, *Crime, Law and Social Change*, 2010, 53, *no. 1*, 1-3

Ponsaers P. and B. Hoogenboom, Het moeilijke spel van wortel en stok - Organisatiecriminaliteit en handhavingstrategieën van bijzondere inspectie- en opsporingsdiensten. *Tijdschrift voor Criminologie*, SISWO, Amsterdam, 2004, Jg. 46, *no. 2*, p. 165-181

Punch M., *Police corruption. Deviance, accountability and reform in policing*. Devon, Willan Publishing, 2009

Punch M., police corruption and its prevention, *European Journal on Criminal Policy and Research*, Vol.8, nr.3, September 2000, 301-324

Rabl, T., M.T. Kühlmann, Why or why not? Rationalizing corruption in organizations, *Cross Cultural Management*, 2009, *no. 3*, 268-286

Shao, R. D., K. Aquino, et al., "Beyond Moral Reasoning: A Review of Moral Identity Research and Its Implications for Business Ethics. *Business Ethics Quarterly*, 2008, 18(4): 513-540

Sutherland E., *White-collar crime*, New York: Holt Rinehart and Winston, 1949

Sykes, G.M. and D. Matza, Techniques of neutralizations: A theory of delinquency, *American Sociological Review*, 1957, *no. 6*, 664-670

Topalli, V., When being good is bad: an expansion of neutralization theory, *Criminology*, 2005, *no. 3*, 797-835

Vander Beken T. *et al.*, Crossing geographical, legal and moral boundaries. The Belgian cigarette black market. In: P.C. van Duyne and G. Antonopoulos, *The criminal smoke of tobacco policy making. Cigarette smuggling in Europe*, Nijmegen, Wolf Legal Publishers, 2009, 77-90

Vande Walle G. (2010), The continuum of conflicts of interest: from corruption to clubbing and the underlying risks at victimisation. In: M. Cools, B. De Ruyver, M. Easton, L. Pauwels, P. Ponsaers, G. Vande Walle, T. Vander Beken, F. Vander Laenen, G. Vermeulen, G. Vynckier, (eds.), *New empirical data: Theories and analyses on safety, societal problems and citizens' perceptions.* Maklu, Governance of Security Research Papers Series, Volume 3, Antwerpen-Apeldoorn, 2010, p. 312

Vaughan D., *Controlling unlawful organisational behaviour. Social structure and corporate misconduct*, Chicago, the University of Chicago press, 1985

Vaughan D., *The Challenger launch decision. Risky technology, culture and deviance at NASA*. The University of Chicago Press, 1996

Vaughan D., Criminology and the sociology of organizations. Analogy, comparative social organization, and general theory, *Crime, Law and Social Change*, 2002, 37, *no. 2*, 117-136.

Vogl, F., Global corruption: applying experience and research to meet a mounting crisis, *Business and Society Review*, 2007, 112: *no. 2*, 171-190

Werner, S. B., New directions in the study of administrative corruption, *Public Administration Review*, 1983, *no. 2*, 146-154

Searching for the contours of the anti-corruption policy in Serbia[1]

Petrus C. van Duyne, Elena Stocco,
Miroslava Milenović, Milena Todorova[2]

Sisyphus' hard labour: Serbian corruption policy uphill?

Among (political) researchers it is common to cast policy making in elegant models consisting of a variety of rationally interacting stakeholders (Freeman, 1984). This rational approach should also apply to the fight against corruption. This phenomenon can even be assigned a 'rational' though unwanted place (Jager, 2003), one may wonder whether this reflects our desire for rational order rather then this shady form of decision making. Also the fight against corruption rarely passes a rational and orderly sequences of milestones, particularly in countries with a long history of mal-governance. There the picture is that of highly promising initiatives followed by a disorderly process of sliding back to 'normal' (for Italy, see Newell, 2004). In such political landscapes rational models do not seem to apply. Instead, the metaphor of the mythical King Sisyphus may be more appropriate. In this ancient Greek myth Sisyphus must push a rock up the hill which in the end rolls back again after which the attempt must be repeated. However, the metaphor does not hold fully. The wily King Sisyphus was condemned to this punishment by the Olympic Gods because he cheated them. But the reverse happens on the 'corruption hill'. The cheaters are the ones who condemn the corruption fighters to do the Sisyphus work: pushing the anti-corruption task

1 This is research in progress. An Earlier version of this article was published in Journal of Financial Crime, Volume 17, Issue 1, Emerald Group Publishing Limited. The first phase of the research project was initiated by the OSCE Mission in Serbia. We thank the Republican Prosecution Office for supporting this research.

2 The first author is professor of empirical penal science at Tilburg Univeristy, Netherlands and head of the Serbian Corruption Project (Petrus@uvt.nl), Elena Stocco is senior researcher in the project and Head Operations (elena_stocco@yahoo.it) Miroslava Milenovic is certified fraud examiner and forensic accountant (k.m@eunet.rs); Milena Todorova is consultant and researcher (milena_al@yahoo.com).

uphill. Meanwhile the corrupters within the public administration are primarily interested in seeing the rock rolling back again even if their official role may be lending support.

Does Serbia reflect the essentials of the King Sisyphus myth: pushing up the anti-corruption rock which rolls back again? And to make it more complicated as well as most intriguing, roles are not defined: who pushes up the stone today may push it down tomorrow.

Of course, metaphors must be given substance in terms of observables. To that end in 2008 a research Serbian-Dutch project set out to reconnoitre the field by taking stock of the available material, whether from the open sources or from the institutions, in particular the data provided by the Republican Public Prosecution Office (RPPO) and Statistical Bureau. These data, even if imperfect, are the basis for the second report of the anti-corruption policy by a selection of administrative institutions and law enforcement.[3] Given the unknown territory it proved to be a true reconnaissance full of pitfalls which we will depict while describing this endeavour.

Before we give an account of this undertaking, we will first project a broader background in the following two sections, as Serbia stands neither alone nor is unique in matters of corruption.

"If left to itself": the prying eye of the EU

When Milošević fell from power (autumn 2000) Serbia returned to the fold of the 'family of European states', even if political instability rendered that process somewhat halting. This return entailed, among other things, working towards 'good governance': fighting corruption, alongside organised crime and money-laundering. These are not isolated phenomena, particularly if one touches political and financial interests being beyond the 'usual suspects' of the rough Serbian underworld, as described by Logonder (2008). At these higher social and economic levels one is likely to find negative and positive influential stakeholders though their roles are rarely clearly recognisable. This induced us to apply the Sisyphus metaphor: attempts to fight corruption and hidden opponent forces which push the reformers downhill.

This is not a surprising observation. Similar observations have been made about the Ukraine (Osyka, 2003), Italy (Newell, 2004), Bosnia and Herzegovina (Datzer *et al.*, 2007) and Macedonia (Karadzoski, 2009). Indeed, tackling corrup-

3 An earlier report was published in *Temida*, 2009, nr. 4

tion can also be compared to a surgical operation which cuts deeply into a social and political tissue. And 'surgical' social operations use to be painful to those who have more to lose than to gain from an effective anti-corruption policy, particularly when corruption has become a daily aspect of personal relationships and a financial completion to one's income.

Thinking about those who stand to lose from fighting corruption one is tempted to think of a cynical political elite, those 'on the top of the hill', who have the leverage of rolling back or slowing down the pace of reform. A well-documented example of such a push-back leverage is the Italian prime-minister Berlusconi who from the moment he came in office succeeded in rolling back the anti-corruption policy with EU Member States devoted to fighting corruption raising an eyebrow (Newell, 2004, p 213; Stille, 2007). But such an elite action would be little effective without sufficient 'co-sinners' within broader layers of the population to whom a bit of corruption means a bit of extra advantage, compensating the bribes they have to pay (Datzer *et al.*, 2007). As a matter of fact, if left to itself, corruption can become firmly rooted in democratic society too, as long as a sufficient number of people feel that profit making out-weights victimisation. One does not need sinister oligarchs to have an enduring corrupt society.

However, "If left to itself . . . " At present, the problem of corrupt regimes is that they are no longer left to themselves (Andvig, 2003). The present economic, socio-political interconnectedness, particularly on the European continent, does not allow anymore that states are left to themselves. Depending on their political and economic power, the states in the 'European space' have to respond to the attention shown by the European Union or the Council of Europe concerning their 'state of corruption'. Of course there are differences, as not all animals in the European 'Animal Farm' are equal. A powerful or an isolated state, such as respectively Russia or Belarus, can display a sovereign indifference to what the Council of Europe or the EU think of them. This does not apply to countries closer to or more dependent on the EU or striving for EU Member State such as the successor states of Yugoslavia. After the last Balkan war these countries, Serbia not excluded, have good reasons for not wanting to be 'left to themselves', certainly not by the EU.

This political situation implies that the present image of widespread corruption in Serbia is not just an internal problem: it also affects Serbia's relationship to the EU. Two years ago, 21 October 2008, Enlargement Commissioner Olli Rehn remarked that (corporate) corruption poses a barrier to Serbia's candidacy for the EU: "*Serbia may gain EU candidate status in 2009 but must crack down on corporate corruption.*" This has a bearing on our Sisyphus metaphor of the Serbian anti-corruption policy, because nobody wants to be branded as a 'roller-down'. Nevertheless, next to active proponents of the anti-corruption policy others may have contrary interests. They cannot demonstrate that overtly but may simply 'sit down', which may be just as effective as 'rolling down'. Or, even more confusing, they may display alternating phases of actively helping a bit and then sitting down again, depending on what interests is at stake.[4] And the interests at stake can be big, as is elaborated in the next section.

'Owning' the state and 'sitting down'

It is usual to depict the anti-corruption policy making in terms of a moral fight of 'good against bad'. But abstracting from such a moral setting, we are actually dealing with rational conduct concerning the stakes in (public and political) decision making. This can be formulated in a formal *decision making* model or a *principal-agent-customer* model (Van Duyne, 2001; Jager, 2004). The decision making approach focuses on the illegal exchange situation in decision making. The principal-agent model concerns the balance between delegating tasks to executive agents, who may act corruptly but controlling them against this is expensive. How to balance? In both models decision making is abused for getting or retaining illegal advantages. In the public domain the spoils are mainly 'public goods' for which there are always many competing bidders. In a (democratic) rule of law bidders should have an equal chance in profiting from such decision processes. This requires transparency in decision making: 'To be seen by all'. This is rational, but only at an abstract, impersonal level. At individual level the converse is true: it is rather rational that every (self-) interesting participant strives for a maximum personal gain and not for the highest degree of transparency, unless it suits him.

Therefore, transparency is not self-evident but requires a constant public vigilance for maintaining it. If this is the case in most countries with a democratic heritage, the situation in countries with a different political heritage will be much more difficult. In socialist countries like former Yugoslavia, the Socialist Party was the monopolist 'owner' of the state. With the disintegration of the Socialist Yugoslavian state, Serbia became (one of) the heir(s) of this one-party state slip-

[4] At the time of finalising this chapter a telling example of 'rolling down the stone was demonstrated by Parliament concerning art. 82 of the Law on the Anti Corruption Agency. This article does not allow elected officials to hold another position. An amendment was considered allowing elected officials a dual position until the end of their mandate. This was withdrawn after media uproar. An independent MP submitted it again. This amendment was accepted in Parliament 28 june and not vetoed by the President Tadic, leaving an angry Anti Corruption Agency appealing to the Constitutional Court and conveying its concern to the EU, the Council of Europe and the UN.

ping into the hands of many owners. Therefore, it is of importance to discuss briefly the issue of 'who owns the Serbian state' in terms of dispensing spoils.

In the literature on public policy making the phrase 'spoils system' has a negative connotation: 'looting the public fund'. While this is not unfounded as far as the effects can be concerned, it concerns an age old public reward system, certainly if the rewards do not consist of direct cash money. During the era of feudalism, lords, usually short of money, rewarded their retainers with lands and titles, as did the kings of the *ancien régime* or the Turkish overlords during most of their rule. In Western Europe this reward system was wiped away by the French Revolution. The unfolding modern (democratic) states could dispense neither land nor titles, but for the ruling elite it remained natural to reward each other with positions, albeit checked by the emerging bureaucracy with its meritocratic rules and democratic control procedures.

However, when democratic control procedures are weak, even multi-party states tend to slide back to the feudal-like reward system in which the role of the lord is replaced by that of political parties. After obtaining power a party rewards its retainers by dispensing them positions-with-income (or power) as if these were 'fiefs'. In addition, the parties themselves need funding too and may be dependent on funds from trade and industry or, rather, the leading businessmen. This happened in many ex-socialist countries, including Serbia, benefitting the business sector. This mutually beneficial dependency is strengthened by changeovers of the actors: businessmen entering parliament (immunity included) and politicians finding well-paid jobs in corporations which interests they used to take care of while being in public office. According to Pesić (2007) this is the 'feudal' socio-political situation in Serbia.

In Serbia the feudal spoils system is to a certain extent stable as from the many political parties four have regularly received sufficient electoral support for staying or returning to power. Each party leadership in a ruling coalition is given control over a part of the public 'reward pool' according to the number of 'their' Members of Parliament. This is implemented per public service column: the spoils in one column (for example, education or health) are all allotted to one party (Begović and Mijatovic, 2007) as long as that party is in power. Rewarded retainers of the previous election may find themselves ousted from their positions to be replaced by other beneficiaries. This is not a matter of some changes in the highest echelons of the political parties or the central administration. Actually, it is an exclusive right of political parties in a ruling coalition to make appointments in all public institutions resorting under the central authorities. With a potential of 40.000 positions this system reaches deep down into most services, down to local libraries or the headmaster of an elementary school in a small village (Pesić, 2007;

p 10). At local power level, the same occurs. Indeed, these positions are held as a modern 'fief', often irrespective of skills or qualifications.

Against this background it is fair to assume that the attitude of the political-entrepreneurial elite to anti-corruption policies will be at least ambiguous. Who 'owns' parts of the state will be more inclined to sit down than rolling the anti-corruption stone up-hill. The spread of interests with many shady strings does not make it easy to indentify at what side the various actors stand. This is the more the case when the flow of information is interrupted by interested actors keen on covering their interests. Therefore, opaqueness prevails, also for researchers.

Searching in twilight

The ambiguity alluded above may correlate with an opaque information landscape which affects research of corruption: the management of facts and figures are likely to reflect this opaque state of affairs. Therefore, our account of taking stock of what can be observed contains due caveats: these concern accounts of policy making products and law enforcement data from the Republican Public Prosecution Office (RPPO), the Courts and the Statistical Bureau.

With single corruption cases we find ourselves soon at the anecdotal level of scandals which use to attract the media. Usually they are highly illustrative for certain situations, but at this stage of the project they are less suitable for a systematic investigation.[5] Therefore, we restrict ourselves to what can be observed as the outcomes of policy making and law enforcement.

In the first place, *policy making*. This encompasses anti-corruption legislation and putting into place institutions intended to combat corruption or to further public integrity. In the next section we will discuss the output of the institutions which proved to be far from clear and accessible, particularly concerning their websites (if existing at the time) and statistics. The Board of the Conflict of Interest had some crude statistics and the Anti Corruption Council has an archive, which has to be sorted out by hand. We postponed this task to the second phase of the research project. Other institutions, like the National Ombudsman, operate more remote from the issue of corruption, though their reports were inspected for references to or complaints about the anti-corruption policy.

---

5 This does not imply that an analysis of publications in the media would not reveal important aspects of the corrupt situation within the county. For example, it is of importance to address the situation of awareness within a country: the size of the coverage (place, preference), the sectors and how they are covered. See Begović and Mijatovic (2007, chapter V)

In the second place, the *law enforcement data*: there are crude statistics of reports, investigations, prosecutions and verdicts. Given the usually most restricted value and validity of such data in Western European countries with more sophisticated IT management, the research team realised to be most careful with processing and interpreting the data they could obtain. Indeed, a preceding project on money laundering in Serbia (Van Duyne and Donati, 2009), served as a serious warning of what could be expected. More detailed methodological aspects concerning these law enforcement data sources will be elaborated in the sections about the criminal law findings.

Despite all the caveats, this first data stocktaking together with the research literature is intended to shed a first ray of light on the Serbian anti-corruption policy and law enforcement.

Findings from institution building

Whether or not under foreign pressure (and rarely without, like the slow unfolding Anti-Corruption Strategy suggests; Begović and Mijatovic, 2007, p 204), anti-corruption institutions and regulations have been proposed, adopted, enacted and put into place, or at least some of them during the past decade. How did these fare?

As there are almost twenty of such regulations and their derivatives (laws, amendments, committees for implementation, commissions plus separate commissioners) which may create a confusing picture, we have 'sliced up' the anti-corruption bundle. We also 'sliced up' the time-path of these measures according to the usual milestones: dates of the start of the proposals, discussion, acceptance, putting into place and last but not least, the output if any dates were available.

We begin with the cluster of the anti-corruption plans. Then we will look at some more specific measures and institutions, some dealing directly, others somewhat more remotely with corruption. Not all are presented in the summarising table below.

a. The anti-corruption plan cluster

Interesting aspects of this summarised history of anti-corruption plans are the time-path, the output, the proposed responsible agents and powers of the proposed institutions or persons.

Table 1
Main anti-corruption clusters and milestones

Milestones	Anti-corruption National Strategy and Plan	Commission for the Implementation of the Action Plan and Strategy	Anti-Corruption Council	Anti-Corruption Agency
Beginning	2004: working group Law and Board on the Conflict of Interest	2006	Oct. 2001	2005
First date of discussion	May 2005: accepted by government, sent to Nat. Ass.			2006: Law on the Agency to fight corruption submitted.
Date accepted as plan or law	Accepted by Nat. Ass. in December 2005. Converted into an Action Plan.	Dec. 2005. March. 2006: the Government accepts its necessity.		Oct. 2008
Date fully implemented	Committee of the Agency to implement: March 2009	July 2006	2003	The Anti-corruption Agency operative January 2010.
Functions	The following fields to be covered: political, police and judiciary, public administration, territorial autonomy, self-government and public services, public finance, economic, participation of civil society and public in combating corruption Strategy implies three key factors:	▪ To make Action Plan for implementation National Strategy ▪ Overseeing the implementation of Action Plan and suggest measures for its improvement ▪ To make sector's action plans for fight against corruption ▪ To make Action plan for implementation GRECO's recommendations; ▪ Overseeing the implementation of GRECO recommendations and suggest measures for their improvement	Governmental working body, not independent; Implementation of anti-corruption measures; Suggestion of new measures and oversight.	▪ overseeing the implementation of the national strategy; ▪ resolving conflicts of interest; ▪ incorporates the Board of the Conflict of Interest ▪ coordinating all the state bodies; ▪ performing functions related to the law of financing political parties; ▪ high degree of independ-

	▪ effective implementation of anticorruption law; ▪ prevention, what means elimination possibilities for corruption; ▪ Increase public conscience and education with the purpose of public support for implementation of anticorruption strategy			ence reporting directly to the National Assembly; ▪ programmed costs: start up € 4,4 ml; salaries € 11 ml, program € 100.000
Challenges as of 2010	Unrealistic time table, no priorities, too broad responsibilities with tasks for Ministries, no estimation of resources needed.	From January 2010, the authorities of Commission will pass on Anti-Corruption Agency.	The Council will remain in place, next to the Anti-Corruption Agency.	Integrating broad input: financial reports of more than 20.000 civil servants and processing data from incorporated Board of the Conflict of Interest.
Observations:	Action plan must be changed, many deadlines were passed.	No known output. No infrastructure or power. Composed of Heads and High-level representatives of state institutions. Rarely meetings, the last one: May 2008	Lacking funds or status to employ staff. No powers of enforcement; the relation with the government is sour.	Has 37 staff of the total of 60 envisaged. Elaborate organisational structure and Board of ACA have put in place. Constitutional issues.

As far as the *time-path* is concerned, the Serbian authorities can correctly maintain that after the fall of Milošević they have been doing every year something on corruption. Politically that was unavoidable as the Council of Europe was watching and evaluating closely.[6] Hence, either an action-plan and strategy has been

6 See: Group of States against Corruption (GRECO), which issued in 2006 an evaluation report on the Republic of Serbia.

suggested, discussed, accepted, or a council, committee or agency established, a law passed and/or implemented. That looks like continually 'rolling the stone uphill'. But did the stone really move? Sometimes the passing of a law or a policy plan was postponed because of the dissolution of Parliament and new elections.

Looking at the *output* the picture is more difficult to interpret. Much seems to have been initiated, but the tangible outcomes are difficult to find. It looks like 'rolling up a bit and sitting down'. This may be due to lack of infrastructure, budget or power of enforcement, as is the case with the Anti Corruption Council, the Commission for the Implementation of the Action Plan and Strategy or the Law on the Financing of Political Parties (Trivunović *et al.*, 2007).

The Anti-Corruption Council assumed a kind of watchdog function, but it has no teeth to bite. In some letters to the government it did bark a bit, which resulted in a soured relationship (Trivunović *et al.*, 2007, p 67).[7] While the response of the government to these notifications remains unknown (or there was no response at all), an ambitious Anti-Corruption Strategy and Plan was drafted.[8] The tangible effects of this strategy are difficult to measure: some of the aims were formulated too imprecise to measure any effect (Begović *et al.*, 2007, p. 143).

All hopes are set on the 'big event' of 2010: the operational start of the Anti-Corruption Agency (ACA) which has taken over wide responsibilities. This had the effect of putting some anti-corruption activities 'on hold'[9], waiting what responsibilities would be transferred to this Agency.[10] For example, the Republic Board responsible for the oversight of the Law on the Prevention of Conflict of Interests has been incorporated in the ACA. Whether this will be the breakthrough is too early to determine. At the time of writing the ACA has 37 staff, partly coming from the previous Board of the Conflict of Interest.

It should be noted that this Agency will not function as a 'super department': it must mainly monitor and report on the progress of the ant-corruption strategy and create networks of cooperation.

---

7 On 15 September, the Council reported on irregularities during the privatisation of "Jugoremedija" Pharmaceutical Factory from Zrenjanin and concluded: "that the actions of the participants in the privatization of "Jugoremedija", both of the Government and the Buyer point to possible corruption." In another letter the same day concerning the privatisation of a Veterinary institute the Council remarked "Such decisions made by the Ministry of Economy and the Agency for Privatization imply that this is a case of either fundamental ignorance of the law, which is inadmissible for the highest state authorities, or corruption." Frank language, but not pleasing to the authorities.

8 Official Gazette of the Republic of Serbia", No. 109/05 from 9 December 2005

9 How the transfer of its expertise and information (particularly raw data) has taken place and how it will carry out its function within the Agency is still unclear.

10 The president of the main board of the Agency denies any absorption of the Anti-Corruption Council.

b. Prevention of conflict of interest

Having a law to further integrity and an institution to enforce it, does not imply that there is real progress in terms of interpretable output. A lot of activities may be going on, while it still remains unclear whether things are advancing or stagnating and for what reasons. A good example is the *Law on Prevention of Conflict of Interest in Discharge of Public Office*, which came into force 20 April 2004, one of the first steps mentioned in Table 1. Naturally, knowledge of the results of the enforcement of this law is of vital importance for obtaining insight into the state of corruption. After all, this law aims at transparency concerning the financial and material backgrounds of public servants. To this end the law specifies (summarised) that civil servants covered by this law shall declare their involvement in other enterprises as well as submit a full disclosure of moveable and unmoveable possessions of themselves as well as of their spouses and next of kin. Of course, to execute this requirement, the civil servants must fill standard forms which are processed, the results of which should be enlisted on the Property Register (art. 14). According to the same article the "*information on the salary and other income received [. . .] from the budget is **public***". Interested persons can evoke the Law of Free Access to the Information of Public Importance to obtain insight in the wealth and income of the obliged civil servants. No information was available whether citizens actually used this opportunity.

As can be seen in Table 2, the number of the annually submitted reports has increased dramatically: from 6.185 in 2005 to 7.685 in 2008 for which the Board has 13 staff for processing and checking. In total 1.253 procedures have been initiated against officials who had failed to submit a report; 108 processes were started against officials performing several public functions contrary to the Law's provisions. For 2008 the Republic Board reported on 102 measures it had pronounced against public servants ('public measures'). However, these are recommendations while compliance with these measures is a responsibility of the institutions or persons involved. The Board expressed its impression that the compliance level is still low. After the elections of 2008, in the expectation of dismissals and new appointments, the level of compliance also decreased. However, this may also be due to the expected transfer of its tasks to the Anti-Corruption Agency inducing an attitude of 'let us wait and see'".

Of other aspects of this law there is insufficient information. For example, "*The Republic Board (its steering body) shall monthly inform the public of irregularities it determines in the course of its work.*" Where is that relevant information? The available statistics are neither clear nor sufficiently broken down for a proper interpretation of what it purports to cover (see Table 2). Their presentation can hardly provide insight into what kinds of breaches of integrity are countered by the responsible institutions obliged to report to the Republic Board. Likewise it is unknown whether there are 'multiple sinners' over the years, leading to multiple counts. Therefore, the Board's efficacy is difficult to determine.

Table 2
Reports to the Republican Board on the Conflict of Interest and initiated procedures

Year	Submitted reports from officials	Procedure for not submitting	Confidential cautions	Public announcement of proposed measures
2005	6.185	193	8	2
2006	6.308	476	205	88
2007	6.926	180	201	76
2008	7.685	404	213	102
Total	27.104	1.253	627	268

Source: Republican Board of the Law on the Prevention of Conflict of Interest.

As already remarked, the Anti-Corruption Agency (ACA) has since January 2010 taken over all the conflict of interest issues. There is no information how the important historic records have been transferred. Safeguarding that information is essential for obtaining insight into four years of addressing conflicts of interest and the coming follow-up effects by the new Agency: it forms the null-measurement from where to start and measure later performance.

c. Protection of citizens' rights

Not all efforts to roll the anti-corruption stone up-hill met with a similar fate. Institutions which demonstrate appropriate determination to pursue their tasks of protecting the citizen's rights, and the right of information are:

- the Commissioner for Information of Public Importance and Personal data protection;
- the National Ombudsman.

These are institutions which have not been tasked to fight corruption directly, but in their task performance they have to deal continuously with the effects of corruption and lack of integrity. This is because they get complaints from citizens about dishonest or malfunctioning institutions which are allegedly keeping something behind. There may be direct corruption involved, for example if a procurement has been tampered with, or the corruption can be more indirect and indicative of foul play: for example, withholding information, postponing decisions for unclear reasons, preferential treatment etc. Providing details goes beyond the framework of this paper, but some selected observations are relevant as background, others because they are in line with other observations.

An essential citizen's right is the 'right to know': from the perspective of Transparency International a central tool against corruption. The Ombudsman cannot work without it and to protect this right Serbia has the institution of *The Commissioner for Information of Public Importance and Personal Data Protection*. This institution was established in 2004, based on the Law on Information of Public interest, enacted in the same year. Meanwhile, the Commissioner has processed many complaints:

Table 3
Complaints about the right to be informed

Year	New complaints	Unsolved in previous year	Total number of Complaints	Solved
2005			693	443
2006	1.741	106	1.847	1.188
2007	1.708	659	2.367	1.539
2008	1.517	828	2.345	1.521

Source: Commissioner for Information of Public Importance[11]

Whether this is to be rated as a success, is difficult to tell. But to the government apparently too successful: spring 2009 the government sent a draft law to the National Assembly, Law on Confidentiality of Information, intended to put restrictions on the freedom of information. This would seriously affect the work of the Commissioner (but also of the Ombudsman). In an open and not very kind letter, the Commissioner protested against this draft law: it "*was prepared, without any public discussion and possibility for the public, public experts before all, to make a contribution which is doubtlessly a prerequisite for such a Draft.*"[12]

Is the Commissioner correct in his concern of seeing another impediment in the up-hill struggle? From his perspective there are sufficient reasons of concern for marginalisation; the office of the Commissioner is seriously understaffed. This is not because of budgetary restraints but because of office space. In spite of all requests the Ministry of Finance does not allow a larger facility in which only 15 staff can be housed.

The effects of the activities of the Commissioner are also difficult to determine. While the Commissioner's decisions are final, he has no power to enforce them. Whether decisions have any effect outside the Commissioner's office is not

11 Reports available in Serbian, at: http://www.poverenik.org.rs/index.php/sr/doc/izvestaji

12 UNDP website, Public announcement, 05-08-2009

known. There is no information feedback to that effect, which makes it difficult to assess the rate of compliance: how often did the authorities *not* comply with the Commissioner's decision? We think this of vital importance as this reflects the real will of the authorities to comply with its own rules, which is more telling than any document on anti-corruption strategy.

Does the government has an 'attitude problem' with communication? If that is the case, it is most unambiguously formulated in the Ombudsman 2008 report. In the introduction the rapporteur was so frank as to point at a characteristic concerning a

> "*tendency of the executive not to react to the needs and problems in exercising human rights through more efficient application of current laws [. . .] but with a propensity to establish new institutions on paper, frequently by poor 'copy/paste' method. Failure to enforce current legislation cannot be continuously justified with its imperfection and the need to enact new laws.*"

This is amplified by the observation that

> "*a number of citizens are faced with an absurd situation – non-enforcement of judicial decisions by administrative authorities. In a high number of cases citizens complain of slow proceedings, stating as a rule corruption, disorganisation and idleness.*"[13]

The ombudsman sent a clear message: all the councils, commissions, strategies, action plans or agencies deployed in the fight against corruption have not made the slightest impression on the Serbian population thus far. Mal-governance, the breeding ground of corruption, is experienced as still being widespread.[14] Even if this may be considered as merely a 'subjective' impression of the population, it has to be countered by a more visible output of law enforcement.

Before crossing over to the criminal law aspects of corruption, it is appropriate to come to an intermediate stock taking. Surveying the past five years it remains difficult to obtain a clear picture of the anti-corruption policy, or rather, its implementation. To reiterate our metaphor: some policy makers and institutions are "rolling the stone up-hill". To which must be added: without adequate facilities, small pay and little help. Others sit still after some ritual stone pushing. Overall, hard evidence is difficult to obtain: if there is any success, it is difficult to know due to lack of precise information. In other words, after five years of anti-corruption policy making opacity still prevails.

---

13 Republic of Serbia, Protector of Citizens, *Report, 2008*, Beograd, 13 March, 2009. Introductory address of Saša Janković, p 6 and 14.

14 According to Transparency International in 2008 Serbia's country score as measured by the Corruption Perception Index is 3,4, shared by Albania and Montenegro as far as the Balkans is concerned. It also has Senegal, India and Madagascar at its same ranking. www.transparency.org. Consulted 8-9-2009

The criminal law picture

When it comes to empirical knowledge of corruption – based on proven 'hard facts' – it appears that systematic research about its extent and nature is rare. Most research is based on the *perception* of the citizens. In some research projects, such as carried out by Begović (2004) and Datzer *et al.*, (2007), and the Transparency International survey 2009[15], respondents have been interviewed about their *own experience*. For example: "*When did you pay your last bribe?*" As a matter of fact, police and criminal law data are scarce. This is not unique for Serbia: researching the prevalence of corruption is difficult in any jurisdiction.[16] Nevertheless, it is telling that in the survey volume of the state of corruption Europe (Bull and Newell, 2003) the chapter on corruption in 'Central and Eastern Europe' does not even mention Serbia (Holmes, 2003).

Apart from definitional problems, corruption is one of the most underreported offences, as it is usually a consensual crime with at least two complicit and often also with two satisfied criminal actors.[17] And even if a complaint has been filed, it is most uncertain whether the police will react or the prosecutor will prosecute. Hence, far from reflecting an underlying state of corruption, law enforcement data tell rather something of the agencies' activities and even then it is a story with many guesses. This does not imply that we should not attempt to tell this story.

Enabling us to research and tell this 'story' the Republican Prosecutor allowed the team to study and analyse the criminal cases handled by the Special Anti-Corruption Unit of the Public Prosecution Office.

Entering a brand new research field requires some scouting of data of which the value in terms of reliability and validity is unknown. Therefore, in the next section we will first discuss the nature of the information sources, which did not only consist of Public Prosecution data, but also of data from the Courts and the National Statistical Bureau. There proved to be no unified penal law data management: databases which should match did not do so. This entails that questions concerning reliability and validity have to be addressed while comparing the information sources. To the extent that the outcomes of the different sources do not match, we will have difficulties in drafting an integrated 'corruption picture'.

---

15 Transparency CPI 2009 and Transparency International Global Corruption Barometer. With score of 20 % Serbia towered above all the other Yugoslavian successor states.

16 For the comparable situation of official corruption statistics in the neighbouring Bosnia and Herzegovina, Maljević *et al.*, (2006; part III)

17 Of course, there is no satisfaction if the corruption amounts to extortion in cases when the citizen has a right to a certain service, but is pressurised to pay for it or for its timely delivery.

Data sources

The first data source consists of the data which the Republican Public Prosecution Office allowed us to inspect. These encompassed annual statistics, (lists of) 'corruption' cases sent by the Municipal and Districts Prosecution Offices to the Special Anti-corruption Department. However, it soon became clear that these data had to be complemented by other sources, for which reason the research team addressed the Statistical Bureau of Serbia. In addition, at the Belgrade District Court a number of finalised cases became available and have been studied too.

a. The Republican Public Prosecution Office (RPPO)

1. The RPPO **statistical database** concerning prosecutions and convictions is based on forms sent by the Prosecution Offices to the Republican Prosecutor's Office. It covers the years 2003-2006; for each year a separate report was issued. It contains penal law categories concerning (a) criminal offences against the economy; (b) crime against official duty and (c) other criminal offences related to a breach of integrity. These are broad categories containing other subgroups the relevance of which vary. The offences taking/offering bribes and illegal mediation, are of course of direct relevance. Of other categories the relevance is less certain, like 'abuse of office' or 'fraud at service'. Whether the latter categories are of real relevance is difficult to determine: nothing is known about a potentially relevant corrupt *conduct*. Fraud can be committed by a single person or by a trespasser paying off a supervisor or a controller. The same concerns 'abuse of office' or 'abuse of authorisation in the economy'.

It is important to bear in mind that in the RPPO database the *counting unit* is the criminal *case*, or more precisely, 'reports' submitted. Individual defendants are counted, but only as 'number of accused', 'position of the accused in the damaged company', 'found guilty/not guilty' and sentences, all differentiated per crime-category. How many suspected persons occur in the *incoming* reports is not mentioned. Therefore a horizontal comparison of the number of incoming reports with the subsequent procedural phases is not possible: e.g. the rejected reports, charged, convicted and punished persons. Basically, all reported/accused persons are aggregated or 'encapsulated' within the separate columns between which there is no statistical connection in terms of an identifiable counting unit.

In essence the RPPO database is an *annual* management instrument. It tallies up the decision steps in the case handling plus a limited number of case variables and characteristics of the accused. A comparison between the years is only possible for cases/criminal acts overflowing from the previous year which together with the pending cases indicate the beginning annual case load (= 100 %). The database is inflexible in the sense that it does not allow an independent breakdown based on identified counting units: what is not mentioned in the columns cannot be known. This implies that it is only suitable for a first description, but not suitable for proper statistical analysis.

2. **Corruption cases for the years 2007 and 2008**. As the Republican Prosecutor was uncertain about the volume of corruption cases at the Municipal and District Prosecution Offices he ordered these offices to submit corruption cases from 2007 onwards. 50 offices complied by sending in cases. The reported cases have been inserted into an excel file, to be discussed later.

b. The Statistical Bureau

The Statistical Bureau (SB) collects data from the Republican Public Prosecution Offices and the Courts. The reporting starts with the RPPO: When at this level a decision has been made, a form is sent to the SB. This happens in case of (a) rejection of the criminal report (no procedure is initiated); (b) a request to the Investigative Judge to start an investigation (the results of which are sent back to the prosecutor); or (c) indictment without investigation.

When the cases are brought to Court they get a process number. When the case has been finalised a form is filled by the Court office and sent to the SB. An important change is made as this form concerns *single defendants, not cases*. The defendant numbers at the SB and the Courts must correspond: with defendant numbers one can find the relevant criminal files at the Courts.

The available annual SB-database output is an aggregated one, based on individual defendants/convicted persons. Its format consists of pre-fixed tables with the offences as the main variables broken down by procedural steps, a time indication and a few offender characteristics like male/female. Statistics on the relevant subjects were available until 2005. After the change of the criminal law 2006, new statistics have been made available.[18] These will be analysed in the next phase of research.

c. The Beograd District Court

18 It is not yet clear how this gap will be bridged. The authors have not been informed of any conversion of transit from the statistics under the old to the new law. The execution of this task is still 'pending'.

In addition to these aggregate databases, the team was enabled to study *12 finalised cases* at the district Court of Beograd. The dates of the reports range from 1995 to 2005. They were sentenced between 2002 and 2007. During a meeting it has been mentioned that more cases would be made available, but during the reporting phase these have not been produced thus far.

The databases of the Statistical Bureau nor that of the RPPO were available in a version suitable for automated processing. Further data processing had to be done by hand. Looking 'behind' the available paper material in terms of studying and processing raw data was impossible.

Main findings

a. Statistical Bureau and Prosecutor data

As remarked before, it must not be taken for granted that the databases of the Statistical Bureau and the RPPO reflect reality in the same way. As a matter of fact, there appeared to be unexplainable, but systematic differences between the statistical output of two sources. They may differ as their (unknown) data processing may different, though no explanation could be obtained. Table 4 presents the differences per relevant crime category for the years 2004 and 2005.

The comparison of the outcomes of the two data sources demonstrates a systematic difference: the RPPO has systematically higher numbers with some exceptions. One difference is really remarkable: the PPPO had no charges for fraudulent documents in 2005 against 216 for the SB and only one such charge in 2004

The difference cannot be explained from the 'case' (RPPO) versus 'perpetrator' (SB) registration, because then the SB would have higher figures assuming that a certain portion of the 'cases' have more suspects. Moreover, that difference should disappear when we compare the categories 'charged *persons*', which should be the same.

When we look at the number of convictions we also find differences between the figures of the SB and those of the RPPO, even though both receive data from the same source.

Table 4

Comparison Statistical Bureau (SB) and Republican Public Prosecution Office (RPPO) 2004-2005: reports and charges

	2004				2005			
	Rejected reports		Charged persons		Rejected reports		Charged persons	
Offence	**SB**	**RPPO**	**SB**	**RPPO**	**SB**	**RPPO**	**SB**	**RPPO**
Abuse off.	1.477	2.190	1.283	1.766	1.414	2.153	976	1.585
Embezz.	105	152	462	556	123	177	440	527
Unconsc. Service	165	191	85	62	145	234	139	43
Fraud	21	25	9	19	5	13	7	9
False. doc	88	1	264	1	125	8	216	0
Crim.off. Civ.serv.	14	18	43	59	18	22	39	78
Taking bribe	20	15	41	50	28	39	49	83
Giving bribe	8	26	24	34	12	35	40	77
Other off.	621	258	47	62	714	382	58	84
Total	2519	2876	2258	2609	2572	3063	1964	2486
Difference	357		351		491		522	

For both years the PPO reports more convictions than the SB, though the differences are less striking – with the exception of 'falsification of official documents' for which the PPO reports no convictions at all.

As in research the validity of databases has to be assessed, we have to conclude that both do not match on any crime category or procedural decision variable. Without further in-depth research the validity of both official Serbian databases on corruption remains indeterminable. But apart from this validity question, in both databases the figures for giving or taking bribes appear to be very low. Even if we take the highest numbers from either database in each year the percentage remains about 3.

Table 5

Comparison of the Statistical Bureau and the Republican Public Prosecution Office: 2004-2005: convictions

	Convictions 2004		Convictions 2005	
Offence categories	**SB**	**RPPO**	**SB**	**RPPO**
Abuse office	461	691	459	687
Embezzlement	314	370	331	398
Unconsc. Service	28	13	36	20
Fraud in service	21	8	16	1
False document	215	0	172	0
Crim.off. Civil. serv.	64	43	66	43
Taking bribe	26	43	22	46
Giving bribe	32	24	34	36
Other offences	9	52	7	63
Total	1170	1244	1143	1294
Difference	74		151	

b. Data from the Public Prosecution Office

The third information source is the Special Anti-corruption Unit of the Republican Public Prosecution Office. In 2007, this anti-corruption department decided to monitor corruption cases for which reason it informed all local Prosecutor's Offices about their obligation to notify this Department of all relevant cases covered by the relevant articles. In principle this should constitute a full database of (potential) corruption cases from 2007 onwards. The results of the compliance to this regulation until August 2008 by 138 municipal and 30 prosecution offices at the District Courts are presented in Table 6.

The table raises doubts as to the compliance to this regulation: only 50 of the 138 municipal and 30 districts offices sent in reports (30 %). Assuming that a proper compliance would reflect the size of the Municipal and District Courts in terms of the number of reports, the outcomes do not correspond to this expectation. The largest district like Beograd submitted only 37 reports in 2007 and 25 in 2008: this represents respectively 6% and 8% of the returned reports. This contrasts with the much smaller provincial district Jagodina, which in 2007 submitted 39 reports: 9%. This score did not last, however, because the following year Jagodina's share sunk back to 4%. Now the small district Vranje scored highest: 13% with 42 reports. Only Kraljevo (two times 39 reports) and Pirot (41 and 31 reports) were somewhat steady in their reporting. However, steady of what? Statistically we do not know what the 100% could be: there was no cross-referencing with the Statistical Bureau.

Table 6
Corruption reports sent to the Republican Public Prosecution Office 2007-2008

District/ municipality	**2007**	**2008** (till August)	**District/ municipality**	**2007**	**2008** (till August)
Beograd	37	25	Novi Pazar	1	0
B.Basta	3	2	Novi Sad	2	0
B. Crkva	8	1	Obrenovac	7	0
Bogatic	11	1	Odzaci	1	2
Boljevac	0	7	Pancevo	0	4
Bor	0	13	Paracin	11	20
B.Topola	8	2	Pirot	43	31
Cacak	9	9	Pozarevac	35	4
Cuprija	1	0	Prijepolje	3	10
Despotovac	4	1	Prokuplje	18	8
Ivanjica	6	2	Raska	11	14
Jagodina	51	13	Sabac	42	2
Kladovo	9	0	Smederevo	7	20
Koceljevo	2	0	S.Mitrovica	36	5
Kragujevac	0	1	Sokobanja	6	3
Kraljevo	39	39	Sombor	1	0
Krusevac	9	3	Subotica	5	0
Kucevo	4	2	Tutin	1	2
Kursumlija	1	0	Uzice	13	1
Lajkovac	3	0	Velika plana	0	0
Lazarevac	12	1	Vladimirci	3	4
Leskovac	3	8	Vranje	16	42
Loznica	14	2	Zajecar	54	6
Majdanpek	5	0	Zrenjanin	6	0
Negotin	8	5			
Nis	4	0	**Total**	573	313

The RPPO did notice some underreporting, indeed, and therefore stimulated the prosecution offices to report broadly. This did not improve compliance, but resulted in over-reporting of cases with little substantial relevance to the corruption issue. This is demonstrated if we break down the input by offence. If we add the two years (2007 and 2008 up until August) and look at the most frequently reported offence categories, we obtain the following picture:

Table 7

Crime categories reported 2007-2008

	Abuse of office	Abuse of auth. Economy	Bribe taking	Bribe giving	Judge & PP corruption	other	Total
2007	278	32	25	8	136	94	573
2008	160	20	22	4	57	50	313
Total	438	52	47	12	193	144	886
%	49,4	5,9	5,3	1,4	21,8	16,3	100

Almost half the reports concerns abuse of office, while the content analysis of many reports hardly reveals corruption (content analysis still in progress). A second category which scores highly consists of complaints about alleged corruption/abuse of office at the *Courts*. However, this is mainly accounted for by the reports of *five* offices, from which 153 of these 193 complaints originated (Jagodina, Pozarevac, Sabac, S.Mitrovica, Zajecar). The suggested explanation is that disgruntled litigants and/or their attorneys almost blindly file such complaints. This could not be verified. Whether (and why) this phenomenon is limited to just a few regions is difficult to tell in view of the irregular compliance.

As far as 'hard-core' bribery is concerned – giving and taking bribes – these categories are hardly represented. Are there so few complaints about bribery? We will address this question later.

It is difficult to attach any specific meaning to these statistics. The compliance rate is low, also due to the fact that non-compliance is not sanctioned. The prosecutors are urged to report and some offices do so abundantly, but if other fail to do so there are no consequences. Perhaps these figures are more interesting for what they fail to tell: a low frequency of corruption cases entering the judicial system despite widespread complaints. In addition, this set of cases contained none of the high profile corruption cases high-lighted in the media: *e.g.* no politically exposed persons were mentioned.[19]

Does this also apply to the Special Prosecutor's Office for Organised Crime (SPO)? Given the likely connection of organised crime and corruption, an input from the SPO should be expected. However, it appeared that the Anti-corruption Department of the RPPO has no informative connections with the

19 It may be that some of the cases with politically exposed persons are processed by the Special Court for Organised crime. But as these cases are not finalised yet, we could not access the criminal files.

SPO and no reports have been forwarded. Nevertheless, the SPO indicted 115 defendants for abuse of office, while in 2006, it indicted 16 defendants of bribery (15 taking and one giving a bribe). All cases are still pending.

During the process of information gathering and analysis the team could not but conclude that an orderly and disciplined data management in the Anti-corruption Department is lacking. In general, it took the team a disproportional amount of time (failed appointments and inconclusive meetings), to move forward, reflecting anything but a sense of urgency to get insight into the own information base on corruption.

c. The Beograd District Court

The team also analysed 12 criminal files of finalised corruption cases at the District Court of Beograd. It goes without saying that this was not a representative sample: it was just what the Court had in stock at the time and subsequently analysed by the team as a try-out for further investigation. Table 8 summarises the main findings.

Far from representing a picture of the actual state of affairs in the Beograd district, the reported cases covered nevertheless a whole decade, during which after years of procedures they struggled to a final verdict. The average process time was well over 4 years (mean, 4,14; median 3,33).

Four cases ended in a not-guilty verdict. In case 5, against a police inspector, this happened after all the 12 witnesses withdrew their statements in appeal: their statements "would have been obtained under pressure". The other two police officers did not fare so well: in cases 7 and 12 the extortion of a simple traffic offender (for 500 dinar) and a smuggler (for a larger fee of 24.000 dinars) ended in a prison sentence of 8 and 10 months prison, but on probation. This sentence modality – probation – appeared to be the most usual punishment: only two custodial sentences were imposed unconditionally. We will return to the issue of sentencing in a later section.

As was the case with the three police officers, most cases concern civil servants demanding or extorting money or goods for services, or neglecting their duty, like the tax officer towards his tax evader. Medical staff also tried to enrich themselves at the expense of the needy patients: refusal of surgery or transport, unless . . . one pays! (cases 6 and 9).

Table 8
Finalised cases at the Beograd District Court

No/year report	Length proc. yr	(not) guilty	No offenders	Sentence	Probation	Nature of facts	Profits in dinars
1 1995	10	guilty	1	1 yr		Embezzlement	5.000.000
2 1999	7,75	not guilty	6			Embezzlement	5.000.000
3 2000	7,25	not guilty	2			false doc	12.700
4 2001	3,5	guilty	1	6 m	2 yr	demand false rep.	6.000
5 2002	3,25	not guilty	1			demand goods	2.100.000
6 2002	1,25	guilty	1	10 m	3 yr	demand surgery	36.000
7 2002	4,58	guilty	1	2 yr	5 yr	demand tax off.	40.000
8 2002	4,08	guilty	1	10 m	4 yr	demand smuggler	24.000
9 2002	2,16	not guilty	2			demand transp ill	unknown
10 2003	0,75	guilty	1	2 yr		demand goods	50.000
11 2004	2,17	guilty	1	6 m	3 yr	demand delivery	2.000
12 2005	1,33	guilty	1	8 m	2 yr	demand traff. off.	500

What kind of perpetrators do we meet here? While realising the danger of undue generalisation from a small sample, the offender picture is that of 'Joe Average': 'married with children', no criminal record and higher education (high school and beyond). And of course, a valuable job, which is the very basis for extorting fellow citizens. Though the criminal files are too few and contain insufficient information to make 'reasoned speculations', the image of the better-off profiting from those who need their services urges itself.

Trends, and what they do (not) tell

The findings thus far are sobering as far as the reliability and validity are concerned: at best the validity is indeterminable. None of the databases match with each other and none can be used as a useful approximation of the corruption situation or a corresponding criminal policy in Serbia. Does this observation entail that the figures of either the SB, the RPPO or the reports from the prosecution offices do not reflect any reality? That depends with what 'reality' one wants to compare them: the 'reality of corruption out-there' or the 'reality of decision making' within law enforcement. For both it may be useful to look at some trend-lines first and compare them with other data.

In the first place we have a rather long nine years time series of the SB concerning the broad category 'crime against official duty', as represented in Table 9 and figure 1. On the one hand, we have the trend of the reporting to the authorities, which – with hesitations – may be interpreted as the citizens' readiness to file a complaint. On the other hand, we have the penal law system response. The two do not appear to correlate: whatever the variation in the reporting rate, the law enforcement system continues to process within comparatively narrow margins.

Table 9
Reports, charges and convictions of offenders against official duty, 1998-2008

Crime against official duty	**'98**	**'99**	**'00**	**'01**	**'02**	**'03**	**'04**	**'05**	**'06**	**'07**	**'08**
Perpetrators reported	4.303	3.169	3.312	4.640	5.312	5.535	5.356	5.253	4.343	4.244	4.140
Perpetrators charged	1.860	1.566	1.583	1.473	1.553	1.566	1.796	1.839	1.896	1.564	1.578
Convicted	1.242	1.133	1.101	983	1.031	1.038	1.170	1.126	1.147	994	913
%	%	%	%	%	%	%	%	%	%	%	%
Charged/ reported	43	49	48	32	29	28	33	35	44	37	38
Convicted/ charged	67	72	70	67	66	66	65	61	60	64	58
Convicted/ reporter	29	36	33	21	21	19	22	21	26	23	22

Source: Statistical Yearbook of Serbia, 2008: p. 404-405

Looking at the reporting line one observes a clear 'bump' upwards after the Miloševič era, which sinks down again after 2004. The line for the charges moves slightly in opposite direction, while the figures of the RPPO and the Courts hardly vary around their arithmetic average. Of course, these figures cannot be interpreted without speculations, but it is fair to hypothesize that the reporting of crime may have been discouraged by lack of response of the judicial system. Already before the decline of reporting in 2004 the ratio of reports versus charges and conviction had decreased sharply. To what extent is this interaction between reporting informants and the judicial system a plausible hypothesis?

Figure 1
Trends in reporting, charges and convictions of crime against official duty

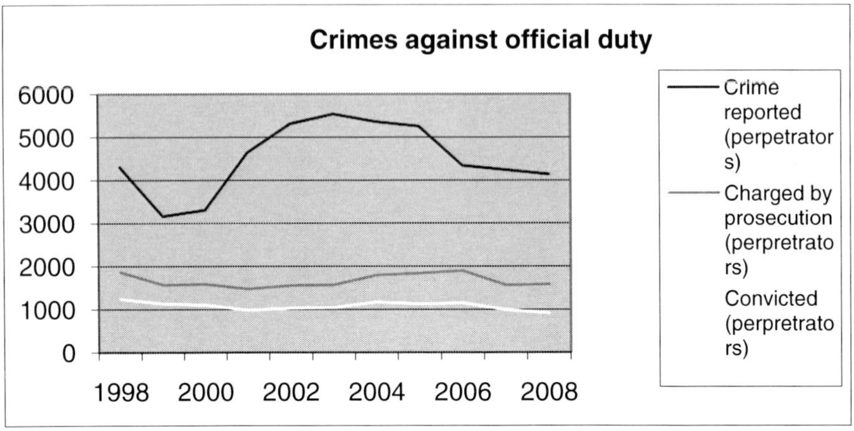

When we project the findings concerning bribery – giving and asking or receiving bribes – one observes a dismal proportion, irrespective whether one takes the figures of the RPPO or the SB for real. According to the SB on average 90 cases of bribe taking/asking and 48 bribe giving are reported (2003-2005). This dwindles into insignificance compared to the total reported crimes against official duty.

Maybe the low reporting frequency in specific categories is due to the fact that the category *abuse of office* 'absorbs' these specific corruption modalities, which are then hidden in the large reporting increase after 2001. That uncertainty has to be investigated. But this is not reflected in the stable trends of charges and convictions over the years (Figure 1).

To find more tokens of corruption the team sifted through the statistics of other crime categories. For the category '*corruption in* [. . .] ' we have the figures of only two years, represented in the following table.

Table 10
Reports, charges and convictions of various corruption categories 2003-2004

	2003			2004		
	Report	**Charge**	**Conv.**	**Report**	**Charge**	**Conv.**
corruption in state administration	18	1	1	17	1	1
Unintentional free use of state funds	1	0	0	4	0	0
corruption in public procurement	0	0	0	12	0	0
corruption in privatisation operations	0	0	0	0	0	0
corruption in administration of justice	11	0	0	12	0	0
corruption in healthcare	13	0	0	5	0	0
Corruption in education system	2	0	0	1	4	4

Source: Statistical Yearbook of Serbia, 2005

It is obvious that these unimpressive figures hardly square with the various corruption perception surveys which have been published during the last years, in particular concerning customs, health care, police and the judicial system. Indeed, the low reporting rate and the subsequently even lower frequencies (or absence) of charges and convictions do not tell us much about corruption in society, but rather about the relevant criminal policy implementation.

If we measure criminal policy making by its outcomes, the present data and the long term 'flat' trends at the prosecution offices and the Courts do not allow any identification of a specific corruption policy. Rather, the picture presented here confirms another story, mentioned in the UNDP report: a "witnesses' lack of readiness to cooperate fully with the police".[20] Clearly, for very good reasons.

The citizen would feel reinforced in this attitude if he would be informed of the length of the procedures in these cases. According to the SB statistics of 2003 and 2004 the procedure of respectively 77 % and 80 % of the cases lasted 'over one year'. However, the SB way of presenting the processing time by a simple month classification under one year and the rest 'over one year' does no justice to the actual processing times. The newest SB data for 2007, which we are in the

20 UNDP Serbia, *The Fight Against Corruption in Serbia: An Institutional Framework Overview*, April 2008, pp. 22,
Available at: http://europeandcis.undp.org/anticorruption/show/05788DCA-F203-1EE9-B164C824E7DA18D7

process of analysing, provides the proper measures: mean and median. In this database the process phases are properly identified so that they allow some comparison of these central tendencies. The preliminary analysis demonstrates again very long processing times (minimum and maximum were not provided):

Total time (report – verdict):	mean = 3,8 years; median = 3,3 years
Trial time (indictment – verdict):	mean = 2,7 years; median = 2,1 years

The range between and within the districts is enormous. For the *total* processing time the range is from a median of 443 day in the district of Zrenjanin to a median of 1938 days in the district of Sremska Mitrovica. This spread is not only due to the pre-trial investigation time: the variation of the median time needed for court processing is equally broad: from 175 days in Zrenjanin (55 cases) to 1092 days in Pirot (29 cases). There appears to be little correlation between the processing time and the number of corruption cases. This reinforces the image of lack of policy in which there is little priority or system in handling corruption cases timely.

From the perspective of measuring policy making by its outcomes sentencing is an important aspect. When after diligent reporting and police investigation cases keep dragging on for years, one cannot expect that witnesses will step forward again, while the police will direct its detective capacity to other priorities. If in addition, the sentences meted out are also lenient, the impression will thrust itself on the public that "they can get away with it". Therefore we inspected the available sentencing data. Though sentencing analysis requires a longer time series we had only the years 2004 and 2005. This does not allow a temporal comparison. To obtain a larger total and to simplify the presentation we put the two years together and calculated the relative frequencies of sentencing modalities and severity.

Interpreting sentencing data is a delicate matter as one cannot deduce causal connections between determining variables and the sentencing outcome, certainly not from the aggregate tables of the SB. Nevertheless, such aggregate statistics do convey a general picture of sentencing.

When we first look at the main categories in Table 11, conditional and unconditional punishments, we observe that most offenders, 70 %, are punished with a conditional sentence. 'Unconscientious services' ('criminal dereliction of duty') and taking bribes appear to be punished most often with unconditional sentences. But while unconscientious services are most often punished with fines, those convicted for taking bribes have a high chance of finding themselves in prison: 77 %. In two cases prison terms of 2-10 years were imposed. Granted, with a national conviction score of 48 over *two* years this may not look as an impressive deterrence. The counterpart – giving a bribe – seems to be dealt with more leniently: 57 % conditional sentence and most prison terms below six months.

Table 11

Sentencing of various crime against official duty: 2004-2005

	< 30 days %	1-6 Month %	6-12 month %	1-2 year %	2-5 year %	5-10 year %	Fine %	Condi. Prison %	Condi. fine %	Sentences= 100%
Abuse office	0,4	20,7	4,5	1,2	0,7	0	0	72,1	0,4	921
Embezzlement	0,6	20,2	6,2	1,9	0,9	0	0	69,6	0,6	644
Unconsc. Service	0	10,9	23,4	9,3	10,9	0	20,3	25,0	0	64
Fraud in service	5,3	21,1	0	0	0	0	0	73,7	0	38
False document	0,5	13,7	1,6	0,3	0	0	0	81,7	2,3	387
Crim.off.Civ.serv.	0,8	20,8	2,3	0	0,8	0	0	70,8	4,6	130
Taking bribe	0	37,5	25,0	10,4	2,1	2,1	0	22,9	0	48
Giving bribe	1,5	36,9	3,1	0	0	0	1,5	56,9	0	65
Total %	0,6	19,9	5,2	1,5	0,9	0,04	0,6	70,2	0,1	2297

Source: Statistical Bureau, 2004-2005

As follows from the previous sections, it is impossible to deduce conclusions concerning anti-corruption prosecution and sentencing *policy*, if there is anything like that. Apart from offence/offender variables, which determine mainly the seriousness of the case, sentencing may be strongly influenced by the variable 'length of procedure'. And with 77-80 % of the procedures lasting more than one year, the likelihood that unconditional prison sentences will be imposed diminishes too. It is a plausible hypothesis that this time variable mainly reflects the (lack of) 'sense of urgency' in this field, which influences again the (declining) reporting rate: see Table 9 and figure 1.

Even if this hypothesis is plausible, to substantiate it we must get deeper into the empirical material. For this we are dependent on the information holders: the SB and the Courts which will be dealt with in the follow-up project.

Present and future: Sisyphus wrapped in clouds or reaching the top?

Surveying the bits and pieces of evidence of the anti-corruption policy in Serbia the picture is that of a silhouette and, returning to our initial metaphor, the silhouette of Sisyphus, but wrapped in clouds. This cloudy image concerns the efforts of the Serbian authorities to fight corruption with specific laws and institutions as well as the outcomes of the efforts of the law enforcement agencies. It proved difficult to assess what and how the administrative institutions as well as the RPPO and Courts process their 'corruption input' to a final output. Neither the uncertainty of the input and processing nor the meagre output convince as a reflexion of a highly prioritised anti-corruption policy of the previous years.

At the criminal law side we started with the uncertainty concerning the nature and quantity of the input. There are differences between the figures of the RPPO and the Statistical Bureau. However, this does not only pertain to corruption cases: this concerns a broader, systematic statistical 'inconvenience'. When Van Duyne and Donati (2008) did research on money laundering in Serbia, they ran into the same problem of unsatisfactory data management. Of course, flaws within such a system are not mended overnight, but even the first step was not visible: showing a minimum of interest or even some curiosity.[21] Naturally, we must take into account that database (in)compatibilities are complex and designing a system for point-to-point comparisons is time-consuming. But given the seriousness of this social problem one would expect more awareness and an accompanying attempt to lift the veils shrouding the anti-corruption policy. Apart from the support by the Republican Public Prosecution Office and the Ministry of Interior, no initiatives to lift these veils have been observed.

The analysis of the criminal database revealed three aspects which have to be researched in-depth.

- The *processing time* in view of the many old cases in our database. But such findings must be projected against the general processing times in the PPOs and the Courts; see the observation of the Ombudsman concerning general lack of 'reasonable time' to see one's case finalized.
- The *sentencing*. Of course, we cannot conclude anything about the severity of the sentencing, which is an evaluative task. Sentencing must be projected against a timeline and the general sentencing level in Serbia and against the third aspect;
- The *nature* and the *seriousness* of the cases. We have the impression that the database does not contain really serious cases, or the kinds of corruption of which the common people complain: corruption in the law enforcement agencies, top officials and health care. This bias towards 'small fry' may be re-

21 Although this is regrettable for the Serbian criminal data management, it is not unique in this regard. Surveying research and data about organised crime and money-laundering in most EU jurisdictions the data management proved to be ramshackle too (Van Duyne, 2007). The chapter of Verhage in this volume provides an account of the poor data management in Belgium concerning money laundering.

flected in the seemingly leniency of the sentencing, also influenced by the amount of time which has passed since the offence.

There may be reasons for this state of affairs, but these have to be researched. In *Politika*, 7-5-2009, the spokesperson Ivana Ramic referred to the 595 suspects awaiting trial at the Belgrade Court for abuse of public function, among them three former managers of the football club *Crvena Zvezda (Red Star)*. Ramic hinted at the time consuming complexity of the cases, particularly if financial constructions are involved and also at the increased workload of the Belgrade Court. These assertions have to be verified. They underline that to obtain clarity the (follow-up) research must be extended to a basic file analysis of a sufficiently large number of cases, in addition to a precise statistical analysis. If Ramic' claims are correct, the research questions are ten: what is the nature of the case input in terms of seriousness and complexity, what is the time variable and what is the sentencing output? This broadening and in-depth analysis will shed light on correlation between the nature of the corruption offences, the (local) sentencing policy and the time constraint. To achieve this, the Courts as well as the Statistical Bureau will have to open up.

At this point we must again stress the limitations of this pioneering phase of the research project: we could analyse only as much as the RPPO and the Courts allowed us to see, and these were finalised cases, which as we have seen, could be very old. Pending cases remained barred for us, even if there were no investigative interests at stake or not the slightest threat to the privacy of the defendants: scientific research must aggregate and anonymise such that no connections between the analysis and concrete (legal) persons can be made. These research principles found little response.

It is a generally correct observation that the penal law system functions as a kind of broom sweeping the dirt left behind and that the real gain is to be made by preventing corruption. This has been the philosophy behind the many commissions and agencies which have been established after 2002. Even if it is difficult to assess exactly their functioning (the all pervasive 'clouds'), it became clear that most were meagrely equipped and maybe were not even really wanted. Did the authorities 'sit down' again? It is most uncertain that the authorities complied with the many decisions or recommendations they received from the organs the government installed itself, which annulled their preventive value. Materially, the government did not display a favourable attitude either. Until the present, the administrative institutions' effectiveness appeared to be not only hampered by lack of staff and infrastructure, but also because the enforcement of their decisions depended on the authorities under their supervision. This implies that the preventive effects of these institutions are low or indeterminable and that the criminal law sag wagon is still badly needed. This underlines the need to make that sag wagon workable. One of the pre-conditions is a proper information management.

It is assumed that the Anti-Corruption Agency will mend much of these defects. As a matter of fact, the coming into force of this body in January 2010 should mean a watershed. Not only because it aims to make the old Law on the Conflict of Interests, which it absorbs, workable, but also because it has two important provisions: (a) it has a criminal law 'tail' in cases of non-compliance (section X Penal Provisions) containing stiff penalties and (b) it solemnly declares to undo the defects of transparency highlighted in this report.
Art 66 of the new law declares:

> "*The Agency shall organise research on the state of corruption and combating corruption, monitor and analyze statistical data, carry out other analyses and research and suggest changes in the procedure for collection and processing of statistical data that are relevant for monitoring of the state of corruption.*"

This is a firm endorsement of the principles of the present research project, or preferably, its intended continuation and cooperation with the new agency. ACA has established a unit for research, though it is still too early to predict future developments: the organisation is still in the state of construction. It should be remarked that the surrounding research community in Serbia is weak: academic research output is extremely scarce which could make ACA's research unit an isolated one.

Thus far, to a large extent the anti-corruption legislation has been 'externally motivated', mainly due to pressure from the EU and the Council of Europe. Without *internal* motivation it is to be feared that the anti-corruption policy proclaimed during election times fades away as soon as the ballot has been cast. But if there is an internal motivation it must be sustained by a feedback of outcomes: facts and figures. The present laws may be fine, but they are like cooking recipes: they may look good and may have been written with the best intentions, but 'the truth of the pudding is in the eating'. That is an outcome that has to be seen and knowable. Then the Sisyphus metaphor will no longer be relevant.

References

Andvig, J.C., International corruption. In: Bull, M.J. and J.L. Newell (eds.), *Corruption in contemporary politics*. New York, Palgrave-Macmillan, 2003

Begović, B., *Corruption in judiciary*. Beograd, Center for Liberal Democratic Studies, 2004

Begović, B. and Mijatović, B. (eds), *Corruption in Serbia; five years later*. Beograd, Center for Liberal Democratic Studies, 2007

Bull, M.J. and J.L. Newell (eds.), *Corruption in contemporary politics*. New York, Palgrave-Macmillan, 2003

Datzer D., A. Maljevic, M. Budimlic, E. Muratbegovic, Police Corruption through Eyes of Bribers: the Ambivalence of Sinners. In: P.C. van Duyne, A. Maljevic, M. van Dijck, K. von Lampe and J. Harvey (eds.), *Crime business and crime money in Europe. The dirty linen of illicit enterprise*. Nijmegen, Wolf Legal Publishers, 2007

Duyne, P.C. van, Will 'Caligula go transparent?' Corruption in acts and attitude. *Forum on Crime and Society*, 2001, vol. 1, *nr. 2*, 73-98

Duyne, P.C. van, Criminal finances and state of the art. Case for concern? In: P.C. van Duyne, A. Maljevic, M. van Dijck, K. von Lampe and J. Harvey (eds.), *Crime business and crime money in Europe. The dirty linen of illicit enterprise*. Nijmegen, Wolf Legal Publishers, 2007

Duyne, P.C. van and S. Donati, In search of crime-money management in Serbia. In: P.C. van Duyne, J. Harvey, A. Maljevic, K. von Lampe and M. Scheinost (eds.), *European crime-markets at cross-roads. Extended and extending criminal Europe*. Nijmegen, Wolf Legal Publishers, 2008

Freeman, R. E., *Strategic management: a stakeholder approach*. Boston, Pitman, 1984

Holmes, L., Political corruption in Central and Eastern Europe. In: Bull, M.J. and J.L. Newell (eds.), *Corruption in contemporary politics*. New York, Palgrave-Macmillan, 2003

Jager, M., The market and criminal law: the case of corruption. In: P.C. van Duyne, K. Von Lampe and J. Newell (eds.), *Criminal finances and organising crime in Europe*. Nijmegen, Wolf Legal Productions, 2003

Jager, M., In quest for essence: the principal-agent-client model of corruption. In: P. C. van Duyne, M. Jager, K. von Lampe en J.L. Newell (eds.), *Threats and phantoms of organised crime, corruption and terrorism*. Nijmegen, Wolf Legal Publishers, 2004

Karadzoski, M., Discrepancies between anti-corruption legislation and practice in Macedonia. In: P.C. van Duyne, S. Donati, Am Maljevic, J. Harvey and K.

von Lampe (eds.), *Crime, money and criminal mobility in Europe*, Nijmegen, Wolf Legal Publishers, 2009

Logonder, A., Who is 'Yugo' in 'Yugo-mafia'. A comparative analysis of the Serbian and Slovene offenders. In: P.C. van Duyne, J. Harvey, A. Maljevic, K. von Lampe and M. Scheinost (eds.), *European crime-markets at cross-roads. Extended and extending criminal Europe.* Nijmegen, Wolf Legal Publishers, 2008

Maljević, A., D. Datzer, E. Muratbegović and M. Budimlić, *Overtly about police corruption.* Sajarevo, Association of Criminalists in Bosnia and Herzegovina, 2006

Newell, J.L., Institutional reforms and attempts to fight corruption: the Italian case. In: P. C. van Duyne, M. Jager, K. von Lampe en J.L. Newell (eds.), *Threats and phantoms of organised crime, corruption and terrorism.* Nijmegen, Wolf Legal Publishers, 2004

Osyka, I., Anti corruption policies in the Ukraine. In: P.C. van Duyne, K. Von Lampe and J. Newell (eds.), *Criminal finances and organising crime in Europe.* Nijmegen, Wolf Legal Productions, 2003

Pesić, V., *State capture and widespread corruption in Serbia.* Centre For European Policy Studies, 2007. Available at: http://www.ceps.be

Stille, A., *The sack of Rome. Media + money + celebrity = power = Silvio Berlusconi.* London, Penguin Books, 2007

Trivunović, M., V. Devine, H. Mathisen, Corruption in Serbia 2007. Overview of problems and status of reforms. Bergen, Chr. Michelsen Institute, 2007

UNDP Serbia, *The Fight Against Corruption in Serbia: An Institutional Framework Overview*, April 2008

Croatia: Fighting EU Fraud a case of work in progress?

Brendan J. Quirke[1]

Introduction

The purpose of this chapter is to consider the experience of Croatia in working to establish effective anti-EU fraud structures and measures. It will elaborate the problems it has encountered, how it has sought to overcome them and the support it has received so far. Attention will be paid to the efforts it will need to make in the future in order to be accepted as well as any wider lessons that can be drawn for prospective entrants to this relatively 'exclusive' club. The chapter will also consider the context within which this application is being made: the political, economic and social circumstances of the country including the extent of corruption. This is important because if Croatia is a country that is prone to and severely affected by corrupt behaviour, then it is not unreasonable to assume that the 'honey pot' of EU funds will prove attractive to corrupt officials and economic criminals. This has implications for the kind of anti-fraud structures that need to be constructed and anti-fraud activities that need to be undertaken.

Background

Croatia is a candidate state for entry to the EU. At present, the hope and intention is that Croatia will become a full member in 2011. Croatia is in the process of transforming itself from a country badly affected by the Balkan war of 1991 – 1995 to a democratic market economy within a very short period of time. The European Union has been described in the introduction above as a 'club', and just as with any club, whether it is the local squash club or the freemasons, there are rules that members have to abide by once they gain membership, and there are

---

1 The author is a Senior Lecturer in Accounting & Finance at Liverpool John Moores University, UK

criteria that have to be met in order to be accepted as a member. It is also reasonable to assume that prospective members want to create a favourable impression and wish to be perceived as being capable of making a positive contribution, once accepted for membership. This paper will consider the efforts Croatia has made and will have to make in the future to become a valued and effective member of the club as well as the kind of support Croatia has received so far in the period leading up to accession.

When one attempts to begin researching into background information about Croatia, any search on the internet will inevitably bring up two key words: 'corruption' and 'mafia'. There is concern about the level of corruption in the country and whether this could lead to a widespread misuse of EU funds. There is also a popular concern about the power and influence of organised crime although in the view of academic observers such as Van Duyne (2006), Croatian organised crime is not as widely developed as that of some of its neighbours, although, according to the taxi drivers of Zagreb: "*Mafia is everywhere*". It can be disconcerting for a first time visitor to be cheerfully informed by his taxi driver that a number of the driver's customers have been either gunned down or blown up by the said 'mafia'!

In terms of corruption, if one consults Transparency International's Perception of Corruption Index, Croatia currently has a score of 4.4. The index scores countries on a scale of 0 to 10, 0 is the most corrupt and 10 is the least corrupt. The current score would appear to indicate that there is a problem with corruption in Croatia (Transparency International Perceptions of Corruption Index, 2008). Croatia's PCI score between 1999 and 2005 was consistently below 4.0 (Budak, 2006). Croatia is attempting to do what is being asked of it by the EU in terms of tackling corruption, such as adopting international protocols, passing domestic legislation and in terms of 'beefing up' its anti-corruption and repressive institutions. In view of the state of affairs concerning corruption in various member states, it is justifiable to pose a reasonable question: Is Croatia not being asked to reach a standard in this respect that none of the established member states could possibly reach at this moment? Is this a case of double standards, or is it a case of politics and the desire to reassure domestic audiences that a tough line is being taken with so-called 'corrupt' countries. The attempts by Croatia to comply with the demands and strictures of the European Union will be considered below.

It would not be feasible, nor would it be sensible or appropriate to study the phenomenon of EU fraud in isolation. For a more complete understanding, one has to consider the broader context within which it operates, such as the political, economic, social and historical circumstances (Scheinost, 2006) which have coloured and affected Croatia and its progress from being part of a communist state (although admittedly a state which had found its own path to communism) to a war torn newly independent country to a democratic, prospective member of the EU.

In Croatia, at first sight, there does appear to be a widespread enthusiasm for EU membership, this is evident at the top of government[2] as well as with more humble members of society – the taxi drivers and waiters/waitresses of Zagreb.[3] Yet nationally, support for membership of the EU has started to wane. According to the Gallup Balkan Monitor opinion poll, 29% of Croats are in support of EU membership, 26% oppose it and 38% are unable to make their minds up.[4] It appears that support has fallen as membership negotiations have dragged on. Whether support for the EU will rise once Croatia has become a full member remains to be seen. This can be compared with the experience of the Czech Republic where the initial enthusiasm for EU membership soon wore off very quickly, once the Czech Republic had become a full member and was replaced by a more Euro-sceptic attitude towards Brussels (Quirke, 2008).

Objectives of the research project

The purpose of the research as outlined above in the introduction, is to consider the experience of Croatia in working to establish effective anti-EU fraud structures, the problems it has encountered and how it has sought to overcome them and how it will seek to become an effective and respected member of this anti-fraud coalition. In previous studies in the Czech Republic and Romania, both of which were former Communist countries with relatively high levels of economic crime, a number of problems/issues were identified in the research. These problems concerned a high degree of fragmentation with multiple agencies involved in the fight against fraud. Some of these agencies were police type bodies, others were administrative bodies such as internal audit departments. Implicitly, therefore there were different approaches and cultures to manage which could lead to inefficiencies and duplication of effort. Also, significant gaps and deficiencies in the training and expertise of staff involved in the anti-fraud effort were identified as well as a lack of knowledge of the OLAF reporting formats for fraud and irregularity. The AFIS (anti-fraud information system) still had not been fully installed in either country upon accession. Given the similar history and background of

2 Interview with Croatian Officials 2009
3 Interviews with Croatian citizens 2009
4 www.balkan-monitor.eu

Croatia, it was therefore reasonable to expect that similar issues may be identified in the Croatian study.

Research Methodology

The approach adopted is similar to that used in previous studies in the Czech Republic and Romania. A number of interviews were conducted with officials from the Independent Department for Combating Irregularities and Fraud (the lead AFCOS body); the Customs Directorate, the Financial Police, the Ministry of the Interior, the State Attorney's Office, the Tax Directorate, as well as representatives from the various payment agencies such as the Ministry of Agriculture, Fisheries and Rural Development and the National Fund. A total of nine officials were interviewed. The interviews were conducted using a semi-structured questionnaire which allowed for flexibility in the sequencing and ordering of questions. A review of secondary materials such as reports from OLAF (the European Anti—Fraud Office), the Croatian Ministry of Finance as well as academic articles was also undertaken.

The new elite (thieves, rogues and war heroes)

In seeking to understand any form of economic crime, such as EU fraud, it is essential to understand the norms and mores that operate within a given society (Quirke, 2008). The fact that in relatively recent history, Croatia has gone through a particularly brutal regional war must have had an impact on Croatian society. Participation in the war was a passport to positions of influence under the first government after independence was gained in 1991. Criminals who had participated with paramilitary units and the official security forces in the worst aspects of ethnic cleansing were promoted to the status of hero and were able to continue their criminal activities after the war ended, thus helping to sow the seeds for organised criminal activities, even if the level of activity has not reached that of neighbouring countries (Stojarova, 2005). Service in the war was also of benefit for people looking for opportunities during the privatisation process. Grubisa (2005) refers to privatisation as the 'original sin' of political corruption in Croatia. The election of the right wing party the Croatian Democratic Union led by Franjo Tudjman paved the way for a complete takeover of all commanding positions in Croatian society (Grubisa, 2005). She outlines that, Tudjman set forth to create capitalism with a Croatian face. This policy was designed to rely on 200 Croatian families that would take over the economy and begin the initial accumulation of capital, thus creating a new entrepreneurial class that would lead the country towards a profound transformation. It was an officially sanctioned form of nepotism. This transformation could only occur by using political power and by eliminating all competitors – i.e. the old managerial class that in the previous twenty years had led the economy and by discouraging foreign investors that could appear and pretend to buy already well established economic ventures.

In the first phase that lasted until the end of the nineties, foreign investors were limited to green field investments and new ventures. As the majority of the well trained and western educated Croatian entrepreneurs and managers did not come back to the country because of the war, the new people in power resorted to people and connections they had confidence in, former military colleagues, and networks based on 'the common acceptance of nationalist fundamentalism' (Bicanic & Franicevic, 2003, p 18) as well as relationships based on familial and political ties. Grubisa (2005) refers to this new class as leading an all-out robbery of state owned capital and transforming it into privately owned capital. It was a form of 'crony capitalism' (Ballinger, 2003). The new 'meritocracy' was geared to participation in the Homeland war and in the war in Bosnia. Veterans were chosen together with relatives and people who shared a similar ideology to be members of the new social group that would be the motor behind the drive of Croatia into capitalism.

Croatian privatisation as Ballinger (2003) identifies, began in 1991 with the passing of the first law on privatisation. As Ballinger (2003) observes, the Tudjman regime maintained a firm grip on the privatisation process. The state remained a major shareholder, the banks held a significant number of shares and there were some shares held by small shareholders (usually employees). The thesis that excessive regulation by law and law enforcement usually leads to non-transparency that favours political manipulation is confirmed in her view by evidence of the legal privatisation procedure. From 1991 to 1996, the law on privatisation was amended and changed twelve times, making it completely non-transparent and confused. The majority of amendments adopted by the parliament were aimed at the protection of small shareholders in the privatisation process. Their (promised) participation was extremely important for the government because it wanted to encourage broad public support for privatisation. This had lost a good deal of its impetus during the first two years of the process over the lack of transparency and the favoured treatment of well connected investors. This was the main reason for the constant amendments to the original privatisation law (Bejakovic 2002). The confusion caused by these constant legal changes enabled the Croatian Privatisation Fund, the extremely powerful state agency created in 1991 to oversee the process, to interpret the law and its multiple and contradictory changes in an arbitrary way. Petricevic (2000) counted ten ways and methods of company takeovers under the explicit co-operation and control of the Croatian Privatisation Fund. As Bejakovic (2002) observes, the Fund had the final decision on the privatisation of a particular company in terms of who to sell to and at what price. Corruption and other irregularities were some of the undesirable side-effects.

In Grubisa's (2005) view, in order for the Croatian Privatisation Fund to maintain its position as the most powerful institution in the country, it needed to act quickly and decisively. There was a need to establish state ownership over the banking system – the banks played a decisive role in enabling a corrupt privatisation. Bankers under political influence and guidance granted so-called managerial loans to those suggested by the political leaders. Since banks accepted mortgages and guarantees on the very same companies that were bought, it became clear that a great number of companies were bought on the basis of the buyer's word of honour. In cases where employees succeeded in buying shares of companies in which they worked, the state intervened by annulling such transactions or by limiting the amount of shares offered to employees (Bejakovic, 2002).

The conclusion must be that the proposed broadening and protection of small investors mentioned above, was little more than symbolism. Small investors were welcome (as this played well politically, in terms of a mass privatisation. But if employees a small investors reached a position where they might gain a controlling interest in a firm, then the government would act to prevent this, as it would threaten potentially the interests of the new elite.

Grubisa (2005) makes the point that during the Tudjman years in the 1990s, 2.650 companies were privatised. In 908 cases, legal proceedings were initiated against the Croatian Privatisation Fund for abuses, but with no practical result. At the end of the century, political change brought an end to Tudjman's authoritarian regime. One of the first moves of the new coalition government led by the social democratic leader Racan was to start a revision of the privatisation process that had transferred an enormous amount of wealth into private profiteering hands. The State Audit Office was instructed to begin an investigation in 2001 into the misdoings of privatisation in Croatia. It reported three years later: out of 1006 cases of privatisation of state owned companies investigated, only in 75 companies did it find that there was no evidence of any abuses or wrongdoing. According to the State Audit Office, the goals of privatisation were not achieved – the value of capital drastically diminished, the number of employees dramatically decreased, 23% of the privatised companies underwent a bankruptcy procedure and no development whatsoever was reported in 64% of the privatised companies. The only goal that was achieved was the transfer of property from state to private hands with the resulting creation of a new class: the nouveaux riches (Grubisa, 2005).

In more recent times, 2007 to be precise, the privatisation fund has been hit by more scandal. Several senior officials were arrested as part of Operation Maestro – an anti-corruption investigation. The operation was carried out by the Interior Ministry, the State Prosecutor's Office, the Office for the Suppression of Corruption and Crime (USKOK) and the intelligence services. Six people were arrested, including three HFP (Croatian Privatisation Fund) vice-presidents. They were suspected of manipulating conditions on the stock exchange to give them favourable conditions in which to buy shares; also of committing frauds with state owned real estate – estimating the real estate at a lower price than it was worth to suit the wishes of individual investors in return for a bribe. The officials allegedly asked undercover agents involved in the 'sting' operation for millions in bribes and the agents had to keep going back to the government to ask for higher amounts of money, bringing the total amounts paid to over 800.000 euros. The chief prosecutor revealed that just for entering a deal, they would ask interested persons for € 50.000 in order to have a coffee with prospective 'investors' – who of course, were undercover police officers. Probably one of the most expensive cups of coffee in the world! Large amounts of cash, € 350.000 had been found in the apartments of those arrested. The Prime minister proposed to close the Privatisation Fund and joining it to existing state agencies such as the Central Office for the Management of State Property.[5]

Inevitably, such corrupt activities are not just confined to one area of the economy. The Judiciary as Budak (2006) observes, is identified by the Croatian public as being the most corrupt institution closely followed by the health service and local government. About 80% of entrepreneurs according to a World Economic Forum & Harvard University Survey between 2002 and 2004 believed that the criteria in policy decision-making and awarding state contracts to specific companies were based on personal acquaintances with government officials. In this process, small companies are most concerned with corruption in contracting of public investments and with the impact of corruption activities on law and policy measures. According to the survey, enterprises in Croatia in their everyday business activities were exposed to or resorted to corruption mostly for the purpose of obtaining public investment contracts (57% of respondents), to influence laws and policy in order to protect their business interests (46%), to obtain a fa-

5 www.vlada.hr/en/

vourable court decision (45%) and for the purpose of obtaining import and export licences (35%). In other words, Croatian entrepreneurs make informal payments most frequently to officials and the public administration to obtain unlawful protection of their business interests or they pay a bribe to circumvent the norms of the rule of law (Budak, 2006).

Corruption and EU Accession

Given the concerns about levels of corruption discussed above in relation to Croatia and other candidate states, as part of the accession process to full membership of the European Union, candidate countries are expected to implement the following measures:

- Adoption and implementation of a national anti-corruption strategy and programme;
- Ratification and implementation of international anti-corruption conventions;
- Enactment of anti-corruption laws and their persistent enforcement;
- Transparency in the work of public employees, rotation of sensitive positions, application of merit criteria in employment, openness of the work of public services and so on;
- Establishment of the principle of accountability of public office and transparency in the work of all public services – judiciary, police, customs office etc.;
- Setting up a code of ethics in the public sector and control of its enforcement;
- Legal protection of persons who report a suspicion of corruptive behaviour;
- Transparent financing of political parties;
- Implementation of these measures is monitored by GRECO – the Group of States Against Corruption who, as well as monitoring, also provide assistance in the implementation of anti-corruption policy.

Croatia is subject to annual monitoring reports of the European Union to ensure that it is meeting her obligations on anti-corruption policy and wider issues as well. It has been obliged to adopt the acquis communautaire which includes enactment of legislation and establishment of institutions for the fight against corruption, as well as to adopt a national anti-corruption strategy.

In response, Croatian legislation has become fully harmonised with the ratified Criminal Law Convention on Corruption and the Civil Law Convention on Corruption of the Council of Europe. (European Commission, 2007). As Budak (2006) identifies, the following key amendments have been introduced into the Croatian national legislation:

- The reach of the criminal law provisions concerning corruption have been extended to include receiving and giving bribes in business operations as well. The bribery includes personal giving or promising of a gift or another benefit as reciprocal favours in concluding business deals or provision of services, as well s mediation in bribery;
- key amendments to the Criminal Act were also introduced for influence peddling;
- the definition of the term 'official person' has been expanded to include official persons in foreign and/or international law;
- besides criminal sanctioning of corruption, preventative activity of combating corruption is also regulated by the law (prevention of money laundering, prevention of conflict of interest).

Together with the establishment of the Office for Prevention of Corruption and Organised Crime (USKOK) and the Economic Crime and Corruption Department of the Ministry of the Interior, Croatia believed it had gone a long way towards meeting the requirements of the international community. Yet, there has been slippage along the way, such as insufficient transparency on the financing of political parties or the strategy of USKOK. This hard nosed approach has had some success to some extent, though as Budak (2006) observes, there is still a lot that needs to be done – judicial corruption is a major concern. The question that can be asked though: are these short term solutions to long term structural problems?

The general situation in Croatia is of concern to officials of OLAF – the EU anti-fraud office[6]. Given that corruption and criminal activities such as smuggling appear to be well embedded in Croatian society, Croatia is seen as a transit country for any criminal cross-border traffic towards northern crime markets using the well-known Balkan Route (Van Duyne, 2006). A profitable branch of tax fraud that affects Croatia concerns high taxed goods such as tobacco and VAT fraud (or the Croatian equivalent) (Van Duyne, 2006).It is not unreasonable to assume that the honey pot of EU funds would prove to be very attractive to economic criminals and corrupt officials. Croatia will receive in the region of three billion euros in pre-accession funds, and obviously many more billions after accession. There may well not be hierarchical criminal organisations plotting to swindle the EU, but organisations can be loose and consist of criminal entrepreneurs on the lookout for opportunities, and it is likely that there will be chances for locally based

6 Interview with OLAF officials 2008

fraudsters to make mischief. In order to counter this threat a system of technical support was offered to candidate countries like Croatia as part of the preparations for the enlargement of the European Union.

Efforts of Croatia to prepare for accession

Given the degree of fragmentation which exists and indeed hampers the EU's fight against fraud which has been illustrated by authors such as Passas & Nelkin (1993), Pujas (2003), Sherlock & Harding (1991), and Sieber (1998) there have been efforts to try at least to harmonise the efforts of member states to secure common definitions of fraud and corruption. Croatia, therefore, is obliged to comply its legal system with the acquis communautaire as part of its preparations for accession. As Murawska (2004) comments, the Community measures about protection of the Community's finances are fairly modest. These consist of three EC Regulations:

- Council Regulation (EC, Euratom) No. 2988/95 of 18 December 1995 on the protection of the European Community's financial interests;[7]
- Council Regulation (EC, Euratom) No. 2185/96 of 11 November 1996 concerning on the spot checks and inspections carried out by the Commission in order to protect the European Communities financial interests against fraud and other irregularities;[8]
- Regulation (EC) No. 1073/99 of the European Parliament and of the Council of 25 May 1999, concerning investigations conducted by the European Fraud Prevention Office (OLAF).[9]

Also, the Croatian government was expected to incorporate into its legal system, the Convention on the Protection of the European Communities Financial Interests (the PFI Convention) together with its associated protocols. The convention as Fenyk (2007) details, requires that member states shall incorporate frauds against the European Communities' financial interests into their criminal code and should take the necessary steps to ensure that fraudulent behaviour and conduct is punishable by criminal penalties that are effective and reasonable and also that heads of businesses and other senior executives that have the power to take decisions and exercise control: "*to be declared criminally liable in accordance with the principles defined by national law in cases of fraud affecting the European Community's financial interests . . .*" (Fenyk 2007, p 2).

7 OJL 312, 23/12/1995: 1-4
8 OJL 292 15/11/1996: 2-5
9 OJL 136 31/05/1999: 1-7

The First Protocol to the PFI Convention requires that definitions on what is termed corruption, both active and passive (Articles 2-3) be assimilated into the criminal code and the Second Protocol to the PFI Convention requires national law to provide that legal persons can be held liable in cases of fraud or active corruption and money laundering that damages or is likely to damage the European Communities' financial interests (Fenyk, 2007).

Croatia's National Anti-Fraud Strategy which is still to be adopted, despite this being planned for mid 2009, stresses the importance of harmonising Croatian legislation with European regulations. The Criminal Code has been amended to include the new type of criminal offence: fraud against the financial interests of the European Communities. So Croatia's progress in this respect is commendable and is a sign of the country's willingness and eagerness to prepare itself for membership. There is unfortunately, a major deficiency in this respect. The penalty for fraud against the interests of the EU is less severe than fraud against the national budget of Croatia – a difference of two years. Croatia has recognised this discrepancy which goes against the spirit of assimilation of laws and penalties and it is due to be corrected in the near future – it is an embarrassing slip up and it is surprising that the Brussels authorities allowed this to go unchallenged, when it was in draft proposal.

It is also of great importance and symbolism that Croatia ratifies the PFI Convention at the same time that it ratifies the Treaty of Accession. Ratification and implementation are important steps towards reducing the fragmentary nature of the legal approaches to fighting fraud in the EU. After a number of self-inflicted wounds on the side of the Commission in this respect in the Czech Republic, Romania and Bulgaria, it is important to learn from these experiences and not repeat them in future enlargements.

Establishment of the AFCOS Network

In order to ensure effective co-operation between OLAF and the national administrations in the candidate countries as well as seeking to have in place organisational arrangements that would be capable of preventing and detecting frauds and irregularities as Murawska (2004) identifies, OLAF supported the creation of independent anti-fraud structures in then candidate countries. The rationale behind such structures was to ensure effective co-ordination between legislative and administrative measures dealing with EU fraud policy (Murawska, 2004). OLAF has provided training and support and although Croatian officials have not made any negative comments about OLAF's role in this respect, by their own admission there are significant gaps in their knowledge both about the technical aspects of policy programmes, investigative techniques and irregularity reporting. These are important areas that need to be addressed. One cannot expect OLAF to provide all the training, but it should facilitate the secondment of national experts from more experienced member states to help in the process – the Dutch have provided some support in this respect. A country like Croatia with a nascent anti-fraud service, with officials who do not have the experience of dealing with the complexities of EU policy regimes as well as not having the experience of investigating transnational frauds obviously are in need of support and nurturing.

The basic functions of the AFCOS network are: co-ordination, co-operation and communication (the 3 C's). These signify the ability:

- to co-ordinate within Croatia, all legislative, administrative and operational obligations and activities related to the protection of the Community's financial interests;
- to co-operate with OLAF and its partner institutions whenever OLAF requires investigation assistance or, on the other hand, whenever OLAF's assistance is required;
- to communicate with OLAF and its partner institutions, with regard to mandatory reporting and information exchange.

Although AFCOS does stand for Anti-Fraud Coordination Structure, woe betide any naive researcher who uses the word 'structure' in any interviews with the Croatian head of AFCOS. They will be firmly rebuked and informed that it is: "*a network and not a structure*!"[10] The AFCOS network was established in July 2008, responsible persons were appointed who would represent the competent bodies within the network, and the tasks of the competent bodies within the AFCOS network were determined.

The AFCOS system in the Republic of Croatia is comprised:

- a network of bodies managing and using EU assistance funds (System for Irregularities Reporting);
- a network of bodies which within the scope of their activities engage in combating fraud, corruption or some other form of system irregularity. The AFCOS network currently comprises ten bodies: the Ministry of Justice, the Ministry of the Interior, the Ministry of Economy, Labour and Entrepreneurship – Public Procurement System Directorate, the Central State Office for Public Administration, the State Audit Office, the Public Prosecutors Office of the Republic of Croatia, the Ministry of Finance – Tax administration, the Customs Administration and the Sector for Budget Supervision.

10 Interview with Croatian officials 2009.

- The Ministry of Finance – Department for Combating Irregularities and Fraud, which act as a system co-ordinator and a contact point for OLAF.

During the second quarter of 2008, the Department for Combating Irregularities and Fraud assumed responsibility for reporting on irregularities. The reports on irregularities were submitted to OLAF and the relevant General Directorates of the European Commission and during June and July 2008 all the bodies within the AFCOS Network confirmed the appointment of 'irregularities officers' who represent the contact point for the Department as part of the operation of the system for combating irregularities and frauds.

The National Anti-Fraud Strategy for the Protection of the European Union's Financial Interest

The strategy is still in its draft form. The intention was to have it approved by the government by mid 2009, but this still has not been achieved. Despite such a strategy being a necessary condition for accession, the Finance Minister did comment: "Why do we need this". This comment was actually hand-written on the anti-fraud strategy document itself and was helpfully translated for the benefit of non-native speakers by the ever helpful Croatian Translation Service (Croatian Anti-Fraud Strategy 2009). This was very surprising and a little worrying! Was he not aware of the criteria which had to be met as part of the accession process!!
The strategy has the following objectives:

- the AFCOS system will provide for the efficient and effective coordination of legislative, administrative, and operational activities relating to the combat of irregularities and fraud, co-operation with the European Anti-Fraud Office (OLAF); and
- will ensure the development of administrative capacities crucial for applying the Community's acquis communautaire including the capacities of judicial bodies which respond to the cases jeopardising EU financial interests.

The Strategy covers:

- prevention of fraud in the context of EU funds through communication, public relations and ethics in the civil service;
- managing EU pre-accession funds and EU own resources;
- proceedings with irregularities;
- criminal investigation and prosecution;
- Financial recovery;
- co-ordination of the fight against fraud and the protection of EU financial interests in the Republic of Croatia (Croatian Anti-Fraud Strategy, 2009).

Assessment of AFCOS Network and Anti-Fraud Strategy

There is a wide variety of organisations involved in the AFCOS network, so the issue of fragmentation has again raised its head. There is a potential for overlap and for duplication of effort. This is a problem that needs to be addressed. Also, there are some organisations within the AFCOS network that have police type powers such as Customs, the financial police, the Prosecutors Office which could undertake on the spot investigations, arrest and interrogate suspects and so on.

There are two sub-groups therefore – one will undertake criminal investigations the other group tends to undertake non-criminal investigations such as internal audit services and these may have no practical experience of liaising with criminal investigative bodies. Just as Quirke (2008) identified in the case of the Czech Republic, here in Croatia, there is the potential for confusion, inefficiencies, duplication and misunderstandings.

Also, having an administrative body like the Finance Ministry at the apex of the AFCOS network could be problematic as they are trying to co-ordinate police and administrative organisations. It might be preferable to place the lead AFCOS body within the Prosecutors Office as was the case initially in the Czech Republic, or at least taking it out of a particular ministry and placing it within the Prime Minister's Office reporting directly to him/her as is the case with Romania – this could enhance the prestige and status of the network.

By their own admission, AFCOS officials were given very little guidance on how to develop the network, they had to "feel their way".[11] More guidance could have been given from Brussels in this respect, although national officials could have consulted more with colleagues from new member states in order to learn from best practice. These findings have been identified in other countries such as the Czech Republic and Romania (Quirke, 2008) and Quirke (2009).

A concern has been expressed about relatively low salaries of public employees and how this might make them vulnerable to corrupt approaches,. Perhaps attention could be given to the Romanian practice of paying such officials a premium (Quirke, 2009), thereby increasing their salaries by a significant amount which might help to some extent in the resistance to bribery and corruption.

---

11 Interview with Croatian Officials 2009

Deficiencies in skills and expertise have been identified. These cover the following areas: managing EU funds and own resources and also dealing with irregularities which includes risk analysis. Also there are deficiencies in the knowledge of officials with regards to administrative proceedings in the case of irregularities concerning own resources and EU assistance funds. There is also a need for education of judges and police officers and prosecutors with respect to amendments of the criminal code and with how to conduct investigations and developing and using tools of international co-operation with OLAF, Eurojust, Interpol, Europol and so on. Financial management procedures with regards to the recovery of wrongly used funds need to be defined (Sigma, 2007). Also, internal audit is tool that needs to be significantly strengthened as an effective system of financial control as a deterrence to the committing of irregularities.[12]

There are some major issues here with profound implications for the effective operation of a system of suppression and repression of fraud and irregularity. The Croatian authorities are aware of this and have put together a training strategy.[13] They need urgent help from Brussels but also from other member states if they are going to adequately address these issues before 2011. Croatian officials have taken the initiative in some respects as they have tried to organise workshops and seminars in conjunction with other member states in order to enhance their expertise on the complexities of EU policy programmes and funding.[14] Perhaps this is something which OLAF could help facilitate as well.

Zagreb has also been warned by the Commission about its casual handling of EU funds with poorly prepared documentation submitted without necessary explanations and management. There was almost an indifference to the application process. Some funds were withheld in 2008 as a warning.[15] This shortcoming in documentation is a serious issue, as it could present opportunities to fraudsters to manipulate and forge paperwork if there are not sufficient checks and controls in place. Properly prepared and checked paperwork is one of the first lines of defence against fraud and irregularity. If this is not being administered adequately, then it does not bode well for the remainder of the control system.

---

12 Interviews with Croatian Officials 2009
13 Interviews with Croatian Officials 2009
14 Interview with Croatian Officials 2009
15 www.neuope.eu/articles/85091.php

Examples of Irregularities

Sugar

Croatia has had examples of irregularities with regards to sugar. Durdevic (2006) identifies fraudulent activities for the sake of manipulation of data about the origin of goods. In November 2000, the EU unilaterally liberalised its farm products market for Croatia and other countries of the Western Balkans. After 2002, when Croatia was allowed to export duty free unlimited quantities of sugar to the EU, on condition that it was of Croatian origin, or that the raw materials were imported into the EU and then processed sufficiently in Croatia, export and imports rose significantly. For this reason, the Commission began to doubt the Croatian origin of all the exported sugar, fearing that it might be highly subsidised sugar from the EU that was concerned together with its re-import into the EU without customs duty. Because of doubts about the origin of Croatian sugar, Italy, Germany and Austria brought in deposits as a special financial fee for exporters from Croatia amounting to €10.000 per truck, practically halting the import of sugar from the country. Analysis of sugar imported into Greece showed the existence of sugar cane sugar when the declaration indicated it was sugar from beet, the raw material from which sugar is produced in Croatia. Criminal indictments were issued against people from the sugar refinery in Croatia who were responsible.

There is also another sugar investigation being undertaken. Apparently, three companies are being accused of avoiding 22 million euros in customs duties by mixing sugar with tea, cocoa and citric acid. Although the companies did not directly break European laws, they used loopholes to sell to the EU sugar imported from Brazil as "processed food" instead of sugar, thus avoiding payment of customs duties, as there are no duties for processed food. According to sources[16], the three companies were given clearance by the Croatian Chamber of Economy to undertake these activities.

Tobacco

Croatia is a transhipment country for cigarettes heading from Bosnia and Montenegro into Western Europe – this point has also been made above by Van Duyne (2003, 2006). Montenegro is believed to play a large role in regional smuggling[17] which causes problems for its neighbours. Croatia is also believed to be involved in local smuggling. Rovinj, the powerful Croatian cigarette monopoly, has bene-

16 Interview with Croatian Officials 2009
17 www.reportingproject.net/new/index2.php

fited greatly from a Bosnian law that keeps taxes low on cigarettes imported to Bosnia from Croatia. Croatian made cigarettes are almost half the price in Bosnia than they are domestically. Some of these cigarettes are then smuggled back into Croatia. Ronhill cigarettes, manufactured by Rovinj, are often found on smugglers.[18]

Cigarettes are such an attractive prospect to smugglers as Von Lampe (2005) makes clear as cigarettes are usually subject to high taxation. He explains how the difference between net (duty-free) prices and legal retail prices provides an incentive for circumventing taxes. If it is possible to acquire untaxed cigarettes (as it is in Montenegro for example), then those who are capable of doing this, can pocket a large share of the difference between the duty-free price and the duty-paid price as profit. (von Lampe, 2005). Von Lampe (2005) also makes the point that a second major factor behind cigarette smuggling is the disparity in retail prices between countries due to different levels of taxation. Depending on the extent of the price difference and on the transport costs involved, it can be lucrative to buy cigarettes in a low tax country and to sell them in a high tax country as appears to be happening in Croatia at present.

This problem is only likely to be exacerbated by Croatia's entry into the European Union with a consequent loss of duty to Croatia's and indeed the European Budget. Maljević (2005) emphasises the point that the Balkans are a centre for illegal trafficking of many kinds with highly organised networks and these will undoubtedly further facilitate the practice of cigarette smuggling.

Public Works Projects

OLAF has been analysing reports on corruption in Croatia's public enterprises owing to alleged corruption in the construction, shipbuilding and public procurement sectors. Apart from tender documentation, MEP's (Members of the European Parliament) have submitted contracts which the Croatian Motorways Authority (HAC) has signed with major contractors over the last five years. The main targets of OLAF's investigation includes Croatian Motorways (HAC), Rijeka – Zagreb Motorway (ARZ), shipyards and a consortium of construction companies represented by Institut IGH.[19] Since this includes projects financed by EBRD[20], it is OLAF's duty to investigate suspected frauds and corruption.

18 www.reportingproject.net/new/index2.php

19 www.seebiz.eu/corporate/european-anti-fraud-office/

20 European Bank for Reconstruction and Development

Conclusions

Croatia has made good progress in some respects in terms of readying itself to adequately protect the financial interests of the EU. It has aligned its legal code with the provisions of the PFI Convention, but has also experienced some self-inflicted wounds such as having a less severe penalty for frauds against the EU's financial interests. Also, Croatia has established its AFCOS network, but there are concerns about the amount of fragmentation with a variety of police type and non-police type organisations involved and the consequent scope for confusion, inefficiency and misunderstandings. Also, major deficiencies have been identified in the skills and expertise of officials involved in protecting the EU's financial interests, these should be addressed with alacrity. The casual attitude of some officials to regulations and paperwork which has deeply concerned European Commission officials could present opportunities to fraudsters – as they continually look for weaknesses in management and controls to exploit. There is an obvious need for a change in culture and attitude here.

Owing to concerns about the level of corruption which are highlighted by the many sharp and shady practices of the privatisation process and by attempts to bribe public officials, attention needs to be given to relative salary levels and the potential to pay a premium to officials involved in AFCOS type work as happens in Romania for example, should be investigated and considered as a matter of urgency. Corruption is deeply engrained in Croatian society and will not disappear with the signing of international protocols and treaties.

Sugar, tobacco and manipulation of the tender process all look to be major areas of concern in terms of the commission of irregularities. The long porous border with the highly corrupt state of Bosnia provides opportunities for criminals to smuggle tobacco and other 'precious' commodities.

Although some of the problems identified above could be considered to be 'self-inflicted' wounds, this does not reflect 'half-heartedness' on the part of Croatian officials. They have received help and training from OLAF and the European Commission and have also taken the initiative in order to arrange seminars and workshops with other member states. Again there is scope for OLAF to help in this respect by facilitating such contacts. With a very small staff and in their opinion, relatively little guidance from Brussels, they have managed to establish an AFCOS network which has the potential to make a significant contribution to the fight against EU budget fraud particularly if the issues identified above are tackled in a robust and coherent manner.

References

Ballinger, P. *Selling Croatia or selling out Croatia?,* The National Council for Eurasian and East European Research, 2003

Bicanic, I. and V. Franicevic, *Understanding Reform: the case of Croatia*, Global Development Network Southeast Europe, 2003

Bejakovic, P. Corruption in Croatia: Institutional Settings and Practical Experiences, *Croatian Political Science Review*, 2002, Vol. 39, no. 5, 128-155

Budak, J. Corruption in Croatia. *Economic Trends and Economic Policy*, 2006, *no.106*, 66-99

Croatian Ministry of Finance. *National Anti-Fraud Strategy for the Protection of the EU's Financial Interests*, 2009.

Durdevic, Z. Fraud adversely affecting the budget of the European Union: the forms, methods and causes, *Financial Theory and Practice*, 2006, vol. 30, *no. 3*, 253-282

Duyne, P.C. van. *Workshop for Police and Customs Officers*, Croatia, 2006

Duyne, P.C. van, Organizing cigarette smuggling and policy making, ending up in smoke. *Crime, Law and Social change*, 2003, *no. 3*, 263-283

European Commission, *Monitoring Report on Croatia*, Office of Official Publications of the European Communities: Luxembourg, 2007

Fenyk, J., The level of implementation of the Convention on the EC's financial interests and of the Follow–Up Protocols in the Czech Republic, *European Law and National Criminal Legislation*, 2007, vol.1, 116-121

Grubisa, D. Political Corruption in Transitional Croatia: The Peculiarities of a Model, Croatian Political Science Review, 2005, Vol.42, no.5, 55-72

Maljević, A., Trafficking in women in Bosnia and Herzegovina. In: P.C. van Duyne, K. Von Lampe, M. Van Dijck and J.L. Newell (eds.), *The Organised Crime Economy*, Nijmegen, Wolf Legal Publishers, 2005

Murawska, A., *Impact of the enlargement on the protection of the financial interests of teh European Community against fraud.* Second Pan-European Conference Standing Group on EU Politics, Bologna, 24-26 June 2004

Official Journal of the European Communities, C316, 27/11/1995, *Convention on the Protection of the European Communities Financial Interests*, pp. 1-8

Official Journal of the European Communities, 312, Council Regulation (EC, Euratom), *no. 2988/95* of 23/12/1995, *On the protection of the European Communities Financial Interests*, pp.1-4

Official Journal of the European Communities, 292, Council Regulation (EC, Euratom) *no. 2185/96* of 15/11/1996, *Concerning on the spot checks and inspec-*

tions, pp. 2-5

Passas, N. and D. Nelkin, The thin line between legitimate and criminal enterprises: Subsidy Frauds in the European Community. *Crime, Law and Social Change*, 1993, vol. 19, 223-243

Petricevic, D. *Organised crime in Croatia: who, how, why*. Abakus, Zagreb, 2000

Pujas, V., The European anti-fraud office (OLAF): a European Policy to fight against economic and financial fraud? *Journal of European Public Policy*, 2003, Vol.10., no. 5, 778-797

Quirke, B., EU Fraud and new Member States: The case of the Czech Republic. In: P.C. van Duyne, J. Harvey, A. Maljevic, K. von Lampe and M. Scheinost (eds.), *European crime markets at cross-roads*, Nijmegen, Wolf Legal Publishers, 2008

Quirke, B., Romania and the fight against EU Fraud: A Balkan Success Story? In: P.C. van Duyne, S. Donati, J. Harvey, A. Maljevic, and K. von Lampe (eds.), *Crime, money and criminal mobility in Europe,* Nijmegen, Wolf Legal Publishers, 2009

Von Lampe, K., Explaining the emergence of the cigarette black market in Germany. In: P.C. van Duyne, K. Von Lampe, M. Van Dijck and J.L. Newell (eds.) *The Organised Crime Economy*, Nijmegen, Wolf Legal Publishers, 2005

Scheinost, M., Some reflections on researching financial and economic crime. In: P.C. van Duyne, A. Maljevic, K. von Lampe and J.L. Newell (eds.), *The Organisation of crime for profit*, Nijmegen, Wolf Legal Publishers, 2006

Sherlock, A. and Harding, M., Controlling fraud within the European Community. *European Law Review,* 1991, Vol 16, no.1, 20-36

Sieber, U., Eurofraud: organised fraud against the financial interests of the EU. *Crime, Law and Social Change,* 1998, vol. 30, *no.1*, 1-42

Sigma, *Public Internal Financial Control Assessment*, OECD Paris, 2007

Stojarova, V. Organised crime in the Western Balkans, *HUMSEC Journal, issue 1*, 2006, pp.91-114

www.vlada.hr/en/ Prime *Minister says Privatisation Fund to be closed, three vice-presidents arrested for fraud*, Accessed on November 3rd, 2009

www.reportingproject.net/new/index2.php. *Smuggling infiltrates the Balkans*, Accessed on January 27th, 2010

www.seebiz.eu/en/corporate/ *European Anti-Fraud Office to investigate suspicious tenders*, Accessed on November 9th, 2009

www.neurope.eu/articles/85091.php *Croatia, under fire, to use or lose more EU funds*, Accessed on November 20th, 2009

www.balkan-monitor.eu *Croats uncertain about EU membership*. Accessed on April 20th, 2010

The holy grail of money laundering statistics. Input and outcome of the Belgian AML system

Antoinette Verhage[1]

Introduction

In this contribution, following the footsteps of Levi (Levi, 1997; Levi & Maguire, 2004; Levi, 2005), Van Duyne (van Duyne & de Miranda, 1999), Harvey (Harvey, 2004; Harvey, 2007) and Fleming (Fleming, 2005), we aim to make an inventory of what is known in Belgium with regard to the outcomes of the Anti Money Laundering system (AML). Our goals are threefold: 1) to map the existing data and the extent to which this data are (public and) available; 2) to study the contents of these data with the aim to obtain insight in the functioning of the AML system and its effects in the field of law enforcement; and 3) to conclude and take stock of the proportion between input and outcome of the anti money laundering system.

Why do we aim to map the knowledge on the outcomes of the anti money laundering chain? Fighting money laundering is a national (cfr. the National Security Plan of the Belgian Police, 2008-2011) and international priority (on the level of the European Union, the US and international bodies like the OCED and IMF) and has been so for over two decades. It may seem obvious that there is a need for an evidence-based policy in this domain, which should be possible after ten to fifteen years of AML activities. After all, the input and effort that is demanded from public and private actors in the prevention and detection of money laundering is rather high (Commission of the European Communities, 2009; Verhage, 2009b).

1 The author is assistant at Ghent University, Faculty of Law, and has finalised her PhD research on anti-money laundering and compliance in 2009. I would like to thank Petrus C. van Duyne for his support and critical comments.

During our PhD study (Verhage, 2009a), we found that gaining access to these sources is not a simple undertaking, implying that either the data are too sensitive to disclose, or that structured data are simply not available. For this reason, in this chapter, we take stock of the available information, combine the different sources and look for methods which may evaluate the functioning of the system. We will do this by making use of each phase in the AML chain, looking for data on each level of activity. We will start by giving a short description of the Belgian AML system and the motives behind its specific nature. After this introduction, we focus on the diverse methods for looking at effects of this system. We will describe why it is important to have a view on the effects of the AML system. Then we discuss the data that were found with regard to the AML system in Belgium, and explain the difficulties in finding these data. To conclude, we will discuss the data that is needed in order to evaluate the AML policy.

AML, the Belgian case

The AML system in Belgium was implemented in 1993[2] by establishing an administrative FIU (functioning as a filter between reporting institutions and law enforcement). It also transformed public and private organisations into 'reporting institutions', by imposing a number of obligations on organisations indicated by law. Through the years, the number of reporting institutions has grown (by the end of 2006, 30.500 organisations and individuals were obliged to report suspicious transactions), along with a steady rise in obligations and requirements concerning AML.

The AML legislation has resulted in an anti-money laundering enforcement chain, consisting of several phases, each phase operating quasi autonomously. After assessment and analysis of transactions and clients, the reporting institutions must report unusual or potentially suspicious transactions to the FIU. The FIU subsequently investigates these reports and differentiates between suspicious and non-suspicious files. The suspicious files will be sent to the public prosecutor's officer, who, after analysis of the file, may decide whether to start an investigation or not. Finally, a small selection of these files may end in court.

2 Through the Law of 11 January 1993 on the prevention of the use of the financial system for the laundering of money and financing of terrorism, *B.S.*, 9 February 1993

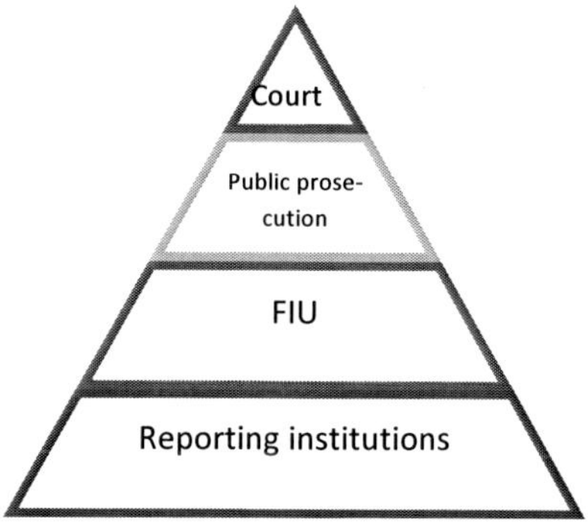

With regard to financial institutions, the Belgian AML regulator has introduced a relatively detailed interpretation of the EU guidelines. In Belgium, financial institutions are obliged to appoint an employee who is in charge of the implementation of AML legislation. Though this is no different from other European countries (as the appointment of a specific AML responsible staff follows in general terms from the second EU Directive[3]), the financial regulator in Belgium has chosen to detail this obligation relatively early in comparison with other countries and has issued a regulation in this respect in 2001. After six years, the detailed directives were converted into law.[4] This has led to the establishment of a specific function, the compliance officer, whose task is focused on (in general) the 'integrity of banking'. More specifically, one of the assigned tasks in this respect is AML. As a result, we have witnessed the emergence of a new and rather professional sector of compliance officers, working in Belgian banks. They are tasked with implementing and leading the 'battle' against money laundering, but principally from their organisational point of view. In contrast with other European compliance officers, the Belgian compliance officer's origins therefore need to be mainly ascribed to the development of AML legislation.

A second characteristic feature in the Belgian AML-system (though not exclusively Belgian) is the administrative nature of the FIU. In the early 1990s, when the AML legislation was developed, the Belgian legislator aimed for an FIU that was "*not a police service, nor a service dependent of judicial authorities*"[5], but a go-

3 Council Directive 91/308/EEC of 10 June 1991 on prevention of the use of the financial system for the purpose of money laundering

4 Wet van 22 maart op het statuut van en de toezicht op de kredietinstellingen (*B.S*, 19 april 1993).

5 Belgische Senaat, 468-1 (B.Z. 1991-1992) Explanatory Memorandum to the bill on the prevention of the use of the financial system for money laundering *22 July 1992 p.39*

between for financial institutions and law enforcement.[6] This administrative nature of the FIU not only has a filter-function, but also functions as a 'black box', in which decision making seems to lack transparency, based on the claim of protection of professional confidentiality. This may also be due to the FIU's specific statute, which paves the way for confidentiality and hence secrecy. In view of aiming for effectiveness – the measurement thereof being the focus of this chapter – this secrecy is a significant obstacle.

Anti money laundering: a construction of 'danger' without knowledge

The international origins of the AML system are well-known and were analysed by several authors (Levi, 1996; Levi & Reuter, 2006; Van Duyne, 1997; Van Duyne *et al.*, 2005; Verhage, 2009b; Verhage, 2009a). They have also shown that the interests behind the implementation of the AML system were of a various nature: economic interests, competition between states and organisations, the war on drugs and – after 9/11 – the war on terror; all have influenced the way in which the anti-money laundering apparatus has been shaped and spread all over the world. The threat image of either the links between money laundering and a potential power-accumulation of organised criminal groups, terrorist groups, or the reputational hazards associated with money laundering, has resulted in a society in which anti-money laundering efforts and investments by private organisations (whose core-task is not crime fighting) are perceived as 'normal' or 'standard' business conduct (Sharman, 2008). The *compliance industry*, as illustrated in earlier contributions (Verhage, 2009c), adds to this threat perception (van Duyne, 2008) by emphasising the risk that is (or might be) associated with money laundering. As we illustrated in earlier contributions, this perception of threat also entails commercial advantages: the higher the risk associated with money laundering, the more AML investments, hence the higher the revenues of the compliance industry. This evolution is not typical for anti-money laundering, however. The last decades have shown an increasing intermingling of public and private actors in the field of crime control, to the extent that "*professional careers and business interests rely upon the continued threat of crime*" (Zedner, 2003, p. 159). This

6 This system is not unique for Belgium: until recently the Netherlands had a similar administrative institution, functioning as a buffer for the processing of *unusual* transactions.

assessment led Bauman to the conclusion that *public* demand for security (and we count financial institutions, for the sake of the argument, as part of the public) is the result of '*a remarkable transfer of anxiety*' (Bauman, 1998, p 116, cited in Zedner, 2003, p. 159). Everyone has to be afraid; in other terms: alertness to risk is of high commercial and policy making importance (Van Duyne, 2008). This tendency has been labelled as the *'commodification of security'* (Loader, 1999, p 373). It is interesting to notice that in this state of fear few requests are made for empirical knowledge. On what knowledge have these fears been based?

One of the examples in this respect is the large accountancy firms. For example, in its 2009 Global Economic Crime Survey, Ernst & Young states that the (perceived) risk of money laundering victimisation by companies has increased during the current financial crisis. Companies now estimate their risk of victimisation as higher than during times of financial stability (Ernst & Young, 2009). Furthermore, of all the companies in the E&Y sample that experienced fraud in the past year (30%), 12% has reported falling victim to money laundering in the past year – money laundering even takes the fifth place on the incident list of financial crimes. This illustrates both the perceived impact of money laundering and the awareness of companies with regard to the incidence of this crime.

Do we need to know the outcome?

In my recently finalised PhD research, I studied these diverse forces that impact on the battle against money laundering. One of the questions that became increasingly urgent during this study was the question to what extent the battle against money laundering is based on facts, instead of on imagery. It soon became clear that facts are surprisingly absent in the money laundering debate and scarce in the research literature. Apart from 'educated guesses' (Schneider & Enste, 2000; Unger, 2006) about the amount of money that is laundered, statistics are unconvincing with regard to the effect of the AML system (Reuter, 2009; Harvey, 2007; Sharman, 2008). A study, carried out in 2009 commissioned by the European Commission[7] concluded that reporting institutions within Europe also question the efficiency and effectiveness of the system. This is partly due to the lack of transparency and knowhow with regard to the outcome of AML policy (Euro-

7 Study on "Best practices in vertical relations between the FIUs and law enforcement agencies and Money Laundering and Terrorist Financing Reporting entities with a view to indicating effective models for feedback on follow-up to and effectiveness of Suspicious Transactions Reports", 2008-2009.

pean Commission, 2008). My own research (Verhage, 2009a; Verhage, 2010) also showed that most reporting institutions are not provided with feedback on their reports, which leads to a system of blind reporting and uncertainty with regard to the quality of these reports.

In short, while financial institutions (and others) are obliged to invest large sums in AML, the authorities are lagging behind with regard to follow-up, feedback, transparency and the granting of access. This is also reflected in the fact that empirical research on the effects of the anti-money laundering system is very scarce, probably also because of the difficulties in gaining access to statistical information of the authorities (Van Duyne, 2007). It may be clear that conducting an evidence-based policy and knowledge-based AML strategy is largely impeded by this lack of data which seems to be due to the attitude of the authorities themselves. Before we further discuss this lack of data, we shortly explain the difference between process and impact effects of AML.

Process Effects

Naturally, we need to have knowledge of the effects of a policy that demand large investments from society at large. However, apart from the 'net' effect of the anti-money laundering policy, this policy also has a symbolic goal. This symbolic goal, based on a moral fear of using criminal money in the legal economy, can also lead to general prevention and can be seen as a *process effect*. This implies that the knowledge of the process of AML in itself has led to an impact on the underlying phenomenon. The same symbolic effect can also be found in 'regular' policing, where the 'net' effect may also be limited (Ponsaers, 2009): (by far) not all crimes are recorded, let alone solved, nor all perpetrators are convicted, which could also lead to the assessment of the law enforcement apparatus in general as ineffective. Still, there is no debate on abolishing the traditional penal chain. Is the anti-money laundering system different?

In our opinion there is a difference in two aspects. First of all, where policing is supposed to lead to the protection of basic principles and democratic rights, and is surrounded with a large amount of checks and balances, the AML policy can be questioned with regard to these values. AML activities regularly balance on the borderline between the general and the individual interest, rubbing against the boundaries with regard to intrusion of privacy and due process. This is all the more pressing since these activities are mainly carried out by private organisations, implying less democratic controls and a potential higher risk with regard to breaches of privacy.

Secondly, the AML system in itself, by its focus on specific sectors (such as the financial institutions) and the risk-based approach that is inherent to AML, unavoidably leads to displacement effects. These displacement effects are different from those with common crime; they will concern the organisation of (financial) business, for which there is ample room of manoeuvre. The preventive effect of the system may therefore be questioned; there are numerous alternative ways to launder money. Reuter and Truman, for example, concluded in their assessment of the US system, that an expansion of the AML system will probably only "*marginally inconvenience those who need to launder the proceeds of their crimes*" (Reuter & Truman, 2004, p 7). Furthermore, the general preventive effect is also very difficult to map. One way of studying this effect could be by asking banks for the number of clients they have refused based on their identification policies, or the number of transactions they have *not* carried out as a result of a money laundering alert. However, although Belgian financial institutions were very helpful during my PhD research, we may doubt whether they would be willing or allowed to share this kind of information, supposing they have this information available.

A second method to study the preventive effect of AML could be by assessing the price of illegal goods: if the AML system has a preventive effect, something must happen at criminal market level. It is to be expected that business costs will increase, at least by making money laundering more expensive. Consequently one would expect the prices of illegal goods to rise. However, as Reuter noted in 2009, an increase in money laundering controls and costs would only have a very small or no effect on the retail price of cocaine (Reuter, 2009). This is confirmed by the UN 2010 World Drug Report: since 1990, whether wholesale or retail, the prices of cocaine and heroin have come down globally (UN, 2010) The effects on the drug markets – if any – appear therefore to be marginal, which may be ascribed to the multiplicity of money laundering methods (displacement) and hence the difficulty to tackle all these methods in one AML regime. However, this is little more than a plausible hypothesis: we have no data to substantiate this.

Impact effects

Impact effects consist of the net effect of criminal cases that flow through the anti-money laundering chain and its impact on crime in general. It refers to the outcomes of the AML chain: prosecutions, convictions, confiscations, or other sanctions. The outcome of the AML chain should be measurable (typically an ideal) by looking at data that are available on the functioning of the penal chain. This may seem to be an easy task. However, as stated above, the lack of access and the limited comparability of data can be major hindrances in this process. This is not only frustrating for researchers, also policymakers have (finally) come to this insight, albeit belatedly (Van Duyne, 2007). At any rate, in the 3rd EU directive on Money Laundering, we may discern some awareness of this defect: policymakers seem to have come to the understanding that an effective policy should be based on the existence of data to measure these policies. In the 3rd Directive, (which was just recently introduced in the Belgian AML legislation – through the law of 18 January 2010), the need for gathering basic data on money laundering and the effectiveness of its approach is emphasised. Countries are therefore obliged to gather these data, under Article 33 of the Directive:

> "*1. Member States shall ensure that they are able to review the effectiveness of their systems to combat money laundering or terrorist financing by maintaining comprehensive statistics on matters relevant to the effectiveness of such systems. Such statistics shall as a minimum cover the number of suspicious transaction reports made to the FIU, the follow-up given to these reports and indicate on an annual basis the number of cases investigated, the number of persons prosecuted, the number of persons convicted for money laundering or terrorist financing offences and how much property has been frozen, seized or confiscated.*[8]"

In addition, in preparation of this obligation in the Directive and in the framework of the EU Action Plan 2006-2010[9], a working group was established, aiming to gather basic data on money laundering with the goal of being able to monitor the implementation of legislation and support the prevention and combat of money laundering by both policymakers and practitioners (European Commission, 7 April 2009). The Financial Crime Subgroup, organised in the framework of the EU Action Plan Criminal Statistics 2006-2010, was composed of experts in the field of money laundering and was set up to advise the European Commission on the set of indicators on ML. The Subgroup established (not surprisingly) that basic data may be available on a national level, but these are often diverse, which hinders international comparisons. The Subgroup therefore aimed to introduce 'efficiency indicators' that would allow the assessment of AML policy. Based on 24 provisional indicators, EUROSTAT gathered information (by sending out requests to Member States in May 2008 – (Eurostat, 2009)) and made a first analysis in November 2008.

They concluded firstly that the data were not suitable for publication, as data are available for only a limited number of Member States. They pointed at the

8 Directive 2005/60/EC of the European Parliament and of the Council of 26 October 2005 on the prevention of the use of the financial system for the purpose of money laundering and terrorist financing

9 This is the EU Action Plan 2006-2010 on "Developing a comprehensive and coherent EU strategy to measure crime and criminal justice"

need to develop a better information flow within Member States, allowing data to become available to contact points for crime statistics.

Secondly, they concluded that data that are available, are not always clear, for example because counting units are different (European Commission, 7 April 2009). Their final report was expected by the end of 2009, but in February 2010, no information could be found on the EU website. An e-mail was sent to one of the members of the Subgroup, to ask for more information. Eurostat answered[10] by stating that they are indeed working on the collection of data on money laundering, but that problems of comparability and data quality have resulted in a delay of their work. They stated that a working paper might be published on this subject in the future, and referred us to the activities of Europol in data gathering.

Europol, as the European police service responsible for the analysis of crime phenomena, has indeed made a round-up of money laundering data in 2009.[11] However, these data are very rudimentary, stating that the number of suspicious transactions reports in EU member states has increased in 2007 to 602.450 reports (an increase of 6,2% in comparison to 2006).

In short, although there are some – very recent – attempts by policy makers to map both the phenomenon of money laundering and its combat, it still is surprising that after almost two decades of AML no valid data are available. Equally surprising, it took an equal amount of time for the European Commission to become aware of this serious data deficiency. Hence, no one knows the magnitude of the crime that is being fought, nor can anyone tell us what the effects are of this intrusive, encompassing and costly AML-system. On the other hand, the fact that the 3rd Directive mentions the need for statistics and the initiatives that are taken with regard to the gathering of these statistics, must be seen as a step in the right direction.

Today, however, the absence of data seems to confirm Van Duyne's analysis of a *camera obscura* with regard to policy formulation (Van Duyne, 2007): policy makers acknowledge to be unaware of the effects of the AML system, and the question may well be: do policymakers really want to know what the effects are?

Outcome of data search: finding pieces of the puzzle

The search for data on (anti) money laundering is comparable to making a puzzle: each small piece needs to be searched for, in order to get the larger picture, and

10 E-mail, Eurostat, on 15/2/2010

11 http://www.europol.europa.eu/index.asp?page=news&news=pr090622.htm

almost unavoidably one or more pieces are mysteriously missing. In the following sections we will describe our search for these data and the results thereof. To be clear: in this paragraph we will look at outcome effects on the level of the criminal law enforcement chain. We have made use of the FIU statistics, the statistics of the Public Prosecutor's Office and police statistics to gain an insight in the AML chain. How do the pieces of the puzzle connect?

To avoid confusion: the counting units discussed differ according to the phase of the criminal law chain.

- in the first phase, the counting unit is 'report' ('reports' are sent from reporting institutions to the FIU);
- in the second phase, the FIU merges these reports into 'files', and sends a selection of these files to the Public Prosecutor. From this phase on, we will refer to 'files' as counting unit.

To remain within the metaphor of the puzzle: not only is it uncertain whether all the pieces are complete, the pieces there are differ in dimensions, one a bit thicker than the other.[12] This disorder may confuse the reader as much as it confused the author in the first place.

Phase 1: input to the FIU

The first phase of the AML chain consists of (public and private) organisations that report a-typical (unusual) or suspicious transactions to the FIU. In Belgium, where a risk-based approach has been adopted with regard to AML reporting (CBFA, 2005) this implies that each organisation is supposed to investigate a transaction before reporting this to the FIU. After all, the risk of the transaction needs to be clarified in advance. A second impetus for the in-house investigation of transactions can be found in the self-protective reflex of the organisations. Banks, for example, are very reluctant to simply report each a-typicality pro forma to the FIU. An internal investigation allows them to filter out the 'genuine' risky transactions and many financial institutions will be inclined to invest in this investigation phase. On the other hand, other financial and non-financial institutions, which are less controlled or less regulated, may choose to report quasi automatically. And there are others who are known for the low number of reports to the FIU (for example, in 2008, real estate agents or diamond dealers have each reported 1 suspicious transaction to the FIU (CTIF-CFI, 2009)). The image and

12 In the Netherlands too, the chain for processing laundering cases starts with reports at the level of transaction, then these are bundled into files and after sent to the PPO the counting unit becomes the single offender.

background of these reporting institutions and their attitude towards reporting is, therefore,very diverse, as is their investment in preventing and investigating money laundering. The reports that are made by the financial institutions (banks) are the ones that are most transmitted in the form of files to the Public Prosecutor: 64,7 % of the files that were sent to the Public Prosecutor were based on reports stemming from financial institutions, while the exchange offices, although once having reported the largest amount of suspicious transaction reports, now only contribute 19,8% of the files. The same can be noted for the amounts of money that are involved (banks are responsible for 79% of the total amount of money involved in the transmitted files).

The total number of reports to the FIU has increased during the last years: in 2004 11.234 reports were counted, while in 2008, 15.554 reports were submitted to the FIU (CTIF-CFI, 2009). The majority of the reports to the FIU are made by exchange offices and financial institutions (banks): together they represent 81% of all reports. Casinos take the third place in reporting. Important to note here is that he Belgian FIU provides statistics for *files* instead of reports: different reports by diverse institutions with regard to the same transaction(s) or client(s), are merged into a file. These files are therefore the counting unit for the transmission to the public prosecutor's office.

Transmission to the Public Prosecutor or dismissal by the FIU

The percentage of reports that have led to a file being sent from the FIU to the Public Prosecutor's office (which could be seen as an indicator of the seriousness of the file) has decreased in 2008. In 2008 only 19,2% of all files were transmitted by the FIU to the Public Prosecutor's office.[13] This could be a first indication that an increase in reporting obligations does not necessarily lead to a more effective system, when counting the files that reach the public prosecutor's office.

We think that more detailed data are needed in order to project these statistics against a proper context and to make an interpretation of what these figures really mean. Again, we must conclude that these data are lacking. Although these aggregate data are gathered on the level of the FIU, no access was given to the raw database.[14]

13 The FIU mentions in their overview that 32% of all *reports* and 19,2% of all *files* were sent to the public prosecutor's office (CTIF-CFI (2009). From this we can derive that 19,2 % of the files consist of 32% of the total number of reports.

14 A letter to the FIU asking for these data in 2009, was answered by a letter from the FIU stating that the FIU was not able to further assist in this research.

Table 1
Overview of phase 1 and 2 of the AML chain

	2004	2005	2006	2007	2008
reports (total)	11.234	10.148	9.938	12.830	15.554
reports merged into files	3.163	3.051	3.367	4.927	4.875
average nr of reports in 1 file	3,6	3,3	3,0	2,6	3,2
files FIU → PP	664	686	912	1166	937
% files to PP	21,0%	22,5%	27,1%	23,7%	19,2%
% dismissal by FIU[15]	68,8%	73,9%	71,6%	68,2%	61,0%

Source: CTIF-CFI, 2009. Columns do not add to 100 % if files are not finalised.

The FIU has dismissed more than 60% of its files in 2008. The annual report mentions that the FIU has dismissed a total of 22.108 files (on a total of 34.878), since the start of its activities since 1993, which amounts to 63% (42,8% of the total number of reports).

In general we see that the number of files that was dismissed at the level of the FIU has decreased. However, the number of files transmitted to the Public Prosecutor's office has also decreased due to number of files that is still pending at the level of the FIU (more than 2.600 files in 2008 – which is more than twice as much in comparison with 2004; CTIF-CFI, 2009).

When looking at the *content* of the files that were sent to the Public Prosecutor, the main category in which files are transmitted concerns racketeering (15,6%) or illegal trade in goods (14,4%) – both concerning legal goods and services (such as cars or jewellery) and illegal goods (such as stolen goods or weapons).

The police: repressive approach

The police statistics for 2008 show that in that year, 661 files on money laundering were registered at the national level. To compare: the statistics for the Brussels police state that 153 files were registered for the judicial district of Brussels.[16]

The activity report of the Federal Police for 2008 states that in that year 732 new investigations were started with regard to money laundering (one of the prioritised phenomena).[17] How this relates itself to the overall crime statistics, is

15 The difference between the dismissal% and the % of transmitted files are files that are still being handled by the FIU: 3,6% in 2005 and 19,8% in 2008.

16 http://www.polfed-fedpol.be/crim/crim_stat_nl.php

17 In total, the federal police is active in 1377 investigations. Activity Report Federal Police 2008;

not clear. From those files, 75 suspects were referred to an examining magistrate. In total, 88 criminal groups were identified as working in the domain of money laundering.

The section financial-economic crime of the Federal Police (CDGEFID) mentions that 20% of their independent, operational files concern money laundering (Federale Gerechtelijke Politie, 2009). Typical for 2008 is, that the majority of their files were started on the basis of a detection of a predicate offence, rather than on the basis of a report by the FIU, which is something that is handled by the FGP's (Federale Gerechtelijke Politie, 2009).[18] In the same activity report, the CDGEFID states that in 2008 for over eleven million euro was seized – however, there are no statistics on the amount of money that was actually forfeited, which would give a more realistic picture. This implies that we do not know what the net effect is of these confiscations.

The COIV (the Central Organ for Confiscations and Forfeitures) should be able to communicate these statistics. They are, after all, also expected to publish an annual report. Unfortunately they have not made their report available at their website. An e-mail, sent to the COIV asking for the most recent version of the annual report or other statistics on this topic, was never answered. We were, however, able to find some information in the FATF mutual evaluation of Belgium. The statistics that were provided for this evaluation showed that in 2003, in 25 files confiscations took place, to an amount of 56.039.846 Euro (FATF, 2005). But here the same remark is made: we do not know how much money was truly confiscated and how much has been returned. In this respect, in a recent interview, even the president of the FIU in Belgium emphasised the fact that the amount of money that is actually recovered by the Belgian State is very small (or, in his words "*next to nothing, especially when compared to the illegal financial flows*" (De Standaard, 28 May 2010).

Public Prosecutor's Office: the mountain brings forth a mouse?

We have concluded that the data on police level is rather limited. We therefore turn to the organisation of the Public Prosecutor for more insight. Unfortunately, here we are faced with comparable problems. First of all we must remark that the statistics of the public prosecutor's office do not differentiate between 'fencing'

---

http://www.polfed-fedpol.be/pub/jaarverslag/pub_jaarverslag2008_nl.php

18 FGP = decentralised directorate of the Federal Judicial Police, present in each judicial district

and 'money laundering'. Both crimes are covered by one denominator: "fencing and money laundering". This makes studying the figures of money laundering very difficult. One of the possible ways to solve this problem would be to ask for the raw data to make an independent analysis. However, gaining access to these data may take a long time, which was not available while drafting this chapter.

Secondly, statistics that are available require some analysis when one wants to look at specific criminal categories. Sometimes this requires the combination of several tables or sets of data.

Furthermore, the public prosecutor does not only receive files from the FIU. Also police departments or other special investigation services (such as the tax inspection) can send money laundering files to the public prosecutor's office. But the FIU report mentions the results of only the laundering files that they have transmitted to the Public Prosecutor. This allows us to refine the data that we have found and enables a comparison between money laundering files 'in general' (stemming from all possible sources) and money laundering files that result from the reporting obligation to the FIU (the outcome of the AML chain).

a. Money laundering files 'in general'

National statistics

In this section we will discuss both the general statistics (national measurements) and the statistics for the Brussels Public Prosecutor's Office. We have studied the statistics for the judicial district of Brussels since this is the court where most of the financial-economic crime cases are handled (35% of the files transmitted by the FIU were sent to the court district Brussels).[19]

In 2008, in Belgium, 4.115 files were started with regard to 'fencing and money laundering' (0,58 % of the total input at the level of the Public Prosecutor). In 2008, the FIU sent 5.045 *reports* to the Public Prosecution Office, divided over 937 *files*. This implies that the majority of cases with regard to 'fencing and money laundering', are not stemming from the FIU. This may however, partly be explained by the fact that two types of crime are combined in one denominator in this statistic.

The output of the Public Prosecution Office (national measurement) shows that in 2008 4.220 files on money laundering *and* fencing were handled in Bel-

19 The FIU report of 2008 also mentions that most files are sent to the Brussels public prosecutor (CTIF-CFI, 2009). We are aware of the fact that this may lead to a bias, but at the same time, these statistics provided the most details.

gium, which adds up to 0,6% of the total output. In general, 52% of these cases were dismissed by the public prosecutor.

Statistics for the Brussels Public Prosecution

For a better view on the relationship between input and output of money laundering cases, we refer to longitudinal statistics, in which a cohort of cases is followed throughout time.[20] These statistics entail the decisions that were made with regard to files that were started in one year (in this case, 2003). The statistics are followed during five years, which implies that we are able to get a view on the handling of files in the course of time. A disadvantage of the longitudinal study is, however, that it only allows for a marginal insight in the flow of files; they can be searched by looking for the type of crime that is studied, and shows us a limited number of decisions. This implies that we see the total of files, and a number of decisions that were taken in the totality of these files, but that a large part of the decisions are missing in the statistics (in the graph these are referred to as 'missing data'). This implies that these data are not able to give us a complete view on the decision making process.

In the longitudinal study, when looking at the district of Brussels, we see an input of 1.523 files in 2003 (0,76% of the total input).[21] In 2008, almost 60% of the files stemming from 2003 are dismissed. Out of these 865 dismissals, again over 60% are dismissed for 'opportunity' reasons or for the sake of expediency (37% is dismissed for technical reasons).[22] This implies that fencing and money laundering is in the sub-top-list of crimes dismissed for 'expediency reasons'. Dismissals for reasons of expediency may be related to the fact that the crime is not a priority for the Public Prosecution, or that the damage is relatively small, or the societal impact is rated as limited. Crimes that are even more often dismissed for these reasons are environmental infractions, drug crimes, public disorder or fiscal fraud.

In 2008 the figures state that 24 cases are still in preliminary investigation, 353 are merged with other files, 5 cases have resulted in a completed finalisation by the public prosecutor, and 31 are still in judicial investigation. The results of the other files (245) cannot be derived from the statistics.

---

20 http://www.just.fgov.be/statistique_parquets/jstat2008

21 http://www.just.fgov.be/statistique_parquets/jstat2008/n/home.html: Tabel 6 Instroom van zaken in de loop van 2008 per rechtsgebied en per type tenlastelegging (N en %): 2,66 % of the dismissals are registered as 'other' in the statistics and can therefore not be counted as either policy or technical dismissals.

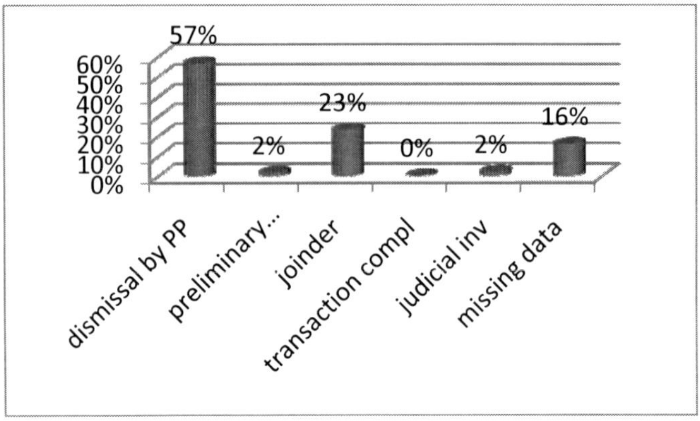

Figure 1: Outcome 'fencing and money laundering' cohort 2003 - Public Prosecution Office Brussels.

Source: Annual Statistics

b. Money laundering files resulting from the AML chain

In the FIU annual report, statistics are provided for the period 1993-2008, based on the results of files sent by the FIU. This implies that the scope is more accurate: these statistics cover only money laundering cases (not fencing), resulting from the reporting duty in anti-money laundering. The statistics are not presented per year, which may create a confusing image. In the judicial district of Brussels, from 1993 – 2008, 3.606 files were started as a result of FIU-reporting. The majority of these files were dismissed by the Public Prosecutor (71%) and a small proportion was discharged by the *raadkamer*[23] (Chambers of Deliberation) (1,3%). In Brussels, 8,8 % of all files on money laundering resulted in a conviction since 1993 (CTIF-CFI, 2009).

When we compare both types of findings, taking into account that this concerns different statistics and different counting units, we get the following procedural outcome: the FIU files are dismissed more often in comparison with the 'general' fencing and money laundering (lumped together) cases. Explanations for this can be various: the inclusion of 'fencing' in the Public Prosecution's statistics might of course have an impact on the way in which these cases are dealt with. It is plausible that 'general' money laundering cases may be more often linked to

23 After a *judicial* invstigation (which is carried out by an examining magistrate), the *raadkamer* (not the public prosecutor) decides on either discharge (dismissal) or referral to correctional court

other, more serious types of crime, which could have an effect on the priority which is assigned to it by the Public Prosecution's office. But these cases cannot be singled out. It is clear that more research or at least better statistics are needed in order to understand more fully the mechanisms behind these statistics of the mountain and the mouse (and subsequently streamline the statistics that are available).

Figure 2.
Outcome FIU 1993-2008, in % of total FIU files sent to PP.

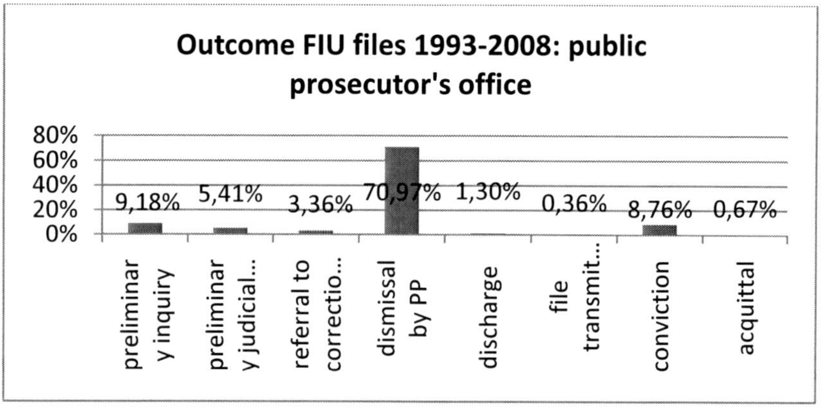

Source: CTIF-CFI, 2009

Figure 3
Comparison results FIU-files - general ML files – In % of total outcome per type of input (FIU or general ML files)

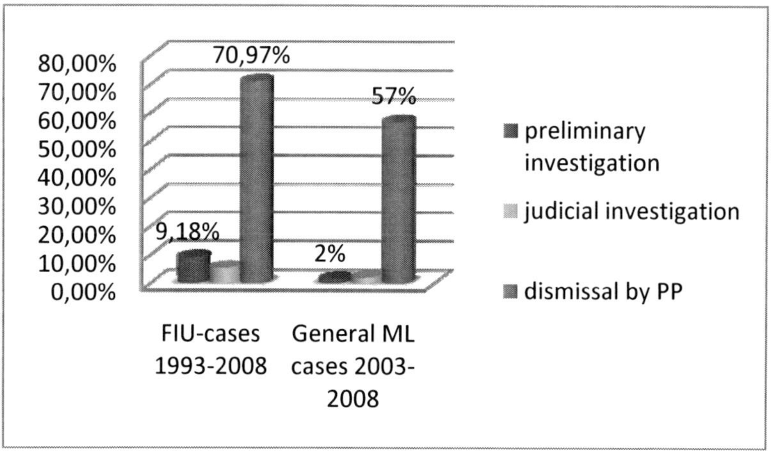

Source: own analysis

Court decisions

The annual report of the FIU states that in the period 1993-2008 10.146 files were transferred by the FIU to the Public Prosecution's Office. In 1209 of these files, the Courts came to a conviction (11,9%) . 'Conviction' can imply a prison sentence, but also a confiscation order of criminal assets and/or a fine. The statistics on convictions in Belgium (on www.just.fgov.be) that are available in the public domain are not detailed enough and hence do not allow the singling out of the money laundering cases, let alone to discern which decisions were taken in these cases, which leaves us with a very unclear picture and leaves us no room to check for the statistics that are provided in the annual report of the FIU. We have asked the department of Justice for more detailed statistics, but they have informed us that statistics on specific money laundering offences are grouped under a more general code, which does not allow for a more detailed view. The Justice Department has, however, provided us with some statistics with regard to convictions under code 505 of the Criminal Law (fencing *and* money laundering). In these figures, the number of convictions with regard to fencing and money laundering are counted, not the number of persons that are convicted. The statistics from 1999-2005 show a relatively stable amount of convictions, but apart from that, provide very little insight in the mechanisms of investigation and conviction. Furthermore, these statistics do not allow for a comparison with the numbers that are given in the FIU report.

Table 2

Sentences in relation to art. 505 Criminal law

	1999	2000	2001	2002	2003	2004	2005
Confinement/treatment	4	6	8	4	6	3	6
Sentence	1646	1783	1963	1941	1910	1987	1813
Suspension of enforcement of sentence	328	315	319	406	270	181	187

Source: FOD Justitie, Service de la Politique Criminelle, 2010

Though we had to be patient, finally the department of Justice has promised us that it should be possible to differentiate for money laundering with regard to convictions in the course of the next few months.[24]

24 E-mail, FOD Justitie, 26/2/2010

A modest result

All in all, after 15 years of AML reporting, investment and investigations, the outcome seems very modest (CTIF-CFI, 2009), while the way the data are handled and the results presented defies further analysis. The same outcome was observed in other countries, where convictions rates seem to remain relatively low too (Levi & Reuter, 2006; Harvey, 2007). This also implies that – based on these statistics – the expected 'general preventive' effect of the AML system might be modest as a result; the chance of getting caught seems rather low, and the chance of getting convicted even lower. Others have also concluded that the AML system has not resulted in more costly or more dangerous money laundering (Blickman, 2009). This not only raises questions with regard to the effects of the system, but also with regard to the priority that the authorities give to money laundering (in contradiction with the threat image they are spreading) and their curiosity about the effect of their own policies.

Conclusion: what do we need to assess AML policy?

The lack of proper statistics

After this expedition for money laundering statistics, we deduce a number of conclusions from our search for the outcome of the money laundering chain.

We can only establish that the priority that needs to be given to (anti) money laundering which is preached by the authorities, is not practised by the authorities themselves.

First of all, it is clear that gathering (detailed) data on both the phenomenon of money laundering (occurrence) and its approach (prosecution and conviction) is very difficult. In some cases, various scattered fragments are found, but putting these together, one ends up with more questions than answers. Attempting to do quantitative money laundering research looks in this respect like 'statistical criminal archaeology'. In this sense, Belgium can be added to the countries that are working in a *camera obscura* (Van Duyne, 2007). The fact that policymakers on a European level have given an impetus for a more elaborately structured data collection is a step in the good direction, albeit after two decades. However, the question (and doubts) remains to which extent this will succeed and to which extent these data will be made accessible publicly, for example for research and what quality these data will have. Nonetheless, we applaud the fact that this topic is now discussed on a European level hoping it will not run aground.

Secondly, in spite of the efforts in recent years, it may be considered surprising – to say the least – that the result of the AML system is unknown. Surprising, because money laundering is considered a serious offence for which reason it has a high priority rating. But how seriously is it taken? First of all, we refer to the alleged threat that is attributed to money laundering (potentially infiltrating the legal economy, resulting in a disruption of the financial flows). In case of such an important threat, one would expect policy makers to be very interested in the effects of a system that aims to reduce this threat and risk. Secondly, the widening of obligations and the broadening of the number of organisations that are obliged to these obligations, suggests the great importance of the AML system for governments and nation states. The costs of AML for banks (and other institutions) are high – as calculated recently by the European Commission: banks invest about 10% of all their financial services regulatory costs in AML compliance (Commission of the European Communities, 2009). These costs are likely to be passed on to the customers as far as it concerns the obliged institution and to the tax payer in all other aspects. This is even the more reason why such a system asks for transparency and control.

Against the background of such high societal and economic costs, governments might be expected to show more interest in the effects of such investments and willing to invest in methods of measurement.

Lack of insight in effects may hamper effectiveness

Gaining insight into the effects of the AML chain is important in developing a more evidence-based policy. Naturally such insight could also be used with regard to enhancing effectiveness of the system. The lack of feedback within the system which we referred to earlier (resulting in reporting institutions that are not aware of the relevance of their reports and hence do not know how to do a good job), results in a potentially ineffective system, as the system lacks well-founded information (Gelemerova, 2009). An investment in acquiring insight in the functioning of the AML chain would therefore also imply an investment in the quality of the system and the value of its functioning. This is confirmed by the FATF, in their statement on the risk-based approach in money laundering (FATF, 2007). In their opinion, in a risk based-policy, sharing information and expertise between reporting institutions and authorities is of utmost importance. Reporting institutions might, after all, in the absence of information, make the wrong assessments and over- or underestimate risks.

The same applies to the gap between the private reporting institutions and law enforcement: criminal investigation and prosecution. As a result of the obligation of reporting institutions to investigate transactions, the knowledge, know-how and expertise is developed. But in a system with no feedback this developed expertise is likely to remain within the private sector and subsequently to stagnate. This may lead to the outcome that the authorities display limited interest for this expertise: there is only an interest in the output in the form of suspicious activity reports. The outsourcing of investigations to other (private) actors in the AML chain may therefore have an unwanted effect.

Furthermore, transparency should prevail in any system that may impact personal and private spheres. Democratic checks and balances are specifically important in case of the anti-money laundering system: clients are largely unaware of the checks and procedures that are carried out while their transactions are passing through the financial channels. Blacklists are used during these checks that are provided by private organisations while the rights of people on these blacklists are very unclear.

What we need

In order to build a transparent policy, there is a need for data. First and foremost, reliable data should be available and easily accessible, for both researchers and practitioners. In addition, as Van Duyne and De Miranda have already noted (Van Duyne & De Miranda, 1999), international data are indispensible in this respect; money laundering is an international phenomenon, enforced on an international level, which automatically implies that international and comparative research is a *conditio sine qua non*. This does not only point at the need of a proper availability of data, but also at a streamlining and harmonisation of data gathering and processing. Different counting units (for example files versus suspicious transaction reports), different registration methods and -systems and different criteria for what is considered to be 'suspicious' hinder comparability and hence transparency. This is underlined by the current difficulties of Eurostat in gathering conclusive statistics.

When we want to measure effectiveness and efficiency, feedback between law enforcement actors and FIUs is also needed. This does not only involve feedback on the statistics of investigations, prosecutions and convictions, but also on the relationship between suspicious transaction reports and criminal files (as is provided by the German FIU) and a feedback on financial intelligence. Ideally, the FIU should also provide this information to the reporting institutions. Hiding behind the professional secrecy may be an easy way out to such feedback task: the example of the German FIU's annual report shows that a general feedback on reporting quality is possible without harming these principles.[25]

25 See for example 2005 Financial Intelligence Unit (FIU) Germany:

Thirdly, and here we must search our own role as researchers, more qualitative research can also shed a light on effectiveness of the AML system. Statistics, after all, need context and interpretation and this is even more true in a system that is characterised by diversity and change. A qualitative approach, in which several types of reporting institutions and sectors are involved, could shed a light on potential displacement effects of the AML system. At least it could clarify how the crime-enterprises have reacted to the AML pressure. Another possibility is to survey clients and staff (first line employees) of reporting institutions, to get an idea on the number of clients that is refused and hence remains out of the financial circuits – to measure a potential preventive effect. This implies that the volume of basic research has to expand.

To round up, we hope that in the near future, given the declarations of risk and knowledge based enforcement, the search for money laundering statistics will no longer be comparable to the quest for the holy (data) grail. This implies that we need solid, reliable data also in addition to transparent and accessible databases and services. Only then will we be able to tell whether there is or is not 'much ado about nothing'.

References

Blickman, T., Countering Illicit and Unregulated Money Flows. Money Laundering, Tax Evasion and Financial Regulation. *TNI Briefing Series,* December 2009

CBFA, Gecoördineerde versie dd. 12 juli 2005 van de Commissie voor het Bank-, Financie- en Assurantiewezen betreffende de voorkoming van het witwassen van geld en de financiering van terrorisme. *B.S.* 12.07.2005.

Commission of the European Communities, Compliance with the anti-money laundering directive by cross-border banking groups at group level. *Commission Staff Working Paper.* 62, 2009.

Council Directive 91/308/EEC of 10 June 1991 on prevention of the use of the financial system for the purpose of money laundering, 1991

CTIF-CFI, 15e Activiteitenverslag 2008, 2009

---

http://www.bka.de/profil/zentralstellen/geldwaesche/pdf/fiu_germany_annual_report_2007.pdf

De Standaard, *Antiwitwascel schrikt van monsterdossier. Witwasfraude steeds internationaler en complexer.* 28 mei 2010

Directive 2005/60/EC of the European Parliament and of the Council of 26 October 2005 on the prevention of the use of the financial system for the purpose of money laundering and terrorist financing

Duyne, P.C. van and de Miranda, H., The emperor's clothes of disclosure: Hot money and suspect disclosures. *Crime, Law and Social Change*, 1999, 31(3): 245-271

Duyne, P.C van, Virtue and reality: an introductory tale of two cities. In: P.C. van Duyne, A. Maljevic, M. van Dijck, K. von Lampe and J. Harvey (eds.), *Crime Business and Crime Money in Europe: The Dirty Linen of Illicit Enterprise..* Nijmegen, Wolf Legal Publishers: 1-14, 2007

Duyne, P.C. van, M.S. Groenhuijsen and A.A.P. Schudelaro, Balancing financial threats and legal interests in money-laundering policy. *Crime, Law and Social Change*, 2005, 43: 117-147

Duyne, P.C. van, Money laundering. Pavlov's dog and beyond. *The Howard Journal*, 1998, *nr. 4*, 395-374

Duyne, P.C. van, Serving the integrity of the Mammon and the compulsive excessive regulatory disorder. *Crime, Law and Social Change*, 2008, 52(1) 1-8

Ernst & Young, *The 2009 Ernst & Young business risk report. The top 10 risks for global businesses.* s.l., 2009

European Commission, *Call for comments from the Financial Crime Subgroup on the draft guidelines for the Money Laundering.* Pilot Project. 7. Brussels, April 2009

Explanatory Memorandum to the bill on the prevention of the use of the financial system for money laundering, *22 July 1992,* Belgische Senaat, 468-1 (B.Z. 1991-1992)

FATF, *Troisième rapport d'évaluation mutuelle de la lutte anti-blanchiment de capitaux et contre le financement du terrorisme.* Belgique; FATF-GAFI, Paris, 2005

FATF, *Guidance on the Risk-based approach to combating money laundering and terrorist financing. High level principles and procedures.* Paris, 2007

Federale Gerechtelijke Politie, Directie Economische en Financiële Criminaliteit, Jaarverslag 2008, Brussel, 2009

Fleming, M., *UK Law Enforcement Agency Use and Management of Suspicious Activity Reports: Towards Determining the Value of the Regime.* London, 2005

Gelemerova, L. (2009). On the frontline against money-laundering: the regulatory minefield. *Crime, Law and Social Change* 52(1): 33-55.

Harvey, J., Compliance and reporting issues arising for financial institutions from money laundering regulations: A preliminary cost benefit study. *Journal of Money Laundering Control*, 2004, 7(4): 1-14

Harvey, J., Just how effective is money laundering legislation? *Security Journal*, 2007, 21(3): 189-211

Law of 11 January 1993 on the prevention of the use of the financial system for the laundering of money and financing of terrorism, *B.S.*, 9 February 1993

Levi, M. and M. Maguire, Reducing and preventing organised crime: An evidence-based critique. *Crime, Law and Social Change*, 2004, 41(5): 397-469

Levi, M. and P. Reuter, *Money Laundering* Chicago, University of Chicago, 2006

Levi, M., Controlling the international money trail: What lessons have been learned? *Global enforcement regimes. Transnational organised crime, international terrorism and money laundering*. Amsterdam, Transnational Institute (TNI), 2005

Levi, M., Evaluating the 'New Policing': Attacking the money trail of organised crime. *The Australian and New Zealand Journal of Criminology*, 1997, 30: 1-25, 1997

Levi, M., Money laundering: Risks and countermeasures. In: A. Graycar and P. Grabosky (eds.), *Money Laundering in the 21st century: risks and countermeasures*. Canberra, Australian Institute of Criminology, 1996.

Loader, I., Consumer culture and the commodification of policing and security. *Sociology*, 1999, 33, 373-392

Ponsaers, P., *Question on the public PhD defense of A. Verhage*, 11/11/2009

Reuter, P., Assessing money laundering controls. Presentation for the AML/CTF conference, Sydney, April 2009

Reuter, P., and E. Truman, *Chasing dirty money: The fight against money laundering*. Washington DC, Institute for International Economics, 2004

Schneider, F. and D. Enste, Shadow economies: Size, causes, and consequences. *Journal of Economic Literature*, 2000, 38(1): 77-114, 2000

Sharman, J., Power and discourse in policy diffusion: Anti-money laundering in developing states. *International Studies Quarterly*, 2008, (52): 635-656

Study on "Best practices in vertical relations between the FIUs and law enforcement services and Money Laundering and Terrorist Financing Reporting entities with a view to indicating effective models for feedback on follow-up to and effectiveness of Suspicious Transactions Reports", Brussels, 2008-2009

Unger, B., *The amounts and effects of money laundering. Report for the Ministry of Finance*. Den Haag, 2006

United Nations Office on Drugs and Crime, World Drug Report 2010, UNODC, Vienna, 2010.

Verhage, A., The anti money laundering complex on a crime control continuum: perceptions of risk, power and efficacy. *Governance of Security Research Papers, Topical Issues in EU and International Crime Control*. M. Cools, De Ruyver, B., Easton, M., Pauwels, L., Ponsaers, P., Vande Walle, G., Vander Beken, T.,

Vander Laenen, F., Vermeulen, G., Vynckier, G., Antwerpen, Maklu: 141-166, 2010

Verhage, A., The anti money laundering complex: power pantomime or potential payoff? Perspectives on practices, partnerships and challenges within the fight against money laundering. *The informal economy and connections with organised crime: the impact of national social and economic policies*. J. Shapland and P. Ponsaers. Den Haag, Boom Juridische Uitgevers: 79-112, 2009a

Verhage, A., Between the hammer and the anvil? The anti-money laundering-complex and its interactions with the compliance industry. *Crime, Law and Social Change* 52(1): 9-32, 2009b

Verhage, A., Supply and demand: anti-money laundering by the compliance industry. *Journal of Money Laundering Control* 12(4): 371-391, 2009c

Wet van 22 maart op het statuut van en de toezicht op de kredietinstellingen (*B.S,* 19 april 1993).

Zedner, L., Too much security?, *International Journal of the Sociology of Law*, 2003, 31: 155-184

Measures against money laundering in Sweden
The role of the private sector

Daniel Vesterhav[1]

Introduction

Money laundering is today a priority issue for Swedish criminal policy, not least as a result of the great international interest in this issue (SOU 2007, p 23).

The backbone of the Swedish anti-money laundering system is, as for most western countries, the obligation for institutions and businesses in cash-intensive branches to report suspicious transactions to the Financial Intelligence Unit (FIU). This means that the reported information plays a crucial role in determining which cases at the end of the day, will be investigated and, possibly, be subject to any kind of measures from the authorities. It is, therefore, important to have insight into what factors actually have an impact on what forms of money laundering are reported to the authorities.

These factors influencing whether or not an input into the judicial system will be made is not the only selection mechanism. As a matter of fact, selection processes take place through the entire judicial system, from the initial institutions' report of a suspicious transaction to the potential final court decision. During its journey, the case passes numerous crossroads, which are crucial for their final outcome. That is a long and tortuous road of which the beginning is of special interest. Therefore this chapter will focus on the very first part of the selection process for the anti-money laundering system: the reporting businesses and institutions on the front-line.

---

1 The author is a researcher at the Swedish National Council for Crime Prevention.

Purpose, research question and method of research

The aim of this chapter is to examine the selection mechanisms that may be relevant for what is reported to the FIU. Formulated in more operational terms, our research question is:

Which factors play a key role in deciding whether information about suspicious transactions is passed on to the authorities or not?

Method

The findings presented in this chapter are based on the results of 96 interviews that were conducted in a study of assets recovery in Sweden. The study was carried out by the Swedish National Council for Crime Prevention between 2007 and 2008.[2] Persons involved in this policy area, both within public authorities and the private sector, were interviewed.

Table 1

Distribution of interviews

Private sector	9
Control Authorities	14
Law Enforcement Agencies	69
Others	4
Total	96

Because of the wide variation in occupations that the study covers, semi-structured interviews were carried out. The point was to give the interviewees an opportunity to speak freely on the basis of his or her own work and experiences, while still remaining within the given theme (Denscombe, 1998). The interviews focused on personal work activities and views on criminal assets recovery and the anti-money laundering system. All the interviews have been tape recorded and transcribed. The time taken for each interview varied between one and two hours. The quotations that are presented in this report are translated from Swedish to English.

2 The authors of the report are, in addition to the author of this article; Malin Forsman and Lars Korsell.

Backgrounds

Before we start discussing the selection mechanisms, a brief review of the Swedish anti-money laundering system will be given.

There is no crime called 'money laundering' in Sweden. In order to get a picture of how money laundering is regulated in Swedish legislation, we must go back to 1991, when the Swedish regulations governing receiving stolen goods were toughened, in order for Sweden to fulfil its requirements under the UN 1988 Drugs Convention. In conjunction with this change in the law, measures were introduced that were aimed specifically at financial transactions which could be interpreted as money laundering (Örnemark-Hansen, 1999).

In 1994, a year before Sweden's entry into the EU, Sweden introduced its first technical legal measures to regulate the fight against and prevention of money laundering. This was done by incorporating the first EU money laundering directive into Swedish legislation, through the Act on Measures against Money Laundering (1993, p 768). The act entailed an obligation on companies, mainly within the financial sector, to check the identity of their customers and to archive documents and information from the identity control. All circumstances that could point to money laundering were to be reported to the police. The companies were also prohibited from consciously participating in transactions relating to funds that could be assumed to have been derived from a serious crime. Companies were also to introduce routines for preventing their own operations from being used for money laundering, and to be responsible for ensuring that employees received information and training for this purpose.

Two years later, in 1996, FATF carried out an evaluation of the anti-money laundering (AML) regime of Sweden, and criticised Sweden's lack of effective penal legislation against money laundering, among other aspects. Three years later, in 1999, the crime of 'money receiving' was introduced in Sweden. The new crime 'money receiving' came to include some of the activities that were then punishable as receiving stolen goods, and was directed against activities intended to hide the origin of property originating from criminal acquisition. In order to achieve a conviction for money receiving, the requirements are that it must be possible to trace the specific profit from crime to the specific crime generating that criminal profit, and that it is someone other than the perpetrator of the specific money generating crime who has carried out the money laundering activities. In other words, this means that laundering profits from crime committed by oneself is not punishable as a crime of its own in Sweden.

` Five years later, in 2005, the Act on Measures against Money Laundering was changed as a result of the second EU money laundering directive from 2001. The change entailed, among other things, that lawyers, estate agents, tax advisers and auditors were also charged with a duty to report any suspected money laundering.

Eight months after Sweden had incorporated the second EU money laundering directive into Swedish legislation, the EU Commission adopted its third money laundering directive. However, it took four years before this was incorporated into Swedish legislation in 2009. The most important changes in the new directive is that yet more sectors have been obliged to report suspicious transactions, that the undertakings are to implement a risk-based approach and that the monitoring of them will become more efficient.

Blind spots in the reporting system

It is too early to determine what effects the third money laundering directive will have on money laundering in Sweden, but while studying how the Act on Measures against Money Laundering (1993, p 768) worked, it became clear that the reporting system for money laundering has major flaws and contains several blind spots.

Similar to the reporting frequency of suspicious transactions in other countries it is only a very small proportion of all companies in Sweden with a duty to report that actually do report suspicious transactions. Of the 14.758 companies who in 2008 had a duty to scrutinise and report all transactions that could be suspected to constitute money laundering or financing of terrorism, only 97 companies (0,7%) reported any suspicious money laundering to the FIU.

As shown in Table 1, the number of money laundering reports varies greatly between the different sectors with a duty to report. Some sectors, such as estate agents, antiques, arts and scrap dealers, jewellers and tax advisers, report nothing, while banks, money agents and exchange bureaus make reports almost on a daily basis.

Table 2
Transaction reporting per sector, 2008.

Money laundering reporters 2008	Number of money laundering reports per sector	Number of businesses reporting	Number of businesses with a reporting obligation
Other Finance Operations	0	0	148
Auction Houses	5	1	300
Bank and Financial Institutes	7.232	57	126
Money Agencies	1.452	7	42
Car Dealers (trading in vehicles)	17	7	1.000
Casino	145	1	1
Estate Agents	0	0	6.100
Fund Managers	1	1	117
Insurance Agencies	1	1	922
Antique and Art Dealers	0	0	150
Scrap Metals	0	0	86
Dealers in Jewels and Precious Metals	0	0	1.000
Credit Market Companies	0	0	67
Life Insurance Companies	0	0	142
Pension Funds	4	2	79
Auditors	2	2	4.117
Tax Advisors	0	0	159
Foreign Exchange Dealers	4.177	13	43
Businesses Issuing Electronic Money	0	0	3
Securities Dealers	5	2	156
Others, with no reporting obligation	7	3	0
Total:	13.048	97	14.758

Source: RKP-rapport 2009:4

Reasons for low reporting frequency

A relevant question when discussing why some actors do not report suspicious transactions is the frequency with which these actors come in contact with criminal funds.. To answer that question we may turn to previous research.

The picture that emerges is that several of the sectors that did not report a single, or only a few, suspicious transactions during 2008 are sectors that in fact are most likely come into contact with criminal funds. For instance, persons with links to organised crime spend a lot of money on jewellery or watches (Junninen, 2006; Skinnari, 2010; compare Hall, Winlow and Ancrum, 2008). Car dealers, auction houses, antiques and art dealers supply objects that are of interest to people with a criminal identity (Brå, 2007, p 4; Van Duyne and Levi, 2005). Even if research suggests that there is not all that much money laundered in Swedish casinos, they do come into contact with illicit or criminal money used for gambling (Skinnari and Korsell, 2010). Other companies that probably would come into contact with persons wishing to launder smaller amounts of money are credit institutes. A strategy used by drugs distributors is a form of "money laundering light". They rarely need to have hundreds of thousands of Swedish kronor laundered, so instead they only get a legitimate source for the cash money the person in question is carrying at any particular time (Brå, 2007:a, 2007:b). This form of money laundering can be, for example, done by the distributor acquiring receipts for gambling revenues or lending money from a credit institution. Using such arrangements, the drug distributors can move around a relatively large amount of money, and at the same time legitimise the origins of the money during a check-up by the police.

It is plausible that there are interfaces between criminal funds and the non-reporting businesses. But, the issue of why they do not report more frequently is still not answered. Could it be that the transactions do not differ from the ordinary operations and are, therefore, not regarded as suspicious transactions?

Of course, the interfaces between criminal funds and the businesses do not necessarily mean that the transactions will be identified as suspicious. It is likely that a large proportion of these transactions blend in with the everyday patterns of trade. Anyway, the Swedish Finance Police indicates large purchases with cash as a sign of suspected money laundering and encourages businesses to report them (RKP-rapport 2009).

There are no data to indicate how common large purchases with cash is but it is unlikely that not a single real estate agent, antiques, art and scrap dealers or jewellers encountered a single a suspicious transaction during 2008 (compare RKP-rapport 2009). The conclusion is that the low reporting rate may not solely be explained by the absence of sufficient cases for reporting. Further explanations for the reason of the low reporting figures must be found elsewhere.

Lack of incentives

One of the problems with the reporting system for money laundering may be that there are not always any obvious advantages for the companies to cooperate, apart from a general sense of justice. The most noticeable reason for cooperation is that they want to comply with legislation in order to avoid sanctions (compare Favarel-Garrigues, Godefroy and Lascoumes, 2008; compare Verhage, 2009b). However, there are also more overarching reasons, such as not wishing to get a bad reputation and be regarded as an irresponsible company, which in turn may influence the competitive situation (compare Harvey and Lau, 2009; Reuter and Truman, 2004; Verhage, 2009a). The consequences of such an incentive can have the opposite effect, however, meaning that the companies report too many transactions instead. Harvey (2004) refers to the Financial Services Authority (FSA), which considered that despite ten years of money laundering regulations in the UK, the companies with a duty to report are still on square one, and produce reports of poor quality (compare Gelemerova, 2009). It appears to be the companies' view that the more cases they report, the smaller is the risk of an inspection visit by the FSA.

Even in Sweden, it is likely that some companies would rather submit a money laundering report too much than risk being subjected to sanctions. Especially after the Swedish FSA imposed a penalty fee of € 5 million on a bank because of structural and recurring deficiencies in its anti-money laundering measures.

However, the problem of over-reporting and poor quality of the reports should not be overestimated. The anti-money laundering system is based on intelligence and requires a large influx of reports to work with. Therefore, an over-reporting is to be preferred instead of a low reporting rate. The anti-money laundering system can be described as a large funnel and the suspicious transactions reported to the FIU only constitute the first step of intelligence gathering (compare Verhage, 2009a). All incoming reports are filtered through different registry checks and are only passed on to a money-laundering official if the case is considered being of substance after the first screening. If it is not considered worthwhile investigating further, the report gets the status 'ad acta' and is put away. The status can be changed to 'active' later if the FIU gets more suspicious transaction reports that can be linked to the case.

When a case is passed on to a money-laundering official a thorough analysis is commenced. If the money-laundering official considers the case to be relevant for an authority, for instance the Swedish National Tax Agency, the Economic Crime Authority, the Customs or a Police department, he or she writes an intelligence report and passes it on. The money laundering report ends up at the receiving authorities' intelligence unit and is subject to further investigation before the case is brought forward for trial. Often, it is the original crime, for example an economic crime, robbery or a drug crime, that is prosecuted and not the crime of money receiving.

As described above, the suspicious transactions are filtered through a lot of different assessments. Due to this, it is not realistic to place a too heavy emphasis on the companies regarding the quality of the suspicious transactions reports. The private actors do not have an overall view and therefore it is hard for them to assess whether a reported transaction will be of interest for the FIU or not. The potential of a case cannot be determined by a single report or a given criteria of a suspicious transaction, it is only one piece of data in a larger pattern of reports, often from different companies and trades. Only when all these reports are linked together by the FIU does it become possible to determine whether it is a case of interest. The problem seems to be rather the companies' apprehension that the FIU is drowning in reports than the actual poor quality of the reported transactions, to which they respond by reporting less.

Our survey showed that the incentives for reporting suspicious transactions are generally low, both for the companies and their employees (Brå 2008). One of the reasons highlighted was that it was felt that the reports did not lead to anything, partly because – as it was put – the FIU is being flooded with reports that they do not have time to look at. Such an outlook, naturally leads to questions being raised regarding the value of spending valuable resources on writing and giving reports (compare Favarel-Garrigues, Godefroy and Lascoumes, 2008; Gelemerova, 2009; Harvey, 2004; Verhage, 2009a; Kochan, 2005; Reuter and Truman, 2004).

One interviewee in our survey expressed himself as follows:

> "*Of course we sometimes feel it is a bit difficult to handle these issues, when we notice that we make reports and nothing much happens, and the behaviour continues.*"
> (Interviewee at a bank).

In line with the international situation, banks and exchange bureaux are the most frequent reporters of suspicious transactions in Sweden. During 2008, they were responsible for just over 87 % of all money laundering reports (see Table 1). Our survey identified three general incentives for these two sectors to work actively with money laundering issues.

Firstly, in line with the above mentioned international research, the businesses do not want to risk their reputation and become associated with money laundering and fraudulent activities. The business of both exchange bureaux and banks are largely based on trust – that is why the management and boards of the companies are well aware of these issues, and prioritise them.

At the same time, the businesses are keen to maintain good customer contacts, which assume that they find a balance between preventing money laundering and safeguarding customer relations. Some interviewees emphasized that the prohibition against informing – that is that company officers are not allowed to inform the customer that he/she has been reported or will be reported – led to cashiers sometimes having to withhold the truth from the customers, which made them feel uncomfortable.

The second incentive is that the interests of public authorities and the financial institutions coincide. There are areas adjacent to money laundering that may cause direct financial damage to banks or exchange bureaux such as fraud. In this way, measures against money laundering are integrated into businesses' high-priority security work against fraud (compare Favarel-Garrigues, Godefroy and Lascoumes, 2008; Verhage, 2009b).

The third incentive is a combination of a general sense of justice and a willingness to comply with the law in order not to risk becoming the target of sanctions. The businesses are, however, profit-driven operations, meaning that they apply the legislation in a way that is as cost-effective as possible. Interviewees within the private sector mentioned that the legislation does provide a certain amount of leeway for how one judges the situation. Of course, some questions have to be asked in the event of a suspicious transaction, but the individual officer could choose to evaluate the answer based on his/her own attitude and understanding, and, according to some of the interviewees, it could be convenient to accept a verbal explanation if it was fairly reasonable.

Another example was that most exchange bureaux and banks would let a suspicious transaction through if the customer identified him- or herself. The bank could then make a report to the FIU afterwards. In this way, the bank or the exchange bureau would earn money from the transaction at the same time as it considered it had done its duty according to the law. The fact that it would entail a loss of income for the companies to refuse to accept these transactions made it difficult to avoid handling them. The following interviewee within the banking sector explained how difficult it is for a company to introduce a policy where all suspicious transactions are refused:

> "*It is difficult for me to take the lead in such a discussion against my own board of directors and say that I propose that we put morals first here, and refuse all these transactions which we actually know are criminal, or where the money has criminal origins. They would then make the immediate response: "Well, what will the other banks do then? Is this a joint thing, or is it just us doing this? Should we loose some hundreds of thousands or perhaps millions a year from these fees when nobody else is doing it?" At a stretch, I would agree with this argument.*"
> (Interviewee at a bank)

In the same way as illustrated in the quotation, several interviewees pointed to the competitive situation vis-à-vis other actors as an important aspect in terms of how companies chose to act on the issue of money laundering (compare Gill and Taylor, 2004). When it came to the banks, the interviews in our survey showed that there was a fairly unanimous view of how to handle money laundering. However, the situation appears to be more problematic for other business sectors. One interviewee from an exchange bureau told us that only a few actors in that branch actually reported suspicious transactions, which led to companies competing on different terms. If an exchange bureau is thorough in checking identification and posing questions to suspicious individuals, there is a big risk that the customer just will go to another exchange bureau instead, where there are less security checks (compare Harvey, 2004). Another interviewee, within the FIU, emphasised that in the long term this will lead to changes in market share, which would result in unsound market conditions.

The proposed solution that was most prominent in the interviews was better monitoring and inspection of the private actors. One interviewee from an exchange bureau emphasized that the control is so much lacking that you almost get the impression that responsibility to report is on a voluntarily basis. The lack of control is deemed to have a direct negative effect on the incentives to report.

> "*What we would really like to see is that everybody complies with this and runs it properly. For while we are a profit-making company, we don't want to shoot ourselves in the foot when we notice that everybody is going elsewhere.*"
> (Interviewee at an exchange bureau)

The third incentive – a combination of a general sense of justice and a willingness to comply with the law so as not to risk becoming the target of sanctions – can therefore be regarded as subordinate to the first two, and in order for it to be sufficiently strong, it is required that:

- all actors in the same sector that are obliged to report should report to the same extent, in order to maintain the competition;
- those with a reporting obligation should feel that the monitoring works and that there is a risk of sanctions.

Another aspect that was highlighted in the interviews is that the private actors requested more feedback from the FIU (compare Gold and Levi, 1994; Verhage, 2009a). The interviewees told us that the banks and exchange bureaux had annual meetings with the FIU, but many actors wanted more continuous feedback when they reported suspicious transactions. Three main reasons were stated:

- incentive;
- cost effectiveness;
- knowledge and improvement.

The reason why feedback is an incentive is that the actors with reporting obligations, particularly at individual level, need confirmation that the extra work they put into the reporting is leading somewhere. To judge from the interviews, this feedback from the FIU does not have to be particularly detailed, nor provided after each reported suspicion. Instead what is requested is to find out, now and then, whether the work carried out has been of any actual importance to the judicial system.

At a more general level, there is also a reason of cost effectiveness. The reporting obligation uses quite a lot of resources from the businesses, and the management therefore wants to know what it is getting for these expenses.

Another reason stated is that feedback from the FIU is important in order to facilitate improvements to routines and working methods. One interviewee within the banking sector likened the collaboration between the private actors and the authorities to an accordion, where it is important that all those involved interpret and implement the law in the same way. In order for this to work, continuous feedback is a prerequisite.

> "*It is important that all parts of the accordion are playing together, so that there is rapid feedback when a money laundering report is made. That this case is not a case of money laundering, or that this is such a case and further supporting documents are required and needed. And that they report that we are now passing this on to the preliminary hearing, to the Swedish Economic Crime Authority, that this accordion of information works. I believe that this is really important. / . . . / That the reporting bank gets information about the progress of the matter. Is anything more expected from the reporting party? Is a decision about further measures still being considered? Or has an assessment been made not to proceed? That the suspicion is not grounds for any further investigation. This communication is important and it is important for the bank's continued relationship with the customer who gave rise to this report.*"
> (Interviewee within the private sector)

The last part of this quote from an interview, that feedback is important in order for the bank to make a decision about how to handle the relationship with the customer who is the subject of a report, is another aspect that recurred in the interviews. Within the private sector, they want to know whether the reported suspicion provides grounds for a continued investigation or not. At the same time, it is important – in the same way as from the reason of incentive – to find a standard for how comprehensive and detailed the feedback should be. It is not realistic to get feedback from each individual case, but an alternative could be that feedback is given for cases with a certain financial profile. Interviewees from the FIU also stated that in some cases they do give feedback – if resources and secrecy regulations permit.

Time and resources

Another reason for the low reporting figures is a lack of time and resources at the companies with reporting obligations. Measures taken by businesses to prevent crime may entail increased costs for the companies (Levi, 2006). Harvey (2004) brings up the work against money laundering in the UK as an example of how an imbalance has grown between public and private resources. A large part of the costs for these measures have been transferred to the private sector (compare Cribb, 2003; Levi, 2006; Reuter and Truman, 2004; Larsson and Magnusson, 2009).

In our survey, a large number of the interviewees, both within public authorities and the private sector, considered that a large burden has been placed on the private sector. As mentioned before, most of the interviewees working within the private sector thought that the reporting liability required a lot of resources. But at the same time, many persons, particularly those employed within exchange bureaux and banks, expressed great understanding for the necessity of the regulation, on the basis of a general sense of justice (compare Gill and Taylor, 2004).

On the other hand, the interviewees were more critical of the amount of work they were forced to put in to satisfy requests from the authorities for bank statements and other supporting documentation. Several interviewees from public authorities confirmed that they issue a lot of requests to exchange bureaux and banks. The requests can also be divided up into two stages: first,statements are requested and analysed; secondly, the supporting documents for the transactions themselves are ordered. These requests can require a fair amount of resources to fulfil, particularly if they consist of older vouchers and forms, as the bank often has to order these from an archive. In order to reduce the burden of work, several interviewees put forward a wish that the requests by public authorities should be made more systematic, coordinated and efficient.

From the interviews, it was possible to interpret that some of the business' actors thought that the authorities over-utilise their right to request supporting documents. This impression arises particularly when various services make requests for information separately without coordination. The following interview quotation is an illustrative example of this view:

> "*What we find irritating is that we send in a large number of reports to the FIU, but still, when the Tax Agency have any questions, they contact us instead of the FIU. If we send this in so that the FIU has a register, why can't the authorities sort this out between themselves? We get the impression that they don't want to use their own resources and look it up in their own archive, instead they come with a new request on the same material and we have to use additional resources to send the information again. Why*

should we be doing it? The information we gave to the FIU in the first place is probably the information that led the Tax Authority on the track. If they contacted the FIU they would surely have received this information from them but still they come to us. It feels like they are using / . . . / the private sector. This seems a bit strange."
(Interviewee at an exchange bureau)

Another problem is that there is no formalised system for how the reports about suspicious money laundering and other information exchanges should be drafted. There was a proposal for a reporting form developed by the FIU, but several of the private actors have developed their own forms. When the survey was carried out in 2008, the reporting system was still totally paper-based, with forms faxed to the FIU. When the information reached the FIU, the administrators had to type in the information into a register, which was both time-consuming and resources intensive. Interviewees both within the FIU and the private sector requested that the authorities develop a computerised reporting and information exchange system. Such a system came into operation in 2009, but has not, at the time of writing, been fully implemented.

Another resource issue that was highlighted in the interviews was the cost of training staff about money laundering issues. Some companies had solved this question by quite simply not training their staff (compare the Swedish Financial Supervisory Authority, 2006).

"*The problem is that a large part of it is knowledge, knowing whether this is suspicious. And we can't afford the money or the time to spend these resources in order to get this training. When they pushed the requirements onto the companies, I think they almost lost more insight.*"
(Interviewee at a company with reporting obligation)

A recurring theme in all interviews with persons in the private sector was a worry about the changes the third money laundering directive might entail. The apprehensions concern whether the new legislation would entail even more work and therefore increased costs for the private actors. Interviewees emphasised that new legislation causes costs, in the form of training, administration and handling.

Knowledge

A study carried out in the UK shows that many of the companies with a reporting obligation request clearer guidelines for how to comply with the legislation (Harvey, 2004). Even if knowledge about the reporting obligation is high, it can be difficult both for companies and individual administrators in practice to determine what should be considered a suspicious transaction (compare the Swedish Financial Supervisory Authority 2006; Harvey, 2004; compare Levi, 1991). There is a tendency for unusual transactions to be reported, rather than suspicious ones (Harvey, 2004; Reuter and Truman, 2004). Some companies choose to make a report rather more frequently than less so (Harvey, 2004; Favarel-Garrigues, Godefroy and Lascoumes, 2008). This is probably linked to what was suggested under the heading 'incentive', that the main ambition is more about complying with the reporting obligation than actually finding concrete cases of money laundering (Harvey, 2004).

Our study shows that an important factor for the reporting obligation to work properly is knowledge among the actors involved. Several interviewees within the private sector gave the impression that to them it was difficult to assess whether a situation was to be considered as a suspicious transaction or not. One reason given was that the money laundering legislation was felt to be unclear.

Banks and exchange bureaux provide basic training for new employees, in which the money laundering act is a standing item. An important part of the training is that staff should be able to make correct assessments. Further internal training on money laundering issues is also provided. At other companies with reporting obligations, internal training is not always provided. If training was to be provided, it is done externally, with the associated costs. Several interviewees therefore requested free training. One interviewee at the FIU brought up the need for more information about money laundering issues to actors within the private sector. The problem, however, is that the FIU does not have sufficient resources to provide such information and for training on any larger scale.

> "*We notice when we go out with information – we have spoken to the Association of Real Estate Agents and various auction houses – then we get a response directly in the number of reports. Unfortunately, we can't quite cope with this bit.*"
> (Interviewee at the FIU)

Even if a company has set up guidelines and trained its staff, at the end of the day the reporting system is dependent on the staff and their subjective assessment of each individual transaction. Several interviewees considered that a great responsibility was placed on each individual to make qualified legal assessments (compare Verhage, 2009c). Even if according to the legislation the staff has a duty to report suspicious transactions, it is very difficult to know what is required in each specific situation to fulfil the requirements of the law. A particular difficulty was the balancing act between not being allowed to notify the customer that there is a suspicion of money laundering, at the same time as the requirement to ask certain questions must be fulfilled. The security manager at a company with a reporting obligation expressed it as follows:

"The assessment is after all always made by our people who work as cashiers. If you have been working for ten years, you are hopefully better at making assessments, but if you have worked there for just a month, then it is obviously difficult."

Concluding remarks

The findings of our research highlight three different selection mechanisms being relevant for the question whether a suspicious transaction is be reported to the FIU or not. Obviously, there is a lack of sufficient incentives, resources and knowledge for the low- or non-reporting commercial sectors to report suspicious transactions.

The perception that the FIU is receiving more reports than they can handle is deemed to have a direct negative effect on the incentives to report. If the private actors do not think that their report will lead to anything, they will probably not be too eager to report. So, why do they believe that their reports are fruitless?

The answer may lie in the rather diffuse conception of money laundering. According to the legislation, the undertaking shall report any circumstances that may be indicative of money laundering to the FIU. This evokes the impression that the authorities will start money laundering investigations and convict persons for money laundering. The problem is, as mentioned above, that there is no crime called money laundering in Sweden and the convictions for receiving stolen money or receiving stolen goods are scarce. This does not mean that the money laundering reports are useless. Actually, they constitute an important part of the intelligence gathering that serves as a base for finding and investigating predicate crimes. Most often it is not the money receiving itself that is brought to for trial but the predicate crime (compare Magnusson, 2009). This means that the suspicious transaction reports, like all intelligence reports, will not be reflected in the criminal statistics. In other words, the effectiveness of the money laundering system cannot easily be measured.

Gold and Levi (1994) make an important point when they suggest the phrase "money movement" instead of money laundering as it conforms better to what the anti-money laundering system actual is supervising. The Swedish system is mainly a system for gathering intelligence information about financial transactions. Some of these reports will turn out not to be related to crime at all but others will, together with information from other intelligence sources, constitute a ground for starting a pre-trial investigation, most often on the predicate crime.

Due to this, it is important for the FIU to explain the conceptual confusion of 'money laundering' in such a way that the private actors can grasp it. If they get a deeper understanding of how the money laundering reports actually are used the idea that their reports are fruitless may change.

Our study was conducted when the act on measures against money laundering (1993, p 768) still was in force. It is now replaced by the act on measures against money laundering and financing of terrorism (2009, p 92) that came into force 2009. Can this legislation be expected to have any effect on the imperfect money laundering reporting? In order to answer this question, we have to look a bit closer at some of the most important changes.

The first change is that even more sectors have become obliged to report. For instance, auditors, businesses that sell newly formed limited companies and anybody with a professional trading where cash payments in excess of € 15.000 are made, have been added. As there were several sectors with a duty to report that did no reporting at all even before this extension, there is a serious risk that the change in the law will result in a further addition of sectors that only report the odd transaction, or none at all. This, in turn, can lessen the confidence in the supervisory system.

The other change is that the reporters are to implement risk-based thinking in order to carry out checks on transactions where the greatest risk of money laundering exists. For such a strategy, the principle of KYC (Know Your Customer) is central, which means that companies shall not only identify their customers, but also find out the purpose and nature of the transaction, and whether there is a real principal or beneficial owner. This type of process will probably work well for banks and exchange bureaus, who even today invest at lot of resources in discovering and preventing money laundering. However, a possible scenario is that it may become more difficult to get the other sectors – not least small companies outside the financial sector which do not even report suspicious transactions today – to introduce a risk-based strategy. Our survey showed that a lack of resources was one of the reasons why some businesses did no reporting. It is reasonable to assume that a risk-based reporting strategy requires both increased knowledge within the companies and more time, which can entail increased costs. If the companies also feel that there is no monitoring of compliance with the regulations, then there is great risk that the companies' commitment to controlling money laundering remains low. However, for the sectors that do report suspicious transactions, the risk-based strategy may be thought to lead to the money laundering reports being of better quality.

A further change is that the monitoring of companies and financial institutions with a reporting obligation will become more efficient. Against the background of the results of our survey, it is felt that improved monitoring was one of the most important changes for enhancing the incentive to report suspicious transactions. The new legislation has resulted in three county administrative boards being appointed as responsible for the monitoring of the newly added sectors with reporting obligations. The county administrative boards should check whether the companies have adopted procedures to prevent money laundering. A coordinating body with representatives from all supervisory authorities has also been formed. Apart from coordination issues, this body shall also provide support to the supervisory authorities on issues relating to training and initiate proposals for changes to legislation, working method and prioritisation. In other words, the changes are so far more of an organisational character, and it remains to be seen what effects they will have on the actual supervision. Our study showed that the incentives for some sector operators to report money laundering are closely linked to a feeling that the monitoring works, and that there is a risk of sanctions.

However, there are two sides of the coin. Improved reporting of money laundering, both in quantity and quality, does not automatically mean better prevention of money laundering. The judicial system also has to have the capacity and ability to use the information received in a way as efficient a way as possible. At the time of writing, the Swedish National Council for Crime Prevention is carrying out a research project, where we investigate the type of selection and processing procedures in the judicial system that influence which money laundering reports will be investigated further, and to what this will lead eventually.

In other words, the story of the Swedish fight against money laundering continues.

References

Brå, Vart tog alla pengarna vägen? En studie av narkotikabrottslighetens ekonomihantering. Stockholm, National Council for Crime Prevention, 2007a

Brå, *Narkotikadistributörer. En studie av grossisterna.* Stockholm, National Council for Crime Prevention, 2007b

Brå:10, Tillgångsinriktad brottsbekämpning. Myndigheternas arbete med att spåra och återföra utbyte av brott. Stockholm, National Council for Crime Prevention, 2008

Cribb, N., Tracing and Confiscating the Proceeds of Crime. *Journal of Financial Crime,* vol. 11, *no. 2*, 168-184

Duyne, P. C. van and M. Levi, *Drugs and money. Managing the drug trade and crime-money in Europe*. London, Routledge, 2005

Favarel-Garrigues, G., T. Godefroy and P. Lascoumes, Sentinels in the banking Industry. Private actors and the fight against money laundering in France. *The British Journal of Criminology*, 2008, vol. 48, *no. 1*, 1-19

Gelemerova, L., On the frontline against meney-laundering. The Regulatory minefield. *Crime, Law and Social change*, 2009, vol.52, *no 1*. 33-55.

Gill, M. and G. Taylor, Preventing money laundering or obstructing business? Financial companies' perspectives on "Know Your Customer" procedures. *The British Journal of Criminology*, 2004, vol. 44, *no. 4*, 582-594

Gold, M. and M. Levi, *Money-Laundering in the UK: an appraisal of suspicion–based reporting*. Cardiff, The Police Foundation and University of Wales College of Cardiff, 1994

Hall, S., S. Winlow and C. Ancrum, *Criminal identities and consumer culture. Crime, exclusion and the new culture of narcissism*. Cornwall, Willan Publishing, 2008

Harvey, J., Compliance and reporting issues arising for financial institutions from money laundering regulations: A preliminary cost benefit study. *Journal of Money Laundering Control*, 2004, vol.7, *no. 4*, 333-346

Harvey, J. and S. F. Lau, Crime-money, reputation and reporting. *Crime, Law and Social Change*, 2009, 52: 57-72

Junninen, M., *Adventurers and risk-takers: Finnish preofessional criminals and their organizations in the 1990s cross-border criminality*. Helsingfors, European institute for crime prevention and control, affiliated with the United Nations (Heuni), 2006

Kochan, N., *The washing machine. How money laundering and terrorist financing soils us*. USA, The Thomson Corporation (Texere), 2005

Larsson, P. and D. Magnusson, The Costs of Money Laundering regulation. *Nordisk Tidsskrift for Kriminalvidenska,*. 2009, *no. 1*. 1-22

Levi, M., Pecunia non olet: Cleansing the money-launderers from the Temple. *Crime, Law and Social Change*, 1991, *vol. 16*, 212-302.

Levi, M., The preventative control of organised crime in Europe: The emerging global paradigm?, In: K. Aromaa and T. Viljanen (eds.), *International Key Issues in Crime Prevention and Criminal Justice*. Heuni, Helsingfors, 2006

Örnemark-Hansen, H., *Penningtvätt. Ett urvattnat begrepp?* Stockholm, Norstedts Juridik AB, 1998

Reuter, P. and E. M. Truman, *Chasing dirty money. The fight against money laundering*. Washington D.C., Institute for international economics, 2004

RKP-rapport 2009:4, *Årsrapport Finanspolisen 2008*. Stockholm, Rikskriminalpolisen, 2009

Skinnari, J., *The financial management of drug crime in Sweden*. This volume

Skinnari, J., L. Korsell, *Swedish international casinos: A nest of organised crime or just a place for ordinary tax cheaters?* This volume

SOU 2007:23., *Genomförande av tredje penningtvättsdirektivet*. Stockholm, Ministry of Finance, 2007

The Act on Measures against Money Laundering (SFS 1993: 768) Stockholm: Ministry of Finance

The act on measures against money laundering and financing of terrorism (SFS 2009:92) Stockholm: Ministry of Finance

The Swedish Financial Supervisory Authority, Penningtvätt och terroristfinansiering - finansektorns förebyggande åtgärder. Finansinspektionen Rapport 2006:17. Dnr. 06-3299-306. Stockholm, the Swedish Financial Supervisory Authority, 2006

Verhage, A., Compliance and AML in Belgium: a booming sector with growing pains. *Journal of Money Laundering Control,* 2009a, vol.12, *no. 2*, 113-133

Verhage, A., Supply and demand: anti-money laundering by the compliance industry. *Journal of Money Laundering Control,* 2009b, vol.12, *no 4*, 371-391

Verhage, A., The beauty of grey? AML as a risk factor for compliance officers, In: P.C. van Duyne, S. Donati, J. Harvey, A. Maljevic and K. von Lamp (eds.), *Crime, money and criminal mobility in Europe*. Nijmegen, Wolf Legal Publishers, 2009c

The financial management of drug crime in Sweden[1]

Johanna Skinnari[2]

Dangerous money?

It is sometimes claimed in general debate, as well as amongst a number of researchers, that money from organised crime, especially drug crime, is a threat to society (see discussions in for example van Duyne and Levi, 2005; Kelly *et al.*, 1994; Naylor, 2004). It is assumed that the money is used for infiltrating and corrupting politics and the business world in order to gain power in society. One concern is that criminal methods, such as threats and violence, spread from illegal markets into the legal business world when criminals become increasingly active there (compare Kelly *et al.*, 1994). In addition to this, there is a perception that society in general will suffer when some individuals become rich as a result of criminal activities. The money or, rather, the proceeds of crime, is described as one of the most important motives for individuals in the drug market (Vesterhav, 2008; Hall, Winlow and Ancrum, 2008; Brå 2007b; Brå 2005).

On the other hand, a contrast is seen in earlier research that hardly describes criminal money as gushing into the legal market. Instead, research on criminal money indicates that it is spent or spills over into the legal market in rather modest amounts (see, for example, van Duyne and De Miranda, 1999; van Duyne, 2002).

Despite the fact that proceeds of crime is a priority for the judicial system, both in Sweden and abroad, there is only limited understanding of how the criminal economy functions (Van Duyne, 2002; Naylor, 2004). An underlying

---

1 This paper is based upon the Brå report ”Vart tog alla pengarna vägen? En studie av narkotikabrottslighetens ekonomihantering” (Brå 2007a). The results from the study have also been published in the chapter “Organiserad narkotikabrottslighet – Går den ekonomiska kalkylen ihop?” in the anthology ”Den ljusskygga ekonomin: Organiserad och ekonomisk brottslighet”.

2 The author works as a researcher at the Swedish National Council of Crime Prevention.

theme amongst those who paint the ominous picture of criminal entrepreneurs trying to take over the legal market is that huge profits are to be made on the drug market. What expenses and revenues drug entrepreneurs have, and whether they really make big profits, are questions that are discussed in this chapter.

Compared to some other countries the system for recovering criminal assets was in its infancy in Sweden, when the research was carried out. It is only recently that the government has stepped up its priorities – particularly through new measures against organised crime and a more severe legislation that allows extended forfeiture (Ds 2008; Brå 2008b; compare Vesterhav, forthcoming 2010). Such measures can have consequences for the financial management in the long run, as drug entrepreneurs see the need for taking extra measures in order to hide and protect their assets. As we will see, this was no great obstacle for the people in this study.

Method

The financial management of drug crime is difficult to study; it is the nature of criminal activities that revenues are either kept secret or separate from the crime. A number of different methods are therefore needed in order to examine the financial management. The four methods that were used for this study are presented below.

Court judgements and preliminary investigation records

The first method, which accounts for the greatest amount of data, is the analysis of district court judgements relating to serious drug crimes or drug smuggling in 2004. This comprises of 284 judgements, or 496 persons prosecuted. From these judgements, 68 underlying preliminary investigation records have been selected for more detailed examination, because they contained data on financial management. Care was also taken to have cases spread proportionally across the whole country and all drug substances, because previous research indicates that different drug markets can differ (compare Naylor, 2004).

Previous research suggests that judgements and preliminary investigation records are suitable data, because they are constant and contain reasonably standardised information that has also been appraised by a court (Schiray, 2000; von Lampe, 2003; Brå 2005; Paoli, 2000; van Duyne and Levi, 2005). They contain details such as transcripts from electronic surveillance and bank records, which are highly objective (Paoli, 2000). At the same time, there are also limitations; they are built solely upon what the authorities know about and have been able to use as evidence, and are therefore the result of a selection process (compare Korsell, 2003). The selection process already takes place at police level, whose data does not necessarily have to do with drug crimes of persons who are representative of the majority. For example, those who deal in closed private environments run less risk of being discovered (Naylor, 2004; Rhodes, 2000; Reuter, MacCoun and Murphy, 1990). Therefore other research methods are needed in order to complement the data and provide a more complete picture of the financial management.

Earlier research has shown that criminal files seldom contain data on how the money from crime has been spent, or even how it was invested, or the connections between the criminal entrepreneur and the legal business world (van Duyne and Levi, 2005; van Duyne et al, 2003). It is also natural that people whose assets are about to be confiscated would want to tone down the size of those assets, and that those 'squealing' on someone else can instead have a tendency to exaggerate, projecting the image that they have access to very important information (Naylor, 2004). In Sweden, the possibilities for confiscation are not as far-reaching as they are in other countries[3], but it is likely, even in the Swedish judgements and preliminary investigations, that the accused will want to appear as insignificant as possible by hiding assets and toning down the proceeds. A particular problem for this study, as remarked above, was also that criminal assets recovery in Sweden was still in its infancy when these preliminary investigations were carried out (Brå 2008b). This means that few cases contained a complete description of the financial situation of the drug entrepreneur.

Since those accused do not normally personally talk about their criminal incomes, the investigators have to gather the figures together from co-defendants, witnesses, direct observations of the lifestyle of the accused, and through studying other evidence (van Duyne *et al.*, 2003). There is, however, usually an inconsistency between figures from different sources, which makes it difficult to use such material as the basis for any definite conclusions about the financial situation of the drug operations (compare van Duyne *et al.*, 2003; Naylor, 2004).

Review of special investigation register

While from an objectivity point of view it is an advantage that judgements and preliminary investigations contain details that are considered as proved, there is also a danger that certain kinds of information remain omitted – for example,

3 See Brå 2008b, English summary.

information that does not need to be investigated further in order to reach a conviction. Such information typically has to do with financial management. For this reason a review was done of intelligence data, the special investigation register on drugs (särskilt undersökningsregister – SUR) kept by a former drug unit within the National Criminal Investigation Department (Rikskriminalpolisen). A SUR can be described as a register where data from ongoing investigations are stored. For this study, thorough examinations were carried out of various drug-related SUR-registries that contained information on financial management.

The data collected from SUR have both strengths and weaknesses. One disadvantage is that the SUR information varies in reliability, because it has not been tested according to the procedural rules of evidence. A lot of the information consists of various pieces of intelligence, which can make it difficult to evaluate the source and the reliability of the data. Together with the other methods, however, the data from SUR has been a valuable complement and has made it possible to identify certain recurring patterns in the material.

Interviews

Important information about financial management comes from 13 interviews carried out with people who were or had been active on the Swedish drug market. Although the interviewees were also found as the result of a selection process, they possessed more knowledge about the financial management than the police have.

Most of the interviewees were found in prisons, and had therefore been convicted, but two persons who had not been prosecuted for drug crimes were also interviewed. Whichever category the interviewees belonged to, they could talk about financial management structures that have never been investigated by the authorities. 12 of the interviewees had been drug distributors, and had collectively dealt with all of the common substances. Previous studies involving interviews with drug distributors have used this method successfully, as it is seen as an important complement to register data (Desroches, 2005; Dorn, Murji and South, 1992; Zaitch, 2002). The method had also been successful in research into large-scale alcohol smuggling (Johansen, 1994; 1996; 2004).

One limitation of these interviews is that it is possible that the interviewees may not want to talk about their experiences, although, since they have agreed to participate, those who did not intend to give away any information have already been excluded. There is also a risk that the information given can either be exaggerated or understated, depending on how the person wants to portray himself or herself. By asking questions about how financial management works on the drug market and why things are done in certain ways (instead of asking about the person's own crimes), the subject was made less sensitive, which encouraged a more open conversation. Even so, in all the interviews, the interviewees spontaneously referred to their own arrangements when they wanted to clarify or illustrate something. The interviewees were not pressed into talking about crimes they had carried out; instead, the focus was on how the financial management can be arranged and the advantages and disadvantages of various options. Discussing costs was easier than calculating income and profits; in some cases because they did not remember/in retrospect could not understand how they could consume such amounts. A couple of distributors were reluctant to reveal where proceeds were kept or on what level incomes were. In general they were however able to give examples that showed actual income levels and spending patterns, especially in comparison to the types of costs discussed earlier. By having data from so many different sources – as has been the case with this study – it has been possible to compare the figures with each other. This has minimised the risk of incorrect information from individual persons influencing the results.

Register checks

As with the methods mentioned above, register entries have been treated qualitatively. A total of 1.715 individuals convicted of serious drug crimes between 2001 and 2005 have been checked against three registers to give an indication of what legal and illegal incomes (aside from drug crimes) they have had. The registers are:

- Brå's register of suspected persons;
- Brå's register of convicted persons, and;
- The Swedish Tax Agency's tax register

Information about the individuals' previous suspected or prosecuted crimes was collected from Brå's *registers of suspected or convicted persons respectively*. The register of suspected persons contains data on those viewed as 'likely suspects' for one or more crimes. These people remain in the register regardless of whether they were later prosecuted for the crime or not. The period studied in the register of suspected persons extended from 1991 to 2005; the period in the register of convicted persons was from 1973 to 2005.

Finally, the research population was checked against *the Swedish Tax Agency's tax register,* including the register of persons in arrears. The information applies to the year before conviction. For a person convicted in 2003, for example, details of his or her income for 2002 were retrieved. The purpose of this processing was to check the individuals' legal finances. One limitation of this register is that the data are to a large extent based on what the persons themselves or their employers declare to the Swedish Tax Agency. In other words, the register entries were mainly to be used as a way to compare (and validate) information gained from interviews and preliminary investigations.

What does the financial management look like?

Figure 1 shows the budget items that can be found in earlier research and in the empirical material. In the next section, some of the most important income and expenses items are presented. Few criminal networks have all of these items. Instead, this list should be viewed as a kind of aggregate budget for drug entrepreneurs. Most striking is the fact that expenses are considerable, compared to revenue. This in itself indicates that drug operations are not as uncomplicated and profitable as is sometimes claimed.

Figure 1.
A model of the most common sources of income and expenses on the Swedish drug market

Expenses Production and logistics ▪ Transportation ▪ Storage Additional costs for criminal activity ▪ Cargo concealment and hidden compartments ▪ Transferring property ▪ Handling cash and money laundering ▪ Debt collecting ▪ Corruption and other forms of unlawful influence ▪ Weapons ▪ Loss and theft Expansion or reinvestment in the drug business Short and long-term credit Private expenses ▪ Food and accommodation ▪ Entertainment ▪ Illegal substances and goods ▪ Gambling ▪ Savings for pension and sickness benefits Investments	**Income** Income from drug related activities Income from other illegal activities Unreported income from work Legal income ▪ Employment or business ▪ Social welfare benefits

The section starts with revenue and then deals with expenses according to the following themes: storage and transport, credit, consumption, and, lastly, investments. The chapter concludes with discussions about the limitations that follow from doing business on an illegal market (as shown in figure 1, not least through the budget items called 'Additional costs for criminal activity') and the connections between legal and illegal markets that are seen in the study.

Rich one day, poor the next?

International studies show how revenues vary over time for individuals involved in the drug market, but also how those individuals adapt and seek to combine alternative sources of income (Junninen, 2006; Reuter, MacCoun and Murphy, 1990; Desroches, 2005; Brå 2006; Svensson, 1996; van de Bunt and van der Schoot, 2003; Mackenzie, 2002; Napoleoni, 2006). The same result emerges in this study.

The most common source of income is, of course, revenue generated from drug dealing. The interviews as well as the preliminary investigations illustrate how income from drug trafficking varies greatly, not just between the different people involved, but also for one individual over time. This is mainly because persons concerned about being detected lie low, or that deals do not materialise due to unforeseen circumstances. Data from the interviews and preliminary investigations relating to the size of the revenue is difficult to validate. As has already been noted, there is a likelihood that suspects are interested in playing down the size of their operations because of the severe sentences they are facing. In any case, the conclusion that can be reached is that it is fully possible to earn a few hundred thousand – in some cases up to a million – kronor (€ 100.000) in a month, but that handling drug shipments of that scale means that deals are not carried out each week, or even each month. In other words, the result is zero income during other months. Large-scale drug operations are unusual (compared to small scale actors) and difficult to conceal.

Income does not necessarily mean money. Especially at the lower end of the drug distribution chain, there is a relatively large potential for barter. Some drug dealers in the data functioned to a certain extent as a receiver of stolen goods, since they accepted payment not only in cash but also in the form of stolen items (compare Brå 2006; Svensson, 1996; Cromwell, Olson and Avary, 1993). Some data also suggest that retailers who sell only to end consumers, sell drugs 'on commission', and get paid – not in cash but in the form of drugs for their own use. There are also examples that show how different drug dealers exchange substances with each other so as to better meet the demands of their customers.

Certain interviewees (and actors from the preliminary investigations) stress that drug operations cannot be combined with either other kinds of crime or legal incomes. One more widespread observation, however, is that the drug market is so unreliable that dealers are dependent on other sources of income, at least periodically. All possible combinations of legal and illegal revenues are included in the data. Those who are most reliant on non drug-related sources of income are naturally the ones who only work temporarily in the drug business or who carry out odd jobs of some kind, such as booking journeys, exchanging money, overseeing couriers, and collecting or storing drugs and money (compare Ruggiero, 1995).

Other income from crime derives from theft, robbery, economic crime and loan sharking. Some drug entrepreneurs have expanded their smuggling activities to or from other commodities such as alcohol, weapons, cigarettes, or even human trafficking, a finding that is also supported by previous studies (Mackenzie, 2002; Bruinsma and Bernasco, 2004). These diversifications have come about with the help of contacts established during the original smuggling activity. Smuggling of stolen goods, such as cars and motorcycles, also features in the material, although it does not appear commonplace (compare Bruinsma and Bernasco, 2004). There are cases where persons have gone from a less serious crime (from a legal point of view) to a more serious one and vice versa. For example, one interviewee who had been convicted of a drug crime regretted that he had not stuck to arms dealing, where he experienced that profits were higher, the risk of detection lower, and that the punishment for the crime was milder than for serious drug crimes.

Some people work within legal business sectors, but without reporting their income. In a handful of cases, details are available on how much these individuals earned whilst working in the illicit labour market, and the amount varies greatly. Most wages are fairly low, considering the working conditions, where the work is hard and working hours long. For these activities, the individuals earned between SEK 5.500 and 14.000 (€ 550-1.400) per month for a full-time job. The fact that some persons have relatively poorly-paid, undeclared jobs besides their often uncertain income from drugs can be understood in several different ways. One interviewee mentions how it is difficult to find legal employment for some people in foreign-based networks, as they are staying in the country illegally. This applies to some of the people with undeclared income, visible in the trial and preliminary investigation material.

Another possible explanation is that it is difficult to keep a legal job at the same time as selling drugs – it is possible that employers who pay undeclared wages do not exactly have the same expectations as do employers who pay declared wages. A further motive for working illicitly is that the people involved have debts and therefore do not want any declared income that can be seized by the Swedish Enforcement Authority. In other words, it may not be unusual for drug abusers and people with debts to take whatever opportunities for income that present themselves (compare Reuter, MacCoun and Murphy, 1990). This mainly applies to persons lower down in the distribution chain, or on the periphery of a criminal network.

Finally, there are also persons with legal incomes – from their own businesses or through employment. As with other sources of income, it could provide extra security, but in addition to this, a legal income can be used to legitimise a high standard of living to the law enforcement agencies (Naylor, 2004). However, one interviewee explained how, in due course, he had problems combining legal work with selling drugs:

> "*I have been to school, I have an education and I worked. I had a legal income on the side. Initially I was working full-time, but due to the demands of the drug operation I had to start working part-time. The problem with having a legal job at the same time as a drug enterprise is that you have to weigh SEK 15.000 per month against SEK 150.000 (€ 15.000) per month. Even if you take all the risks into account, it's hard not to be tempted.*"

About 40 percent of the research population (people convicted of serious drug crimes) checked in the Swedish Tax Agency's register had declared income from employment or self-employment the year prior to their being prosecuted for drug crime. An additional explanation for why such a large proportion lacks a registered income is that many in the study are foreign citizens; even foreign couriers can be prosecuted for serious drug crimes (in combination with serious drug smuggling). Where income was registered, it was often very low, significantly less than the equivalent of € 1.500 per month. This could indicate part-time work, poorly-paid and sporadic work or benefits. Contributions from the social benefits system are most common at the lower levels of the distribution chain. Income support from the social services is the most common kind of benefit amongst the people involved in the study, followed by unemployment benefit and sickness allowance.

There are, however, a handful of persons who have very high declared incomes, as well as some who have taken large sums from their own businesses. A possible explanation for this is that there are some amongst these individuals who have only small assignments on the drug market, who may have been given those assignments due to their being established on the legal market. This is a subject that will be developed below.

The sectors in which those with legal incomes work are almost exclusively so-called high-risk sectors for economic crime: construction, restaurants, cleaning and vehicle workshops (compare Persson and Malmer, 2006). It is not surprising that drug entrepreneurs set up their own businesses in the restaurant sector. As we shall see, this is a sector that is familiar to them because of their lifestyles, and it is probably handy to engage in a familiar kind of operation (Larsson, 2009). There are also lines of business with a natural connection to drug trafficking – such as import/export and haulage – and to retail drug selling, such as the service industry (compare van de Bunt and Van der Schoot, 2003). The data contains cases where security guards and other persons who have worked for restaurants and bars, have used the access to clientele in drug crimes.

Not only are revenues uncertain for the great majority of persons within the drug market, but at times they are also rather meagre. Despite the fact that individuals get income from several sources, there are not many who bring in large amounts of money. Large income should not to be confused with making large gross profits: as we shall now see, net revenue is much lower because there are also considerable expenditures.

Transportation and storage costs vary greatly

Sweden is not a production country for drugs. Practically all illegal drugs have to be purchased and transported from abroad (RKP 2007). The costs for tasks such as cutting and repackaging the drugs are described as negligible by the interviewees. Instead, it is transportation and storage that can result in considerable expenses. The size of these expenditures, however, varies greatly depending on the set-up chosen.

The sender normally covers the cost of transporting the drugs to Sweden, but it is compensated for by a higher purchase price. Because of this, some buyers organise their own shipping. In most of the cases of drug smuggling included in this study, the cost of a courier is greater than other travel costs. The actual travel costs are not especially great, involving car expenses, airline/train/ferry/bus tickets and sometimes a few nights at a hotel. When cars are used, they are either rented or owned by someone other than the drug entrepreneur. In some cases, cars were rented from normal car hire firms. If the car is borrowed or bought the owner was someone without any direct link to the drugs, or the car was signed over to the courier, sometimes with the promise to keep the car as part of the wages. Although great effort is often put into getting the courier to blend into the normal flow of traffic, this is accomplished by simple means and has only a marginal impact on the costs (compare Brå 2005; RKP 2007). There are a few cases where more expensive methods of transport have been used, mainly lorries, but we know little about the expenses involved in this mode of transport. The few cases that were detected do not tell us much about such smuggling methods. It may be that the courier pays for the costs of the truck or other means of transport himself and is compensated with a higher fee. In spite of all of this, the actual transportation does not comprise a large portion of the total expenses compared with other costs incurred in the drug operation.

The amount that a courier is paid varies greatly, as do the couriers' backgrounds. However, preliminary investigations and interviews indicate that couriers often are outsiders (mainly for security reasons), who know only about their limited assignment and have very little knowledge about the drug operation as a whole (Brå 2005; compare van Duyne and Levi, 2005). This is to protect those responsible for the operation, should the authorities discover the drugs. Since couriers are persons on the periphery of or outside the criminal network, they are paid in cash, and the smuggling is rarely done for reasons of friendship or similar motives. Some prosecuted couriers state that they are in debt to the person who assigned them to work, but even if that is certainly true in some cases, the interviewees say that such information should be taken with a pinch of salt (compare Brå 2005). They claimed that if someone has become indebted through mistakes made during earlier assignments from drug distributors, that person has not exactly qualified himself for new high-risk assignments.

The courier fees mentioned in the prosecutions and preliminary investigations vary greatly. The payments range from SEK 1.000 to 55.000 (€ 100-5.500). Most couriers received between SEK 7.000 and 25.000 (€ 700-2.500) per trip, though. The highest paid couriers were those who were well established in legal society, such as lorry drivers, employees in the tourist sector or, in some cases, retired Swedish women. Such persons were employed in an attempt to reduce the risk of detection, because some drug entrepreneurs' did not think that customs officials watch out for these groups. This is not entirely true, since those couriers did show up to a certain extent in the court judgements and preliminary investigations. What is clear is that persons established on the legal market require more money when risking their freedom and position by transporting drugs. In such cases, the couriers' wages exceed other transport costs by a large amount.

There are, however, cheaper ways of minimising the risk of detection than choosing a more expensive courier. The most common method was to keep the drugs stowed in secret compartments in cars. The costs involved here are mainly for the labour involved in making the secret compartments, but no large sums are involved because the vehicle can be used for more than one smuggling trip. In some cases, cover cargoes were used, but these cover cargoes were often items such as vegetables or sweets, which could later be sold on the legal market, thereby avoiding any significant extra cost. In some cases the drug entrepreneur had an import/export firm that was used for this, which kept expenses down (but involved other risks). In other cases the drug distributor had recruited someone employed by, or the owner of such a firm (compare Brå 2005).

Domestic travel is viewed as less problematic, and the drugs are not hidden in the same way. Sometimes, the person transporting smaller amounts of drugs in a bag or inside a jacket does so as a service to a friend or in return for some drugs for personal use. As domestic transports are not seen as sensitive as international ones, they can be left to people within the drug network. So the remaining costs, then, are for the train tickets or, if the person uses a car, fuel. Whether or not this result is the outcome of selection – that the more careful ones are not detected because they hide their drugs well – is hard to say. The fact that neither of the interviewees mentioned that they invested resources in hiding drugs during domestic transportation suggests that the preliminary investigations give a fairly accurate picture. The security strategy that was emphasised was to avoid transporting the drugs yourself and instead let someone else do it (compare van Duyne and Levi, 2005; Brå 2005).

It is not only the drugs that need transporting; the operation also requires that payments are made regularly. Sometimes this is done through electronic money transfers, for example through payment agents such as Western Union. However, such methods leave paper trails, so it is hardly surprising that cash is also transported over the borders or between cities in the same country (compare Reuter and Truman, 2004). Although the number of documented cash transports in the study is low, it is likely that the same shipment method is used for these as for drug shipments.

Since only a few cases of cash transports are observed in the data, it is difficult to determine their expenses, apart from the trip itself. Some interviewees mention that the cost is around five percent of the amount to be transported; others think that drug couriers cost more, as this is a more dangerous assignment. Finally, some interviewees have simply transported the money themselves, without help from anyone else.

The data contain cases where cash is transported in the hand luggage on commercial flights, or in cars. Payment for larger consignments can be difficult to take as hand luggage, though, since the banknotes take up a relatively large amount of space. In some cases, the courier has been hired to deliver the drugs and return with a part-payment, and sometimes with the entire sum. In other cases, the individual in charge, or someone close to that person, will collect the money personally. It also depends on the conditions of payment; there are examples where the buyer has not been able to collect enough money to pay the supplier on time. This has resulted in a need for sudden trips for payment, leading to several problems for the drug entrepreneur. Firstly, the amount of money involved is too much to entrust to just anyone in the network. Money is more likely to be stolen than drugs, and there are cases where the person giving the assignment has been cheated out of money and drugs by his own colleagues. In addition to this, sudden trips or altered travel plans can mean increased exposure to the authorities. The data contain a few examples where persons have called or visited a travel agency in order to buy tickets for the next flight somewhere. Stressed, nervous people who are less concerned with costs and more with getting to a place as soon as possible can expose the network and increase the risk of discovery.

As with transportation, the drug distributors avoid storing the drugs themselves (compare Brå 2007b). Consignments are sometimes spread across several smaller storage places or sold quickly, in order to avoid being found in possession of too large a consignment (compare Desroches, 2005; Zaitch, 2002). Some of the persons appearing in the preliminary investigations and interviews have routinely hidden smaller consignments in the forest, removing the need to arrange for storage. A more expensive arrangement can involve people who are established in society; examples from the data sources include government employees or students. These persons are likely to require payment, although our findings indicate that they receive less than couriers with the same background. There can also be fees for renting a storage facility or other premises.

Money, which is extremely attractive to thieves, could also be stored by people other than the drug entrepreneur. However, the few cases that occur in the material involve close family members or friends, preferably people outside the criminal network. The interviewees explained that this was done as a favour or for nominal compensation and therefore did not involve any great expenses. In addition, family members were sometimes unaware that money was being kept in their home.

Transportation and storage both involve certain risks. In addition to the law enforcement agencies, there are competitors, but also collaborators who are mainly interested in embezzling money as well as drugs in large or small quantities (van Duyne *et al*, 2003). A clear indication of the importance of trying to minimise the costs brought about by losses and theft are the stories told by two interviewees, about insured drug consignments. They both said that it was possible to sign an insurance policy, which meant that the supplier was responsible for the shipment as far as the Swedish border. After that, it was the recipient who would bear the loss if the consignment was seized, damaged or stolen. The insurance was paid for through a higher price for the drugs. One of the interviewees paid SEK

6-8 per gram of cannabis without insurance and SEK 15 (€ 1,5) with insurance. Prices quoted by a single individual should, of course, be interpreted with caution, but this does illustrate that lost shipments can involve great expenditure for drug entrepreneurs. And indeed, some are willing to pay about twice the purchase price in order for the supplier to share some of the risk.

Handling cash carries an element of risk, and to reduce such risks various forms of straw men are used. Some of our sources mentioned contacts who enabled them to exchange money illegally. However, this also carries a risk. In one case, the person carrying out the exchange for a network received the exchange rates and fees written on a Post-It note, figures that he altered in order to embezzle money.

Therefore, for some drug entrepreneurs theft and losses can add up to greater expenses than storage or even transport costs. On the other hand, safety-conscious entrepreneurs have external costs for insurance and make use of people who are established in society, whenever possible, in order to reduce the risk of getting caught. Moreover, they have more people involved in the drug operation, meaning that the business costs accumulate to a substantial burden even if some only receive nominal payments.

Credit – a necessary evil?

As with many international drug markets, the Swedish one is in many ways a credit-based economy (compare Paoli, 2003; van Duyne et al, 2003). At the lower levels of the distribution chain many retailers and end consumers sell drugs to partly finance their own drug use, and therefore have small margins. They therefore often need credit to be able to buy drugs. At the same time, the drugs present a danger to the sellers – the longer they keep the consignment, the greater the risk that the law enforcement agencies will seize the contraband (compare Desroches, 2005). In addition, risk of theft or loss increases over time. In order to dispose of consignments quickly, drug entrepreneurs have to offer credit to at least some customers. Competition also often forces them to offer favourable terms of payment, in which credit is an important aspect (Brå 2007b; Desroches, 2005). However, credit is not just a necessary evil but has also security aspects. Granting credit ties the buyer to the seller, meaning that they do not have to move around looking for new sellers or buyers, which would increase the risk of police intervention (compare Desroches, 2005).

The credit system is often costly for the market parties. Preliminary investigations and interviews testify that unpaid debts are commonplace. In the worst cases, payment problems at the bottom of the distribution chain (near the end consumers) can propagate themselves up the chain to high-level distributors, although a number of measures are taken by the distributors to clear their own debts. The study reveals several such measures. A common measure is to offer credit only to certain individuals – especially to reliable customers, which is not much different from what the next door grocery store does (compare Desroches, 2005). In other cases, the largest possible portion of the consignment is sold for cash so that the drug entrepreneur can pay his own debts, while only the profits – or part of the profits – are put at risk (compare Desroches, 2005; Brå 2007b). One drug distributor explains:

> "*The most common method of payment was that the customer got 50 percent on credit. Customers that you were uncertain about had to pay for 70 percent and got 30 percent on credit ... I always tried to get 50 percent of the consignment paid for in cash, so as to cover certain expenses.*"

Some of the people in the study also had the habit of regularly driving around to their resellers to collect money, as they knew that the money would otherwise easily disappear due to other expenses, mainly consumption.

Some interviewees also mention something similar to the credit rating system for the legal market, although the version used on the drug market is less effective and formal. Cautionary rumours are circulated about those who neglect to pay their debts, and, even if it may take some time for the rumours start to go around, distributors listen out for them. Information about fellow traders and business partners fills an important function on the market, where individuals risk not only severe punishment but also a great deal of trouble if they do business with the wrong people (Desroches, 2005; van Duyne *et al*, 2003). Apart from making it more difficult to find new partners because of neglected debts, having such a reputation also increases the risk that the authorities will start to get suspicious. Therefore, there are many good reasons for trying to keep payments under control.

According to the interviewees, when payments have been neglected the usual approach is to try to solve the problem smoothly. Threats and violence are to be avoided as far as possible, since they attract attention (Brå 2009, Korsell, Skinnari and Vesterhav, 2009; compare Wästerfors 2007; van Duyne and Levi, 2005; Desroches, 2005). One interviewee said that he established payment plans to try to solve the problems. Particularly in the preliminary investigation material, several individuals say that they carried out various assignments on the drug market in order to pay off debts, but the interviewees do not believe that this is as widespread as people may believe. The reason they give is very plausible: those who get into debt have usually messed up, so why give them more assignments when more mistakes can lead to even more damage? Some mentioned that they were more benevolent if a person had lost drugs or money because of actions taken by the authorities or the competition, while the person himself had fulfilled his part of the assignment. However, the most common reason for debts usually involved the person prioritising other expenditures.

Some said that they would rather write-off debts than collect them. The explanation they gave was that it is less problematic in the long run to waive a debt and cancel a partnership with a person who does not behave properly. At the same time, it is important not to waive too much – some interviewees claimed that if a distributor has a reputation for being weak and that there are no sanctions for misconduct and deceit, other customers could start neglecting their payments too. In other words, the challenge is to have a *reputation* of force and violence, while avoiding to use such measures.

For the person who does try to collect debts that are due, and where diplomacy has failed, there are a few options. Collection methods commonly include threats, but less often violence – the point is to get people to pay up, not frighten them into the arms of the authorities or injure them so seriously that they become unable to pay at all (compare Desroches, 2005; Brå 2008a). The preliminary investigations contain examples where a distributor had several resellers, one of which had the job of collecting money. In this way, it becomes known throughout the sales circuit that action is taken against those who do not pay on time. There are also examples of more professional collectors being paid in cash for collecting debts, although it is most common that the entire debt is sold to such a collector. Reasonably, this further reduces the possibility for the debtor to work off his debts. One interviewee explains what he did when there were credit problems:

> "*I usually tried to solve the problem in as diplomatic a way as possible. If that didn't work, a way out was to sell the debt. There are two ways to sell a debt: one is to sell, for example, a SEK 100.000 (€ 10.000) debt for SEK 50.000 (€ 5.000). Another way is to sell the debt for the whole sum (€ 10.000) and let the collector add interest himself when doing the actual collection. The people that the debts are sold to are for the most part not in the drug market, they are usually from other criminal backgrounds.*"

These collectors are presented as providing collection services as a business concept, and it is hardly surprising that, with their fees, they are amongst the highest paid in the drug market. They often come from gangs with established means of intimidation, known names, intimidating symbols and previous experience of threats and violence. These individuals are also relatively active in using unlawful influence on persons in authority, so it could be said that they specialise in assignments involving threats, collection and extortion (compare Brå 2009; Korsell, Skinnari and Vesterhav, 2009).

Normally, the part of the consignment that is purchased on credit is somewhat more expensive than that bought in cash (compare Desroches, 2005). Even so, the impression given is that mismanaged credits cost most distributors more than they gain due to higher prices. It is not possible to increase prices to fully make up for the losses that mismanaged credits bring about. Mismanaged credits lead not only to reduced profitability and revenue, it also creates disorder in the drug market. When debts are not paid, contacts are made that are not normally done and people get angry and talk without using code words etc (compare Brå 2007b). Safety consciousness is reduced. When people think that they have been fooled, they are also more likely to help the law enforcement agencies. All of this means that the costs are greater than the direct losses suffered by the entrepreneurs when debt is not repaid or is sold to a collector for a lower price.

Consumption as the means and goal

Consumption represents one of the most important expenditure items for drug entrepreneurs. Several interviewees say they got involved in the business because of the money, but money has no value if it is not used. As we shall see, there can also be some strategic advantages in staying in certain places of entertainment.

The word 'consumption' perhaps does not lead to immediate thoughts about an individual's own drug use, but it does in fact become a considerable expense for many, especially at the lower levels of the distribution chain. For such individuals, personal drug abuse can be a strong motive for starting to sell drugs (compare Svensson, 1996; Snertingdal, 2006; Blanken *et al.*, 2000). There are, of course, distributors who never use drugs themselves, but many of them have certain expenses relating to personal use, even if they do not view themselves as abusers or addicts (compare Brå 2007b).

The interviewees, however, were more inclined to emphasise their consumption of licit goods. The fact that a high level of consumption can be a way of showing success even amongst criminal entrepreneurs, is known from earlier research (Hall, Winlow and Ancrum, 2008; Naylor, 2004; Junninen, 2006; Zaitch, 2002; Adler and Adler, 1992). In this study, entertainment was emphasised as an expense item. The fact is that, for many interviewees, it is seen as such a central part of life as a drug entrepreneur that they regard it as a necessary work-related expenditure. Spending time in the right environments can bring information about potential co-workers, and also about how the authorities work or whether specific persons in authority have various weaknesses that can be exploited (compare Brå 2009; van Duyne *et al*, 2003; Desroches, 2005). Although these possible benefits are very important and can render the drug enterprise and its related financial management more effective, they bring with them a number of direct expenses. One interviewee explains:

> "*I could blow SEK 15.000-20.000 (€ 1.500-2.000) in the bar every night, it was always possible to arrange more money the day after. Taxi rides could also add up to a few thousand per evening.*"

Money is also spent on gambling or holidays abroad with varying degrees of extravagance (compare Junninen, 2006). Consumer items that show up in the study and could have a certain lasting value are designer watches, jewellery and expensive cars. However, some entrepreneurs have realised that the insurance for expensive cars costs a great deal (for young men), and have chosen to lease a car instead. While lowering the costs for insurances, it also makes it easier to change cars later. For some individuals, the expensive lifestyle has become a goal and an addiction in itself – an addiction that can be hard to break (compare Korsell, Skinnari and Vesterhav 2009; Larsson 2008). Several interviewees describe a high paced lifestyle with a lot of parties, drugs and alcohol, together with indescribable worry about things that could go wrong with the operation (compare Brå 2007b; Korsell, Skinnari and Vesterhav 2009). Stakes are high – both the competition and the authorities are waiting for a mistake to be made. Such a desire for consumption can also bring about difficulties in paying debts and reduce reinvestments in the criminal operation, as well as making it impossible to invest in a quieter future life. A person who was interviewed in prison explains:

> "*I have financial back-up on the outside. The reason I bought a house and a flat was to have an investment for the future, a retirement fund. If you don't secure a little money, you risk spending it all.*"

However, not all of the persons involved are as visible in their pattern of consumption. Those with a more cautious image choose instead to eat out more often, but in simpler restaurants, to acquire better housing, buy clothes or furniture. In addition, some entrepreneurs apply the principle of living modestly while in Sweden, where their standard of living corresponds reasonably to their official incomes, while a large part of the year is spent abroad, where they live a completely different lifestyle with more extensive consumption (compare Junninen, 2006; see also van Duyne and Levi 2005, Zaitch, 2002).

Another method of hiding consumption is to register properties, cars and other expensive items in the names of family or friends (compare Kopp, 2004). This does not entail any direct extra costs; rather, it is an advantage when it comes to cars – since the young men who use the car can get lower insurance costs by signing the car over to a woman.

Little need for money laundering, despite investments

As we have established, entertainment and other forms of consumption are addictive for some drug entrepreneurs. Several interviewees also stress that it was safer to invest in real estate or businesses, as the money was otherwise easily spent on consumption (compare Junninen 2006, see also van de Bunt and van der Schoot, 2003). Real estate can be viewed as a form of investment, especially property purchased abroad for retirement later in life (or periodic use while involved in drug dealing) (compare van Duyne and Levi, 2005; compare van Duyne, Soudijn and Kint, 2009). The interviewees said that buying real estate or establishing their own businesses could be done in their own names, since the Swedish authorities either did not look for property abroad or found it difficult to get information quickly from the countries in question. Sometimes, they invested in real estate or businesses in Sweden or abroad under a family member's name.

The 'threat' described in the introduction, that criminal entrepreneurs are investing in businesses with the intention of controlling the legal market, does not come to light in this study. It is true that money from drugs is invested in legal businesses – either in Sweden or abroad – but legal activities are usually kept separate from the criminal ones (compare, for example, van Duyne and Levi, 2005). Preliminary investigations, interviews and other research all point in the same direction. An interviewee explains:

> "*There are some investments made on the legal market. Usually, this isn't about having a legal 'front'. On the contrary, people are very careful to keep legal activities separate from the drug operation. They don't want a stain on their reputation. The investments should, instead, be viewed as a successive springboard away from the drug-related activities. Even if you pull out of the drug market, you keep your contacts and relations in the criminal world, so that you have something to fall back on if the legal business doesn't go so well.*"

Seen in that light, the drug market can be said to function as a kind of criminal welfare benefits system. According to several interviewees, running a legal business was not as simple as they had thought at first; there are a lot of formal requirements for e.g. book keeping and a lot of expenses they had not expected. To save the legal business – which is seen as the future – they have gone back to the drug market and carried out limited assignments in order to bring in money. These are attempts to save a business that is not making a profit rather than downright money laundering, if the interviewees are to be believed. In fact, the interviewees saw a very limited need for money laundering; most of the time it worked just fine to consume or make investments with their criminal money, without any overly difficult questions being asked.

Furthermore, a great deal of the money is reinvested in the drug market (compare Junninen, 2006). The interviewees found it difficult to specify how much was reinvested, but answers ranged from around the same figure they spent on consumption up to twice that amount. For many, investments are mostly made in criminal activities and concern legal objects only to a limited extent. Certain more daring individuals reinvested all of their profits into new shipments of drugs, aiming to double their profits. Others reinvested about half of the profits. Some of those interviewed or visible in the preliminary investigations had money put aside in case a good smuggling or purchase opportunity came up, so the reinvestment did not necessarily happen immediately (compare Brå 2005; Reuter and Truman, 2004; Junninen, 2006).

For many drug entrepreneurs, it is important to have a financial management that results in a lifestyle which does not draw too much attention. This can be achieved, as we have already seen, by signing property in the name of others. Another solution, which is closer to money laundering, is to take out a small bank loan, which enables them to have the same amount available in cash. However, most of the people involved in this study lacked a well thought out arrangement and referred to an inheritance or winnings from gambling in the hope that nobody would question their stories, or, preferably, they had old winning tickets or wills. In other words, these arrangements hardly constitute real money laundering, as a false legitimate source often is lacking (compare Reuter and Truman, 2004; van Duyne *et al.*, 2003).

Overall, there are just a few examples of 'proper' money laundering in the study. Money laundering costs around 5 to 25 percent of the total amount laundered, according to the few details provided in the interviews, which is also in line with what other researchers have found (Masciandaro, 1999; Reuter and Truman, 2004). On top of this are costs in terms of risks, as other people need to be involved which in itself increases the risk of detection.

In order to reach such large amounts that problems arise from handling the money in a legal context, income from other, more profitable, crimes is also required. The money that the interviewees say that they laundered came from robbery, human trafficking and arms dealing. There are cases in the court judgements and preliminary investigations that involve money laundering in connection with economic crimes, tax offences and smuggling of cars, alcohol or cigarettes. Where economic crimes are concerned, an individual's private business could be used. In the perhaps most simple arrangement, buyers paid drug money into the seller's legal business account, meaning that the revenue appeared as legal income from business activities. At the same time, this was not particularly difficult for the authorities to unravel once they had uncovered the drug operation. The principal in another case had acquaintances that functioned as fronts for economic crime. In further cases, the persons prosecuted had insolvent companies, where the basis for the transactions was to some extent missing. These cases show signs of more advanced attempts at money laundering. In addition, one case involved a drug entrepreneur with a history of being a bank clerk; it is hardly surprising that this individual also used the bank system to a relatively large extent. Whilst these examples are few, other researchers have noted that money laundering requires a detailed understanding of the financial system, something that is not learned through drug dealing (compare Reuter and Truman, 2004).

Another explanation as to why money laundering is not more common in the data is that, after covering all expenses, most individuals in the Swedish drug market do not have particularly large sums of money left. There are only a few persons in the study who had money left for investing in legal objects. The main reasons for this were that consumption and reinvestments in the illegal enterprise took up a lot of resources. The investments in real estate or businesses that did take place were not of a socially subversive size, but rather, to enable a middle-class existence and withdrawal from the drug market.

Legal markets and the limitations of an illegal operation

The conclusion of this study is that only a few drug entrepreneurs make large enough profits to allow for investments. A large part of the explanation lies in the fact that they are running an operation that is completely illegal. Operating outside the legal market's more effective system creates difficulties in developing efficient financial management. To name one example, a formal credit rating system that can warn about notoriously untrustworthy customers is missing. The need for such a system becomes visible in the rumour-based informal version on the Swedish drug market. If debts are to be collected, there is no enforcement authority to turn to; instead, reliance has to be placed on a much more expensive criminal person. The same applies if a person wants to insure the drugs – the 'insurance premiums' mentioned in this study are very expensive. When new employees are needed, drug distributors have to ask around, since it is not possible to have open recruitment procedures and call and check references (van Duyne *et al*, 2003). Interviewees testify that the costs of hiring the wrong person are substantial, both in terms of lost money and increased risks.

Of perhaps greater concern for the drug operation, however, is the need for reducing the flow of information. Safety-conscious individuals in the study make sure that each worker knows only as much as they absolutely need to know about the others involved, the size of the operation and new smuggling projects. Neither do they report back on everything that happens, since contact should not be made unnecessarily. This limits the drug entrepreneurs' overview of the operation, making it difficult to make activities and the financial management more efficient, such as noticing theft and loss (compare Reuter, 1985). The problem is made clear in interviews where offenders actually found it difficult to answer certain questions, not because they were unwilling to, but because they did not really know where the money had gone. Although they enjoyed the informal and flexible nature of the drug market, where book keeping often was avoided (all documentation of such nature is potential evidence in the hands of the authorities), a more organised book keeping would probably have made it possible to achieve more efficient financial management.

Unlawful influence, especially in the more hidden form of corruption, is a strategy used by some individuals to lower the costs for the drug enterprise. Friendship corruption, i.e. using contacts within the law enforcement agencies to get information on what the authorities' know about the drug network, and warnings if there is a need to lie low for a while can help keeping losses down (compare Brå 2009; Desroches, 2005). A few drug entrepreneurs suspected that competitors had told the police about them, meaning that the law enforcement agencies can also be used to improve the market conditions for the individual's own goods (compare Passas, 1998). As previously mentioned, connections to key figures in the legal society are important.

Non-criminal circles are utilised to compensate for certain weaknesses on the drug market. This becomes clearest when considering those individuals who have supplementary income from legal work or social security benefits. The more safety-conscious drug entrepreneurs in the study in particular are also quite skilled in taking advantage of manpower on the legal market, in order to minimise the risks. People who work in import and export businesses, the tourism industry or restaurants can justify journeys and payments from abroad. Moreover, people in the restaurant business can identify clientele and new employees, which is why they are of interest as collaborators in the drug market.

However, the perhaps most obvious dependency on the legal market has to do with consumption. Even if a lot of money is spent on illegal goods and services, the criminal market does not offer the same range of supply (compare van Duyne *et al*, 2003). The really desirable consumer objects, the ones to show off to others, are all legal. For the same reason, interviewees wanted to invest in legal businesses in order to be able to live openly and leave the criminal world. In other words, drug entrepreneurs in general may be more dependent on legal society than those who fear infiltration are willing to admit.

The danger of crime-money reconsidered?

In this chapter we set out from generally stated doctrine about the dangerousness of crime-money and laundering, particularly concerning the 'integrity of the financial' system. The assumption that money from drug dealing for example, causes harm to the financial system has been used as one of several motives for putting in place one of the most expensive global financial surveillance systems (see for example Magnusson and Larsson, 2009, van Duyne and de Miranda, 1999). So it is appropriate to look closer and more critically at the criminal finances. In line with other researchers we did so concerning the Swedish drug market, but not from the usual assumptions of large sums being laundered, but from the earthly level of 'what criminals do with their money'. The answer is amazingly simple: "Very little of real economic interest". Doing crime-business appears to be more expensive than expected; the income distribution is very skewed (few own much and many own little); and the few more well-to-do drugs entrepreneurs' go in their economic dreams little beyond having in the end sufficient savings for a bourgeois life: "house with garden". In this regard the findings did not deviate from the (scarce) earlier research.

Is that all and does that mean a rejection of the commonly accepted assumptions? Not necessarily. Firstly, we have only looked at the Swedish drug market. A market that the Swedish authorities have prioritized to combat. It is possible that other types of crime are more profitable (as they are not prioritized by the authorities in the same way as drug crimes), and that such criminal entrepreneurs are more interested in investing the crime-money in legal markets. One main obstacle for the drug distributors was the fact that they deal with criminal goods, and could not use the legal systems to protect their enterprise or income. Those who earn their crime money from tax fraud can often hide the actual crimes within (their own) legal enterprises. We are therefore currently studying the financial management of that criminal market. Secondly, as we and a few other researchers looked at what criminals do, financially and economically, the findings were conditioned by what could be observed locally from criminal files and interviews. This approach and methodology differ from those of the FATF, OECD or World Bank, which issued such grave warnings. Between the two there is apparently a gap, which has to be bridged. Rigorous behavioural research and statistical analysis of basic data may be a proper approach along the line of 'conjectures and refutations': either to bridge that gap or to reconsider the crime-money danger hypothesis.

References

Adler, P. A. and P. Adler, Relationships between Dealers: The Social Organizations of Illicit Drug Transactions. *Sociology and Social Research*, 1992, no. 67, 261-277

Blanken, P., C. Barendregt and L. Zuidmulder, Retail-level drug dealing in Rotterdam, In: EMCDDA Scientific Monograph Series, no. 4, *Understanding and responding to drug use: the role of qualitative research.* Luxemburg, European Monitoring centre for Drugs and Drug Addiction, 2000

Bruinsma, G., and W. Bernasco, Criminal groups and transnational illegal markets. A more detailed examination on the basis of social network theory. *Crime, law & social change*, 2004, no. 41, 79-94

Brå, *Narkotikabrottslighetens organisationsmönster.* Stockholm, The Swedish National Council for Crime Prevention, 2005

Brå, *Häleri: Den organiserade brottslighetens möte med den legala marknaden.* Stockholm, The Swedish National Council for Crime Prevention, 2006

Brå, *Vart tog alla pengarna vägen? En studie av narkotikabrottslighetens ekonomihantering.* Stockholm, The Swedish National Council for Crime Prevention, 2007a

Brå, *Narkotikadistributörer. En studie av grossisterna.* Stockholm, The Swedish National Council for Crime Prevention, 2007b

Brå, *Otillåten påverkan mot brottsoffer och vittnen. Om ungdomsbrott, relationsvåld och organiserad brottslighet.* Stockholm, The Swedish National Council for Crime Prevention, 2008a

Brå, *Tillgångsinriktad brottsbekämpning. Myndigheternas arbete med att spåra och återföra utbyte av brott.* Stockholm, The Swedish National Council for Crime Prevention, 2008b

Brå, *Polisens möte med organiserad brottslighet. En undersökning om otillåten påverkan.* Stockholm, The Swedish National Council for Crime Prevention, 2009

van de Bunt, H.G., and C.R.A. van der Schoot, *Prevention of organised crime. A situational approach.* The Netherlands, Meppel, Boom Juridische uitgevers, 2003

Cromwell, P., J. Olson and D. W. Avary, Who buys stolen property? A new look at criminal receiving. *Journal of Crime and Justice*, 1993, no. 16:1. 75-95

Desroches, F. J., *The crime that pays. Drug trafficking and organized crime in Canada.* Toronto, Canadian Scholars' Press Inc, 2005

Dorn, N., K. Murji, and N. South, *Traffickers. Drug Markets and Law Enforcement.* London, Routledge, 1992

Ds, *Nationell mobilisering mot den grova organiserade brottsligheten. Överväganden och förslag*. Stockholm, Ministry of justice, 2008

Duyne, P. C. van, Crime entrepreneurs and financial management, In: P.C. van Duyne, K. von Lampe and N. Passas (eds.), *Upperworld and underworld in cross-border crime*. Nijmegen, Wolf Legal Publishers, 2002

Duyne, P. C. van, M. Pheijffer, H. Kuijl, A. van Dijk, G. Bakker , *Financial investigation of crime. A tool of the integral law enforcement approach*. Nijmegen, Wolf Legal Publishers, 2003

Duyne, P. C. van and M. Levi, *Drugs and money. Managing the drug trade and crime-money in Europe*. London, Routledge, 2005

Duyne, P. C. van and H. de Miranda, The emperor's clothes of disclosure: Hot money and suspect disclosures. *Crime, Law & Social Change*, 1999, no. 31, 245-271

Duyne, P.C. van, M. Soudijn and T. Kint. Bricks don't talk. Searching for crime money in real estate. In: P.C. van Duyne et al. (eds) *Crime, money and criminal mobility in Europe*. Nijmegen, Wolf Legal Publishers, 2009

Hall, S., S. Winlow and C. Ancrum, *Criminal identities and consumer culture. Crime, exclusion and the new culture of narcissism*. Cornwall, Willan Publishing, 2008

Johansen, P. O., *Markedet som ikke ville dø, Forbudstiden og de illegale alkoholmarkedene i Norge og USA*. Oslo, Rusmiddeldirektoratet, 1994

Johansen, P. O., *Nettverk i gråsonen*. Oslo, Ad Notam, 1996

Johansen, P. O., *Den illegale spriten*. Oslo, Unipub, 2004

Junninen, M., *Adventurers and risk-takers: Finnish professional criminals and their organisations in the 1990s cross-border criminality*. Helsinki, European institute for crime prevention and control, affiliated with the United Nations (Heuni), 2006

Kelly, R.J., R. Schatzberg and K. Chin, Turning black money into green: money laundering, In: R.J. Kelly, R. Schatzberg and K. Chin (eds.), *Handbook of organized crime in the United States*. Westport, Connecticut, Greenwood press, 1994

Kopp, P., *Political economy of illegal drugs*. London & New York, Routledge, 2004

Korsell, L., *Bokföringsbrott – en studie i selektion*. Dissertation. Department of criminology at Stockholm University. Edsbruk, Akademitryck, 2003

Korsell, L., J. Skinnari and D. Vesterhav, *Organiserad brottslighet i Sverige*. Malmö, Liber, 2009

von Lampe, K., Organising the nicotine racket. Patterns of criminal cooperation in the cigarette black market in Germany, In: P.C. van Duyne, K. von Lampe and J.L. Newell (eds.), *Criminal finances and organising crime in Europe*. Nijmegen, Wolf Legal Publishers, 2003

Larsson, P., Up in smoke! Hasch smuggling the Norwegian way. In: K. Ingvaldsen and V. Lundgren Sørli, *Organised crime. Norms, markets, regulation and research*, Norway, Unipub, 2009

Larsson, P. and D. Magnusson, Hvitvaskingsreguleringens kostnader. *Nordisk Tidsskrift for Kriminalvidenskab*,. 2009, *no. 1*, 3-25

Mackenzie, S., *Organised crime and common transit networks.* Trends & issues in crime and criminal justice, No. 233. Canberra, Australian institute of criminology, 2002

Masciandaro, D. The financing of criminal organizations, money laundering and the banking and financial system: Europe in an international context, In: *Organized criminality. Security in Europe.* Working paper. European commission, Forward studies unit, 1999

Napoleoni, L., *Oheligt krig. Den moderna terrorismens ekonomiska rötter.* Stockholm, Anderson Pocket AB, 2006

Naylor, R. T., *Wages of crime. Black markets, illegal finance, and the underworld economy.* Revised edition. Ithaca & London, Cornell university press, 2004

Paoli, L., Qualitative methodology at the edge: assessing Italian mafia groups' involvement in drug trafficking, In: EMCDDA Scientific Monograph Series, no. 4, *Understanding and responding to drug use: the role of qualitative research.* Luxemburg, European Monitoring centre for Drugs and Drug Addiction, 2000

Paoli, L., The 'invisible hand of the market': the illegal drugs trade in Germany, Italy and Russia, In: P.C. van Duyne, K. von Lampe and J.L. Newell (eds.), *Criminal finances and organising crime in Europe.* Nijmegen, Wolf Legal Publishers, 2003

Passas, N., A structural analysis of corruption: The role of criminogenic asymmetries. *Transnational organized crime*, 1998, vol. 4, no. 1, 42-55

Persson, A. and H. Malmer, *Svartköp och svartjobb i Sverige. Del 1: Undersökningsresultat.* Solna, The Swedish National Tax Agency, Rapport 2006:4, 2006

Reuter, P., *The organization of illegal markets. An economic analysis.* Honolulu, Hawaii, University press of the Pacific, 1985

Reuter, P., R. MacCoun and P. Murphy, *Money from crime. A study of the economics of drug dealing in Washington,* D. C. Rand, Drug policy research center, 1990

Reuter, P. and E. M. Truman, *Chasing dirty money. The fight against money laundering.* Washington D.C., Institute for international economics, 2004

Rhodes, T., The multiple roles of qualitative research in understanding and responding to illicit drug use, In EMCDDA Scientific Monograph Series, no. 4, *Understanding and responding to drug use: the role of qualitative research.* Luxemburg, European Monitoring centre for Drugs and Drug Addiction, 2000

Ruggiero, V., Drug economics: A fordist model of criminal capital?, In: Capital & Class, 1995, no 55, 130-150

RKP, *Den illegala drogsituationen i Sverige 2007*. Stockholm, National Criminal Investigation department, Swedish Customs, 2007

Schiray, M., Illicit drug distribution organisation in France: methodological experimentation at three levels of research, In: EMCDDA Scientific Monograph Series, nr 4 *Understanding and responding to drug use: the role of qualitative research*. Luxemburg, European Monitoring centre for Drugs and Drug Addiction, 2000

Skinnari, J., Organiserad narkotikabrottslighet – Går den ekonomiska kalkylen ihop?, In: T. Alalehto and D. Larsson (eds.), *Den ljusskygga ekonomin: Organiserad och ekonomisk brottslighet*. Umeå, department of sociology at Umeå university, 2008

Snertingdal, M. I., *Om metodiske utfordringer ved kvalitative intervjuer med heroin omsettere og importører*. Paper for Nordiske Sosiologikongressen, Turku, Finland, 2006

Svensson, B., *Pundare, jonkare och andra. Med narkotikan som följeslagare*. Stockholm, Carlssons, 1996

Zaitch, D., *Trafficking cocaine. Colombian drug entrepreneurs in the Netherlands*. Haag, Kluwer Law International, 2002

Vesterhav, D., Narkotikadistributörer – Vilken typ av personer är verksamma som grossister på den svenska narkotikamarknaden?, In: T. Alalehto and D. Larsson (eds.), *Den ljusskygga ekonomin: Organiserad och ekonomisk brottslighet*. Umeå, department of sociology at Umeå university, 2008

Vesterhav, D., *Measures against money laundering in Sweden. The role of the private sector*. Forthcoming, 2010

Wästerfors, D. *Fängelsebråk. Analyser av konflikter på anstalt*. Lund, Studentlitteratur, 2007

Swedish international casinos: A nest of organised crime or just a place for ordinary tax cheaters?

Johanna Skinnari and Lars Korsell[1]

Times, they are a changing

Sweden is in many ways a modern country, with more than half of the young population pursuing higher education studies, providing a home to several multinational companies and recording a high proportion of Internet users (Ekonomifakta 2010, Internetstatistik 2010). Further to this some forty percent of the population between the age of 25 and 34 has a university education (Ekonomifakta 2010).

This small country in the north also has a strong tradition of regulating vice (Bruun and Frånberg 1985). Wine, beer and spirits cannot be purchased in the local supermarket or at an off-licence. Instead, alcoholic beverages are bought at the Swedish Alcohol Retail Monopoly, better known as Systembolaget. It exists for one reason only: "*To minimize alcohol-related problems by selling alcohol in a responsible way, without a profit motive*" (Systembolaget, 2006). Drugs are considered a major threat to society, and the punishment for drug offences is severe (Tham, 1992). Drug use is an offence and many drug users – victims of addiction – are punished (Paulof and Lindström, 2000). Sweden is quite unique in an international perspective in that the purchase of sexual services, but not selling, is forbidden and the police carry out surveillance on the buyers (Hagstedt, Korsell and Skagerö, 2009).

Against this background, therefore, it comes as no surprise that gambling in all forms is regulated and the most popular games are owned and run by the state.

---

1 Johanna Skinnari is a researcher at the Economic and Organised Crime Research Unit at the Swedish National Council for Crime Prevention. Dr. Lars Korsell is a researcher and head of the unit.

The state owned company Svenska Spel – Swedish Games – is the largest gambling company in Sweden. Svenska Spel always stress that a share of the profit goes to non-governmental and sports organisations for children and youth. That is how the Government is taking responsibility while conducting business as usual.

Considering these circumstances, it is quite surprising that the Swedish Government has allowed Svenska Spel and its subsidiary company Casino Cosmopol AB to establish four international casinos in Sweden. During the years 2001-2003, these casinos were opened in the capital Stockholm; the second and third largest cities Gothenburg and Malmö; and the northern city Sundsvall (SOU 2006). The casinos resemble other casinos in Europe, and if you walk into one of them you will see decorations in red and gold, janitors in uniforms, gambling chips, neon lights, luxurious restaurants and bars.

However, Sweden is currently undergoing significant and potentially harmful changes in the area of vice. There is political pressure from the European Union to liberalise the alcohol monopoly, and recently there have been changes in customs regulation for private imports of alcohol that in practice mean that travellers can, more or less, bring as many bottles and cans as they like for 'private use'. At the same time, it is very difficult to maintain regulations in the gambling industry because of the Internet and the global gambling scene. There are no restrictions online where you can gamble on horses, play poker and even bingo (Lotteriinspektionen 2010). There are games for all seasons and all potential clients. Svenska Spel provides online gambling to keep up with the competition. In the light of this development, the establishment of the casinos can be seen as a fairly innocent way of adjusting to the "new times".

With this background in mind, it is not surprising that the four international casinos are subject to a lot of speculation and myths about casinos as a criminogenic and sinful environment. Swedish newspapers, the tabloids in particular, frequently stress all kinds of problems like prostitution and gambling addiction, often in connection with embezzlement, violence, alcoholism, drug abuse and other crimes or problems. There are headlines such as "*Black money turned white at Casino Cosmopol*", "*Sky-high records of gambling addicts banned from Casino Cosmopol*" and "*Money laundering at the Government's casino*" (Expressen 2007a, Expressen 2007b, SVT 2005). This leads to politicians to ask questions (motion 2008/09:Ju3, Skiftlig Fråga, inquiry 2005/06:149), such as "*Is there any truth behind these headlines?*"

Not surprisingly, a Government committee was established in order to evaluate different aspects of the casinos, for example criminality. The committee's report was published in 2006 (SOU 2006). The general conclusion was that the casinos are well-managed and regulated; they had foreseen and tried to prevent most of the problems that occur in this environment.

This article is based on a small-scale research project which we carried out for the committee (Skinnari and Korsell, 2006). The project presented an opportunity to use registers, some of them hardly ever used for research purposes, in order to contribute to a better understanding of how money is distributed and consumed in the Swedish society.

The aim of this article is to describe casino visitors' criminal background, whether illicit money is spent in casinos, whether such money is being laundered and from what kind of criminality or illegal business the money derives. The Government committee was particularly interested in the casinos' connections to organised and economic crime. Therefore, indicators of these two types of criminality were carefully analysed.

An appropriate way of analysing illicit money is to differentiate between the grey and criminal economy. The grey economy refers to law breaking in licit commercial sectors yielding undeclared incomes. The commercial activities are legal, but the crimes are committed and embedded in the licit businesses. The grey economy is therefore close to the term economic crime.[2] This is seen as different from the criminal economy where 'the enterprise' *per se* is illegal, for example trafficking in drugs, arms, alcohol, cigarettes or humans. In actual cases the difference between the grey and criminal money is not necessarily clear, but we have still chosen to make this distinction in the survey (see Ruggiero 1996).

Method

Swedish regulations, in line with other European countries, require that all casino visitors identify themselves with an identification card. Their personal identity number is then registered and a photo is taken of the person. In this research project the personal identity numbers of all visitors to the casinos during the period July 2004 – June 2005 were checked against the following registers.

2 Other terms include, for example, black economy (Björklund Larsen, 2010), hidden economy (Henry, 1978) and shadow economy (Gaertner and Wenig, 1985; Pedersen, 2003).

- Register of people suspected of offences (registered suspected offences during the period July 2000 – June 2005)
- Register of people convicted of offences (convictions during the period 2000 – 2004)
- Tax registers (most recent available information)
- Money laundering register (information available in December 2005)

The total number of visitors with Swedish personal identity numbers was 213.252, which serves as the population in the study. Foreign visitors are registered with their date of birth only, so it was not possible to check them against the registers mentioned above (approximately 22.000 persons).

Out of the 213.252 visitors, 61% were men. The visitors are quite young, as 29% are between 20 and 29 years old and 26% are between the age of 30 and 39.

Convictions and suspected crimes were collected for a five year period, in order to obtain information about crimes committed less frequently and crimes that require a lengthy investigation. The register of suspected persons contains data on those viewed as 'likely suspects' for one or more of these crimes. These people remain on the register regardless of whether they were later prosecuted for the crime or not.

The Swedish Tax Agency's tax register is to a large extent based on what the persons or their employers declare to the Swedish Tax Agency. The register contains data on more or less the entire population. The purpose of this processing was to check the individuals' legal finances. Due to restrictions regarding privacy, the Swedish Tax Agency was prohibited from delivering data on each individual person and instead delivered tables with results. Therefore, it was not possible to produce any cross tables.

The money laundering register contained 11.000 individuals at the time of the register check. It is based on reported suspicious transactions mainly from currency exchange offices and banks, but also from dealers in expensive goods and real estate such as jewellers, brokers, auction houses and car dealers (see Vesterhav, forthcoming 2010; Örnemark Hansen, 1998). According to the Finance Police, it is possible that close to 80% of the reports in the money laundering register are related to tax fraud and other economic crimes (Skinnari and Korsell, 2006). Because of the strict privacy regulations, the Swedish National Council for Crime Prevention was not allowed to connect the results on an individual basis from the money laundering register to the corresponding results from the registers of people suspected or convicted of offences. But they could be used for comparison with the data on the individual casino visitors.

This method gives us a limited picture of the visitors and their backgrounds. The registers only contain information that the authorities have on the individuals, or in case of the Tax register, the information the taxpayers themselves have reported. Even if we had been allowed to connect the results from the four registers to each casino visitor, we would not have been able to show the use of either grey or criminal money through the register studies. However, with references to other research, in connection to our results from the register checks, it is possible to make general assessments and discuss the likelihood of grey or criminal money used by casino visitors. In this article, we attempt to use this method.

To conclude, the data, supported with other forms of research, can only be used to make assumptions or interpretations about the origin of casino visitors' money. In order to get a more complete picture of the money, we would have to gather data in other ways; for example through questionnaires and interviews with casino visitors. However, this would only result in a slightly better picture. Measuring the use of money from the grey or criminal economy is very difficult, as people have good reason to hide such sources of income (RRV 1998). Still, this small scale research project, based on register checks, did reveal some interesting features of the casino visitors.

Results

What kind of offences?

The proportion of visitors who had been *suspected* of committing offences at least once was 10,4%. In comparison with the Swedish population (6,3%), visitors have a higher rate of suspected offence. However, the visitors are younger, have a higher proportion of men and – given where the casinos are situated – are more likely to live in big cities. These are all well known criminogenic factors which explain the higher relative frequency of these features among casino visitors.

The same pattern can be seen in the results from the register of people *convicted* of offences. The proportion of visitors who had been convicted of a crime during a five year period was 8%, while the only data available for the Swedish population at large is for a six year period and adds up to 5,4%. This difference can be explained by the same factors as the results of the register checks on people suspected of offences. When compared to people suffering from alcoholism (19,4%) or substance abuse (40%), the figure is low (see Skinnari and Korsell 2006 for more details).

What kind of offences have the visitors committed? According to table 1, the most frequently recorded offences concern physical violence against other people. As previously mentioned, 61% of the visitors are men, and they are also young.

When considering the high proportion of young men in the casino population, and that casinos are part of the 'night scene', this figure is hardly surprising. Young men are responsible for a high proportion of violent crime, and there is also a connection between alcohol consumption and violence (Estrada 2008, Kühlhorn 2004).

Drunk driving offences (1,71%) and drug offences (1,66%, mainly consumption) are also relatively common among the casino population. However, drug offences should not be seen as an indicator of organised crime among the visitors, as those offences mainly concern personal use and not drug distribution.

Table 1.
Casino visitors in relation to a comparison population (age: 15-52 years). Proportion of certain forms of crime. In percent.

Form of crime	Casino visitors	Comparison population
	(n= 176.191) %	(n= 4.397.192) %
Crime against life and health (Chapter 3 of the Criminal Code)	4,00	1,88
Crimes against freedom etc. (Chapter 4 of the Criminal Code)	0,72	1,47
Criminal damage etc. (Chapter 12 of the Criminal Code)	1,01	0,72
Fraud, embezzlement, accounting offences, crimes against creditors etc. (Chapter 9-11 of the Criminal Code)	2,22	1,27
Crimes against public officials etc. (Chapter 17 of the Criminal Code)	1,40	0,60
Traffic violations (not drink driving)	2,04	0,93
Drunk driving offences	1,71	0,91
Drug crimes	1,66	0,66
Smuggling offences	0,13	0,11
Tax offences	0,32	0,12
All crimes	**15,21**	**8,67**

It is noteworthy that the less frequently represented crime categories in the table concern various types of white-collar crime, or offences pertaining to economic crime: tax offences, accounting offences, fraud, embezzlement, crime against creditors, smuggling offences. These are systematically more frequent among visitors compared to the Swedish population: 2,22% of all casino visitors had been suspected of fraud, embezzlement, accounting offence, crimes against creditors etc. compared to 1,27% of the comparison population. Corresponding figures for tax offences are 0,32% for casino visitors and 0,12% for the comparison population. Although the differences between the two populations are small in numbers, they are large in percentage and are worth a closer look, especially in the other registers.

What kind of people are behind these figures? It is apparent that the population of casino visitors does not only consist of ordinary young conscientious salary men, who are going out to have a good time. There are also self-employed people and other businessmen among the visitors. Accounting offences and crimes against creditors can only be committed in connection with a business (Levi, 1987; Korsell, 2002; Korsell, 2003). According to Swedish regulation, petty tax crimes are handled as misdemeanours with administrative measures, while tax crimes are defined as more serious crimes, typically in connection with businesses. Most of those who were suspected of a specific form of white-collar crime – accounting offences, crimes against creditors and tax fraud – were 30 years of age or older. This is quite natural, as these types of offences require an established position in the business sector for which at least a university education, training or several years in the business is needed (Weisburd and Waring 2001; Korsell, 2002; Shover and Hochstetler, 2006). It is also noteworthy that a rather high proportion of the suspects were 50 years of age or older.

Thus far, we can conclude that, among casino visitors, there is a group of people who have money earned from economic crime. Let's return to the data to find out more.

Risky businesses?

Where does the money that is being spent come from? The tax register gives us a basic idea. Table 2 illustrates the most common commercial sectors represented by the self-employed and business owners (who constitute around 12% of the frequent visitors[3]). Note that the five most common sectors are restaurants, taxi, construction, cleaning and hairdressing enterprises. Previous research into white-collar crime has identified these sectors as 'high risk' areas for tax evasion and other forms of economic crime (c.f. van Duyne and Houtzager 2005, Alalehto, 1999; Persson and Malmer, 2006; Larsson, 1995; RRV 1998; Punch, 1996; Appelgren and Sjögren, 2001). According to the figures in table 2 the self employed

3 Frequent visitors are people who visited a casino at least four times during the twelve month study period. Some of the checks against the tax register are done only for this group. They comprise 32.184 persons in total, and approximately 15% of the total number of visitors. However, their visits make up 75% of the total number of casino visits during this time.

visitors in restaurant, taxi and construction sectors alone account for almost 60% of the visitors and 61% of the visits.

Table 2.
Self employed casino visitors according to commercial sectors.

Sectors	Number of people	Number of visits	Visits per person
Restaurant	527	13.228	25,1
Taxi	220	6.543	29,7
Construction	178	5.133	28,8
Cleaning	101	3.377	33,4
Hairdressing	137	2.878	21,0
Smaller food shops	101	2.863	28,3
Mixed agriculture	80	1.966	24,6
Other technical consulting	64	1.612	25,2
Paintwork	49	1.530	31,2
Literary and artistic work	99	1.450	14,6
Total/average	1556	40.580	26,1

International research suggests that some of these sectors, the most obvious example being the restaurant sector, have connections to 'organised crime', as well as economic crime (cf. van de Bunt and van der Schoot, 2003; cf. Johansen, 1996). In the case of Sweden, research suggests that people involved in organised drug crime may start their own businesses in order to leave the drug market, and that they often choose sectors they are familiar with, such as restaurants (Skinnari, Vesterhav and Korsell, 2007; cf. Larsson 2009). Therefore, a small number of casino visitors may have a background in organised crime without it showing in the registers of people suspected or convicted of related offences, as those visitors are likely to have more or less left the drug market.

Another interesting finding from the tax registers is that a higher proportion of casino visitors are in the lower income categories compared with the Swedish population. This is clearly the case for frequent visitors (at least four visits): 35% of them have declared a salary or income from self employment that does not exceed SEK 100.000 per year (roughly EUR 10.000) or state zero income. In addition, the casino visiting population (frequent visitors) also contains a higher percentage of people (5% compared to 3,1% for the Swedish population) who have not filed their tax returns or people from whom no information on income exists at all, at least to the knowledge of the Tax Agency (non-filers)[4]. The Swedish Tax Agency has conducted studies on non-filers, and one of their conclusions was that there are people who function as straw men and individuals with income from crime in this group (Persson, 2006; Skinnari and Korsell, 2006).

In other words, there are clear indications that casino visitors have a lower average income than the total population. This is especially the case for frequent visitors. So how should these results be interpreted? Could it be as simple as that people with low income are trying to improve their economic situation by visiting casinos (cf. Westfelt, 2003)? Or is it a sign of undeclared income, i.e. that there are visitors who in fact have a higher income than they have stated to the Swedish Tax Agency? A reasonable assumption is that at least some of the people with low declared income, who visit casinos frequently, also have undeclared income (cf. Persson and Malmer, 2006).

From previous research we know that a substantial part of undeclared money is used for 'luxurious' consumption (RRV 1998; Skinnari, Vesterhav and Korsell, 2007). One study concluded that those who had undeclared income were more likely to work 'additional' hours at the same work place or somewhere else, in order to marginally strengthen their financial position (RRV 1998; Persson, 2006). The money was used for all sorts of expenses, ranging from occasional extravagance to a more permanent high standard of living, e.g. buying clothes or travelling more often. Visiting casinos fits very well into this lifestyle of consuming undeclared money.

We have already concluded that high-risk tax evasion sectors were common among the self-employed casino visitors (see table 2). What about the employees working in these sectors? The tax register does not contain information on the commercial sector in which an individual is employed. However, we know from previous studies that undeclared salaries to employees are quite common in the high-risk tax evasion sectors (c.f. van Duyne and Houtzager 2005, Alalehto, 1999; Persson and Malmer, 2006; Larsson, 1995; RRV 1998; Punch, 1996; Appelgren and Sjögren, 2001; SOU 1997; SOU 2002). If employers who pay undeclared wages visit the casinos, it is reasonable to think that their employees do the same. In other words, the risk sectors would be over-represented among employees as well.

Visiting a casino is a form of luxurious consumption that attracts money from economic crime, tax crime in particular. The register checks show that there is a higher degree of people suspected of various forms of economic crime than in the comparison population. Other results such as low registered income, the instance

---

4 Not including children, who seldom have income. Only people born between 1944 and 1979 were included in this variable.

of non-filers and visitors with businesses in commercial 'risk sectors' are also indicators of grey money, as shown in previous research. Taken together, these indicators suggest that a group of casino visitors have undeclared income. As these registers could not be checked against one another, it is impossible to say how large a group this is, but that was not the aim of this small-scale research project.

The second point of interest for the government committee was whether money from organised crime was spent at the state owned casinos.

What about organised crime?

The results show that money used at the casinos to some extent comes from the grey economy; undeclared income from tax evasion. This may be a surprising result, as the general view is that casinos and gambling are connected to organised crime rather than economic crime (cf. Cressey, 1969; Davidson, 1997; Block 1991). As previously stated, some casino visitors had committed economic crime, or more specifically, tax fraud and accounting offences. But were there any signs of organised crime? In addition to the previous discussion on the restaurant sector and its connection to organised crime, there was also a relatively high percentage of drug offences. The latter turned out to concern consumption rather than trafficking or selling drugs. In order to spread more light on this matter, we have studied the money laundering register.

As in many other countries; banks, exchange bureaus, casinos and other institutions are obliged to report suspicious transactions to the Finance Police (cf. Vesterhav forthcoming 2010). Casino visitors were checked against the 10.000 persons in the money laundering register. Only 0,61% of the visitors appeared in the register. However, roughly 12% of the suspects in the money laundering register had visited a casino at least once during the year we studied. As Sweden has only four casinos, and this is an advanced form of gambling, this was a surprising result. As with the previously mentioned results, the proportion is higher among *frequent visitors* who are found in the money-laundering register (see table 3). 0,33% (or 486 visitors) of those who had visited a casino once in a year were found in the money laundering register, while the corresponding figure for those who had made 53 visits or more was 2,94% (or 91 visitors). As most people had only made one casino visit, frequent visitors formed proportionally the largest group of visitors found in the money laundering register (37,4% or 486 visitors).

Table 3
Casino visitors in the money laundering register according to visits. Number and %.

Number of casino visits	N. of visitors found in the money laundering register	% of the visitors found in the money laundering register	% of the number of casino visitors in each category
1 visit (n=146.655)	486	37,4	0,33
2-3 visits (n=34.412)	279	21,5	0,81
4-12 visits (n=19.427)	263	20,3	1,35
13-26 visits (n=6.049)	104	8,0	1,72
27-52 visits (n=3.612)	75	5,8	2,08
53 or more visits (n=3.096)	91	7,0	2,94
Total	**1298**	**100**	**0,61**

The next question regards the amount of money these persons have reportedly been handling in a suspicious manner. Fortunately, the money laundering register has this information. We found a small group, 13,7% of the visitors who were suspected of money laundering, and who had handled at least one million Swedish crowns, roughly € 105.000, on a single occasion.

12% of the people in the money laundering register, or 1.298 individuals, had visited a casino. This is noteworthy, considering that it is a relatively high figure and that the money laundering register contains intelligence information about suspicious transactions. According to the Finance Police, it is possible that close to 80% of the reports in the money laundering register are related to tax fraud and other economic crimes (Skinnari and Korsell, 2006). A characteristic of the Swedish money laundering register is that only a small part concerns actual money laundering, in the sense of hiding the source of the money. Instead, some actors have a need, not to launder money to hide its criminal origin, but to hide the recipient of the cash (Carlström and Lantz Hedström, 2007, Skatteverket 2009). Legitimate contractors who order construction work, for example, pay the bills in a regular way, i.e. by transferring money to a construction company's account. A problem arises when the company needs to withdraw a large amount of cash to pay undeclared wages to their workers and at the same time avoid being reported to the Finance Police. From an analytical point of view, this process is the very opposite of money laundering, although reports of such activity are collected in the same register as the suspected money laundering. In other words, a typical report concerns a person who has money (in SEK) transferred to an exchange office, from where they withdraw a large sum in cash (still in SEK) (Skatteverket 2009; Finanspolisen 2009). When asked about what the money is for, no reasonable explanation has been given.

The register is based on the assumption that suspicious transactions are a sign of very serious criminality. One possible interpretation of the result is that this group of visitors includes many people involved in either organised crime or economic crime, since they have been reported for handling cash in a suspicious way. It is therefore interesting that over a tenth (1.298 individuals) of the persons in the money laundering register are casino visitors, and that over 40% of these are frequent visitors (533). While 56% of the visitors in the money laundering register had only been reported once, there is a small group (68 persons) who has been reported for suspicious transactions at least ten times. So who are these people?

If we start with the small group that had been reported for suspicious transactions at least ten times, it is likely that most of them have withdrawn cash from accounts in order to transform legitimate money into undeclared wages (cf. Skatteverket 2009).

In order to avoid being reported, some actors use several accomplices; each of whom makes smaller withdrawals. In international literature, these persons are often referred to as 'smurfs' (Rose, 2003; Reuter and Truman, 2004). Our interpretation is that there is probably a smaller group of such smurfs among the casino visitors, since these individuals had been reported frequently. As explained above, the money laundering register mainly contains reports on cash withdrawals that may later be used for undeclared wages. As the smurfs regularly make cash withdrawals, they run a higher risk of being reported to the Finance Police. The smurfs may be gambling with the money they have earned from their services to the criminal entrepreneurs, rather than trying to launder money at the casinos. Previous research indicates that many of the money carriers were in the low income range, often receiving social security benefits (van Duyne *et al.*, 2003), which is in line with our findings on the frequent visitors. Only 31 persons were reported for suspicious transactions by the casinos themselves, and the previously mentioned evaluation of Swedish casinos, which concluded that money laundering is unusual at casinos because of all the security measures being taken, seems to be correct (SOU 2006).

Despite the probable small group of smurfs, it is important to remember that the majority of suspected money laundering casino visitors probably belong to a very heterogeneous group. This group contains everything from small-scale tax cheaters to white-collar criminals dealing with huge sums of money that has to be laundered outside of the casinos. Others work for criminal entrepreneurs in the construction business. In other words, what can be observed in the Swedish casinos is mainly the handling of black and illegal money, alongside the far greater flow of licit money. But why does this consumption occur at the casinos?

The consumer society

The consumerist spending patterns in the illicit economy will hardly be any different from the licit economy. Other Swedish studies on organised drug crime and on tax cheaters clearly state that consumption is a strong motive for committing these crimes (Vesterhav, Skinnari and Korsell, 2007; RRV 1998). Consumption seems to make everyone happy, but what kind of consumption are we talking about? Preferences vary depending on the individual, but often involve exclusive clothes, watches, jewellery, restaurant dinners, cars, holidays, new furniture and everything that "makes life worth living" (Skinnari, Vesterhav and Korsell, 2007; Hall, Winlow and Ancrum, 2008). Gambling fits very well into this lifestyle, and we have seen that tax cheating visitors visit the casinos fairly frequently.

Why are the drug dealers not more visible in the casinos? One reason is that the casino visitors were only checked against the registers of people suspected and/or convicted of offences during the past five years. Aggravated drug offences usually lead to longer prison sentences than five years. If our assumption is correct, the results of the checks against the two different criminal registers would not yield an identical result. Instead, we would see a different structure of suspected crimes compared to the structure of convictions. For example, there would be a higher percentage of people suspected of trafficking and selling drugs than of people being convicted (and therefore imprisoned) of those crimes.[5] However, this was not the case.

One explanation is that many drug dealers, especially at the higher levels, are very cautious and use different kinds of security systems in order not to be found or get caught (Vesterhav, Skinnari and Korsell, 2007). It is important to remember that a limitation with the registers is that they only contain information that is known to the authorities. The authorities discover this information as a result of a complex process of selection (Korsell, 2007). Therefore, it is hardly the 'able criminals' who end up in the registers (cf. Walsh, 1977).

Security is of great importance to many drug dealers. Therefore, a plausible explanation as to why they are not part of the casino clientele is that some of them suspect that the police will use the pictures and registrations of visitors in their investigations (cf. Korsell, Skinnari and Vesterhav, 2009). As a result, careful

---

5 The average prison sentence for aggravated drug crimes is almost five years (Brå 2009).

drug dealers who want to gamble, choose to do so elsewhere. Our knowledge of the gambling habits of drug dealers indicates that they see more appropriate gambling options than casinos, such as private poker games or the horse track (cf. Skinnari, Vesterhav and Korsell, 2007). A third and very important explanation is that there are more tax fraudsters than drug entrepreneurs, which is reflected in the previously mentioned results. If the tax fraudsters and drug entrepreneurs are just as likely to visit casinos, then the tax fraudsters would be in a clear majority, as they are in this study.

Money makes the world go round

The results from this research project are part of a wider field of research on criminal markets. By using register checks we have found further support for the theory that participation in the criminal environment only rarely yields substantial and lasting fortunes (cf. van Duyne and Levi, 2005). If this were not the case, this study would have found more people suspected and convicted of theft and serious drug offenses among casino visitors. Instead, there are various findings showing that money from other forms of crime is being spent at the Swedish casinos. To conclude, the grey economy is more efficient and widespread than the criminal economy, and therefore generates more substantial amounts of money to a larger number of people compared to the criminal economy (cf. Naylor, 2004). A reason for this is that criminal enterprises are managed relatively inefficiently from a financial point of view, and that they have many persons on their pay roll (Van Duyne and Levi, 2005; Korsell *et al*, 2005). The grey economy is more efficient, as it can use the legal economy and take place within regular companies. The routines and possibilities for hiding black labour in a legitimate environment contribute to a reasonably efficient economy, which can generate large turnovers for luxurious consumption, such as casino visits (cf. van Duyne *et al,* 2003).

As of a few years ago, asset recovery has been a supplementary law enforcement tool; "following the money" instead of only punishing the offender has become a mantra in Government strategies (Vesterhav, Forsman and Korsell, 2008). One of several questions that arises from this strategy is "assets from whom?" Casinos and other places for consumption of grey and criminal money – jewellers, dealers of expensive cars, designer shops, travel agencies, watchmaker's shops and restaurants – are therefore strategic spots for gathering intelligence.

The results presented in this chapter suggest that there are close ties to grey money rather than criminal money at the four Swedish casinos. The fact that grey money is being consumed at casinos is not surprising, as previous research have indicated that illicit money appears everywhere, and that it is especially likely to be used for expenses that "make life worth living"., This study presented the researchers with a unique opportunity. With the help of four registers we could get an initial impression of how criminal and grey money is being spent. We already had deep and widespread knowledge on the various origins of crime money. However, while it might not be possible to prevent either the crimes or indeed the consumption of their profits it might at least identify and trace the perpetrators through their consumption. This could be termed consumption surveillance.

References

Alalehto, T., *Motiv eller tillfälle? En studie om ekonomisk brottslighet i restaurangbranschen.* Stockholm, Atlas, 1999

Appelgren, L. and H. Sjögren (eds), Ekonomisk brottslighet och nationalstatens kontrollmakt. Stockholm, Gidlunds förlag, 2001

Björklund Larsen, L., *Illegal yet Licit. Justifying informal purchases of work in contemporary Sweden.* Stockholm, Stockholm University, 2010

Block, A. A., *Perspectives on organizing crime. Essays in opposition.* Dordrecht, Kluwer, 1991

Bunt, H.G. van de and C.R.A. van der Schoot, *Prevention of organised crime. A situational approach.* Meppel, Boom Juridische uitgevers, 2003

Bruun, K and P. Frånberg, Utblickar, In: Bruun, K and P. Frånberg, Den svenska supen. En historia om brännvin, Bratt och byråkrati. Stockholm. Prisma, 1985.

Brå, *Kriminalstatistik 2008.* Stockholm The Swedish National Council for Crime Prevention, Report 2009:17, 2009

Carlström, A. and H. Lantz Hedström, *Fina Fasader med Fixade Fakturor - Kriminella entreprenader i byggbranschen.* Stockholm, The Swedish National Council for Crime Prevention, Report 2007:18, 2007

Cressey, D. R., *Theft of the nation. The structure and operations of organized crime in America.* New York, Harper & Row, 1969

Davidson, R. L., Asian gangs and Asian organized crime in Chicago, In: P. J. Ryan and G. E. Rush, *Understanding organized crime in global perspective. A reader.* Thousands Oaks, Sage, 1997

Duyne, P.C. van, and M.J. Houtzager, Criminal sub-contracting in the Netherlands: the Dutch 'koppelbaas', In: P.C. van Duyne, K. von Lampe, M. van Dijck and J. L. Newell, *The organised crime economy.Managing markets in Europe.* Nijmegen, Wolf Legal Publishers

Duyne, P.C. van and M. Levi, *Drugs and money. Managing the drug trade and crime-money in Europe.* London, Routledge, 2005

Duyne, P.C. van, M. Pheijffer, H.G. Kuijl, Th. Van Dijk and G. Bakker, *Financial investigation of crime. A tool of the integral law enforcement approach.* Nijmegen, Wolf Legal Publishers, 2003

Ekonomifakta. www.ekonomifakta.se, 2010

Estrada, F. Misshandel, In: L., Ekström, *Brottsutvecklingen i Sverige fram till år 2007.* Stockholm, Brottsförebyggande rådet, rapport 2008:23

Expressen. *Svarta pengar blev vita på Casino Cosmopol.* 2007-01-18 *Expressen,* 8 January, 2007a

Expressen. Rekordmånga spelmissbrukare portade från Casino Cosmopol. 2007-01-08. *Expressen,* 18 January, 2007b

Finanspolisens årsrapport 2008, Stockholm, Finanspolisen, 2009

Gaertner, W. and A. Wenig, *The economics of the shadow economy.* Berlin, Springer, 1985

Hall, S., S. Winlow and C. Ancrum, *Criminal identities and consumer culture.* Cornwall, Willan Publishing, 2008

Hagstedt, J., L. Korsell, L. and A. Skagerö, In the land of prohibition? Clients and trafficked women in Sweden, In: A. di Nicola et al (eds.), *Prostitution and human trafficking: focus on clients.* New York, Springer, 2009

Henry, S., *The hidden economy. The context and control of borderline crime.* Oxford, Martin Robertson, 1978

Internetstatistik. www.internetstatistik.se, 2010.

Johansen, P. O., *Nettverk i gråsonen. Et perspektiv på organisert kriminalitet.* Oslo, Ad Notam Gyldendal, 1996

Korsell, L., *Ekobrott – utvecklingen av några centrala brottstyper.* Stockholm, The Swedish National Council for Crime Prevention, Report 2002:1, 2002

Korsell, L., *Bokföringsbrott – en studie i selektion.* Stockholm, Stockholm University, 2003

Korsell, L., A theory of selection in response to economic crime. *Monatsschrift für Kriminologie und Strafrechtsreform, Special issue: Crossing the borders. Economic crime from an international perspective,* 2007, no 2-3, 2007, 140-157

Korsell L., Heber, A., Sund, B. and D. Vesterhav, *Narkotikabrottslighetens organisationsmönster.* Stockholm, The Swedish National Council for Crime Prevention, Report 2005: 11, 2005

Korsell, L., J. Skinnari and D. Vesterhav, Organiserat arbete i Sverige. Stockholm, Liber, 2009

Kühlhorn, E. Misshandel, In: L. Dolmén, *Brottsutvecklingen i Sverige 2001-2003.* Stockholm, Brottsförebyggande rådet, rapport 2004:3

Lotteriinspektionen. *Spelmarknadens utveckling i Sverige och internationellt 2009.* Strängnäs, Lotterinspektionen

Larsson, P., *Svarte klipp. Om skatteunndragelser i frisørnaeringen.* Oslo, Norges forskningsråd, 1995

Larsson, P., Up in smoke! Hash smuggling the Norwegian way, In: K. Invaldsen and V. Lundgren Sørli, *Organised crime. Norms, markets, regulation and research.* Oslo, Unipub, 2009

Levi, M., *Regulating fraud. White-collar crime and the criminal process.* London, Tavistock publications, 1987

Motion 2008/09: Ju3. *Motion med anledning av skr. 2007/08:167 Handlingsplan mot prostitution och människohandel för sexuell exploatering*

Naylor, R. T., *Wages of crime. Black markets, illegal finance, and the underworld economy.* Ithaca & London, Cornell University Press, 2004

Paulof, A. and P. Lindström, *Kriminaliseringen av narkotikabruk. En utvärdering av rättsväsendets insatser.* Stockholm, The Swedish National Council for Crime Prevention, Report 2000:21, 2000

Pedersen, S., *The shadow economy in Germany, Great Britain and Scandinavia. A measurement based on questionnaire surveys.* Copenhagen, The Rockwool Foundation Research Unit, 2003

Persson, A., Dolda inkomster och folkbokföringsfel bland nolltaxerade. Skatteekonomiska meddelanden no 52, Solna, The Swedish National Tax Agency, 2006

Persson, A. and H. Malmer, *Svartköp och svartjobb i Sverige. Del 1: Undersökningsresultat.* Solna, Riksskatteverket, Rapport 2006:4, 2006

Punch, M. *Dirty business. Exploring corporate misconduct. Analysis and cases.* London, SAGE publications, 1996

Reuter, P. and E. M. Truman, *Chasing dirty money. The fight against money laundering.* Washington D.C., Institute for International Economics, 2004

Rose, R. M., Another deal, another dollar. *Security management*, 2003, vol 47, no 6, 21-127

RRV, *Svart arbete 3. Struktur.* Stockholm, Riksrevisionsverket, Rapport 1998: 29, 1998

Ruggiero, V., *Organized and Corporate Crime in Europe. Offers that Can't Be Refused.* Dartmouth: Aldershot

Shover, N. and A. Hochstetler, *Choosing white-collar crime*. Cambridge, Cambridge university press, 2003

Skatteverket, *Slutrapport uthyrning av arbetskraft, "Svartjobbsgranskning en" 2006-2008*. Stockholm, Skatteverket, 2009

Skinnari, J. and L. Korsell, Svart på rött - statliga kasinon, skattekriminalitet och svart konsumtion, In: SOU 2006:64, *Internationella kasinon i Sverige. En utvärdering*. Stockholm, Fritzes, 2006

Skinnari, J., D. Vesterhav and L. Korsell, *Vart tog alla pengarna vägen? En studie av narkotikabrottslighetens ekonomihantering*. Stockholm, The Swedish National Council for Crime Prevention, Rapport 2007:4, 2007

Skriftlig fråga 2005/06:149. *Brottslighet på svenska kasinon*

SOU, *Branschsanering och andra metoder mot ekobrott*. Report 1997:111 Stockholm, Fritzes, 1997

SOU, *Skärpning gubbar! Om konkurrensen, kvaliteten, kostnaderna och kompetensen i byggsektorn*. Report 2002:115, Stockholm, Fritzes, 2002

SOU, *Internationella kasinon i Sverige. En utvärdering*. Report 2006:64, Stockholm, Fritzes, 2006

Systembolaget, www.systembolaget.se/eng, 2006

SVT. Uppdrag granskning. Penningtvätt på statens egna kasinon. 2005-10-11.

Tham, H., Narkotikakontroll som nationellt projekt. *Nordisk Alkoholtidskrift*, 1992, vol. 9, nr 2, 86-97

Vesterhav, D., J. Skinnari and L. Korsell, *Narkotikadistributörer. En studie av narkotikamarknadens grossister*. Stockholm, The Swedish National Council for Crime Prevention, Rapport 2007:7, 2007

Vesterhav, D., M. Forsman and L. Korsell, *Tillgångsinriktad brottsbekämpning. Myndigheternas arbete med att spåra och återföra utbyte av brott*. Rapport 2008:10, Stockholm, The Swedish National Council for Crime Prevention, 2008

Vesterhav, D., Measures against money laundering in Sweden. The role of the private sector. Forthcoming, 2010

Walsh, M. E., *The fence. A new look at the world of property theft*. Westport, Connecticut, Greenwood press, 1977

Weisburd, D. and Waring, E., *White-Collar Crime and Criminal Careers*. Cambridge, Cambridge University Press

Westfelt, L., *Kasinoetablering, spelvanor och spelproblem – Situationen före och efter etableringen av statliga kasinon i Sundsvall och Malmö*. Delrapport från SoRADs forskningsprojekt, Stockholm, Centrum för socialvetenskaplig alkohol- och drogforskning (SoRAD), 2003

Örnemark Hansen, H. Penningtvätt. Ett urvattnat begrepp? Stockholm, Norstedt Juridik AB, 1998

Ponzi finance and state capture
The crisis of financial market regulation

Nicholas Dorn[1]

Introduction

How can we understand the systemic crisis in global financial markets ('credit crunch') that emerged from 2007 onwards, the frauds that the crisis uncovered, and the failures of financial market regulation? The belated regulatory activism and policy responses of 2008-9, including rescuing private sector actors who had taken unsustainable market positions, remain controversial on both the right and the left: 'socialism for the rich and capitalism for the rest of us' (Caprio, 2009). The crisis and the rescues will have consequences that will be felt for decades. We need tools for understanding the regulators' role in these events and to ask what (if any) room for manoeuvre may exist for future public policies on financial markets.

This chapter attempts a theorisation of the crisis. Three interlocking analyses are explored: on 'Ponzi finance' (asking whether market malfeasance and regulatory tolerance are unfortunate exceptions or are key features of contemporary markets); 'state capture' (a version of regulatory capture theory, extended to take on board the phenomenon of regulatory *rapture*, or political swooning, over financial markets); and the work of sociologist Pierre Bourdieu. Unfashionable as it might be, considerations of social class and of its relation to knowledge, emotions and regulation can help us to understand the structural conditions in which Ponzi finance became a generalised *habitus*, intellectually capturing and emotionally rapturing regulators and policy makers. Such an analysis also guards us from any notion that 'quick fixes' are available: they are not, since both the crisis and the capture that allowed it are historically and politically deep-seated, as this paper seeks to show. In particular, whilst the criminal law is being applied in minor and selective ways, assuaging public outrage by picking off a few sacrificial lambs (for example, Madoff, discussed below), this constitutes a distraction from the task of

1 The author is Professor of International Safety and Governance, Department of Criminology, Erasmus School of Law, Erasmus University Rotterdam.

understanding the wider issues: not simply a few 'rotten apples' but rather systemic failures of financial markets and of their regulation.

In order to meet this conceptual challenge, lawyers, criminologists and other students of harm need to borrow, and to build upon, work in regulatory studies and sociology. In a way, we may take inspiration from the intellectual challenge offered by the so-called 'law and economics' movement (Rowley and Schneider, 2003; 341), which represents the incursion of economic, market thinking into legal and social studies. What is proposed here is the converse: the incursion of the social sciences into market thinking.

The approach taken here no doubt raises as many questions as answers. Some scholars and commentators might protest that financial markets and their governance are best analysed by economists and allied technicians, and that social scientists should stick to traditionally socio-cultural matters. However, any such division of intellectual labour would continue to privilege market-based conceptions of the economy, and private ('expert') discussion of them, undermining wider public debate and political action. Transgression of disciplinary lines is scientifically defensible, and is clearly in the public interest when existing, *mono-disciplinary* approaches have failed to provide policy with a robust knowledge base.

Other scholars and commentators, although broadly sympathetic to the objective of understanding regulatory shortcomings, may not follow certain aspects of the analysis presented here. For example, the notion of 'state capture' is conventionally deployed in relation to less-developed, post-conflict and 'transitional' countries (for example some in Eastern Europe). It may be disconcerting to find it applied to leading market economies and to their most advanced, innovative and profitable sectors. However, one consequence of the global financial crisis is that (further) doubt has been cast on notions of the superiority of western models of governance, potentially opening these up to further scrutiny, even if much remains to be done in order to deepen the analysis.

Ponzi finance: the exception or the rule(s)?

The basic facts about the emergence of the financial crisis are not in dispute. Rapid expansion of financial markets 'assets' from the mid 1990s onwards was followed by even more rapid value loss from 2007. This is illustrated for one bank in Figure 1 below. A similar story can be told in relation to other banks, non-bank entities that have arisen in the international financial system, companies and indeed some countries.

Figure 1

Banking, a visual history: 'assets' and market value

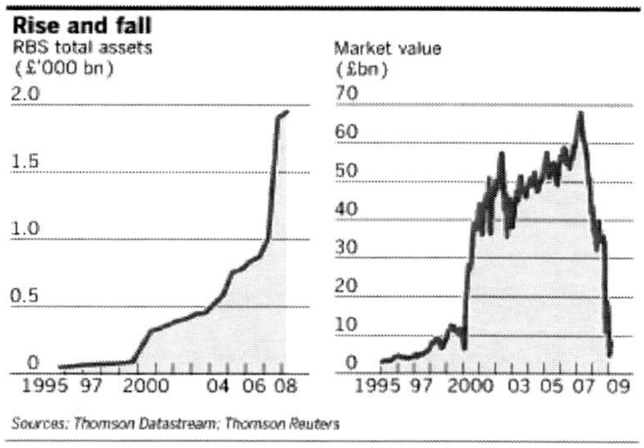

Legend to Figure 1. The first graph shows growth in assets of a particular bank (Royal Bank of Scotland) over a period of aggressive international expansion (acquiring Natwest, ABN Amro and others). The second graph indicates what the market thought about the bank's value, as reflected in its share price, just prior to a government bail-out in February 2009. (Larsen, 2009)

Market innovations in the 1990s included the construction of complex and opaque financial instruments (in US parlance, 'securities') involving high levels of leverage and ever-greater levels of trading – so that eventually the supposed value of these markets greatly exceeded the underlying physical markets that they supposedly referenced (for example mortgages). These globally-disseminated and legal market innovations share the key feature of illegal Ponzi frauds – they can continue until a significant proportion of market participants seek to made withdrawals. Saying this is not to imply widespread fraudulent intent within markets. Rather, from a regulatory point of view, intent is not the issue; effect is the issue. The formal distinction between (i) fraud (passing on unsustainable risk to market participants freshly drawn *into* a scheme) and, (ii) innovation (passing on unsustainable risks to market participants *outside* the scheme) distracted policy-makers and regulators from doing their job. The systemic issue was (un)sustainability of risk, not its distribution.

Ponzi frauds – illegal but inviting

In December 2008, in the midst of the crisis, a very major and long-running fraud came to light at an investment service, Bernard Madoff Investment Securities. Mr Madoff admitted that, over the life of the funds, ten years or more, his investment activity had been "all just one big lie" and "basically, a giant Ponzi scheme". A Ponzi scheme is an investment fraud in which incoming money from new investors is used to pay apparent profits to existing investors. Such a scheme can continue as long as the flow of new investors offsets the payments to existing investors, thus it is vulnerable to any decrease in new investors. This appears to have been the trigger in this case for Mr Madoff to give up. It is possible that, had the financial downturn not triggered investors to draw back some funds in order to cover losses elsewhere, the Madoff fraud might have been able to continue for an even longer time.

There are many features of the Madoff case that should have scared off sophisticated investors, which included not only very rich individuals but also investment firms such as Fairfield Greenwich Group, Man Group and Nomura, as well as many large banks including Santander, BBVD, Union Bancaire Privée, BNP Paribas, Nomura Holdings, Neue Privat Bank, HSBC and Royal Bank of Scotland. For example, some investment managers, who spoke with Mr Madoff at the instigation of clients who were interested in investing with him, were unable to understand the nature of his business and for this reason did not recommended the clients to invest (*Financial Times*, 2008a). (This lack of transparency was widely known in investment circles, however, the same goes for many hedge funds.) Also, Madoff's declared profits were not only high but also remarkably stable from one year to the next, showing none of the ups and downs that characterise most genuine investments. Finally, his operation involved a small staff, several family members and little external oversight – all 'red flags' for fraud that could (should) have alerted the authorities. In short, as the Financial Times put it,

> "*regulators may also have to explain how such a scam could have gone unnoticed for years, especially since Mr Madoff's consistently high returns had previously aroused suspicions and sparked complaints to the SEC [Securities Exchange Commission]. There were other potential red flags: lack of third-party oversight; a very small accounting firm for the size of the operation; his own broker/dealer operation.*"(Financial Times, 2008b)

The Securities Exchange Commission conducted inquiries, finding that some rules were broken in relation to broker-client relations, however it did not forward the issues for enforcement action. What is curious, and what needs to be explained, is that those investigations seemed not to have concerned the matters mention above. Part of the answer may lie in the good repute of Mr Madoff and his firm, his support for charities, his social and political connections (CNBC, 2008) and the fact that the firm took care to involve itself in SEC consultations over rules and regulations (SEC, 2005), as would a reputable firm concerned with regulatory details that might affect its business. Another part of the answer may lie in the ways in which regulators tended to allocate their supervisory and investigation resources – focussing on surveillance of new and smaller firms, on the basis that risk controls there may be below an acceptable standard – whilst allowing longer-established and larger firms to run their own risk assessments. In the wake of the financial market problems, which most definitely involved larger firms, regulators have largely abandoned (Financial Times, 2008c) their previous assumption that big firms do not need much direct oversight.

Ponzi mortgages – the shifting boundaries of legality

The sensational and front-page nature of large alleged Ponzi-type frauds should not divert us from the smaller but much more commonplace forms of fraud (and knowledge of it), the effects of which permeate the financial crisis. Turning to sub-prime mortgages, for example, knowledge of wrong-doing was quite widespread in financial circles. Simply put, too many sales were being made to people who previously would never have dreamt of taking such a contract, with little attempt to check whether they had the means of repayment. It was widely known that, in the event of downturn, mortgage holders could simply return the house keys, then being free of all obligations: hence, purchase was a one-way bet, with an easy exit when/if the market soured. This is what happened to a bundle of 2.393 subprime mortgages that had been rated AAA by the rating agency Moody's.

> "*Usually, people who finance a home stay current on their payments for at least a while. But a sliver of folks in XYZ fell behind within 90 days of signing their papers. After six months, an alarming 6 percent of the mortgages were seriously delinquent. (Historically, it is rare for more than 1 percent of mortgages at that stage to be delinquent.) Moody's monitors properties lacked sod [grass lawn] or landscaping, and keys remained in the mailbox: the buyers had never moved in. The implication was that people had bought homes on speculation: as the housing market turned, the buyers walked. [. . .] In April 2007, Moody's announced it was revising the model it used to evaluate subprime mortgages. [. . .] Amy Tobey began to make inquiries with the lender and were shocked by what they heard. Some, leader of the team that monitored XYZ, told me, "It seems there was a shift in mentality; people are treating homes as investment assets." Indeed. And homeowners without equity were making what economists call a rational choice; they were abandoning properties rather than make payments on them.*" (Lowenstein, 2008, p 1)

Mortgage fraud was rife in the United States in particular in the mid-2000s, being driven by investor demand for securitised products; by the fees to be made by those who sold the mortgages to the retail purchasers; and by the slowness of the authorities to stem what were (in retrospect at least) millions of abuses.

> "*The shortfall in mortgage servicing from this sub-prime lending should have been anticipated by the originators and by the arranger who acquired the stream of payments and structured them; it was not a random shock. Some have rightly stressed the agency problems involved: in effect arguing that some originators and arrangers knew but did not care that they were selling on substandard products.*" (Honohan, 2008, p 20)

If so many observers knew that there was fraud or at least misrepresentation in the system (or could have known had they enquired) then why was insufficient action taken by the regulators to restrain these fraudulent practices? One answer would be that these frauds were structurally quite similar to wider phenomena in the financial markets: presenting the financial situation in unduly favourable terms. Many sectors of the economy including energy, communications and environmental services have seen high-profile business embarrassments, difficulties and collapses from the 1990s onwards, including Enron, Xerox, Waste Management, Cisco Systems, AOL Time Warner, Tyco, WorldCom and Ahold (Markham, 2003). Most of these have involved attempts, through improper accounting, to give the impression that companies' profits were more stable than in fact they were, with a general attempt to represent overall profits as higher than in fact they were. Two techniques of income smoothing and income manipulation commonly used from the 1990s onwards were 'channel stuffing' (inflating earnings in one period by shipping more goods than could reasonably have been sold in that period – this is effectively borrowing sales from the future), and 'cookie jar reserves' (putting profits into a reserve fund against future liabilities, where no such liabilities exist, allowing that income to be realised in a future period when sales might be slower) (Markham, 2003, p 773-775). The numbers of accounting restatements, reflecting such practices, ballooned from the late 1990s onwards. Some commentators have argued that such practices were provoked in part by performance-related pay and bonuses for senior management, which created a corporate culture sympathetic to the idea of steady and rising income and profits streams. Critical commentators also draw attention to de-regulation in the Reagan years, which include relaxation of accounting rules (Coffee, 2002). This implies that de-regulation should be reversed. Others argue, somewhat to the contrary, that a cure for misrepresentations and frauds would be to further relax disclosure requirements upon companies, thus promoting a free market in disclosures regimes – from which 'menu', investors could choice according to their notions of and appetite for risk (Markham, *op cit*; 795 *et seq*.). Leaving aside such prescriptions, most commentators agree that rather shady practices became almost normalised amongst companies from the 1990s onwards. Some point out that something similar may have happened to accountancy firms (Sikka, 2008).

The wider financial markets – lawful but awful[2]

Turning to wider theories of capitalist development, there is a body of thought that sees economies as going though successive waves of crisis, as speculative over-borrowing is followed by panic selling. Followers of the thought of (now deceased) Hyman Minsky refer to so-called 'Minsky Moments' – crisis points during which even cautious investors are forced to sell good assets in order to pay back their loans. These are seen as intrinsic characteristics of market economies.

> "*The first theorem of the financial instability hypothesis is that the economy has financing regimes under which it is stable, and financing regimes in which it is unstable. The second theorem of the financial instability hypothesis is that over periods of prolonged prosperity, the economy transits from financial relations that make for a stable system to financial relations that make for an unstable system. In particular, over a protracted period of good times, capitalist economies tend to move to a financial structure in which there is a large weight to units engaged in speculative and Ponzi finance.*" (Minsky, 2003, p 203)

What Minsky meant by this is that conservatively-operated financial units – meaning ones that can meet their payment obligations out of their cash flows – become edged out of the market by more 'speculative' units, and by the even more adventurous 'Ponzi' traders.

- In 'speculative' finance, cash-flows from the business are insufficient to meet operating needs, and so periodically there is a need to issue new debt. The financial health of such firms (or sectors) is contingent on continuation of benign market conditions, which condition however the speculative units themselves may undermine. Speculative finance occupies a middle ground between conservatively managed forms and Ponzi units.
- In 'Ponzi finance' debtors are paid out of new income from new investors. There may be little or no cash generation within the business (expenses outweigh any profits). However, by using investors' money in a circular manner, the unit can give an appearance of financial viability and can continue to attach the investment it needs in order to continue. This is inherently very unstable. Madoff's firm seems to have been such an operation.

---

2 Regarding the subheading 'lawful but awful', the author acknowledges Passas, 2005.

Minsky suggests that periods of stability lull market players (and regulators) into thinking that the stability is an inherent and defining aspect of the financial system.[3] In such a situation, more risky financial tactics are adopted, as investors believe that they can have high profits without risk (risk having been 'banished' in this sphere of stability). More speculative patterns emerge and, as this way of thinking spreads from the professional investment world to the whole population, Ponzi styles of investment become generalised. Minsky (*op cit*, 203) says that 'the greater the weight of speculative and Ponzi finance, the greater the likelihood that the economy is a deviation-amplifying system'.

The suggestion is that, far from being a departure from market norms, Ponzi schemes become the emerging norm at a certain (turning) point in the cycle (Wray, 2008, 15). This perspective has until recently been of little interest to orthodox economists, however, it appears to be an idea whose time has come.

> "*Markets are ruled by fear and greed, they say, but those two ingredients are not the whole recipe: ideas play a part, too. And, as all bankers worth their Blackberry know, the current big idea is the 'Minsky moment'*" (Guardian, 2007).

Whether in the longer terms Minsky's views will become mainstream economic theory, as well as the stuff of newspaper headlines, remains to be seen. Not all economists – indeed not all lawyers – would be happy with a blurring of the distinction between, on the one hand, frankly criminal Ponzi schemes and, on the other hand, highly-levered financial speculation that attract some civil fraud claims but not action under criminal law. Nevertheless, ideas can have their own effects,[4] and from 2007 onwards the belief that a 'financial meltdown' was occurring became one of the drivers of that process (just as, previously, the belief that markets could only go up was one of the drivers pushing it up).

Nevertheless, the question remains, why were these issues *previously* dismissed as minority views – why did the regulators not see the problems coming? The debate as of 2008-2009 revolved around two big issues, how (if it is at all possible) to stabilise the financial system, and what to do about the regulators. The view from the markets and from policy-makers seems to be that the first priority must be to take action to arrive at systemic stability – after which one might have a debate to what to do about the regulators. This might seem pragmatic, however it assumes that the regulators, mildly reformed or reconfigured, could be capable of

3 See for example talk in the 1990s of a 'new financial paradigm' and, in the 2000s, of 'the great moderation', underpinned by market innovation and/or regulatory fine-tuning. "One of the most striking features of the economic landscape over the past twenty years or so has been a substantial decline in macroeconomic volatility" (Bernanke, 2004)

4 Self-fulfilling hypotheses in the social sciences are roughly equivalent to 'performativity' in economics, see Callon, 2007.

understanding and dealing with the problems. This assumption might not be safe, for reasons now explored.

State capture: private models for public regulation

Conflicts of interest arise when a policy-making system, a regulator or a part of the private sector on which regulators may rely for information – ratings agencies, for example – have both a private interest in a matter, and perform a public duty, leading to the possibility that these might clash (Davis and Stark, 2001). When conflicts of interest are institutionalised – as they have become in financial market regulation, as the regulators became dependent on private sector thinking, 'models', data and mood – then the situation becomes one of 'regulatory capture' by the market: the thinking of regulatory agencies is structured by the thinking of the market. When this situation is not only accepted but also encouraged by governments in major financial centres, then one can talk of state capture, just as when any private interest circumscribes state policy.

The ratings agencies

Following recognition of the crisis, it is now recognised that conflicts of interest have been very widespread. For example, the chairman of the US Federal Reserve has said (albeit unfortunately several years too late) that "*We [regulators] will review our own use of credit ratings as a risk metric*" (Bernanke, op cit, p 4). The reliance of the regulators on the ratings agencies is one of the most obviously egregious aspects of current situation.

> "*Ratings agencies have been subject to a great deal of criticism because their primary purpose is to evaluate the risks of the products or entities that they rate. They seem to have done badly in rating structured financial products, and the agencies themselves are reviewing their processes. A major worry is the potential conflict of interest they face because rating agencies are well rewarded for rating structured finance products.*" (Mizen, 2008, p 561)

Not only did the regulators allow the ratings agencies to develop and maintain client-friendly methods that sent to the market so positively-biased signals (the ratings agency only got business and got paid if they could give a rating acceptable to the ratee). More troubling is that the US authorities built into regulatory standards a requirement that certain categories of market participants must take account of ratings from state-licensed agencies – and licensed a very small number of rating agencies.[5] In short:

> "*Regulatory deference or outsourcing facilitated the manipulation of both the information inputted into models and the selection and design of models to justify predetermined [rosy] decisions [and so] subverted risk management principles and corrupted risk models.*" (Gerding, 2009, 10)

The result was that many institutional investors, including pension funds and the like, instead of making in-depth enquiries of their own, all followed the samc advice – thus ensuring a 'Gadarene swine' effect, deepening collective risk and the depth of the eventual crisis.

> "*Too much homogeneity among risk management strategies among financial institutions can increase systemic risk. If firms have the same strategies and similar portfolios, market shocks can cause the firms to sell the same types of assets at the same time to cover their positions. A widespread sell-off would cause values of these assets to plummet and trigger a sell-off of yet another class of assets. Homogeneity of risk management and models can thus lead to spiraling market declines. There has [been] some concern that this is already occurring in the subprime crisis; prices of certain less risky assets have plummeted, as financial firms sell off 'good assets' to cover their losses on the 'bad'. At first blush, it may seem odd that firms can have homogenous risk models and risk management practices. But, widespread reliance on rating agency's ratings operating with similar models and with a similar financial stimulus toward upward rating can create this homogeneity.*" (Gerding, 2009, p 64-65)

Moreover, the regulators in part constructed their own worldview from such data. It must be expected, in any regulatory system, that day-to-day working relations between firms and the regulator, friendship, alliance and criss-crossing career paths form a close net of shared orientations and forms of knowledge. However, the regulators' formal reliance on the same worldview, risk methodologies and market data as that used by market actors must deepen systemic risk. Even allowing for high levels of professionalism and commitment to independence, still the regulators were captured in terms of their knowledge base. 'Groupthink' developed.

Problems with the ratings agencies have led many commentators (including some in the European Commission) to call for more effective regulation of the rating agencies. This seems to imply a more coordinated approach. However,

5 For an attack on the relationship between the state and the ratings agencies, written a decade before the crisis, see Partnoy, 1999. http://ssrn.com/abstract=167412.

other commentators have taken the opposite approach, advocating deregulation and more competition in the provision of risk information, on the basis that multiple sources and methods of calculating risk would improve quality (White, 2009, 8). The present author has made a broadly similar suggestion in relation to the structure of strategic (not operational) police intelligence in the European Union (Dorn, 2009c). Be that as it may, the creation of such a narrow information base has been such a key element in risk assessment practices that possibly *any* radical change would be an improvement – whether that is the 'freeing' of information on risk, or its tighter control by the state.

Two practices of the ratings agencies that have attracted particular commentary are their (a) *optimistic ratings* (over and above the positive bias that characterises analysts' ratings in general), and (b) *symbols* (AAA mortgage-backed bonds were seen by the market as meaning something similar to AAA sovereign debt, for example US Treasury bonds) (Mizen, 2008, p 563). Some commentators have said however that 'the market was not fooled' by this symbolism (Danielsson, 2008, p 14). Market professionals perfectly understood that an AAA rating on a quite new and highly structured product referred to a comparison within that category of product, rather than being equivalent to dissimilar, longer-established products that promised a lower rate of return (*ibid*). The implication is that the ratings agencies used the same symbol because this allowed the highly structured products to be sold to a wider base of (risk-averse) investors, who were lured by these symbols of safety. Fund managers, who throughout the 1990s were under pressure to improve performance – to attain so-called 'alpha' or out-performance – 'bought the story'. Their high demand in turn stimulated the invention and supply of new securities, etcetera. The regulators presided over this process.

When the market finally 'turned', regulators blamed problems at the retail (so-called 'origination') end of the securitisation process: fickle and irresponsible lenders and loan-takers were portrayed as being responsible for the financial crisis. Yet an alternative (or complementary) view, as put forward by Coffee and Sale, is that retail investors were drawn in by the promotion of debt, which was created on an ever-increasing scale by financial institutions, in order to generate the considerable fees involved (Coffee and Sale, 2008, p 19). During the same period, financial market regulators observed, and allowed, the emergence of other new, 'innovative' markets that, being new, were outside the scope of existing regulation. New and largely unregulated spaces were opening up, not only the (in)famous Hedge Funds (speculative investment vehicles) but also 'off balance sheet' financial vehicles of the banks (spinning off subsidiary entities, into which the banks' debt was put, thus keeping the debt off banks' own balance sheets: see below).

Where were the regulators?

Why did the regulators not enlarge the scope of regulation in order to bring these activities within the net?[6] Possibly because they were preoccupied with competition between national financial centres and interests. Market participants may be involved in 'jurisdictional shopping' (also called 'regulatory arbitrage'), relocating trading operations to less burdensome regulatory centres (Prentice, 2005). Thus, although regulators were fully aware that much or most of the international financial system was escaping regulation, there were pressures upon them, both from the market and from policy-makers, not to bring regulation to the new market spaces and products. Off-balance-sheet-vehicles emerged as a way for banks to get round the capital adequacy rules required by the Basle I regime for bank regulation: by transferring debt and risk to a wholly-owned subsidiary, the beneficial owners of banks were able to continue to take on risk. Additionally, even on-balance measures of bank debt shot up in the period to 2008. In the US, regulatory reforms encouraged this for the biggest financial institutions (Coffee and Sale, 2008, 20-21). Regulatory competition may have been a factor (De Fontnouvelle *et al*, 2005), as US traders and regulators sought to minimise the extent to which US traders would be subjected to European regulation (Dierick, 2004). Also, European banks took on more risk. For example, as one economist and journalist put it:

> "*UK bank assets jumped from a manageable twice gross domestic product in 2001 to almost 4,5 times by 2008. These, then, are [like] undercapitalised hedge funds with liabilities large enough to destroy the solvency of the British state. What on earth were the authorities thinking?*" (Wolf, 2008, 9)

The situations in other European countries varied somewhat, however, the general trend has been the same in all. When one considers the regulators' tolerance of banks building up such large debts *on* their balances sheets, alongside ballooning *off-balance*-sheet debts, then it is clear that the deregulatory trend in this period was strong.

Meanwhile, the rules (sometimes rather loose and amorphous understandings, as it turned out) for wholesale trading in levered debt instruments were made by

---

6 Regulatory quietism obviously cannot be analysed in terms of explanations (familiar to criminologists and others) such as 'bureaucratic interest', or 'moral crusade', or 'criminology of the other' – all such concepts having been formulated in order to explain instances of regulatory or policing *activism* (defining new 'problems', in order to claim a higher level of reassures, expansion and power). Much social theory (following Foucault) and criminological theory (á la Garland) have been preoccupied with questions of whether and how the state organises the private sphere (through the creation of subjectivities and categories, through surveillance and responsibilisation).

private associations, not by regulators. It seems that the view of the regulators was that, where trading occurred between large and sophisticated firms, who should be capable of assessing their own 'risk appetite', they and their private associations could be left to self-regulate in relation to derivatives and other highly levered products such as CDS (credit default swaps, essentially a form of insurance against default on an underling instrument, such as a bond issued by a company or a country).

As finance law academics Coffee and Sale (2008) observe, 'the unique fact about financial institutions in general, and investment banks in particular, is their fragility'. This is because:

> "*They [financial institutions] finance their business using short-term [borrowed] capital to hold long-term illiquid assets. This mismatch exposes investment banks to liquidity crises, and, as the crisis mounts, their counter-parties back away and refuse to trade with them. This has happened before cyclically, well within the memory of the chief executives running these institutions. Then as now, the SEC [Security and Exchange Commission, US regulator] was not effective in dealing with this problem.*" (Coffee and Sale, 2008, p 29)

Characteristically, financial institutions borrow, sometimes on a day-to-day basis, in order to have enough finance to cover the longer-term obligations. Every now and again there is a shortage or withdrawal of that short-term finance and then there is a problem ('crisis').

Alongside reliance on ratings for purposes of regulation of wise investment choices, and for their own worldview, the regulators came to rely on private sector risk models in relation to banks' needs for capital reserves. Martin Hellwig recounts that, when in 1993 the Basel Committee on Banking Supervision consulted on a standard approach to bank capital requirements, "*the banking industry responded with intensive criticism, arguing that such regulation would represent a step back from the very sophisticated risk management procedures that they themselves had started to implement on the basis of quantitative models*" (Hellwig, 2008, p 54). The banks won and their 'model based' approach was codified 1996. Hellwig suggests that, although the standard approach was 'clumsy' in comparison with the risk management methods that the banks were already using, something was lost at this point.

> "*[I]n this discussion, the notion that there is a difference between private interests and the public interest in risk management and risk control of a bank seems to have been lost. I think of this process as regulatory capture by sophistication. The question of how to protect the public interest against possible flaws in the quantitative risk modeling does not seem to have been given much attention. [. . .] Nor was any attention paid to the possibility that the bank's quantitative risk model might be inherently incapable of capturing*

exposures to systemic risk that result from the activities of other institutions [. . .]". (Hellwig, 2008, p 54-55)

The seriousness of this cannot be overstated. How then did the banking industry convince regulators to put individual private interests before collective private and public interests? Hellwig suggest that public policy makers were influenced by consideration of the competitive advantage that might accrue to their countries' banks.

"*In particular, for countries with banking institutions at the forefront of change, most prominently the United States, the introduction of the option to rely on the banks' own model-based approaches to risk assessment (rather than on a stricter regulatory requirements) seemed like a chance to have 'their' institutions benefit from their advantages in global competition in newly developing markets. Even if many bank regulators involved in the negotiations with the banks may have had their doubts about the change, the political environments from which they came provided them with little leeway to express these doubts, let alone have them prevail in the international deliberations.*" (*ibid*)

And in relation to derivates such as futures:

"*A similar logic may have been at work in the late nineties when Federal Reserve Board Chairman Greenspan, Treasury Secretary Rubin, and Securities and Exchange Commission Chairman Levitt, all three of them with strong ties to the investment banking community, used their influence to stop attempts to bring derivatives trading into the domain of statutory regulation* [. . .]. (*ibid*)"

The fundamental issue here is that the regulators should have their own requirement for strategic information. This follows from the point of view of regulators' ability to take an evidence-based view on the level of collective risk in parts of the international financial system. Then they have to build up an understanding of systemic risk in the system as a whole, through consideration of the interlocking of risks between counterparties. It is the regulators who should define the risk models and methods to be used by the private sector, and they should define what data to be supplied to them. That this very basic requirement of governance was let slip suggest that the regulatory system as a whole was improperly influenced by special interests. If power is knowledge, then the regulators rendered themselves powerless and blind.

Explanations given by regulators as why in the recent past they pursued a style of regulation that is now seen as insufficient revolve around three points: (a) the regulators now see that their acceptance of, and reliance upon, private sector assumptions and models was a mistake; (b) this mistake was part of the 'light touch regulation' (in some financial markets) or lack of regulation in others (for example in derivatives markets in the US and in 'over the counter' transactions between financial institutions); but (c) these mistakes were driven by policy makers. In an exchange before the Treasury Select Committee in the UK House of Commons in February 2008 this was characterised as a 'Nuremburg defence' – that we do X and Y because our masters tell us to.

> "*Lord Turner [chairman of the UK financial market regulator, the FSA] has just given evidence to the Treasury Select Committee and his words may not be exactly welcomed in Number 10 [the Prime Minister's official residence] and the Treasury. Essentially, the new FSA chairman said that political "pressure" for "light touch regulation" was partly to blame for fuelling the current banking crisis. [. . .] "a philosophy of regulation which was in retrospect mistaken". [. . .] "That existed within a political philosophy where all the pressure on the FSA [regulator] was not to say "are you looking more closely at these business models?" but to say "Why are you being so heavy and intrusive? Can't you make your regulation a bit more light touch?" [. . .] The MPs were not exactly convinced, with [MP] Michael Fallon claiming Turner was using 'the Nuremberg defence'.*" (Waugh, 2009)

It should be noted that policy makers' subversion of regulatory agencies is just one of several perspectives that may be taken on the relationships between them. The converse perception, to be found in the law and policy literature, is that regulatory agencies are all too eager to alter, widen, narrow or effectively subvert, their purposes (Cohn, 2001), be that for reasons of institutional aggrandisement, market favour and career-making, professional advancement or intellectual preference.

Towards a historical understanding of state capture: collapse of cultural difference

> "*When centrist economists start to blog about Bourdieu, the French structuralist Marxist sociologist, something important is happening.*"(Price, 2009)

Pierre Bourdieu's work helps us to contextualise regulatory failure in terms of a historical shift, from (i) regulatory thinking being grounded in a *tension and balance* between cultural capital (related to traditional and localist ideas about 'club' or gentlemanly regulation) and economic capital (market models and other forms of knowledge developed by private interests), to (ii) the ascendance of the second, lacking cultural restraints. This results in a one-dimensional knowledge base for financial market regulation, opening the door to the misapprehension that private sector knowledge and models are suitable for public regulation. Regulatory rapture induced market over-confidence, herding behaviour, shared blind spots and systemic risk. Crucially, not only market participants but also the regulators themselves come to use the same risk assumptions – derived from private sources.

Bourdieu, a sociologist and more specifically an anthropologist, would have been wary of being called a structuralist (since structuralism implies that things cannot change) or a Marxist (if only because he was too immodest an academic to admit to following anyone, according to one reviewer: Jenkins, 1992). For some contemporary commentators, Bourdieu raises more heat than light, being seen first and foremost as a political activist, a critic of neoliberalism as a programme for the destruction of collective interests. For example, regulator and academic John Braithwaite finds Bourdieu's and others' perceptions of neoliberalism to be just a 'fairy tale' (Braithwaite, 2008). It is certainly the case that in his later life Bourdieu made many public statements hostile to neoliberalism in the sense of deregulation (Bourdieu, 1998) – a sentiment that may have become more widely shared as a result of the crisis in financial markets.

Bourdieu's theoretical apparatus (Bourdieu, 1984, 1993, 1996) is at heart very simple (Allen *et al*, 2000; King, 2005), even if his own expositions are at times abstruse (Jenkins, *op cit*). The key concepts are *forms of capital* (including economic property, social networking and cultural resources); *habitus* (habits derived from background, family and, within and sometimes against these parameters, personal choice); *field* (the space within which the above are deployed); and *reproduction* (of all the above). Capital includes not just static forms of property but also the potential and power of social strata to reproduce and, to some extent, re-invent themselves. Cultural capital stems from sources including family and schooling (a particular focus in Bourdieu's work) and is acquired as tastes and preferences within the circles within which the individual moves, becoming 'second nature' or habitus.

All strata of society are internally differentiated in terms of having more or less economic capital and cultural capital, those at the top of the tree having more of both than those lower down. Concerning the relationships between economic and cultural capital, the former may be traded for the latter (elite schooling being an important mechanism, especially in Bourdieu's time, see his 'The State Nobility', 1996). Once acquired, cultural capital can be deployed in order to 'open doors'. For example, in former times, getting a job in the City of London was easier for those whose possession of culture meant that they could be expected to 'fit in'. Thus, in certain circumstances, there can a circular relationship between cultural capital (being 'cultured' and respectable, having 'taste' and 'good manners') and economic capital (a seat on the Board).

On the other hand, historically Bourdieu observed something of a struggle between, on the one hand, traders possessing economic capital (for example, the *nouveau riche*) – and, on the other hand, certain historically constructed notions of good taste, breeding and cultural capital. Cultural and economic capital kept each other in check, even as they intermingled. Thus, financial market regulation might be based in part on cultural considerations of 'the done thing', as well as on 'vulgar' market calculation – as illustrated for the UK by the tale about the Governor of the Bank of England ruling out certain behaviour by the merest twitching of his eyebrows. A silly story perhaps, however it nicely epitomises what a number of eminent scholars of government and regulation have called 'club' regulation (Marquand, 1988; Moran, 2003, 2006; Vogel, 2008). Prior to the 1970s in the UK, checks and balances were provided (to some extent) by the availability of cultural reservoirs of tastes, knowledge and power underpinning rather localist, sectorally specific and indeed idiosyncratic forms of club regulation.

However, that precarious balance between economic and cultural capital was destroyed in the UK in the 1970s, as financial elites turned outwards and began to network globally for their cultural and economic reference points. At that point, economic capital as a way of thinking and social reproduction got the upper hand over cultural capital, leaping across social classes – finance capital, packagers, intermediary strata (retailers) and purchasers – there being inadequate (traditional) checks and balances at any social level, or between levels. The new men did not understand the eyebrows of Governor of the Bank of England; indeed the eyebrows themselves no longer twitched quite as they had done traditionally. As club regulation, with its particularistic cultural preferences, was historically undermined, so a double victory was achieved by economic capital: ascendancy both within national boundaries and across them.

In the UK and subsequently many other countries with the notable exception of the US, this homogenisation was taken further through the creation of a single regulator.[7] As economic capital as a corpus of knowledge and 'common sense' displaced cultural capital and club regulation, so the state *nominally* took charge, whilst in practice ceding the lead to private sector influences. As this shift progressed, so regulation changed – from sectoral, club, self-regulation (although that is really much too individualist a term), to greater attentiveness to the wishes of international firms (Briault *et al.*, 1997). In the new context, Ponzi finance flourished and regulatory capture become institutionalised.

7 As of 2009, considerable energy was being expended on the prospects for fine-tuning these structural arrangements, see *inter alia* Pellerin et al, 2009.

Conclusion

Levels of analysis: ponzi, capture, culture

Cutting across distinctions between economic and social analyses, this chapter explores three levels of analysis of the recent systemic instability in financial markets and the complicity of market regulators. Ponzi finance is most commonly invoked in its 'exception' version: malfeasance is the exception, rather than the rule(s). According to that version, frauds by market participants and corruption of regulators are unfortunate but isolated events, which need to be criminally prosecuted and/or civilly contested. In a more 'cynical' version, fraud and corruption are widespread, because of market innovation, which continuously creates new and unregulated market spaces, within which greater risk and rewards may be pursued. This vision blurs the line between exceptional wrong-doing and systemic innovation. It does not point to a solution – it risks becoming dissipated into moral outrage and cynicism – arguably not a good basis for citizens' greater involvement in debate on market regulation. However, a sensitivity to Ponzi finance does raise questions about continuities between financial market innovation, specific frauds, governance and the wider crisis.

The second level of analysis is capture/rapture, here meaning not capture by the market of particular staff or sections within financial market regulators, but rather a wider process of intellectual capture of the framework thinking, *and mood*, of regulators, central banks and state treasury departments. Capture/rapture is a sign of the reversal of the familiar and comfortable notion of public-private cooperation and governance (and of associated social and criminological theory, see for example Garland, 2002). Capture/rapture is a marker of the dominance of private-public dynamics (private interests in the ascendancy and leading the public interest). As demonstrated by recent events, private interests regulate the regulatory bodies, their thinking, models, data and rule making. The challenge is whether it could be possible to reverse this state of affairs.

The wider structural pre-conditions which facilitated the emotional as well as intellectual capture of regulation and policy have been explored here by making selective used of Bourdieu's concepts. The historical ascendance of economic capital over cultural capital – using these terms not just in terms of power but also in terms of knowledge and emotion – adversely impacted the intellectual resources available to people in the private sector, as well as in government and the regulatory agencies. By the beginning of the second millennium, 'good taste' and 'the done thing' had been relegated to cultural history, leading private sector managers and regulators to share a single culture. The lack of diversity of backgrounds, cultures and worldviews resulted in intellectual convergence, a lack of the capacity for challenge, and a captive (indeed rapturous) regulatory environment, so reinforcing the tendency for market 'herding'. On these grounds, the prospects for the reform of regulation look somewhat glum. Looking forward, are there any alternatives?

A restoration of nineteenth Century and early twentieth Century class and cultural contours is hardly feasible, even were it to be desirable. Another stumbling block is that Bourdieu's analysis of cultural capital being quintessentially European, the implications for *international* financial regulation do not flow smoothly. What needs to be found is some other moorings that might replace historically defunct cultural resources for intellectual challenge and systemic stability. There seem to be two (somewhat contradictory) possibilities: democratisation and globalisation.

More active democratic steering of regulatory policy – politicisation of issues hitherto regarded as technical and as the private possession of experts – would open up the possibility of regulatory challenge and diversity. Local political constituencies can be expected to differ in their understanding of the issues, and in their policy preferences, opening up the prospect of diversity in regional and national regulatory regimes. Hitherto, financial regulation has 'floated off' from its potential moorings in democratic politics. Had financial regulators at national and/or regional (eg, EU) levels been held democratically accountable (through elected representatives, even by referenda on controversial issues), then inevitably regulators would have been somewhat constrained from convergence with their market constituencies at international level. For the future, the strategy of democratic steering may become interesting, although it must be admitted that signs of its emergence in a robust form are rather few (Dorn, 2009a, 2009b, 2010).

The second but possibly determinant factor, is the rocky road of globalisation. As the influence of western financial centres wanes (as a result not only of their financial losses but also of the reputational damage they have incurred), newer financial centres based in and across other countries and regions are coming more to the fore. So the prospects are opening up for a new global patchwork of market and regulatory mentalities, having one foot in diverse local political conditions and one in the global markets. The consequences for financial regulation are highly contingent and there is no reason in general to think that such developments would lessen systemic risk: doubtless new crisis tendencies will emerge.

Beyond crime and punishment

The reader of a book on cross-border crime and inroads on integrity might well now ask how such an analysis of the financial crisis and of regulatory failure/capture fits in with traditional notions of crime, including 'organised crime'. The frank answer is that the fit is poor: but why is that? Possibly it is because, over the years in which the financial crisis has been brewing, 'organised crime' functioned as an attention-deflecting device, in two senses. First, it directed attention to those outside the financial markets, who might 'penetrate' them (Mafioso, etc); second, 'organised crime' as a concept directed attention to criminality, as defined in criminal law. Yet, where were the greatest harms actually being created? As the present author has argued elsewhere, the financial crisis was created through conflicts of interest and through capture in locations where the criminal law and 'organised crime' were least present:

> "*It is received wisdom that the locus of corruption is outside the EU and US – for example, eastern Europeans siphoning off a proportion of incoming funds and using political influence and/or the courts to slow down investigators. Meanwhile, however, US Treasury people run round financially significant capitals, urging public and private investors to prop up US financial 'institutions' that built a huge Ponzi scheme through encouragement of unsustainable mortgage debt, repackaged it as 'bonds' and the like and sold it on to the unwary.*" (Dorn, 2008)

Although what has occurred in global financial markets seems (and largely remains) *like* a Ponzi scheme (in the sense that new investors' funds were used to pay off old investors – see preceding sections), most of what occurred was entirely legal: lawful but awful, to borrow again the phrase of Passas (2005). As the present author has put it:

> "*Let's leave aside for a moment the legal question of how widespread criminal frauds have been in the creation of the crisis: part of the dark beauty of the current mess is that, in terms of law, financial regulation and rule-following, much of what transpired was allowable, indeed for many years it was regarded as smart. Criminal prosecutions will occur only in minor and the most egregious cases, although some civil actions may dig deeper and more profitably. Being smart meant being in a position to write and interpret the financial rulebook so that one could create a bubble, on the bursting of which one calls in the taxpayers of west and east – if they are remain amenable, in the face of what to some may seem like an extortion racket in which they are invited to pay more to decrease the already unknown chance of not losing what they already paid.*" (Dorn 2008)

For some, the question may arise of whether (and if so, how) to criminalise at least some aspects of the conduct that led to the financial crisis. That debate is part of a broader one on criminalisation of the harms of capital. For the present author, however, such discussion is irredeemably idealist, meaning that 'it ain't gonna happen': one would have to attack not isolated individuals but whole social swathes. In reality, the opposite has happened, with the responsible institutions and social class being re-capitalised at public expense. Neither are we likely to see regulators or policy-makers prosecuted criminally for their roles in the financial crisis: even civil actions against regulators seems largely absent (as of late 2009), Yes, there is public anger, but trying to stoke it higher is likely to result in bringing down just a few vulnerable individuals, whilst further distracting attention from the historical dynamics that have brought us to this juncture.

The global financial crisis – its historical roots in social class and cultural shifts, the phenomenon of state capture by the mentality of financial markets, the resulting regulatory failure, and the resulting social injustices and harms – all this is yet another illustration of the limitations and superfluity of the concept of 'organised crime' as an academic and policy project (Dorn 2009c). The largest social and economic harms will always escape the label of crime (organised or otherwise), leaving us just a few wretched sacrificial victims (like Bernard Madoff).

A deeper analysis is required. Ponzi finance *as a generalised, global system of finance* is the historical child of market and class developments over the past decades. Financial market regulation has been shown up as being more like the midwife for dangerous 'innovations' in financial markets, than as a gatekeeper. Meaningful reforms will not be achieved through legal actions, be they criminal or civil, nor by extending the reach of the criminal law. (As for changes in regulatory institutions and rules, the reader is invited to follow the limited progress expected from 2010 onwards.) On the wider canvass, changes in markets and in their regulation will occur as part of wider geo-political processes, involving the de-centring of western power and the rise of new historical forces (including 'class' forces, for those wishing to try to integrate that aspect into the social and cultural analysis). Our hope is that the concepts employed here – Ponzi-like finance, state capture and collapse of cultural difference – may provide useful levers for future analysis of financial market regulation, crises and crime.

References

Allen, D., E. McGoun and G. Kester, A sociological explanation of financial market growth. *International Review of Financial Analysis*, 2000, vol. 9, 421-432

Bernanke, B., *The great moderation*. Remarks by Governor Ben S. Bernanke at the meetings of the Eastern Economic Association, Washington, DC, 20 February 2004 http://www.federalreserve.gov/BOARDDOCS/SPEECHES/2004/20040220/default.htm

Bourdieu, P., Cultural reproduction and social reproduction. In Brown, R (ed.), *Knowledge, education and cultural change*, London; Tailstock, 1993

Bourdieu, P., *Distinction: A social critique of the judgment of taste*. London: Routledge, 1984

Bourdieu, P., *The state nobility: elite schools in the field of power*. Stanford: Stanford University Press, 1996

Bourdieu, P., The essence of neoliberalism. *Le Monde Dipomatique*, 1998, http://mondediplo.com/1998/12/08bourdieu

Braithwaite, J., *Regulatory capitalism: how it works, ideas for making it work better*. Cheltenham: Edward Elgar, 2008

Briault, C., A. Haldane and M. King, Independence and accountability. In I. Kuroda, (ed.), *Towards more effective monetary policy*. London: Macmillan, 1977

Callon, M., What does it mean to say that economics is performative?. In D. MacKenzie, F. Muniesa and L. Suit (eds.), *Do economists make markets? On the performativity of economics*. Princeton: Princeton University Press, 2007

Caprio, G., US bad banks and bad plans: why capitalism requires "nationalisation". *Financial Times economists forum*, 23 February, 2009 http://blogs.ft.com/economistsforum/2009/02/us-bad-banks-and-bad-plans-why-capitalism-requires-nationalisation

CNBC, Madoff was a smooth operator [says] former SEC official. *CNBC*, 2008, retrieved 15 December 2008 from http://www.cnbc.com/id/28237248

Coffee, J., *Understanding Enron: it's about the gatekeepers, stupid*. Columbia Law & Economics Working Paper 207, 30 July 2003 http://ssrn.com/abstract=325240 http://ssrn.com/abstract=325240

Coffee, J. and H. Sale, Redesigning the SEC: Does the Treasury Have a Better Idea?', *Columbia Law and Economics Working Paper, no 342*, November 2008, available at SSRN: http://ssrn.com/abstract=1309776

Cohn, M., Fuzzy legality in regulation: the legislative mandate revisited. *Law and Policy*, 2001, vol. 23, *issue 4*; 469-487, available at SSRN: http://ssrn.com/abstract=942475m

Danielsson, J., Blame the models. In A. Felton and C. Reinhart (eds.), *The first global financial crisis of the 21st century*, 13-16, London: Centre for Economic Policy Research, 2008 http://www.voxeu.org/reports/subprime/report.pdf.

Davis, M. and A. Stark, *Conflict of interest in the professions*. Oxford: Oxford University Press, 2001

De Fontnouvelle, P., V. Garrity, S. Chu and E. Rosengren, *The potential impact of explicit Basel II operational risk capital charges on the competitive environment of processing banks in the United States*. 12 January 2005, Boston: Federal Reserve Bank of Boston, available at the Federal Reserve System http://www.federalreserve.gov/generalinfo/Basel2/docs2005/opriskjan05.pdf

Dierick, F., *The supervision of mixed financial services groups in Europe*. European Central Bank Occasional Paper number 20, August 2004, available at SSRN, http://ssrn.com/abstract=752069.

Dorn, N., European Strategic Intelligence: how far integration? *Erasmus Law Review*, 2008a, vol. 1, *issue 5*, 163-180 http://www.erasmuslawreview.nl/files/issue_5_Article4.pdf

Dorn, N., Just where does the locus of corruption lie? *Financial Times*, letters page, 28 July 2008(b), p. 12, hard copy. Downloadable from http://www.ft.com/cms/s/0/cb11610e-5c3c-11dd-9e99-000077b07658.html

Dorn, N., Financial market systemic regulation: stability through democratic diversity. *VoxEU.org*, 2009a, 18 December 2009; 3. VoxEU.org is a refereed policy portal of the Centre for Economic Policy Research *et al*, funded by the EU. http://www.voxeu.org/index.php?q=node/4411

Dorn, N., Systemic regulators' accountability to parliaments: advantages for stability of global financial markets, 2009b, 30 September 2009; 12, a response to the UK Treasury White Paper on reforming financial markets. Available at http://ssrn.com/abstract=1497505 or with other consultation responses at http://www.hm-treasury.gov.uk/d/rfm_academic_responses.pdf.

Dorn, N., The end of organised crime in the European Union. *Crime, Law and Social Change,* 2009c, vol. 51, *no 2*, 283-295 http://www.springerlink.com/content/7362g96063141748

Dorn, N., The governance of securities: Ponzi finance, regulatory convergence, credit crunch. *British Journal of Criminology*, 2010, vol. 50, *issue 1*, 23-45 (originally published 10 September 2009; 1-23)

http://bjc.oxfordjournals.org/cgi/content/abstract/50/1/23

Financial Times, 'Wealthy lured by apparent history of success', 2008a, retrieved 15 December from: http://www.ft.com/cms/s/0/3f5ea4aa-c87f-11dd-b86f-000077b07658.html

Financial Times, 'SEC under fire over Madoff failings, 2008b, retrieved 15 December from http://ft.onet.pl/0,18622,sec_under_fire_over_madoff_failings,artykul_ft.html

Financial Times, 'Altered remit spurs 'better' regulator', 2008c, 1 December, retrieved 15 December from: http://www.ft.com/cms/s/84e8e3a8-bf49-11dd-ae63-0000779fd18c

Garland, D., *The culture of control*. Oxford University Press, 2002

Gerding, E., The subprime crisis and the outsourcing of financial regulation to financial institution risk models: code, crash, and open source', 25 September 2009 pre-publication draft; 82 http://ssrn.com/abstract=1273467 and forthcoming in Washington Law Review.

Guardian, 'In praise of Hyman Minsky', *The Guardian* (UK newspaper), editorial, 22 August 2007 http://www.guardian.co.uk/commentisfree/2007/aug/22/comment.business

Hellwig, M., *Systemic risk in the financial sector: an analysis of the subprime-mortgage financial crisis*, November 2008. Preprint 43; 75, Bonn: Max Planck Institute for Research on Collective Goods http://www.coll.mpg.de/pdf_dat/2008_43online.pdf

Honohan, P., *Risk management and the costs of the banking crisis*, National Institute Economic Review, 2008, volume 206, *no 1*; 15-24.

Jenkins, R., *Pierre Bourdieu*. London: Routledge, 1992

King, A., Structure and agency. In A. Harrington (ed.) *Modern social theory: an introduction*. Oxford: Oxford University Press, 2005, 215–232.

Larsen, P., Goodwin's undoing. (Press story on ex-Chairman of the Royal Bank of Scotland), *Financial Times*, 24 February 24 2009 http://www.ft.com/cms/s/0/dbcc20aa-02a0-11de-b58b-000077b07658.html

Lowenstein, R., The ratings game. 27 April 2008, *New York Times* (and reprinted in M. Lewis (ed.), *Panic: the story of financial insanity*, 2008, London: Penguin, 2008; 316-329)

Markham, J., Accountants make miserable policeman: rethinking the federal securities laws. *North Carolina Journal of International Law and Commercial Regulation*, 2003, vol. 28, *issue 4*; 725-812

Marquand, D., *The unprincipled society: new demands and old politics*. London Jonathan Cape, 1988

Minsky, H., The financial instability hypothesis. In F. Stilwell and G. Argyrous (eds.), *Economics as a social science: readings in political economy.* (p. 201-203) North Melbourne: Pluto Press, 2003

Mizen, P., The credit crunch of 2007-2008: a discussion of the background, market reactions, and policy responses. *Federal Reserve Bank of St. Louis Review,* 2008, 90; 531–6

Moran, M., *The British regulatory state: high modernism and hyper-innovation.* Oxford & New York, Oxford University Press, 2003

Moran, M., The transformation of the British State: from club government to state-administered high modernism. In J. Levy (ed.), *The state after statism: new state activities in the age of liberalization,* Harvard: University Press, 2006

Partnoy, F., The Siskel and Ebert of financial markets: two thumbs down for the credit rating agencies. *Washington University Law Quarterly,* 1999, vol. 77; 619-712, http://ssrn.com/abstract=167412.

Passas, N., Lawful but awful: 'legal corporate crimes'. *The Journal of Socio-Economics,* vol. 34, *issue 6,* 2005, December, p. 771-786

Pellerin, S., J. Walter and P. Wescott, The consolidation of financial regulation: pros, cons, and implications for the united states. *Economic Quarterly,* 2009, vol. 95, *no 2,* spring; 121–160 https://www.richmondfed.org/publications/research/economic_quarterly/2009/spring/pdf/walter.pdf

Prentice, R., Regulatory competition in securities law: a dream (that should be) deferred. *Ohio State Law Journal,* 2005, vol. 66, *no 6;* 1156-1230, http://moritzlaw.osu.edu/lawjournal/issues/volume66/number6/prentice.pdf

Price, T., Bourdieu & the crisis: leverage your social capital. *Open Democracy.* 28 April 2009 http://www.opendemocracy.net/article/economics/bourdieu-the-crisis-leverage-your-social-capital

Rowley, C. and F. Schneider, *The Encyclopaedia of Public Choice* (chapter on law and economics), New York, Kluwe 2004

SEC, *Final rule: regulation NMS,* 2005, (17 CFR PARTS 200, 201, 230, 240, 242, 249, and 270, Release number 34-51808, File No. S7-10-04), 523 pages, Washington: Securities and Exchange Commission, retrieved 15 December from http://www.sec.gov/rules/final/34-51808.pdf

Sikka, P., *Enterprise culture and accountancy firms: new masters of the universe,* Working Paper 08/01, January 2008, Colchester: University of Essex, Centre for Global Accountability.

http://www.essex.ac.uk/afm/research/working_papers/WP_08-1%20ACCOUNTANCY%20FIRMS%2020Masters%20of%20the%20universe.pdf

Vogel, D., Private global business regulation. *Annual Review of Political Science*, 2008, vol. 11; 261–82

Waugh, P., 'Turner blames bank crisis on Brown's "light touch"', *Evening Standard*, 25 February 2009
http://waugh.standard.co.uk/2009/02/turner-blames-bank-crisis-on-browns-light-touch.html

White, L., Free bond information market from its shackles. Letters page, *Financial Times*, 2009, 25 February 2009, http://www.ft.com

Wolf, M., What to do with Britain's banks? *Financial Times*, 12 December 2008, page 9, retrieved 11 December 2008 from
http://www.ft.com/cms/s/2774a1f0-c7a8-11dd-b611-000077b07658.html

Wray, L., *What can we learn from Minsky?* 2008, Public Policy Brief number 94, New York: The Levy Economics Institute of Bard College; 53, http://www.econ.uoa.gr/UA/files/1663905189..pdf and
http://papers.ssrn.com/sol3/papers.cfm?abstract_id=161024.

Lifting the veil on SOCA and the UKHTC
Policymaking responses to organised crime

Jon Spencer and Rose Broad[1]

Introduction

> "*If 'everybody knows' how things 'really' work, why do the [policy analysis] models persist in leaving out such knowledge, and why do such inaccurate models persist? It would seem that tacit knowledge plays a key role in maintaining supporting silences in public discourse.*" (Yanow 1995:111)

The making of public policy in criminal justice has been a frequent, if not at times, a frenetic activity in the UK over the past two decades. A cursory investigation of public policy highlights the competing dynamics within the production of criminal justice policy. There are different agendas and aims of policy-making: some policies are made to enhance the law and order credentials of a particular minister or government; some policies are made to shore up the weak side of government against focused attacks by opposition parties and yet others constructed to be in step with what is thought to be public opinion. No doubt, some policies are the outcome of 'thoughtful' policy-making. That is: consultative and incremental, what we might term a 'considered' approach to public policy.

This paper takes the issue of crime as a significant area of public policy-making and explores the process of public policy in relation to 'organised crime'. It considers the policy foundations of recent UK responses to organised crime. First, there is a brief consideration of issues of criminal justice policy making. Second, the discussion turns to issues related more specifically to organised crime. Third, the Serious Organised Crime Agency (SOCA) and the United Kingdom Human

1 The authors are respectively director of the Anglo-Baltic Criminological Research Unit, University of Manchester and Research Assistant University of Manchester.

Trafficking Centre (UKHTC) are discussed as a policy-making response to 'organised crime'.

Criminal policy research: Poverty and questions

The *making* of criminal justice policy does not appear to be a significant concern of criminologists. There is little criminological literature that addresses the process of criminal justice policy making. Jones and Newburn (2005) comment on the dearth of analysis in this field and make a contribution that is focused on international policy making. The lack of a literature that focuses on the policy-making process begs the question of whether the discipline of criminology is implicated, by an act of omission, in contributing to the 'supportive silence' (Yanow 1995) that allow prevailing definitions and ideas to persist. As Jones and Newburn (2005) argue the main focus of criminologists in relation to policy making has been on the 'content and impact' of penal policy 'rather than its origins' (Jones and Newburn 2005, p 59). Apparently, political scientists have not identified criminal justice policy-making as an area of research (Jones and Newburn 2005) and so there is little empirical research that can assist in unravelling the dynamics of policy-making in the field of criminal justice. Therefore, in attempting to go one step further and unravel the policy-making dynamic in relation to 'organised crime' we face a paucity of empirical research and analysis of how policy is made in this area.

Policy-making is a process that orders the concerns and what is perceived to be pertinent information into a series of questions and policy is an outcome of how interpretative frameworks are utilised to structure the questions that the policy attempts to answer. Policy is also an attempt to mediate between a range of competing political interests (Turnbull 2006) and so is the consequence of a series of compromises in order to reach a politically viable solution. However, as Turnbull (2006) argues there is a very real difficulty in being able to theorise policy-making because of the uniqueness of each set of policy questions and the variety of policy decisions available. Crime policy is no exception to the difficulties of theorising about policy-making; indeed, crime policy is contentious. Johnstone (2000) argues that current penal policy is subject to a form of penal populism and that this has replaced 'elitist' policy making.

Policy is formulated through a process of asking questions, of accommodating varying political interests and mediating between them, of attempting to secure a resolution to a series of conflicts and in so doing provides anew sets of conflicts that require a policy resolution. Policy direction is in part determined by the social construction of the problem that it is addressing. Importantly policy is not universal but only focuses on those issues that are defined as problematic and deemed to be in need of a policy response. Criminal justice in general and 'organised crime' in particular are areas where there is a surfeit of policy at the national and EU level, and yet there is a lack of policy analysis in the field organised crime and it is getting to grips with this thorny issue that we must now turn.

Unravelling the Policy Dynamic

Levi (2006) has commented that there are particular difficulties in the framing of policy in relation to organised crime:

> "*Almost every country seeking the power to do something about social nuisances – from motorcycle gangs in Canada and Scandinavia to Balkan and Chinese people smugglers – wants the definition of organised crime to include those nuisances.*" (Levi, 2006, p. 823)

This lack of a framework within which to understand what is meant by organised crime results in a fluidity of policy so that one way of understanding the policy-making process is to perceive it as a market and policy-makers are consistently attempting to push the boundaries of the 'market' to achieve policy outcomes that they desire (Levi 2006). In relation to organised crime Van Duyne and Vander Beken (2009) have considered some of the discourse that surrounds such policy, especially in relation to the approach taken by the EU. They argue that the fear of organised crime or the articulation of the threat of organised crime interacts with what can be described as 'knowledge based policy making', much of which seems to be the restructuring of the 'facts' to fit with the articulated fear. To maintain this articulated fear, the pretended 'knowledge based policy making soon degrades to a 'knowledge *denied*' policy-making (Van Duyne and Vander Beken 2009). It is the lack of empirically based knowledge in organised crime policy that is of concern to Van Duyne and Vander Beken (2009). They suggest that policy-makers are engaged in achieving tangible results which are demonstrated through legislative action or apprehending offenders (Van Duyne and Vander Beken 2009)

The formation of policy in part relies on the way in which the substance of the policy is constructed in the public domain. Using the example of sex trafficking, Weitzer explores how many of the current perspectives of this aspect of organised crime are problematic, can be falsified and have acted as a foundation for policy (Weitzer, 2007). Weitzer (2007) considers the role of moral crusades and resulting public perceptions in raising the profile of sex trafficking and consequently leading to policy developments which can be seen to be based on unsubstantiated evidence. It is through establishing 'social evils' (Weitzer, 2007, p. 450) the discourse focuses on particular themes of a given concept. Thus, by emphasising the extent to which the organised crime is a blight on a community, official discourses, the media and the public view organised crime as a 'social evil'. The policy discourse provides a shortcut to what is being referred to without the need to define it.

The structure of the 'organised crime' policy discourse, with its myriad of definitions, has not been challenged within the mainstream of criminal justice policy-making. On the contrary, policy-makers have embraced the dominant discourse and presented policies based on worthy sentiments and political banalities (Van Duyne and Vander Beken 2009). The policy debate in relation to organised crime has not been a rational one but has taken the dominant social constructions of organised crime uncritically. For example the UK government's White Paper *One Step Ahead* (Stationery Office 2004) defined the organised crime problem in the UK in the following terms:

> "*Organised crime reaches into every community . . . It manifests itself most graphically in drug addiction, in sexual exploitation and in gun crime. Its influence corrupts government and law agencies in many states world-wide which desperately need good and honest government as a foundation for economic prosperity, order, security and political liberty.*" (Stationery Office, 2004, p 1)

This wide ranging 'definition' – if it deserves this qualification – of the impact of 'organised crime' demonstrates that the discourse of policy-making is socially constructed to fit more within pre-conceived understandings of organised crime rather than what the research evidence might suggest. This supports Turnbull's view that "*. . . policy problems do not appear in an unambiguous fashion to allow objective, analytical treatment*" (Turnbull, 2006, p 6). What appears to happen in relation to organised crime is a form of policy-making that does not ask questions but relies on commonly held assumptions about organised crime to formulate and implement policy. One consequence of this approach to policy-making is the current structure of the law enforcement response to organised crime in the UK.

The UK government presents a 'joined up' approach to the problem of organised crime. First, they claim to have created a sharper prioritisation of policy and operations through a more efficient use of intelligence that allows for "*. . . a comprehensive understanding of the scale of the problem, and the working methods of organised criminals*" (Stationery Office, 2004). This greater understanding they claim has resulted in better national priorities in tackling the problem of 'organised crime'. The second element of the government's response is the Serious and Organised

Crime Agency (SOCA), a dedicated law enforcement agency that has as a main priority 'the fight against organised crime'. The third policy element is that of co-coordinating police action against serious and organised crime and the fourth element is that of increased police powers to tackle the 'threat'. The final element is that of exploiting existing powers more fully.

The problem with aims such as these is that they lack substance: all of them, except the formation of SOCA, are essentially the rhetoric of policy-making. Such rhetoric makes accessing the policy-making process more problematic as it is one of the elements that makes public scrutiny more difficult. It is unclear on what basis the priorities of policy are established, for as Van Duyne and Vander Beken (2009) argue there is very little that is reliable in the Organised Crime Threat Assessment (OCTA) because of the lack of robustness of the assessment instrument. It is possible that as Van Duyne and Vander Beken (2009) argue the process of policy-making is based on a form of ritualism. One of the main issues of this approach to 'organised crime' is that government policy is designed to deal with the populist social constructions rather than basing a policy approach on what is known. Furthermore, there is such a lack of evidence on the outcomes of policy that they are never properly scrutinised:

> "*The impact of anti-organised crime measures on outcomes in the United Kingdom and elsewhere remains insufficiently analysed, since there are little reliable data on the before or after (a) levels or (b) organisation of drugs and people trafficking, European Union fraud, and so on*" (Levi, 2006, p 847).

This lack of scrutiny of policy outcomes is not surprising given the basis on which policy is developed. It can also be evidenced in practice and research. Levi and Maguire (2004) concluded that there were no structured analyses of the effectiveness of strategies to combat organised crime. In evaluating the activities of law enforcement against organised crime Levi and Maguire (2004) concluded that there was a dearth of structured impact assessments of the strategies and initiatives to deal with 'organised crime' and few attempts to understand the structure and activities of 'organised crime' groups. They conclude that the failure to take an analytic approach resulted in an over concentration on 'operational goals' (Levi and Maguire 2004). This is a serious indictment of the UK government's policy in relation to organised crime. The next section will consider the issues raised here in more detail with special consideration of SOCA and the United Kingdom Human Trafficking Centre (UKHTC).

John Spencer and Rose Broad

The Secrets of Organised Crime Policy

Flawed policy or a failing agency; the case of SOCA

The Serious and Organised Crime Agency (SOCA) was created in 2006 to replace the National Crime Squad (NCS) and the National Criminal Intelligence Service (NCIS). SOCA was not only formed to meet the needs of the UK to tackle organised crime but was congruent with concerns of the EU to develop innovative ways of working towards combating organised crime. According to Harfield (2006) SOCA was intended to introduce into the policing of organised crime an 'intelligence-led' form of policing that was to be effective and efficient in stemming the rise of organised crime through the apprehension of serious criminals, the disruption of their markets and the easier confiscation of their assets (Harfield 2006). The structure and operational remit of SOCA were the subject of a lively debate. It was argued that the introduction of SOCA would be detrimental to the UK traditional model of policing, one that is visible, accountable and local (Harfield, 2005; Bowling and Ross, 2006). The structure of SOCA and the fact that it blurs the boundaries between police and a range of other law enforcement agencies, for example immigration and customs, would allow SOCA to "*. . . undertake their new policing role with unprecedented intrusive and coercive powers*" (Bowling and Ross, 2006, p 36). So for many commentators the main issue concerning the introduction of SOCA was about the extent of its powers and the autonomy of the Director-General. Commentators (Segell 2007, Harfield 2005) also suggested that the creation of SOCA represented a new shift in the way that intelligence services were to be structured and the process of intelligence gathering. As Segell (2007) and Harfield (2005) have noted SOCA, so the official narrative went, would be more open and less shrouded in secrecy. Accountability of SOCA, and the assessment as to whether it meets the aims defined for it, has been complicated by the government's insistence that SOCA is not a police organisation and yet the similarities with the police service suggest that it should be subject to the same scrutiny (Harfield, 2006).

However, the outcome of the introduction of SOCA is much different to that envisaged prior to its introduction. SOCA has been mired in allegations that it is inefficient and ineffective. The tales of SOCA's ineffectiveness are 'legendary' and since its inception it has been subject to periodic press criticism. For example, in 2007, approximately eight months after it was established, SOCA was criticised for not investigating the number of drug cases referred to it by Customs and Excise (The Times 2007). In 2008 there were press reports that were highly critical of SOCA's performance claiming that SOCA's strategy was based on 'flawed intelligence' (The Times, 2008), and in May 2009 further criticisms were aired in the press when a critical report on SOCA was published by Her Majesty's Inspectorate of Constabulary (HMIC 2009). The Guardian quoting police sources indicated that:

> "*. . . there was a gaping hole in the country's ability to tackle organised criminals because SOCA was focused on gathering intelligence and, at the other end of the scale, most police forces have neither the resources nor the experience to tackle serious organised crime effectively.*" (The Guardian 2009)

In July of 2009 the appointment of Sir Iain Andrews as Chair of SOCA raised further complaints because he had no 'crime fighting experience': he had experience in the governance of the Ministry of Defence Police but no experience in operational or serious and organised crime policing.

Collectively, these criticisms describe a specialised policing agency that costs in excess of four hundred million pounds, looks inefficient, a safe haven for retired bureaucrats and has its ability to meet the objectives set for it regularly brought into question.

The current aims of SOCA are set out in the Serious and Organised Crime and Police Act 2005 (Stationery Office 2009). The strategic approach utilised by SOCA is realised through intelligence led policing and partnership working with other relevant agencies in order to meet the requirements of the UK Threat Assessment. However, as discussed, SOCA has been consistently criticised for failing to meet these objectives. The drip-drip effect of these reports has resulted in a loss of political confidence in SOCA and serious questioning of its substantial annual four hundred million pound plus budget. The HMIC Inspection's overall verdict on SOCA's intelligence gathering and analysis was that it could do much better (HMIC, 2009, p 6).

A cursory scrutiny of SOCA highlights many 'failures' in meeting its agreed targets. It is surprising, considering the criticisms of SOCA, that there is little detailed scrutiny while SOCA is an agency with such a substantial budget. When SOCA was established it was stated that it would not be measured by number of arrests or amount of drugs seized but by educating the public and using intelligence to spot trends (Segell, 2007, p 217). Therefore, from the beginning, SOCA had only very vague concepts by which to measure its effectiveness. This lack of potential scrutiny because of lack of 'hard' measures of effectiveness is not so remarkable when SOCA can shroud itself in a form of secrecy based on the notion that to be an open and accountable organisation would be injurious as security would be compromised. This resistance to transparency is one reason why there is little academic literature that focuses on SOCA: the institution keeps its doors and windows closed. The considerable budget inhibits internal motivators for change while the external political motivators to increase transparency and accountability are also weak because with such a substantial budget it is difficult to allow SOCA to be perceived as a failure of policy. The words of Yanow (1997) come back to haunt us as this analysis of SOCA suggests that 'supporting silences' exist. Although the press regularly publishes critical reports, these appear to have little impact on policy. Despite the official discourse acknowledging the evidence regarding the failures of SOCA, the policy model in relation to the policing of serious and 'organised' crime remains the same, and there is considerable evidence that such a policy approach is flawed.

Immigration and Trafficking:

The case of the UK Human Trafficking Centre

There are a number of target areas that are identified for SOCA, one of which is 'Organised Immigration Crime' which is defined as being:

> "*. . . the organised facilitation of immigrants to the UK ('people smuggling') and the trafficking of people for criminal exploitation, for example as prostitutes or forced labour ("human trafficking").*" (SOCA, 2009)

Despite organised immigration crime appearing as a specific target area for SOCA, in 2006, a specialist agency was established to address the 'increasing' problem of human trafficking: The United Kingdom Human Trafficking Centre (UKHTC). The UKHTC since the 1st April 2010 has been located within SOCA to ensure budgetary oversight, and whilst the UKHTC does not have independence to undertake its own 'operations' it liaises closely with other law enforcement agencies, in particular the police and SOCA. The UKHTC has a number of seconded police officers and Crown Prosecutors. The UKHTC resembles SOCA in that it is not part of a police force or any other law enforcement agency: it is located outside of the normal law enforcement systems and it is accountable to the Home Secretary, although its actual lines of accountability are opaque. It has an annual budget of over two and half million pounds of which just under a half is salaries (£955.000). So, whilst it is perhaps not a law enforcement agency within the strict definition it is located within the law enforcement nexus and is presented very much as a law enforcement agency. In policy development terms it is difficult to conceive of UKHTC acting significantly differently from SOCA. The very existence of an agency with such a similar remit suggests an interesting policy making process in this area.

During the past three years the UKHTC has taken a role in the training of police officers and of establishing human trafficking on the agenda of police forces in the UK. However, the UKHTC appears to have been politically astute in building a coalition of interests which includes campaigning groups, media interests, religious groups and academics to promote the idea of human trafficking as a prevalent and significantly serious problem demanding of significant government resources and attention. Despite these lofty undertakings, it is difficult to find anything other than the most general of information concerning the work of the UKHTC. As a matter of fact, a recent report in The Guardian (2009b) was the result of a lengthy legal action to gain access to information about the performance *Operation Pentameter II* in which the UKHTC was centrally involved. Opacity prevails.

During 2007 the UK government authorised a large scale anti-trafficking operation known as *Operation Pentameter II* following on from the first *Operation Pentameter* a few years earlier. There were significant claims made of the success of *Operation Pentameter II* and an analysis suggests that the claims of success were in general accepted uncritically.[2] Such claims of success managed to keep all the constituent elements of the UKHTC satisfied and their agendas intact. However, the legal application by The Guardian in 2009 for the UKHTC analysis of the *Operation Pentameter II* data revealed that in fact the operation led to no convictions for human trafficking even though they made over 500 arrests and raided over 800 premises.

The failure of the UKHTC to meet its objectives within *Operation Pentameter* does not appear to have been a 'one off' but indicative of a systemic failure across the whole of the agency. There has been no significant increase in offences of Trafficking for Sexual Exploitation since 2006 when the UKHTC came into existence. This is remarkable especially considering that the definition of human trafficking in the UK is much wider than that agreed within the Palermo convention and includes 'internal' trafficking regardless of whether the woman participated willingly. In light of this we could expect to see a rise in the number of Trafficking for Sexual Exploitation Offences. As Table I indicates, there was no substantial rise that would justify the initiation of a specifically targeted, independent 'multi-agency' centre. A failure to achieve convictions for Trafficking for Sexual Exploitation Offences may have led to an increase in Exploitation of Prostitution Offences as a subsidiary or alternative charge. Again, Table 1 indicates that there was no substantial rise in these figures:

---

2 See: http://www.ukhtc.org/about-ukhtc#Pentameter

Table 1
Recorded offences of (Trafficking for) Sexual Exploitation

Offence	2003-04	2004-05	2005-06	2006-07
Trafficking for Sexual Exploitation	No Offence	21	33	43
Exploitation of Prostitution	186	117	153	190

(Source: Home Office 2009)

Due to the low number of recorded offences these figures could be as much an artefact of reporting and recording practices as an indication of a genuine increase in these forms of crime. For both crime types the numbers are so small attempting to theorise from the trends in the figures would be a very hazardous project.

In May 2009 the Home Affairs Select Committee reported on Human Trafficking and the Committee made some specific comments in relation to the UKHTC. These comments are not particularly flattering, whilst taking account of the relative newness of the Centre the Committee made the following observation:

> "*. . . the UK Action Plan placed a huge emphasis on UKHTC's role as a multi-agency body, the central repository of all data on human trafficking, offering strategic and operational support and a 24/7 support line for advice, including on the care of victims. It is therefore disappointing that so many of our witnesses suggested it was not really multi-agency, being dominated by the police and UKBA*[3]*; that it was not doing much work to produce the badly-needed estimates of the scale of trafficking; that it was not fully aware of the needs and rights of child victims; and that recent operations and individual cases had shown a lack of clarity in responsibilities and a failure to give useful advice on the support available for suspected victims.*" (Stationery Office, 2009, Para 189)

Following in the footsteps of SOCA, the UKHTC does not fare well under the gaze of scrutiny. Whilst the Select Committee used soft political language it delivered a serious indictment of the UKHTC's competence to meet stated objectives and it placed a responsibility on government to report back by March 2010. We can only speculate, but it is probable that the report will not be able to provide substantial evidence for the efficacy of the UKHTC.

3 United Kingdom Border Agency

Policy Sense – Practical Use?

The UKHTC and SOCA are agencies located within the law enforcement nexus, the latter with an operational law enforcement remit and the former with a law enforcement brief, and both created specifically to meet the perceived demands of 'organised crime'. They appear to sit outside the normal forms of accountability and scrutiny and are opaque in the way they are presented to the public. However, when they come under public scrutiny they are found lacking and failing to meet their stated objectives. Furthermore, the UKHTC have been accused of failing to overcome the problems of multi-agency working, which is surprising taking into account that it was established as a multi-agency approach to the issue of immigration crime drawing from the Home Office experience of REFLEX Teams[4]. The question arises, how can it be possible that after over a decade of New Labour where public agencies have been held under public scrutiny and subject to targets, key performance indicators and management by objectives, we find two public agencies that appear to be a throwback to the 1970s? To answer this question we need to return to the policy making process.

In establishing the UKHTC there were a number of interests that were at play and that no doubt had a significant effect on the structure and approach of the UKHTC. First, the political 'hot potato' of immigration influenced the policy approach to transgressions of immigration laws. The concept of migrant, or the 'other' is a central element in the criminalisation of migrants: migrants are constructed as criminal because they are outsiders and therefore their right to residence is consistently under scrutiny on the assumption that they are in the country illegally (Melossi, 2003, Young 2003). Second, the process by which undocumented migrants arrive in the UK is constructed as being a significant activity of 'organised crime', despite the evidence for such assumptions being, at best, partial.

Undocumented migrants arrive in the UK through a series of different means. Some arrive through organised routes although these are expensive to access and are only available to the wealthy. For the majority the routes are dangerous. Criminal networks can be involved in this process but their participation is fragmented and accessed at the local level. However, the law enforcement response constructs an approach that views the migratory process as being inherently criminal. Politicians agree to this construction as it provides an easy means of

4 REFLEX Teams were multi-agency teams established by the Home Office and located in police force areas with specific task of tackling organised immigration crime. REFLEX teams were varied in their activities, some were intelligence gathering and others were operational.

managing the political problem of migration. In addition, it defines the terrain on which part of the migration problem can be located as 'organised crime'. Undocumented migration is constructed as a problem: very simply about there being too many people wanting to enter the UK without the required papers. And then 'organised crime' offers its services. However, migration is much more complex than this over-simplified analysis suggests but it does allow for policy to appear rational and problem focused.

If we explore some of the themes of the problematic of migration we see a different set of issues to those which are placed at the forefront by law enforcement. For example, migration is essentially concerned with individuals attempting to provide a greater level of security and safety for themselves and their families. This can be physical security and safety in relocating to a place that is free from political oppression and politically motivated violence. There can also be a desire to relocate oneself or relatives to a place of economic security and to find a community that is less ravaged by the effects of poverty. However, these issues raise difficult questions for governments in relation to foreign policy strategies and so on. As Melossi (2003) has argued there is a dynamic between source and destination countries that has economic, social and political outcomes. For example, in Italy the prominence of the Northern League is one of the consequences of the way in which immigration is structured as a law enforcement problem (Melossi, 2003).

The construction of migration as a crime problem is an outcome of the process of problem defining;

> "*While some problems are so obvious that we need not reflect upon them, most social problems do not appear to us ready-made by a determinate reality. We must work through a process that gives order to our worries by converting them into a defined problem. We can approach the same problem in different ways and different people can hold differing interpretations of the problem at the same time. Policy-making does not proceed from obvious problems and correspondingly clear solutions but commences from a point where we have only questions.*" (Turnbull 2006, p 6)

One of the ways in which migration becomes a law enforcement problem is preventing the transgression of borders by non-documented migrants. How to tackle this movement across borders becomes the framework of questions that are designed to lead to a solution. (Spencer *et al.* 2005). As this form of questioning is developed, law enforcement responses are constructed in relation to 'organised crime' so that the Serious and Organised Crime Agency becomes a direct response to the perceived threat. The website of SOCA demonstrates such an approach:

> "*Organised crime covers a very wide range of activity and individuals involved in a number of crime sectors. The most damaging sectors to the UK are judged to be trafficking of Class A drugs, organised immigration crime and fraud.*" (SOCA ,2010)

Here we see Levi's (2006)political market at work and with a wide range of activities being included in order to maintain a focus of 'organised crime' as a very real threat. The political and public attractiveness of the aims and objectives of SOCA and the UKHTC provide nebulous statements that define the operational approach of the organisation. These statements and therefore the working practices of the organisations are difficult to evaluate as the statements are not based on robust research, but populist notions of what 'organised crime' is, the dangers it poses and the action that needs to be taken.

It is here that two distinct practices are at work. Firstly, the construction of the problem by those responsible for the implementation of the state's protective strategies; these strategies are designed to counter the threat of human trafficking for sexual exploitation and 'organised crime'. The problem is presented as an imminent threat that requires action. The call for action is supported not only by law enforcement agency intelligence but also by the coalition of interests that have coalesced around the 'issue' and which have engaged with law enforcement agencies. Government by refusing to take action will be viewed as being negligent and so is sensitised to the potential electoral traps that inaction or a contradiction of law enforcement 'knowledge' might create. In many instances government becomes a willing partner in the construction of the problem as it provides a populist platform to justify further restrictive state powers.

The second element is that 'knowledge is denied' about the effectiveness of the particular law enforcement agencies, even when the critical accounts concerning the specific agencies are from government endorsed institutions. So, SOCA is heavily criticised by an HMIC report and yet the government does little to review the work or effectiveness of the agency. One reason may be that SOCA has been defined as being at the forefront of countering human trafficking for sexual exploitation and so is seen as being more difficult to dispense with its services.

The UKHTC, although non-operational, has also been heavily criticised by parliament but yet retains its influence in the debates concerning human trafficking for sexual exploitation. Such influence is retained not by a critical analysis of the data but by being one of the definers of the problem. It is these prominent roles that allow SOCA and the UKHTC to retain their high profile role in addressing the problem. However, it is our contention that such processes place constraints on research that would provide a more complex and multilayered explanation of the issues. This approach is sacrificed at the expense of permitting agencies that fail to meet their statutory aims and objectives, to continue to provide a one dimensional analysis that essentially can be seen to be self-serving.

The policy of the British government towards trafficking appears to be informed by an agenda that is established primarily by law enforcement and associated agencies that have a vested interest in maintaining the issue of 'sex trafficking' as one of being seen to be an activity of 'Organised Crime' rather than a consequence of the much larger, and thornier, political problem of migration. Despite working under such an important banner, law enforcement agencies do not meet their objectives. But it may be that by political process they succeed in obfuscating such failure by making the issue of 'sex trafficking' a political Achilles heel, thereby diverting the attention. For a government be seen as a one that fails to take the issue of sex trafficking seriously, as defined by law enforcement agencies, will be seen to be not taking the issue of 'Organised Crime' and sex crimes seriously. The government succeeds in avoiding this impression by shrouding her organisations in fog through a 'knowledge denied' policy.

However, the government is not taking the issue seriously because if they were, they would require much more evidence of the problem and insist on law enforcement engaging in an active debate that constructs the 'problem' according to the data. Instead, the government is making it to fit within those reinforced stereotypes that will ensure funding streams for those parts of law enforcement engaged in 'combating organised crime'. That aspect appears to be taken most seriously.

References

Adams, J., Alien animals and American angels: The commodification and commercialization of the Progressive-Era white slave. *Concept An Interdisciplinary Journal of Graduate Studies*, 2005

Bowling, B. and J. Ross, SOCA: the Serious and Organised Crime Agency, *Criminal Justice Matters*, 63: 1, 8 – 36

Duyne, P.C. van and T. Vander Beken, The incantations of EU crime policy making. *Crime, Law and Social Change*, 2009, vol. 51, p. 261-281

Harfield, C., SOCA: A paradigm shift in British Policing, *British Journal of Criminology*, 2006, *46*, p.743-761

HMIC, *Getting Organised: A thematic report on the police service's response to serious and organised crime*. Home Office: London, 2009

Home Office (2009) Crime in England and Wales 2008/09' Vol. 1, Findings from the British Crime Survey and Police Recorded Crime Home Office : London

Johnstone, G., Penal policy making. *Punishment & Society*, 2000, vol. 2, *no. 2*, 161-180

Jones, T. and Newburn, T. (2005) Comparative Criminal Justice Policy Making in the the US and the UK *British Journal of Criminology* 45, p.58-80

Levi, M., The making of the United Kingdom crime control policies. In C. Fijnaut and L. Paoli, L (eds.), *Organised Crime in Europe*. Springer, Netherlands, 2006

Levi, M. and M. Maguire, Reducing and preventing organised crime: An evidence-based critique. *Crime, Law & Social Change*, 2004, vol. 41: 397–469

Melossi, D. In a peaceful life. Migration and the crime of modernity in Europe/Italy. *Punishment & Society*, vol. 5, *no. 4*, 371-397

Segell, G., Reform and transformation: The UK's Serious Organised Crime Agency. *International Journal of Intelligence and Counterintelligence*, 2007, 20, p. 217-239

SOCA Serious and Organised Crime Agency Annual Report 2008-09 Home Office: London, 2009

SOCA (2010) www.soca.gov.uk

Spencer, J., K. Aromaa, M. Junninen, A. Markina, J. Saar and T. Viljanen, *Organised crime, corruption and the movement of people across borders in the new enlarged EU: A case study of Estonia, Finland and the UK*. HEUNI, Helsinki, Finland, 2005

Stationary Office (2005) *Serious and Organised Crime Police Act 2005* Stationery Office. London

Stationery Office, *The Trade in Human Beings: Human Trafficking in the UK*. (House of Commons Home Affairs Select Committee. Sixth Report Session 2008-2009). Stationery Office, London, 2009

The Guardian, *Gordon Brown steps in as agency fails to tackle organised crime gangs*. The Guardian, Monday, 27 April 2009a

The Guardian, *Inquiry fails to find single trafficker who forced anybody into prostitution*. The Guardian 20 October 2009b

Times (2009) 'Failing Serious Organised Crime Agency to be overhauled' http://business.timesonline.co.uk/tol/business/law/article6272391.ece

Times (2008) SOCA abandons hunt for crime lords
http://www.timesonline.co.uk/tol/news/uk/crime/article3919686.ece
Times (2007) SOCA performance slammed
http://www.timesonline.co.uk/tol/news/uk/article1295810.ece
Turnbull, N., How should we theorise public policy? Problem solving and problemasticity. *Policy and Society*, 2006, *no. 1*, p. 3-22
Weitzer, R., The social construction of sex trafficking: ideology and institutionalisation of a moral crusade. *Politics and Society*, 2007, vol. 35, p. 447-475
Yanow, D., Practices of policy interpretation, *Policy Sciences*, 1995, 28: I 11-126
Young, J., To these Wet and Windy Shores; Recent Immigration Policy in the UK. *Punishment & Society*, 2003, vol. 5, *no. 4*, 449-462

'Organised crime' and migrants in the labour market

The economic significance of human smuggling and trafficking in Greece

Georgios Papanicolaou and Georgios A. Antonopoulos[1]

Introduction

In a recent paper examining the stolen car and car parts market in Greece (Antonopoulos and Papanicolaou, 2009) we have shown how the forms of organisation and the activities that are now routinely associated with 'organised crime' are but one aspect of a wider 'dirty economy' (Ruggiero, 1997). In this economy the overlap of the licit and the illicit helps to sustain an extensive business sector built around the commodity of the automobile. We were thus able to raise questions about mainstream, particularly official approaches, which define illicit activities as 'organised crime' and treat it in isolation from the wider circuits of economic activity and the web of social relations in which they occur. We suggested that what in official accounts is represented unequivocally as a parasitical structure that feeds on legitimate economic activity and also undermines the established institutional order, is in effect a simplified image of a more complex process that unfolds across the boundary of upperworld and underworld. The label 'organised crime' engenders a severely distorted view of the configuration of actors and actions in the 'dirty economy'. This in turn, evokes a range of disproportionate, yet ineffective law enforcement and criminal justice responses which have little impact because of the low priority of the illegal vehicle market.

In the present work we return to explore the above problematic in the case of the illegal labour market, and more specifically the segment of that market that involves illegal *migrant* labour. Here, compared to the automobile market, we are confronted with a radically different situation. Notions of 'organised crime' have

1 The authors are senior lecturers in criminology at Teesside University, UK. They would like to thank the reviewers for their comments and suggestions on earlier drafts.

been routinely associated with cross-border mobility and the employment of migrants, to such an extent that the couplet 'organised crime *and* migration' has captured the centre stage of crime and disorder debates in Greece from the early 1990s and up to the most recent general election of October 2009. As migrants seemed to 'take over' the city streets and everyday life of Greece, the media were quick to adopt the idea of 'transnational mafias' taking over the Greek 'underworld' (e.g., Nikolakopoulos, 1997; Mandrou, 1999; Tsarouchas, 2002). Furthermore, important policy measures targeting illegal migration have been advanced by invoking the threat of 'transnational mafias'. Examples are the creation of a special Border Guard agency (Papanicolaou, 2006), and consecutive legislative interventions, including substantive revisions of the Greek penal code (e.g., L.2928/2001, see Lambropoulou, 2003, p 83–84).

Linked with human smuggling and trafficking, the notion of 'organised crime' has come to dominate policy agendas in Greece, and has acquired a meaning which is now directly comparable to definitions used elsewhere (see Naylor, 2004; Paoli and Fijnaut, 2004). This concern about 'organised crime' emerged gradually in the 1990s, primarily through media accounts and official declarations rather than criminological research and appears to have reached a status of an all-menacing phantom (see Van Duyne, 1995); for example, the active minister of Public Order[2] reportedly regards

> "*exceptionally dangerous the certain, as far as [the minister of Public Order] is concerned, contact between 'organised crime' and the new terrorism". As he confides in private conversations: "If the relationship expands and the ties stabilise, then the situation may get out of hand in the field of security and disturb decisively the stability of the economy*" (Karakousis, 2009, our translation).

However, there is a lack of evidence from research or official data and reports containing meaningful and accessible information that could corroborate the above claim about the extent and potency of 'organised crime' in Greece, let alone any ties with terrorism (see Lambropoulou, 2002; Savona *et al.*, 2005). Rather, the evidence from the emerging literature is at odds with official statements, and with established public, especially media representations of 'organised crime' (see e.g., Antonopoulos and Winterdyk, 2005; 2006; Antonopoulos, 2008; 2009; Antonopoulos *et al.*, 2010; Kostakos and Antonopoulos, 2010; Lambropoulou, 2003; Papanicolaou, 2008; forthcoming).

2 The former Ministry of Public Order (see Rigakos & Papanicolaou, 2003), having been demoted to a general secretariat between 2007 and 2009, has been recently restored to its prior status and renamed, quite tellingly, to 'Ministry for the Protection of the Citizen'.

There is nothing exceptional about the observation that the official use of the notion of 'organised crime' builds on a knowledge base that is simply inadequate to support it or, indeed, sometimes virtually absent (see Van Duyne and Soudijn; Van Duyne and Nelemans, forthcoming). Historically, official definitions and understandings of the issue have involved a use of the available evidence that has been selective enough to legitimise intensive and intrusive law enforcement measures that the public would have difficulty in accepting otherwise (Naylor, 2004). Internationally, the development of debates about definitions and the emergence of various conflicting paradigms and approaches in the study of 'organised crime' have engendered considerable scepticism about the nature of the phenomenon and about the established ways of dealing with it (see von Lampe, 2001; Van Duyne and Van Dijck, 2007).

In Greece, however, the development of any theoretical debate is short-circuited by the fact that there is very little communication between criminological research and criminal justice policy making (Lambropoulou, 2005). In addition, whatever communication did exist has become less meaningful by the fact that the legislative changes introduced in the early 2000s to deal with 'organised crime' appear to have been dictated by a rush towards an alignment with established approaches in other western countries rather than a concern for the actuality of whatever could be understood as 'organised crime' in the country (Xenakis, 2004). Considering the above, the idea of 'organised crime' does not appear to refer to clearly identified patterns of criminal organising and activity in Greece, nor, importantly, to provide a solid foundation for rational and effective policy responses.

The consequences of this above disconcerting situation are, we argue, particularly evident in the case of the illegal migrant labour market. In this chapter we aim to investigate the idea of 'organised crime' by focusing on the significance of criminalised phenomena related to migrant labour for sectors of the Greek economy in which they appear to play an important role. In the vein of our previous work, we argue that the social organisation of human smuggling and trafficking, which both are activities pertaining to the mobility and exploitation of migrant labour, is adaptive and functional to the structures of particular sectors of the Greek economy. But notions of 'organised crime' engender a special mode of state intervention that is unable to capture and address effectively the causes of criminal violations and harmful outcomes that do occur in these economic sectors. The distortive effect of the 'organised crime' lens thus becomes fully visible.

Given the paucity of useful official data, our account is still exploratory, and relies on a variety of both official and 'unofficial' sources of data: official statistics from the Greek authorities; interviews with law enforcement agencies; interviews with migrants and employers of documented and undocumented migrants as well as interviews with two migrant smugglers.

The issue with migration in Greece, 1990–2009

We begin with a general overview of the issue of migration and migrants in Greece without differentiating between types of migratory movements or how many individuals may be involved in. This may include legal or illegal migration as well as exploitative situations such as human trafficking. The term 'migrants' refers here in a neutral way to all economic immigrants, political refugees, asylum seekers and immigrant ethnic Greeks, and includes individuals whose country of origin varies considerably (Gent, 2002). Nevertheless, the term migrant has acquired a very particular flavour in Greece since 1990. It has been associated with non-western European migrants, who have been predominantly the ones around whom negative understandings of the 'other' coalesce. It is these non-EU nationals whose mobility is primarily restricted by the legal framework of migration and who are also preponderantly targeted by law enforcement in Greece.

Greece's transformation in the 1990s

Historically, levels of migration to Greece had been low, and in the 1970s and 1980s they mostly consisted in return migration of Greek people from Western European or other countries that received the earlier large Greek migratory wave in the 1950s and 1960s. Numbers of EEC nationals or others, who, on the basis of bilateral or multilateral agreements, entered Greece legally for work or as refugees and asylum seekers were also relatively low. Official data and estimates vary according to the source, but the population of foreign nationals (legally) resident in Greece appears to have been around 200.000 in 1989 (Linardos-Rylmon, 1993; Petriniotis, 1993).

The situation changed dramatically after 1989 due to the geopolitical changes of that time. There was a sudden influx of migrants with the arrival of large numbers of immigrant ethnic Greeks from the Soviet Union after that country[3] had relaxed regulations concerning travel abroad. These were in their vast majority

3 Immigrant ethnic Greeks have been residing in Southern part of Russia and Ukraine as well as Georgia and Armenia for centuries. Such immigrants, who are foreign citizens of ethnic Greek descent, are subjected to many of the processes that foreign immigrants of non-Greek descent are subjected to; they are marginalised and excluded, and they are in need of integration assistance as much as other migrants (see Tsoukala, 1999).

legal migrants and enjoyed special status leading to 'fast-track' naturalisation after legislative changes in 1991.

The vast majority of migrants to Greece after the late 1980s have not been of Greek descent, a characteristic which brought to an abrupt end a long historical pattern: Greece was transformed from a sending to a receiving country. The vast majority of migrants were Eastern Europeans, particularly Albanian nationals, who entered the country and its labour market illegally. It appears that the Greek economy was in a position to employ the migrants primarily in low-status, low paid jobs in the primary and secondary sectors of the economy, or, especially in the case of women, domestic services. It could increasingly do so throughout the 1990s, as it was set on a course of convergence with Europe. With time, Greece also became a destination or transit country for people migrating from other regions such as Africa or the Greater Middle East and, to a lesser extent, Southeast Asia.

The migrant population

It is very difficult to provide accurate figures regarding the number of migrants, as there is (still) an unknown number of undocumented migrants in the country. Though there is a florishing literature on migration (Kyriakou, 2004; see, *e.g.* IMEPO, 2008), the esimates of migrants vary according to the chosen methodology. In addition, they also reflect the results of the consecutive 'legalisation' programmes implemented after the mid-1990s. Indicatively, the number of illegal migrants residing in Greece has been estimated to be 471.000 in 1995, around 300.000 in 2001, between 227 and 235 thousand in 2004 and between 184 and 275 thousand in 2005 (IMEPO, 2008). All these estimates support the argumentation that the number of illegal migrants as a proportion of the total population residing in Greece is considerably high.

As far as demographic characteristics are concerned, and to get an idea of the dramatic change of Greece's social outlook since 1992, it is safer to examine the data regarding *documented* migrants. According to the most recent Greek Census, in 2001 the total number of documented migrants was 693.837 (ESYE, 2001). With a total population of 10.964.020, migrants at that time constituted 6,4% of the total population of Greece. The largest migrant group by far were Albanians, which constituted 63,7% of the total population of documented migrants, and were followed by Bulgarians, Georgians, Romanians, Russians and Ukrainians. The rest of the migrant population is spread over national groups, each less than 1 % (Table 1).

Table 1:
Migrant population in Greece, by country of origin and % of each migrant group in the total migrant population: 2001 Greek Census

Country	N	% of migrant population
Albania	443.550	63,7
Bulgaria	37.230	5,4
Georgia	23.159	3,3
Romania	23.066	3,3
Russia	18.219	2,6
Ukraine	14.149	2,1
Poland	13.378	1,9
Pakistan	11.192	1,6
Turkey	8.297	1,3
Egypt	7.846	1,1
Armenia	7.808	1,1
Others	85.943	12,3
Total	693.837	100*

* 100 per cent due to rounding

Source: Data elaborated from ESYE (2001)

According to data from Greece's National Statistical Authority (ESYE) the majority of documented migrants in Greece are male (2001). Specifically, out of 693.837 documented migrants, 388.776 are male and 305.061 female. Given that the total male and female population of Greece is 5.431.816 and 5.532.204, respectively, documented male migrants constitute 7,1% cent of the total male population, and documented female migrants constitute 5,5% of the total female population. The representation of male and female migrants in each migrant group is, however, different as there are some groups composed mostly of men and others mostly of female members. The proportion of male and female members in the Albanian community, as mentioned the largest migrant community in Greece, is 59% and 41%, respectively. Finally, there are some groups that are almost exclusively composed of male members such as the Bangladeshi (96,6% male), Pakistani (95,7% male), and Indians (92,8% male) (ESYE, 2001). As far as the age distribution of migrants is concerned, more than half of migrants are younger than thirty years old (51,7%), whereas the vast majority (91%) are below the age of forty-four years.

The concentration of the migrant population of Greece in specific geographical areas is almost identical to the concentration of the Greek population. Specifically, the largest percentage of migrants (44,2%) live and work in the greater Athens area, whereas 15% live and work in the area of Central Macedonia, and specifically in the city of Thessaloniki. Over 80% of this population is concentrated in urban areas (Kritikidis, 2004).

The immigrant population of Athens is characterised by considerable variety. According to the 2001 Census, Albanians constitute the majority in the migrant population and total up to about 5% of the total Athens population. But Athens and the nearby prefecture of East Attica comprise a very varied mixture of nationalities including not only Eastern Europeans, such as Polish, Bulgarians, Romanians and Ukrainians, but also a significant presence of Pakistanis, Iraqi, Turks and Filipinos (Baldwin-Edwards, 2005).

The above characteristics and the fact that immigrants are estimated to take up some 25% of the rented housing market (Baldwin-Edwards, 2005) which is itself concentrated in inner city areas, may account to a large extent for the negative representations of migration and migrants. This is especially the case among the native population of Greece's capital, which apart from the majority of policy makers includes the country's most powerful opinion makers. These negative representations have been amplified by official policies that added to the migrants' marginalisation, either by failing to foster integration or by actively criminalising migrants.

Legislative responses to migration in Greece since 1991

The sudden reversal of historical patterns of migration to and from Greece was initially met by a distinctively disorganised reaction of the Greek state. It gave rise to legislative actions that complicated rather than attempted to resolve issues. The large numbers of Albanians entering the country in 1991 generated a sense of threat and urgency. Under this pressure new legislation was introduced in the same year (L.1975/1991) to replace the existing 1929 legislation. The character of that early response defined the subsequent approach to and the (negative) perception of the migration, as migrants have been seen to pose a national security threat and have been stereotyped as 'dangerous'.[4] Consequently they have been discriminated against and excluded, and ultimately, they have been severely criminalised (see Antonopoulos, 2009).

---

4 E.g. Terror Over the City (*Ta Nea,* 25/11/1991), Deportation of the Foreign Criminals (*Kathimerini*, 31/05/1991), The Albanians Come First in Criminality (*Ta Nea*, 18/03/1998), The Albanians Kill With No Mercy (*Eleftheros*, 20/03/1998), The Mafiosi Killed the Farmer (*Eleftheros Typos*, 21/03/1998), Greece, a country-hostage of the Albanian criminals (*Ta Nea*, 15/07/1999), The Mafia of the Greek Riviera (*To Vima*, 30/07/2000), Crime in Greece Speaks Albanian (*Adesmeftos Typos*, 05/06/2002).

Under the real weight of numbers, a first legalisation programme was implemented with the Presidential Decrees 358 and 359 of 1997, and was put into effect in 1998. These decrees established a process of 'temporary' legalisation embodied in the obtainment of, firstly, a 'white card', a card of six months residence that would then lead to the obtainment of a 'green card', a residence card valid for between one and three years. In effect, obtaining the 'white card' was a requirement for someone to obtain a 'green card'. Presidential Decree 358/1997 set the requirements as well as the procedures for the legal stay and employment in Greece of foreigners, who were not citizens of an EU Member State. Several conditions had to be satisfied for a 'white card' to be issued, but this would often be impossible, due to practical obstacles. For example, migrants needed to have a passport, or an ID card, not an easy task given that many identification papers were kept by those smuggling the migrants in the country. And (in some cases) if they had an ID, it was seized or destroyed by the police during checks. The obtainment of the 'white card' also required the submission of a social security stamp book, or a proof of applying for one. However, this was very rare, given the conditions under which migrants were employed. Only few employers were willing to pay the migrants social security contributions. And these were mainly those having the same migrants as their employees for a long period of time and for a series of jobs, and thus they did not want them to be deported (see Kapsalis, 2004).

Migrants arriving in the country after 28th November 1997 when the decrees came into action were not eligible for a 'white card' (and in consequence the 'green card'). With criteria like these, legal entry for a number of migrants after the enactment of these two Presidential Decrees was virtually impossible. As a consequence a very large number of migrants were not recorded, and 75% of those recorded were not able to obtain a 'green card' (see Youth Against Racism – Greece, 2000). At any rate, this first legalisation process occurred within conditions of a "*complex culture of discretion . . . [with] nationalist and neo-entrepreneurial overtone. [The state] does not perceive immigrants as their clients, but the local employers and Greek society as a whole*" (Jordan *et al.*, 2003, p 383).

The subsequent Laws on Aliens 2910/2001 and 3386/2005 have been credited with extending some rights to migrants, such as the right to be informed in a language they understand of the reasons for their detention, and with safeguarding some other civil rights, such as the right to social security, and creating an obligation to provide nine years of education for migrant children, including the children of undocumented migrants. The 2001 Law, which introduced the system of the so-called 'Green Card II', still encouraged the identification of migration with public order and national security issues. It also failed to address issues of trafficking and forced labour (including prostitution). It had 'no realistic mechanism for labour recruitment' (Baldwin-Edwards, 2004). The Green Card II system also failed to curb long delays in the handling of residence permit requests, as well the culture of 'discretion' or arbitrariness, despite some transfer of competence for deciding on these permits to local authorities.

Overall, these legislative changes made it very difficult for migrants who were not already residing in the country before 2001 and 2004, respectively, to become lawful residents. In consequence, migration to Greece continues to be seen as a historic phenomenon that was officially ended when the 2005 law came into force that defined who is entitled to stay in Greece. In so doing, it created an army of permanently disaffected migrants, a large number of which exist in a limbo between legality and illegality. The presidential decrees of 1997, and the laws 2910/2001 and 3386/2005 focused on the management of migrants as labour force, while simultaneously limiting important work rights such as seeking a job in every part of the Greek territory.

Further dimensions of the legislative response

The above responses of the Greek state have left a mark on the migrants' social situation that still persists today. Firstly, the entry of these populations has been connected with the formation of new relatively isolated social spaces. These were particularly to be found near central areas of Greece's urban centres, where migrants congregated in search of cheap housing. These areas also provide relative security from the persecution of the authorities, as they are not so frequently policed. Also important is the easier access to employment, since these neighbourhoods assumed the character of an open air labour market. Psimmenos (2004; Psimmenos, 2000), in his studies of the living conditions and the social exclusion of migrant workers in Athens, has understood these areas of congregation as *periphractic spaces (fenced–off spaces)*: hidden from the public eye and organised around the places where low grade mass accommodation could be found. Such collective spaces form "*an amorphous environment full of physical and moral humiliation and unable to care for the physical, spiritual and emotional needs of the population*" (Psimmenos, 2000, p 92). These extreme conditions of social exclusion and isolation have also been found in a series of other studies (Lazaridis and Romaniszyn, 1998; Lazaridis, 1999; Labrianidis and Lyberaki, 2001).

It should be evident that the Greek state's share of the responsibility in the perpetuation of these conditions has been substantial. The common denominator of all the legislative initiatives since the beginning of the 1990s has been the consistent raising of barriers denying immigrants opportunities for integration in the country's economic and social life under the organised supervision of the state (see, e.g. Amnesty International, 2005). In fact, a review of the various legislative measures suggests that the primary rationale of state intervention related more to the political and perhaps narrowly fiscal consequences of the presence of a large foreign population within Greek territory. The question of integration into the country's economic and social life remained virtually untouched by legislative hands.

At the same time, one should recognise how at the level of legislative rationale the immigration laws constitute a relatively coherent whole with the legislation dealing with human smuggling and trafficking introduced in the wake of the 2000 UN Convention on Organised Crime. For example, the provisions of the special anti-trafficking legislation introduced in 2002 (Law 3064/2002), despite taking an aggressive stance towards trafficking offenders, are at the same time rife with reservations about the victim's standing. The victim must exhibit a willingness to cooperate with the authorities as witness against the traffickers if any modifications to his/her status as an illegal alien are to be effected. While victims of trafficking formally constitute for the purposes of that legislation a special category of third country nationals, the procedure is conditioned by the victim's value to the investigative procedure. The issuing of the special stay permit for victims of trafficking depends in the first instance on the characterisation of the individual as 'victim' by the public prosecutor; a reflection period is also granted by a special order of the public prosecution service, depending on the results of the police screening. The actual issuing of the stay permit depends on 'whether the extension of the stay of the said person is deemed expedient, in order to facilitate the ongoing investigation or penal process', whether 'the above person has demonstrated clear will to cooperate', or whether the individual 'has broken all relations with the alleged traffickers'. Conversely, the stay permit is not extended or is recalled, when the authorities (the prosecution service) considers that the cooperation or report of the victim is malevolent or abusive, or when the victim stops cooperating.

The fact that regression to the status of an unwanted alien is always a possibility once the victim fails to cooperate with the investigative authorities, shows that the status of victim is merely instrumental to the investigation and prosecution. It is evident that any considerations regarding the welfare of the victim and the provision of support have been entirely foreign to the rationale of the law (Papanicolaou, forthcoming). This has given rise to consistent and highly problematic patterns in the treatment of trafficking victims by the authorities (as documented by Amnesty International, 2005; Amnesty International, 2007).

Employment, migrants and the social organisation of migration

The legislative treatment of migration to Greece is the formalisation of a continuum from discrimination and negation to criminalisation of migratory movements. It has had an intimate relation with discourses about the grave threat of 'organised crime'. Secondly, with the factors influencing migratory flows being equal, any (non-EU/'respectable' westerners') migratory movements to and within Greece have been treated as something involving a criminal irregularity. This valuation did not take into account the different types or economic and social situations associated with the position of migrants in the labour market or the characteristics the social organisation of migratory flows into Greece. We briefly discuss these below.

Migrants in the Greek labour market

Research has shown that in the beginning of the 1990s, documented migrants in Greece were mainly employed in restaurants and hotels, with fewer numbers in the field of transportation and industry (Petriniotis, 1993). According to Linardos-Rylmon (1993, p. 16), the biggest percentage of undocumented migrants was employed in seasonal agricultural or fishing works, or as cleaners and builders (construction). They were paid less than half the wage of a Greek worker. Given that employers did not pay social security contributions, and could hire and fire them at will, the real labour cost may have been, as low as one quarter of the Greek rate (King *et al.,* 1998). There were certainly instances in which the difference may have been even greater.

The last Greek census did not show any difference as to the sectors of employment of migrants, but rather in the patterns of employment of migrant groups. Predictably, male migrants are employed in labour intensive industries: construction and agriculture and fishing works, as well as industry, commerce, removals, mining, and tourism or as street vendors. There were also two small categories/sectors of employment called 'uncertain' and 'other' (ESYE, 2001; Kritikidis, 2004).

Nationalities

In respect to specific migrant groups, Albanian male migrants, who have been characterised as the 'helots' of our days (Lazaridis, 1999), were primarily employed in construction (about 70.000), and agriculture (about 40.000), and a further 40.000 are employed in industry and tourism (ESYE, 2001). Albanians are also the migrant group most heavily involved in running a small business. According to the Athens Chamber of Commerce and Industry (*Emporiko kai Viomechaniko Epimelitirio Athinon*), 26,1% of foreigners enrolled come from Albania (Galanopoulos and Dionysopoulou, 2003).

Overall, the different nationalities are not evenly distributed in the various sectors of the economy. Markova and Sarris (1997) suggest that Bulgarian men were primarily employed in fruit picking in Northern Greece, although there was a number of Bulgarians, who pick strawberries in southern Greece as well. Poles and Georgians are primarily employed in the construction industry, together with Romanians and Russians. Moreover, there are a number of Sub-Saharan Africans, and Chinese migrants who work as street vendors selling CDs/DVDs, toys, and other ornaments at the bazaars and flea markets,–situation not unknown elsewhere (*e.g.*, Nelken, 2006). Finally, there are about 14.000 migrants, who are employed as seamen on Greek commercial ships. Most of these seamen are from Pakistan, India, Sri Lanka, Indonesia, and the Philippines (SOPEMI, 1997).

Migrant women

Generally, the majority of women migrants are employed as domestic servants, babysitters, caretakers, and in agriculture. Albanian female migrants are primarily employed in agriculture and as domestic servants, as workers in small and medium industries, and as cleaners. A significant number of them are unemployed or housewives (ESYE, 2001; Hatziprokopiou, 2003). Bulgarian females are typically employed in agriculture, tourism and in domestic services, and so are Romanian, Russian, Ukrainian and Georgian women. Philippino women almost exclusively work as domestic servants. The percentage of Philippino women, who follow this line of employment exceeds 90%, according to data from the ESYE (2001) (Fakiolas and Maratou-Alipranti, 2000).

Additionally, an issue which was brought to the centre stage of public concern, particularly in the second half of the 1990s involved the number of women working in the sex industry and the conditions under which this had occurred. It would not be an exaggeration to state that the first main public policy debate concerning the notion of 'organised crime' concerned sex trafficking. The concern about this phenomenon was instrumental for the comprehensive introduction of the provisions of the UN Convention on Transnational Organised Crime in Greek criminal law in the early 2000s (Dimitrainas, 2003; Papanicolaou, 2008). This development had been preceded by considerable media coverage of the issue, and also considerable mobilisation of civil society and other international actors (Papanicolaou, 2008; Papanicolaou, forthcoming; Papanicolaou and

Boukli, forthcoming). However, the actual evidence about the extent of migrant women's involvement in the sex industry and about the conditions of their exploitation has been disputed. It is certain that the influx of migrant women radically reversed the ethnic composition within the sex industry. However, the generation of estimates about the number of women involved in the sex industry, showing a rise from just over 2000 in 1990 to a population of over 20.000 in 2000 (Lazos, 2002; Lazos, n.d.), has been criticised for methodological obscurity (Papanicolaou, 2008; Sykiotou, 2009). Furthermore, another heavily contested issue has regarded the extent of forced prostitution as well as the nature and the role of 'transnational organised crime' (Lazaridis, 2001; Lazos, 2002).

The role of clandestine migration flows

We conclude this section with an assessment of the patterns of distribution of migrant labour in the various sectors of the Greek economy. The preceding discussion, which draws from data recorded by the 2001 census and other sources, strongly suggests that migrants have been mostly confined to performing unskilled manual labour within the more traditional or labour intensive sectors of the economy (OECD, 2001; Kritikidis, 2003; Baldwin-Edwards, 2004). In these sectors they have been over-represented compared to the indigenous labour force (Table 2). Baldwin-Edwards (2008) has found that the overall trend since 2001 has rather involved a movement away from the agricultural sector into construction, household and cleaning and tourism (a trend which for the beginning of the decade can be related with the organisation of the 2004 Olympic Games in Athens), rather than towards occupational variety.

Table 2
Aliens employed by economic sector

Sector	**% of migrant labour**	**comparison with native labour force**
Agriculture	3,5	
Mining and manufacturing	19,3	*
Construction	26,6	*
Wholesale, retail and accommodation	19,0	
Health, education and social services	5,9	
Households	19,9	*
Public administration	0,8	
Other services	5,0	

* overrepresented in comparison with native labour force
Source: OECD (2001: 174)

One should take into account the extent of the informal economy, which in Greece is strongly associated with the labour intensive sectors where migrant labour has been concentrated. Add to this the general lack of the enforcement of tax, social security and social welfare legislation. One may then understand more clearly why the Greek state's prolonged indifference to the migrants' economic and social situation engendered extreme exploitative and exclusionary conditions. Of course, the employment and exploitation involving violation of labour and social security legislation can be considered as a common characteristic of both indigenous and migrant black labour. However, the thorough social marginalisation of the migrant population was directly connected to the prohibitions instituted by the state: the latter induced an exclusive reliance on informal or illegal networks in order to satisfy the demand for labour.[5] As Linardos-Rylmon observed in 1993:

> "... *The Greek experience shows that in many cases it is possible to satisfy the demand for cheap labour by legal means, while the rigid prohibition creates now the conditions for the development of illegal networks that come to offer a labour force that is dispersed in turn to the rest of the economy*" (Linardos-Rylmon, 1993, pp. 21, 25).

'Organised crime' and the labour market

The preceding section has provided an overview of the available information about the position and role of migrants in the Greek labour market. Before we evaluate in more detail the participation of migrant labour in particular circuits of the Greek economy, we must take a step in a different direction and offer an overview of law enforcement and criminal justice responses to the issue of illegal migration. Recall that our claim is that such responses do not rely on rational, evidenced evaluations of how illegal migrants operate in the labour market. Rather, they constitute action against an abstract criminal threat, 'organised crime.' We have already pointed out that Greek criminology and criminal justice did not possess a native language of 'organised crime'. Such language was imported from elsewhere and grew on the fertile ground of the discrepancy between the real and the perceived effects of (illegal) migration. It endowed with a semblance of cohesion and legitimacy responses that have been essentially knee-jerk and heavy-handed, as much as they have been misinformed. We discuss below this contradiction by considering the available evidence about the nature of the

5 Van Duyne and Houtzager (2005) describe similar issues around organising black labour service in the Netherlands.

relation between migration and 'organised crime' and the extent to which this relation exists.

How much organised crime?

As Greek law enforcement lacked any concept of 'organised crime' in the early 1990s, the initial fire-brigade style response had to do more with the control of a visibly exploding migrant population. The most common measure, which is still being widely used even today, has been the so-called 'sweep operation'. As the word indicates, the police would simply stop and detain any migrants congregating in public places, particularly in cities. The detainees would then be forwarded to the border for expulsion (see Petriniotis, 1993, p 16). As records for the results of these operations have not always been available, various sources report different numbers or come to different estimates. An early 1993 study, referring to a Ministry of Public Order source, reported 167.204 repatriations of Albanian nationals between 1991 and June 1992 (Linardos-Rylmon, 1993, p 16). Another report (Karydis, 1996), quoting a press source, mentioned a total of 948.956 Albanian nationals repatriated ('re–forwarded') between 1991 and 1995. Other calculations indicate that between 1990 and 1996 about 1,1 million Albanians had been deported (Lambropoulou, 2000).

These reports should not be taken as unrealistic. Between 2001 and 2008, the Hellenic Police and the Hellenic Coast arrested 794.137 migrants for illegal entry and/or residence in Greece. The majority of those migrants (527.080, or approximately 66%) were Albanians (Table 3). Albanians were followed by nationals of Asian as well as African countries. It is also interesting to note that from 2001 to 2006 there were 9.479 and 10.255 arrestees from Bulgaria and Romania (two countries that were admitted in the EU in 2007), respectively.

These are numbers of arrestees only: evidently, there is at all times a largely unknown number of undocumented migrants, who either reside in Greece or travel without documents through Greece. This stock is continuously renewed, despite the heightened policing of border areas and sea routes and also despite the restriction of their opportunities within Greece. Migrants still enter the country because they would do anything to escape hunger and persecution in their home countries (see *e.g.* Kitsantonis, 2009). The futility of 'fire brigade style' measures is somehow underscored by the degree of cross-border return mobility of those expelled. Particularly the Albanian nationals simply cross the border again the next day.

Table 3
Migrants arrested by the Hellenic Police and the Hellenic Coast Guard for illegal entry and/or residence, 2001-2008

Year	Arrestees	Albanian	% Albanian
2001	219.598	173.957	79,2
2002	58.230	36.827	63,2
2003	51.031	35.789	70,1
2004	44.987	31.637	70,3
2005	66.351	52.132	78,5
2006	95.239	57.466	60,3
2007	112.364	66.818	59,5
2008	146.337	72.454	49,5
Total	**794.137**	**527.080**	**66,4**

Source: Hellenic Police (2009)

Overall, the rigid framework of immigration law in Greece, the treatment of irregular migrants as a security risk, and the contribution of Greece to 'Fortress Europe', have resulted among other things in (a) the high numbers of migrants deported from Greece, (b) a low number of asylum applications compared to other countries of the EU, (c) the small percentage of successful applications, and (d) a high number of deaths (see Moulopoulos, 2009).

Migrant smuggling

While the sheer volume of people involved in cross-border movement underscores that the nature of the process is as disorganised as it is desperate, migrants often resort to smugglers and take the associated personal risks as well as the infringement of their rights during the smuggling process. As Rebwar, a Kurdish migrant from Iraq and close friend of one of us, put it: ". . . *the kaçakçi*[6] *do good. How could we come here if it wasn't for the kaçakçi?*" (Antonopoulos and Winterdyk, 2006, p 448).

According to official *police* statistics, the majority of arrested people smugglers in Greece are Greeks. Specifically, they constituted 58,4% of arrested smugglers in the first eight months of 2000 and 53,2 % in the first eight months of 2001. Albanian nationals are also heavily involved in the smuggling of migrants, primarily from Albania. They accounted for 16,1% in the first eight months of 2000, and 25,2% in the first eight months of 2001. The third nationality in terms of arrested

6 The *kaçakçi* are, according to the Kurdish participants in Antonopoulos & Winterdyk's (2006) study, those individuals who assist in the illegal crossing of borders. However, the term can be roughly applied to someone involved in illegal markets in general.

migrant smugglers is Turkish, who accounted for 7,4% and 6,9% of the arrested human smugglers in the first eight months of 2000 and of 2001, respectively. Bulgarians, Iraqis, Romanians and Russians are also involved (Antonopoulos, 2009). According to official data which were made available recently, the majority of arrested smugglers in the first 8 months of 2009 are now foreign nationals (Hellenic Police, 2009). Nevertheless, the participation of Greek nationals is considerable and accounts for the 21% of the arrestees, whereas Albanians and Turks comprise 41% of the population of arrestees (Hellenic Police, 2009).

Human trafficking

The information that the Hellenic Police began to make available about human trafficking after the introduction of special legislation in 2002 offers a less conclusive picture about the extent and nature of (cross-border) 'organised crime'.

Table 4
Human trafficking offenders 2003-2008

	2003	2004	2005	2006	2007	2008	Total
SUM	284	352	202	206	121	162	1327
Greece	166	207	133	142	48	70	766
Romania	20	5	28	9	18	32	112
Albania	22	22	13	28	4	13	102
Bulgaria	1	15	12	12	26	10	76
Russia	30	10	3	4	12	7	66
Ukraine	12	5	1	1	7	1	27
Moldova	8	4	3	0	2	4	21
Nigeria	0	0	5	4	0	6	15
Lithuania	5	0	0	0	2	3	10
Other	20	20	4	6	2	16	68
Unknown	0	64	0	0	0	0	64

Source: Hellenic Police, no date

Firstly, data about the number of identified offenders (the number of individuals being investigated), tabulated by country of origin, are usually made available each year alongside the rest of the information about victims and forms of cooperation with other agencies (see, *e.g.* Hellenic Police, n.d.). Table 4 presents the data for 2003-2008, which include offenders of all forms of human trafficking. In the course of these years, the Hellenic Police has encountered diverse forms, such as labour trafficking or baby trafficking. For example, the OC report for 2004 includes a particular mention to both these forms, as a number of criminal networks had been targeted and dismantled successfully in that year. It notes however, that in the case of baby trafficking the investigations had not been successful in discovering details about the Greek 'baby adoption' demand side. With the above qualification it can be observed that although the 5-year period data reveal an involvement of Romanians, Albanians, Bulgarians, and Russians to a lesser extent, the majority of trafficking offenders (almost 60% of the total number of investigated individuals) have been Greek nationals.

Significance of official data

The now discontinued annual reports of the Hellenic Police on Organised Crime offered an overview of the national situation by compiling the yearly activity reports by the various divisions of the Hellenic Police. While a number of doubtful distinctions[7] have been superimposed on the raw data (which were not made available), they were important in that they offered some information about the social organisation of 'organised crime', such as the size and structure of 'criminal organisations', as well as their *modus operandi*. The official definition of 'organised crime' found in article 187 of the Greek Penal Code which was introduced by Law 2928/2001 speaks of a 'structured and continuously active group (organisation)' of three or more members that purports to commit specifically named felonies (see Hellenic Police, 2005; Hellenic Parliament, 2001). This is roughly in accordance with the international definition of 'organised crime' (Convention on TOC). Casting the police data in this mould, the police reports offer information on the number of members of the 'criminal organisations' that were targeted each year by the Hellenic Police.

As it can be seen in Table 5, the majority of investigated 'criminal organisations' barely exceed the legislative threshold of three members. More than two thirds of these groups involve 6 members or less, which appears to be approximately the average membership of human trafficking groups (as ratio of suspects to investigated groups) (Hellenic Police, 2004; Hellenic Police, 2005; Hellenic Police, 2006).

7 For example, the distinction between 'homogeneous' and 'heterogeneous' criminal organisations on one hand, and the distinction between 'indigenous', 'non–indigenous' and 'indigenous and non-indigenous' on the other (see, e.g. Hellenic Police, 2006). What made the problem worse is that the reports did not include cross-tabulations of the above two categories–something which would have resulted in much more meaningful information.

Table 5
Size of 'criminal organisations' under investigation, 2003-2005

No. of members	2003	2004	2005	Total
(2)*/3	35	38	26	99
4	36	40	32	108
5	32	25	20	77
6	20	17	20	57
7–10	21	37	30	88
11–15	8	12	8	28
16–20	4	2	3	9
>20	1	7	0	8
Total	157	178	139	474

* The 2006 report includes a separate category for 2–member criminal organisations
Source: Hellenic Police (2004; 2005; 2006)

Because of their obvious limitations, the statistics cited here offer indications only, and they should be treated with caution. At a minimum, they may leave out a potentially large number of persons operating in countries other than Greece. This may distort the picture of smuggling networks. As a matter of fact, Kurdish immigrants in Greece, as well as Kurdish people smugglers, for instance, suggested that there were Pakistanis, Syrians and Turks as well as Greeks in their smuggling groups, all involved in a coordinated effort. Furthermore, the fact that many individuals arrested for these offences in Greece are Greek nationals may simply be the result of their greater exposure to the national authorities (Antonopoulos and Winterdyk, 2006). In addition, variations in arrest totals reflect not only the productivity of the authorities but also their shifting priorities. It is reasonable to assume that the same observation applies for the case of human trafficking.

Smuggling, trafficking and the migration process

Nevertheless, since these are the available official data, sense must be made of what they reveal, especially when one considers the rhetoric surrounding 'organised crime' and the threat it poses. Firstly, if organisational membership is an indication of the extent of the threat an organised criminal group poses because of its purported power then, one must conclude, that the imagery of powerful clandestine criminal organisations conjured up by official discourses appears unwarranted. Secondly, the considerable degree of involvement of Greek nationals indicates that the process of human smuggling and trafficking is not taking place in the absence of indigenous agents, but rather it involves them as active and critical components. Thirdly, to single out aliens as the primary actors in these criminal activities is congruent to a particular threat imagery, but completely fails to explain the economic and social significance of these activities.

Rather, what we know about the social organisation of human smuggling and trafficking and the ways migrants find their way into the informal economy moves us away from the usual Transnational Organised Crime (TOC) image. Empirically we must move away from the idea that what is involved in the phenomenon relates to robust, ethnically homogeneous organisational forms. Firstly, with regard to the smuggling of migrants into Greece, the typical case involves loose forms of cooperation between groups (see, for instance, Antonopoulos and Winterdyk, 2006). In its simplest form, when there is no need for great sophistication, individuals simply bring the bulk of migrants to the intended destination. As Greece is both a transit and a destination country, this may entail a smuggler-to-smuggler approach that does not allow any individuals to be lost during the process. Depending on difficulties or the presence of obstacles as the process unfolds, other individuals or groups that may have been unrelated to the original smugglers may take over the smuggling operation (Antonopoulos and Winterdyk, 2006). This general configuration of the process involves, in organisational terms, networks, not hierarchies, and clearly explains both the strong presence of Greek nationals in the population of smuggling arrestees. The individuals who know the 'smuggling map' of the region, are likely to hold a key position in the moving of migrants via the maritime routes in and out of Greece. Similarly, it accounts for the very strong presence of nationals of the neighbouring Albania and Turkey.

The situation with human trafficking, whose definition in the Greek penal Code (art.323A) now matches closely that introduced by the Protocol to Prevent, Suppress and Punish Trafficking in Persons, especially Women and Children supplementing the 2000 UN Convention,[8] is more obscure, since the wording is not so much related to the ways by which trafficked persons enter the country (as these may be legal), but rather to the places and ways they are being exploited within the Greek territory. These may include legal and illegal bars, nightclubs, brothels, construction sites, sweatshops and other small businesses, as well as activities in the streets, as in the case of informal street selling of CD/DVDs, lighters and other gadgets, and of services such as window washing and so on. A potentially key point in the understanding of the labour situation regards the social profile of the businesses where migrants may be found in conditions of extreme

---

8 'Every person who, with the use of force, threat or any other means of coercion or through imposing or abusing power, hires, transports, promotes [transportation] within the country [Greece] or outside the country, detains, harbours, delivers with or without benefit in return, or receives from another a person for the purpose of removing organs from this person's body, or exploiting this person's labour for his/her benefit or for the benefit of another . . .' (English translation obtained from IOM, no date).

exploitation. This is in the first place of importance because 'exploitation' is a component of the UN Palermo Convention. In the second place, it reinforces the idea of mafia–type transnational organisations, 'ruthlessly exploiting' their victims. However, Greek as well as international research point to typically small groups.[9] The groups are likely to be interconnected and heterogeneous overall (see also Bruinsma and Bernasco, 2004) as the space they have to cover is, by the nature of the core business (foreign labour), large. In the end there are significant ties with legitimate endpoints: the market of end users for the cheap labour service. Whether licit or illicit, their output consists of cheap licit output, commodities and services, for mainly local customers. Hence, a strong indigenous presence is indispensable to the whole 'exploitative process'. In other words, the 'circuit of exploitation' is embedded in (a) the whole chain of handling illicit labour and (b) the economic situation of small-scale business and entrepreneurship (Papanicolaou, 2008).

This understanding is congruent with research results obtained from the examination of the social organisation of various illegal markets as well as the provision of other illicit services in Greece. This concerns -amongst others- the trafficking of goods such as cigarettes, stolen cars and car parts. Official accounts tend to underplay the significance of the indigenous elements in the processes involved. They shy away, particularly from the overlap with the shady activities of labour providers and establishments associated with legitimate businesses and entrepreneurship (see Ruggiero, 1997). Thus, in the case of the stolen car market, for example, we have noted that the illicit "*business would not be viable without the legitimate actors, who are essential in orchestrating the criminal network. These legitimate actors drift from legality to illegality and back always within the confines and protection of their legal business*" (Antonopoulos and Papanicolaou, 2009, p 163).

Furthermore, the shift of focus that this approach entails acknowledges the need to disengage from the terminological and conceptual 'minefields' spawned by recent attempts to define the various types of migration in isolation from the conditions within which it takes place. It involves a move towards an understanding of migratory movements not merely as an outcome, but rather as a process of a complex undertaking. On the part of the migrants it is complicated as it depends critically on the environment within which it takes place. Where will the end result, for the migrants, fall on the continuum between safety and harm or extreme exploitation (see Bangladesh Thematic Group on Trafficking, 2004)? It follows that an analysis of the economic, social and legal environment of the migratory destination is indispensable.

9 E.g. Labrianidis and Lyberaki (2001); Lazaridis (2001); Lazos (2002); Spencer (2007; 2008); Zaitch and Staring (2007)

The economic significance of smuggling and trafficking

The final piece of our account consists of a more concrete examination of the economic, social and institutional environment in which the migration process has taken place in Greece.

The positive contribution of (legal and illegal) migrants to the Greek economy and even the rapid economic recovery in the 1990s can hardly questioned, despite the rather limited data flow and the relative scarcity of research (in comparison to Western Europe and North America). A study of migration policy conducted for the General Confederation of Greek Workers has noted how "*it is clear that [as regards the relation between migration and economic development] the economic developments of the past 10–15 years would have followed a rather different course, had the migrants that were so quickly integrated in economic activity not been available*" (Linardos-Rylmon, 2003b, p 10).

As far as labour markets are concerned, the case of Greece appears to confirm that there is no relationship between migration and unemployment (Baldwin-Edwards, 2002). Nor is there an overall effect of migration on the level of wages, with the exception of unskilled labour. Econometric studies have shown that, as far as relations of income distribution are concerned, (illegal) migration is macro-economically beneficial. It also impacts beneficially the better-off classes of Greek households in terms of real disposable income. It allows households to reduce expenses so that those that were formerly rich become richer under illegal immigration. However, Greek urban households headed by an unskilled person are likely to lose income (and jobs) due to the influx of illegal migrants at their level of employment, even though, under different scenarios, they could also obtain better incomes from other sources such as self employment (Sarris and Zografakis, 1999).

It appears, therefore, that the influx of migrant labour has provided a unique opportunity for the satisfaction of demand for cheap labour in a series of productive sectors of the Greek economy. These included agriculture, with migrant workers being involved in the formation of a wage-labour population in the countryside 'for the first time after several decades'.[10] Also manufacture benefits: construction and services, where low wages played a role in the ability of these

10 In 2008, the mobilisation of migrant workers at strawberry plantations in Northwest Peloponnese was making headlines in Greece, and revealed the extent not only of the dependence of this niche agricultural sector on migrant labour (approximately 3.000 workers from Bulgaria, Romania and Bangladesh), but also of their miserable conditions of living and exploitation with wages ranging between €3 to €5 per hour (see, e.g., Ta Nea, 2008).

enterprises to sustain competitiveness. In addition, the redistribution of income in favour of certain social strata during the late 1980s made possible the employment of migrants in domestic services (Linardos-Rylmon, 2003b, p 9).

However, with the segregation of migrant labour as given, what needs to be explicitly questioned is the structure and nature of the economic sectors that primarily accommodated the influx of migrants. Although the knowledge gaps in this respect are quite pronounced, the existing literature does tend to emphasise the relation of (illegal) migration with the shadow economy (Baldwin-Edwards, 2002).

In the case of Greece, such a connection would firstly involve a significant amount of economic activity that takes place in the country, since estimates of the shadow economy's extent have ranged between 25–30% of Greece's GDP (see Pavlopoulos, 1987). Secondly, and perhaps more importantly, the connection would be mainly concentrated in labour intensive sectors of the economy, namely small manufacture and commercial enterprises (such as bars, night-clubs *etc*) as well as agriculture. It is in those sectors that the informal economy is prevalent in Greece and abroad (see Sakellaropoulos, 2001; Vettori, 2009).

In this light, it is possible to situate most forms of the exploitation of migrant labour within known and widely diffused indigenous economic practices in the 1990s. To explain these mechanisms there is no need for 'mafia' terminology. While the absence of any legal (and perhaps moral) status certainly removed employers' inhibitions, the experiences of migrants are nevertheless situated on a continuum of practices from some of which Greek employees would have no qualms to benefit themselves. We do not of course deny the fact that extreme-harm outcomes in the migratory process of an unknown number of individuals have occurred. What we argue is that harmful outcomes, which through the lens of 'organised crime' legislation appear as exceptional and isolated, are rather characteristic of the general conditions under which migration to Greece, as a destination country, takes place.

Such an approach would explain the Greek state's prolonged indifference to the issue of humane migrant integration to the country's economic and social structures. Evidently, the principle of least regulation has made perfect sense at a time when the intensive exploitation of migrant labour had been instrumental at revitalising important sectors of the economy that suffered most from the economic crisis of the 1980s. In the end of the 1990s and after, this prolonged indifference was replaced by a re-conceptualisation of the issue as 'organised crime' and therefore with an increasingly aggressive punitive stance towards it.

Some tentative conclusions: combating 'organised crime' as avoidance strategy?

By relating the social organisation of migrant smuggling and trafficking to processes in Greece's labour market, our analysis has sought to advance a very simple point: the problem with current approaches towards human smuggling and trafficking is that the authorities view these phenomena in isolation from the context in which they occur. Smugglers and traffickers are active in the wider processes linking migration and labour markets. Therefore, it is important to examine the objective significance of clandestine migratory movements for the destination contexts in order to assess their role and the impact of their activities. The fact that smugglers and traffickers often define their activities as a service (Antonopoulos and Winterdyk, 2005; Antonopoulos and Winterdyk, 2006) is an indicator of the objective role they hold both within these movements and within the economic circuits into which migrant labour is channelled. In some respects, and contrary to the idea that their role is largely parasitic, they make a functional contribution to both, as far as they create some order in an otherwise chaotic process. In a sense, 'organised crime' may describe more the effect these individuals and groups bring about in their environment rather than the organisational forms their activities assume.

On the basis of the preceding analyses, our account of the relation between illegal migration and 'organised crime' unfolds along the following lines: as Greece enjoyed levels of growth and standards of living comparable to other western countries, it became a migratory destination for people experiencing the devastation of the economic and social changes of the early 1990s (primarily) in her Balkan and eastern Europe neighbourhood. The Greek economy had the capacity to provide employment to migrants and continued to do so throughout the 1990s: cheap migrant labour revitalised various sectors of the economy and reinforced growth. Ultimately, this process helped sustain inward migration flows, leading to an even larger migrant population. But Greece lacked the material and institutional infrastructure to cope with her new position. Conditions in the inner city deteriorated under the weight of large migrant populations, just as the last fuelled anxieties about the migrant 'other'.

It follows that the current mainstream discourse about 'organised crime' articulates more an expressive reaction to an imagined threat, rather than a rational response to real social issues pertaining to exploitation and social marginalisation. In Greece, a popular explanation of the escalation of repressive state reaction has indeed been derived from the idea of a moral panic ignited by the sudden influx of large numbers of foreigners in a country which not only had been ethnically homogeneous but also one that contributed to international migration as a sending country. The sudden change in its economic and social environment quickly generated stereotypes of the 'criminal migrant' (see Karydis, 1996), and therefore 'organised crime' policy represents under this approach a rational response at curbing the processes impacting migratory inflows. However, in the light of the positive economic contribution of migration inflows, the approach itself is far from rational. Rather, it is a convenient substitute for evidence-based, carefully planned policies aiming to harness the contribution of migrants for the benefit of the economy as a whole as well as the fiscal interest, and also to foster a process of social and cultural integration of migrants.

References

Amnesty International., *Greece: Out of the spotlight. The rights of foreigners and minorities are still a grey area.* Report EUR 26/016/2005, October 5, 2005. Available online from
http://web.amnesty.org/library/index/engeur250162005.

Amnesty International., *Greece: protection of rights of women and girls victims of trafficking for sexual exploitation.* Athens: Amnesty International Greek Section, 2007 (in Greek)

Andreas, P. and E.A. Nadelmann, *Policing the globe. Criminalisation and crime control in international relations.* New York: Oxford University Press, 2006

Antonopoulos, G.A., The Greek connection(s). The social organisation of the cigarette–smuggling business in Greece. *European Journal of Criminology*, 2008, 5(3), 263–288

Antonopoulos, G.A., 'Are the "others" coming?': evidence on 'alien conspiracy' from three illegal markets in Greece. *Crime, Law and Social Change*, 2009, 52(5), 475–493

Antonopoulos, G.A. and G. Papanicolaou, 'Gone in 50 seconds': the social organisation and political economy of the stolen cars market in Greece'. In P.C van Duyne, Donati, S., Maljevic, A., Harvey, J. and von Lampe, K. (eds.) *Crime, Money and Criminal Mobility in Europe.* (pp. 141-174) Nijmegen: Wolf Legal Publishers, 2009

Antonopoulos, G.A. and J.A. Winterdyk, Techniques of neutralising the trafficking of women. A case study of an active trafficker in Greece. *European Journal of Crime, Criminal Law and Criminal Justice*, 2005, 13(2), 136–147

Antonopoulos, G.A. and J.A. Winterdyk, The smuggling of migrants in Greece: an examination of its social organisation. *European Journal of Criminology*, 2006, 3(4), 439–461

Antonopoulos, G.A., G. Papanicolaou and M. Simpson, 'Entertainment Starts With an E': The Ecstasy Market in Greece'. *Trends in Organised Crime,* 2010, 13(1) (special issue on 'Drug Markets'), 31-45

Baldwin-Edwards, M., *Southern European labour markets and immigration: a structural and functional analysis.* Athens: Mediterranean Migration Observatory, 2002

Baldwin-Edwards, M., *Immigration into Greece, 1990–2003: a southern European paradigm.* Paper presented at the UNECE European Population Forum 2004, Geneva, 2004, January 12–14

Baldwin-Edwards, M., *The integration of immigrants in Athens: developing indicators and statistical measures.* Athens: Mediterranean Migration Observatory, 2005

Baldwin-Edwards, M., *Immigrants in Greece: characteristics and issues of regional distribution.* Athens: Mediterranean Migration Observatory, 2008

Bangladesh Thematic Group on Trafficking., Revisiting the human trafficking paradigm: the Bangladesh experience. Part I: trafficking of adults, 2004. Retrieved 15 November 2009 from http://www.iom.int//DOCUMENTS/PUBLICATION/EN/Full_BangladeshTrafficking_Rpt.pdf

Bruinsma, G. and W. Bernasco, Criminal Groups and Transnational Illegal Markets. *Crime, Law and Social Change,* 2004, 41, 79-94

Chtouris, S. and I. Psimmenos, *Migrant groups in Athens.* Mytilene: University of the Aegean, 1998

Dimitrainas, G., Combating human trafficking after L.3064/2002 (presentation). In E. Symeonidou-Kastanidou (ed.), *The new Law 3064/2002 on human trafficking* (pp. 87–156). Thessaloniki: Sakkoulas Publications, 2003 (in Greek)

Duyne, P.C. van, The Phantom and Threat of Organised Crime, *Crime, Law & Social Change,*1995, 24(4), 341-377

Duyne, P.C. van, The Creation of a Threat Image: Media, Policy Making and Organised Crime'. In van Duyne, P.C., Jager, M., von Lampe, K. and Newell, J.L. (eds.) *Threats and Phantoms of Organised Crime, Corruption and Terrorism: Rhetoric and Critical Perspectives.* (pp. 21-50) Nijmegen: Wolf Legal Publishers, 2003

Duyne, P.C. van, OCTA 2006: The unfulfilled promise, *Trends in Organised Crime,* 2007, 10, 120-128

Duyne, P.C. van and M. Houtzager, Criminal subcontracting in the Netherlands: the Dutch 'koppelbaas' as crime-entrepreneur. In: P.C. van Duyne, K. von

Lampe, M. van Dijck and J.L. Newell (eds.), *The organised crime economy. Managing crime markets in Europe.* Nijmegen, Wolf Legal Publishers, 2005

Duyne, P.C. van and M. van Dijck, Assessing Organised Crime: The Sad State of an Impossible Art. In: F. Bovenkerk and M. Levi (eds.) *The Organised Crime Community: Essays in Honour of Alan A. Block* (pp.101-124) New York: Springer, 2007

Duyne, P.C. van and M. Nelemans, Transnational organised crime. Thinking in and out of Plato's cave. In: F. Allum (ed.), *The Routledge Handbook of Transnational Organised Crime.* London, Routledge, forthcoming 2011

Duyne, P.C. van and M. Soudijn, Crime-money in the financial system. What we fear and what we know. In: M. Evans (ed.), *International Criminology Encyclopaedia.* Nijmegen, Wolf Legal Publishers, forthcoming, 2011

ESYE, *Census 2001*, 2001. Retrieved 9 November, 2009 from http://www.statistics.gr/portal/page/portal/ESYE/PAGE-database

Fakiolas, R., and L. Maratou-Alipranti, Foreign female immigrants in Greece. *Papers*, 2000, 60, 101–117

Galanopoulos, A., and V. Dionysopoulou, The communities of migrants. *Eleftherotypia*, 6 December 2003, retrieved May 5, 2008 from http://www.enet.gr

Gent, S., *The root causes of migration: criticising the approach and finding a way forwards.* Brighton: Sussex Centre for Migration Research, 2002.

Hatziprokopiou, P., Albanian immigrants in Thessaloniki, Greece: processes of economic and social incorporation. *Journal of Ethnic and Migration Studies*, 2003, 29(6), 1033–1057

Hellenic Parliament, *Report on draft law 'Amendment of provisions of the Penal Code and Code of Criminal Procedure regarding the protection of citizens from punishable acts of criminal organisations'.* Athens: Directorate of Scientific Studies, Hellenic Parliament, 2001 (in Greek)

Hellenic Police, *Annual report on organised crime in Greece 2003, open edition.* Athens: Hellenic Police, Hellenic Ministry of Public Order, 2004

Hellenic Police, *Annual report on organised crime in Greece 2004, open edition.* Athens: Hellenic Police, Hellenic Ministry of Public Order, 2005

Hellenic Police, *Annual descriptive report on organised crime in Greece 2005, open edition.* Athens: Hellenic Police, Hellenic Ministry of Public Order, 2006.

Hellenic Police, Table of arrested migrant smugglers by police and coast guard authorities, by nationality, first 8 months of 2009, 2009. Retrieved 15 November, 2009 from
http://www.astynomia.gr/images/stories/STATS/021009meta7.pdf

Hellenic Police, Offenders of human trafficking-procuring (articles 323A and 351 PC), no date. Retrieved May 12, 2008 from http://www.ydt.gr/main/Article.jsp?ArticleID=94800

IMEPO, *Estimate of the volume of migrants illegally residing in Greece*. Athens: Hellenic Migration Policy Institute, 2008 (in Greek)

Ioakimoglou, E., and Milios, J., Accumulation and profitability of capital in Greece (1964–2004). *Theseis,* 2005. Retrieved September 16 2009 from http://www.theseis.com/76-/theseis/t91/t91f/ioak-mil.htm (in Greek)

IOM, Country specific information on trafficking in human beings. No date. Retrieved November 15, 2009 from
http://www.belgium.iom.int/AGIS2003/pdf/Country%20Sections/Greece.pdf

Jordan, B., Stråth, B., and Triandafyllidou, A., Comparing cultures of discretion. *Journal of Ethnic and Migration Studies*, 2003, 29(2), 373–395

Kapsalis, A., *Presentation of results from interviews with target group of immigrant workers in construction, fuel and clothing sectors*. Athens: EKA, 2004

Karakousis, A., What Mr. Chrysochoidis knows. *To Vima*, 1 November 2009. Retrieved from
http://www.tovima.gr/default.asp?pid=49andct=1andartid=296818

Karydis, V., *The criminality of immigrants in Greece*. Athens: Papazisis, 1996 (in Greek)

King, R., T. Iosifides and L. Myrivili, A Migrant's Story: From Albania to Athens, *Journal of Ethnic and Migration Studies,* 1998, 24, 159-175

Kitsantonis, N., Migrants reaching Greece despite efforts to block them. *New York Times,* 19 November 2009. Retrieved November 19, 2009 from http://www.nytimes.com/2009/11/19/world/europe/19iht-greece.html?_r=1andpartner=rssandemc=rssandpagewanted=print

Kostakos, P. and G.A. Antonopoulos, The 'Good', the 'Bad' and the 'Charlie': The Business of Cocaine Smuggling in Greece, *Global Crime,* 2010, 11(1), 34-57

Kritikidis, G., Migration in Greece. 2003. Retrieved 19 October, 2009 from http://www.inegsee.gr/Μετανάστες.doc

Kritikidis, G., Migrants in the country's regions. 2004. Retrieved October 15, 2009 from
www.inegsee.gr/ΜΕΤΑΝΑΣΤΕΣ%20ΚΑΤΑ%20ΠΕΡΙΦΕΡΕΙΑ.doc

Kyriakou, I., *Statistical data on immigrants in Greece: analytical study on the available data and proposal for the harmonisation with the standards of the European Union.* Report for IMEPO, Mediterranean Migration Observatory IAPAD Panteion University, Athens, 2004

Labrianidis, L. and A. Lyberaki, *Albanian immigrants in Thessaloniki. Journeys of prosperity and aberrations of public image*. Thessaloniki: Paratiritis, 2001 (in Greek)

Lambropoulou, E., The routes of mafia. The georgaphy of organised crime in

Eastern Europe and the Balkans. *To Vima*, 30 January 2000, p. A47.

Lambropoulou, E., Greece. In M. den Boer (ed.), *Organized crime. A catalyst in the Europeanization of national police and prosecution agencies?* (pp. 261-307). Maastricht: European Institute of Public Administration, 2002

Lambropoulou, E., Criminal 'organisations' in Greece and public policy: from non-real to hyper-real. *International Journal of the Sociology of Law*, 2003, 31, 69-87.

Lambropoulou, E., Crime, criminal justice and criminology in Greece. *European Journal of Criminology*, 2005, 2(2), 211-247.

Lazaridis, G., The helots of the new millennium: ethnic-Greek Albanians and 'other' Albanians in Greece. In F. Anthias and G. Lazaridis (eds.), *Into the margins: migration and exclusion in Southern Europe* (pp. 105–121). Aldershot: Ashgate, 1999

Lazaridis, G., Trafficking and prostitution: The growing exploitation of migrant women in Greece. *European Journal of Women's Studies*, 2001, 8(1), 67–102

Lazaridis, G. and K. Romaniszyn, Albanian and Polish undocumented workers in Greece: a comparative analysis. *Journal of European Social Policy*, 1998, 8(1), 5-22

Lazos, G., *Prostitution and transnational trafficking in modern Greece, vol. 1: the prostitute.* Kastaniotis Publications , 2002 (in Greek)

Lazos, G., Transnational trafficking and forced prostitution in Greece of 2002, no date. Retrieved 26 March 2007, from http://www.stoptrafficking.org/database/STOPNOW_REPORT_en_2002.pdf

Linardos-Rylmon, P., *Foreign workers and labour market in Greece.* Athens: INE/GSEE, 1993 (in Greek)

Linardos-Rylmon, P. Forms of internationalisation and issues in immigration policy. In K. Kasimatis (ed.), *Immigration policies and strategies of integration. The case of Albanian and Polish immigrants* (pp. 283-305). Athens: Gutenberg, 2003a (in Greek)

Linardos-Rylmon, P., The need for a new approach of immigration. *Workbooks of INE*, 2003b, 24, 5–12

Mandrou, I., The business of organised crime. *To Vima*, 1999, p. A28

Markova, E. and A.H. Sarris, The performance of Bulgarian illegal immigrants in the Greek labour market. *South European Society and Politics*, 1997, 2(2), 57–77

Marvakis, A., D. Parsanoglou and M. Pavlou (eds.), *Immigrants in Greece.* Athens: Ellinika Grammata, 2001 (in Greek)

Mediterranean Migration Observatory (2004) *Statistical Data on Immigrants in Greece: An Analytic Study of Available Data and Recommendations for Conformity*

With European Union Standards. Athens: Mediterranean Migration Observatory, 2004

Naylor, R.T., *Wages of crime. Black markets, illegal finance and the underworld economy* (Revised ed.). Ithaca: Cornell University Press, 2004

Nelken, D., Immigrant beach selling along the Italian Adriatic coast: deconstructing a social problem. *Crime, Law and Social Change*, 2006, 45(4–5), 297–313

Nikolakopoulos, D., This is the Greek mafia. *To Vima*, 28 September 1997, p. A42

Ode, P., Nigerian community of Greece. In A. Marvakis, D. Parsanoglou, and M. Pavlou (eds.), *Immigrants in Greece* (pp. 351–352). Athens: Ellinika Grammata, 2001 (in Greek)

OECD, *Employment outlook*. Paris: Organisation for Economic Cooperation and Development, 2001.

Paoli, L., and C. Fijnaut, Introduction to part I: the history of the concept. In C. Fijnaut and L. Paoli (eds.), *Organised crime in Europe. Concepts, patterns and control policies in the European Union and beyond* (pp. 21–46). Dortrecht: Springer, 2004

Papanicolaou, G., Greece. In T. Jones and T. Newburn (eds.), *Plural policing: a comparative perspective* (pp. 77–97). London: Routledge, 2006

Papanicolaou, G., The sex industry, human trafficking and the global prohibition regime: a cautionary tale from Greece. *Trends in Organised Crime*, 2008, 11(4), 379–409

Papanicolaou, G., *Sex trafficking and transnational policing in southeast Europe: policing at the highest stage of capitalism*. Houndmills, Basingstoke: Palgrave Macmillan, forthcoming

Papanicolaou, G. and E. Boukli, Sex, trafficking and crime policy in Greece. In L. Cheliotis and S. Xenakis (eds.), *Crime and punishment in contemporary Greece*. Oxford: Peter Lang, forthcoming.

Pavlopoulos, P., *The hidden economy in Greece. A first quantitative outline*. Athens: IOBE, 1987 (in Greek)

Petriniotis, X., *Migration to Greece. A first recording, classification and analysis*. Athens: Odysseas, 1993

Psimmenos, I., *Immigration from the Balkans. Social exclusion in Athens* (2nd ed.). Athens: Papazisis Publications, 2004 (in Greek)

Psimmenos, I. and S. Georgoulas, Migration pathways: a historic, demographic and policy review of the Greek case. In A. Triantafyllidou (ed.), *Migration pathways: a historic, demographic and policy review of four European states* (pp. 38–32). Florence: European University Institute, 1999

Psimmenos, I., The making of periphractic spaces: the case of Albanian undocumented migrants in the sex industry of Athens. In F. Anthias and G. Lazaridis (eds.), *Gender and migration in Southern Europe. Women on the move* (pp. 81–101). Oxford: Berg, 2000

Rigakos, G.S. and G. Papanicolaou, The political economy of Greek policing: between neoliberalism and the sovereign State. *Policing and Society*, 2003, 13(3), 271–304

Ruggiero, V., Criminals and service providers: cross-national dirty economies, *Crime, Law and Social Change,* 1997, 28(1), 27-38

Sakellaropoulos, S., *Greece after the political changeover.* Athens: A.A. Livanis, 2001 (in Greek)

Sarris, A. H. and S. Zografakis, A computable general equilibrium assessment of the impact of illegal immigration on the Greek economy. *Journal of Population Economics*, 1999, 12, 155–182

Savona, E. U., C. Lewis and B. Vettori, (eds.), *EUSTOC: Developing an EU statistical apparatus for measuring organised crime, assessing its risk and evaluating organised crime policies.* Trento/Milano: Transcrime in cooperation with Centre National de la Recherche Scientifique, University of Huddersfield Applied Criminology Group and EUROPOL, 2005

Sheptycki, J.W.E., Against transnational organized crime. In M. E. Beare (ed.), *Critical reflections on transnational organised crime* (pp. 120–144). Toronto: University of Toronto Press, 2003

SOPEMI, *Trends in international migration: annual report 1996.* Paris: OECD, 1997

Spencer, J., The illicit movement of people across borders. The UK as a destination country and the disorganisation of criminal activity. In P.C. van Duyne, A. Maljevic, M. van Dijck, K. von Lampe and J. Harvey. (eds). *Crime Business and Crime Money in Europe: The Dirty Linen of Illicit Enterprise.* (pp.111-129) Nijmegen: Wold Legal Publishers, 2007

Spencer, J., Media constructing organised crime concepts in an extended criminal Europe: Trafficking women for sexual exploitation. In P.C van Duyne, J. Harvey, A. Maljević, K. von Lampe and M. Scheinost (eds.). *European Crime-Markets At Cross-Roads: Extended and Extending Criminal Europe.* (pp.43-61) Nijmegen: Wolf Legal Publishers, 2008

Sykiotou, A.P., Gendered criminality: an attempt towards a critical approach. In N. E. Kourakis (ed.), *Gendered criminality: penal and criminological approach to gender* (2nd ed.) (pp. 83–458). Athens: Ant. N. Sakkoulas, 2009 (in Greek)

Ta Nea, Violent fights for 5 Euro. War climate in Manolada of Ilia after the uprise of foreign workers for wages. *Ta Nea*, 21 April 2008, p. 13 (in Greek)

Travis, A., Chief drug adviser David Nutt sacked over cannabis stance. *The Guardian*, 30 October 2009, retrieved on 30 October 2009 from http://www.guardian.co.uk/politics/2009/oct/30/david-nutt-drugs-adviser-sacked/print

Tsarouchas, K., The turnover of prostitution is 600.000.000. *To Vima*, 10 March 2002, p. A44. (in Greek)

Tsoukala, A., The Perception of the 'Other and the Integration of Immigrants in Greece. In Geddes, A. and Farell, A. (eds) *The Politics of Belonging: Migrants and Minorities in Contemporary Europe.* (pp.109-124) Aldershot: Ashgate, 1999

Vettori, B., Safety crimes in the enlarged Europe: Between economic and social drivers. In P.C. van Duyne, S. Donati, J. Harvey, A. Maljevic, and K. von Lampe (eds.) *Crime, Money and Criminal Mobility in Europe.* (pp.361-393) Nijmegen: Wolf Legal Publishers, 2009

von Lampe, K., Not a Process of Enlightenment: The Conceptual History of Organized Crime in Germany and the United States of America, *Forum on Crime and Society*, 2001, 1(2), 99-116

von Lampe, K., Organised crime research in Europe: development and stagnation. In P.C. van Duyne, J. Harvey, A. Maljević, K. von Lampe and M. Scheinost (eds.), *European crime markets at cross roads. Extended and extending criminal Europe* (pp. 17–41). Nijmegen: Wolf Legal Publishers, 2008

von Lampe, K., The study of organised crime: An assessment of the state of affairs. In K. Ingvaldsen and V. Lundgren Sørli (eds.), Organised Crime: Norms, markets, regulation and research (pp.165-211) Oslo: Unipub, 2009.

Xenakis, S., International norm diffusion and organised crime policy: the case of Greece. *Global Crime*, 2004, 6(3), 345-373

Youth Against Racism – Greece, *To Imerologio tou Ratsismou stin Ellada: Theseis kai Protaseis gia tous Metanastes.* Athens: Youth Against Racism – Greece, 2000

Zaitch, D. and R. Staring, Trends and Policies on Women Trafficking in the Netherlands, *Crime and Justice International,* 2007, November/December, 15-22

Extortion rackets in Europe: An exploratory comparative study

Stefano Caneppele and Francesco Calderoni[1]

Introduction

This chapter presents an exploratory research performed on data concerning extortion rackets across twenty-seven EU Member States (Member States).[2] The article begins by defining extortion rackets and discussing the difficulties encountered when analysing it in a comparative manner. We then move on to explain how and what information is available on extortion rackets across the EU.

Extortion racket between extortion and criminal protection

The concept of 'extortion racket' is not generally used in the literature. As a matter of fact, it associates two different, but interrelated concepts: extortion and racket. In the general language, extortion is "*the action or practice of extorting or wresting anything, especially money, from a person by force or by undue exercise of authority or power*" (Oxford English Dictionary, 2008). In general, extortion is an offence under criminal law and is punished with relatively high penalties.[3]

---

1 Università Cattolica di Milano & TRANSCRIME (Joint Research Centre on Transnational crime - Università Cattolica di Milano, Università degli Studi di Trento).

2 The findings produced in this study are the result a the project "Study on Extortion Racketeering the Need for an Instrument to Combat Activities of Organised Crime". Mentioned project was carried out for the European Commission (October 2008-July 2009) by Transcrime – Joint Research Centre on Transnational crime, Università Cattolica di Milano – Università degli Studi di Trento.

3 For example, Article 312-1 of the French Criminal Code punishes extortion with up to seven years of imprisonment; Article 629 of the Italian Criminal Code punishes extortion with imprisonment between five and ten years; Section 21 of the United Kingdom Theft Act 1968 punishes blackmail with up to fourteen years of imprisonment; Section 253 of the German Criminal Code punishes extortion

The term 'racket' refers to "*a criminal enterprise, especially one conducted by an organized group*" (Oxford English Dictionary, 2008). Since the mid 19th Century, the concept of racket has generally been applied to illicit forms of business. In the first half of the 20th Century the expression was still significantly broad and "*used so loosely as to include a great variety of things one does not like 'graft, violence, monopolistic exactions, etc.'*" (Millis & Montgomery, 1945, p. 670). As Cohen notes, "*little has changed over the past six decades. For the public, racketeer is a general synonym for gangster*" (Cohen, 2003, p. 576). In the 1920s, Gordon Hostetter attempted to apply this notion to the illicit behaviours committed by members of trade unions. However, Hostetter did not succeed in his attempt and the concept of racket came to refer to gangs and organised criminal activities, most notably extortion, including those crimes committed *against* trade unions (Cohen, 2003).

Nowadays the concept of racket or racketeering is based mainly on an American criminological and legal perception that, for the most part, refers to 'organised crime' (see the famous Racketeer Influenced and Corrupt Organizations Act of 1970). This evolution highlights the character of the 'historical artefact' of the concept of racketeering (Cohen, 2003, p. 591) and its close connection with organised crime. The contents of both concepts is highly debatable and in especially the concept of organised crime has virtually been 'analysed to death' (Von Lampe et al., 2006; Van Duyne and Van Dijck, 2007).

In fact, racket is frequently a synonym for extortion, a type of extortion (Konrad and Skaperdas, 1998, p. 474) or, contrarily, extortion is a type of racketeering (Schelling, 1967, p. 63). Further, some scholars argue that extortion is "*the defining activity of organised crime*" (Konrad and Skaperdas, 1998, p. 462), while others state that extortion is not its 'defining feature'(Varese, 2006, p. 412). Although the extortion-racket connection is frequent, the previous examples show that there are some differences in the analyses of the specific relation between the two components. This is also because the concept of extortion frequently overlaps with the provision of criminal protection.

It is important to distinguish between extortion and criminal protection. Extortion implies a predatory action which involves a victim. The offender obtains a benefit through intimidation, threat or violence and against the will of the victim, who does not benefit from the crime. The presence of a victim may cause reporting to the authorities.

Criminal protection implies a collusive agreement in which all the parties involved receive advantages. Criminal protectors can protect from conventional

with up to five years of imprisonment. Article 243 of the Spanish Criminal Code applies from one to five years of imprisonment in addition to the penalty provided for the acts of violence actually perpetrated.

criminals, from police intervention, from competitors in a market. They can also provide illicit advantages, for example, granting access to politicians, public administrators and securing public contracts and funds. Unlike extortion, criminal protection requires extensive resources which are unlikely to be accessible to a single offender. Usually criminal protection is a service provided by criminal groups, such as mafia-type groups, and supplied to one or more enterprises. Since all the parties profit from the deal, there is no victim to report the crime. Therefore, its detection mostly depends on the investigative skills of law enforcement agencies. Further, these behaviours, once discovered, are rarely defined and prosecuted as extortion, but rather fall into the concepts of corruption, embezzlement and bribery.

Notwithstanding their differences, extortion and criminal protection are often confused (Varese, 2006, p. 412). In fact, it is not always easy to distinguish between extortion and criminal protection (Konrad & Skaperdas, 1998, p. 475). It may be more appropriate to view extortion and criminal protection as two poles in a *continuum*. The first pole is represented by a single episode of violent extortion against a victim who refuses to pay. This is a predatory crime which can be committed by single criminals as well as by groups. The second pole is represented by a collusive agreement between several actors where some provide illicit services and favours and some provide other benefits in exchange (e.g. money). At the first pole the involved parties are in contrast and the criminal behaviour results in the prevarication of the victim. At the second pole the involved parties are partners and the criminal behaviour results in an illicit agreement.

In the literature, a few contributions analyse extortion from a mainly economic perspective (Konrad & Skaperdas, 1998, p. 462, Shavell, 1992). Criminal protection has received more attention (for detailed references, see Varese, 2006: 412), namely in relation to the criminal protection provided by mafia-type groups. In particular, some scholars analysed criminal protection from an economic perspective. Some pointed out that mafia-type groups provide criminal protection to a market, therefore supplying a demanded service (Gambetta, 1996). This approach aligns criminal protection to other illicit goods and services (e.g. drugs, prostitution, weapons) and focuses on the reasons why some markets are demanding criminal protection (e.g. lack of trust towards national authority in the Southern Italian society). This approach enjoyed significant consensus in the international literature (Van Duyne, 2003, p. 30).

The Italian literature, however, raises several criticisms to it (*nemo profeta in patria*). Scholars argued that the mafia, with its violent activities and its control over some territories, is the initial cause of the market demand for protection.

The lack of trust in the legal institutions is therefore a consequence of the presence of mafia-type groups rather than of some peculiar elements in a society. The focus shifts from the demand of criminal protection to its supply (Catanzaro, 1994; Armao, 2000, pp. 157-158). Other scholars refuse to dedicate their attention solely to the protection market as they sustain the argument that mafia-type groups not only supply protection, but also enjoy protection from other parts of a given society (e.g. law enforcement, politics). Ultimately, the mafia is a complex phenomenon which is in relation with other actors in a multiplicity of possible interactions. It should be considered as an element of the structure of power within a given society (Santino, 2006, pp. 42-44).

These different interpretations and distinctions influence research carried out on extortion rackets. For the purposes of this research, the concept of extortion racket means *systematic* extortion carried out by a *group of criminals*. Using the continuum discussed above in this paragraph extortion–criminal protection, extortion racket is between the two extreme poles. This type of systematic extortion has been rarely addressed by specific studies (Konrad & Skaperdas, 1998). However, it presents several features that make it different and more dangerous than simple single episodes of extortion. Its systematic (continuous and repeated) nature is likely to affect the economy and the development of a community, affecting the decisions of entrepreneurs and citizens. Further, extortion racket is extremely difficult to detect and enforce. It is likely to be very underreported, since the victims may fear retaliation by the criminals. For example, mafia-type groups in Southern Italy frequently resort to extortion racket by exploiting their specialisation in the use of violence and their established criminal reputation allowing them to obtain advantages through intimidation and threats. In these cases, extortion racket is one of the instruments to establish a criminal control over a territory. Indeed, the profits of extortion rackets may appear like taxes imposed by a state-like entity which is competing with the legitimate state for power and tax collection.

Extortion racket is a crime that requires further empirical research. The literature on organised crime has mostly focused on the provision of criminal protection. However, this activity has some remarkable differences from extortion racket being on the other end of the continuum. It can be expected that this one-sided attention affects also the availability of data on extortion rackets. Apart from that, most scholars do not provide data on extortion, extortion rackets or criminal protection, but rather base their different approaches on theoretical constructions and interpretations. A data based research is clearly wanted.

The challenge of comparative and cross national analysis of crime

The comparative analysis of crime in different countries faces important difficulties. More specifically, in the field of quantitative analysis, the difficulties lie in the conceptual validity and reliability of crime data. Scholars have pointed out that the main purpose of crime statistics is administrative and not scientific research (Aromaa & Joutsen, 2003, pp. 3-6). Consequently, official crime statistics mainly serve the purposes of state authorities and law enforcement agencies, and reflect what a state chooses to criminalise and what the law enforcement agencies choose to actually deal with (Deflem, 1997, p. 154).

When attempting to compare crime among different countries the difficulties increase. The number of countries taken into consideration multiplies the issues relating to all the factors affecting the validity and reliability of crime statistics. Differences in national cultures, criminal justice systems and legal definitions make comparison extremely difficult. A few examples may clarify this. First, legal qualifications and definitions may vary significantly among jurisdictions and this implies that crime statistics measure different phenomena. For example, the theft of a motor vehicle is one of the crimes showing less variance in its legal definition among countries. Nevertheless, this category includes attempted theft in Bulgaria, it includes motorboats in Finland and it excludes motorcycles and mopeds in Greece (Eurostat, 2009, p. 25). Clearly, these differences influence the levels of recorded crimes among countries. Secondly, the dark figure (i.e. unreported crimes) may vary significantly among countries. For any given type of crime, this depends on several factors, such as the population's trust in the criminal justice system in general, the efficiency of data collection procedures and the socio-economic conditions of the population. For example, studies have demonstrated that both the likelihood of reporting crimes and the police capacity to gather crime data are related to the level of economic and development indices (Neuman & Berger, 1988, p. 299; Andrienko, 2002; Soares, 2004, pp. 167-173; van Dijk, 2009; van Dijk, Manchin, van Kesteren, Nevala, & Hideg, 2005, pp. 109-110). Thus, high levels of recorded crimes are more likely to reflect the higher propensity of the population to report crimes than the actual volume of criminal activities. For example, the rate of insurance against theft in a country influences the reporting of property crime. Thirdly, the data collection procedures and the statistical techniques change amongst countries and this inevitably affects any comparison (Aebi, 2008).

In response to these problems, since the 1960s, additional data collection methods have been developed. These are victimisation surveys, which entail interviewing people about their crime experiences. Victimisation surveys can be considered as complementary information that allows for a more complete analysis. The integration of both sources (and possibly the triangulation with socio-economic data) has provided significant improvements in cross national comparison of crime (Mugellini, 2010, p. 40). However, victimisation surveys still encounter various hindrances (e.g. cultural differences, sampling of respondents, memory of the respondents and willingness to respond) which also include their frequency and costs.

The difficulties in comparing crime amongst countries are even graver for non-conventional crimes.[4] Undoubtedly, extortion rackets falls within the category of non-conventional crimes. Official crime statistics in this field are extremely unreliable, or even "*a source of disinformation*" (van Dijk, 2007, p. 40). As for comparative cross-national analyses in general, the most recent contributions include data from different sources and in particular victimisation surveys (Van Dijk, 2008, 2007, p. 145). Victimisation surveys may help in the analysis of non-conventional crimes. They partially overcome the critical problems relating to differential definitions among countries, since these surveys are based on common definitions which are independent from the definitions provided by national criminal law. Further, victimisation surveys frequently ask whether the respondents reported the crime to the police and therefore provide information also on unreported crimes (Alvazzi del Frate, 2008, pp. 229-231).

Comparing extortion rackets at international level

In the light of the arguments outlined above, the international comparison of extortion rackets is a daunting task. The difficulties encountered relate to at least two different issues. First of all, as observed in the previous section, extortion racket is an unclear and under-researched topic which is affected by the problems related with research on organised crime. Secondly, comparative or cross-national analysis of crimes faces the problems as discussed: the validity and commensurability of concepts and reliability of crime data gathered on extortion racket across countries. In addition, data on non conventional crimes such as extortion rackets are seldom available and hardly ever reliable or may be recorded under different criminal qualifications.

---

4 Generally, conventional crimes (or common/volume crimes) include theft, burglary, rape, assault. Non conventional (complex) crimes include, for example, corruption, money laundering, terrorism and organised crime (van Dijk, 2008, p. 17).

In the light of the possible difficulties that can be encountered while performing research on extortion rackets, this study conducted an exploratory analysis of the presence of extortion rackets and available data on them among EU Member States.

Methodology: exploring information on extortion rackets across the EU

In this study extortion racket refers to the crime of extortion coupled with three additional elements:

- Two actor's elements: 1) extortion committed by a group of three or more people; 2) extortion committed by people who are not public officials
- One skill element: 3) the offence is committed regularly/on a professional basis.

The goal of the study was to explore the different data sources on extortion rackets among EU Member States. This included the collection and analysis of administrative crime statistics and victimisation surveys on extortion rackets. Further, additional information has been collected through national experts.

Sources collected

In order to provide an exploratory analysis of data on extortion rackets among EU Member States, the research followed two steps.

The first step consisted of literature research and review. As highlighted above, academic literature on extortion rackets is rare, theoretical and focuses mainly on criminal protection by organised crime.[5] Only in a few cases do some scholars specifically address extortion racket namely in countries such as Italy, Bulgaria and Germany (Gambetta, 1996; Varese 2006, Gounev 2006, Ohlemacher 1999 & 2002, Tzvetkova, 2008). Similarly, reports by European and national law enforcement and research institutions rarely deal with the extortion rackets in detail. The literature research also focused on national criminal legislation concerning extortion rackets, covering substantive criminal law, procedural criminal law and

5 The sources used mainly include documents in English even if, where possible, sources in different languages (Italian, German, French and Spanish) were considered.

additional legislation which provide protection programmes for victims, witnesses and collaborators with justice.

The second step entailed the administration of a questionnaire to 27 national experts (February-July 2009). The experts were initially selected from those who attended the Seminar on "Counteraction of Extortion Racket" held in Frascati, Italy in 2007 and arranged within the framework of the AGIS Programme. Most of the selected national experts were members of law enforcement agencies, although some of the selected experts were staff members of NGOs and universities. The questionnaire aimed to provide additional information and also to fill the information gap which still existed after desk research. It included a thirty-six open and closed questions divided into four sections aiming at collecting information on extortion rackets, the legislative framework and measures implemented to counteract this phenomenon, and the best practices employed at national level in response to this type of crime. Subsequently, the research team drafted a country profile for each EU Member State. The country profiles were then validated by the national experts.

Extortion rackets in European Countries

This study shows that very limited information is available on extortion racket across EU Member States. This applies to both administrative crime statistics and victimisation surveys. Nevertheless, the collected information, integrated with scientific literature, reports from national and international law enforcement agencies and research institutions, added to the information provided by national experts allowed us to assess the presence of extortion rackets among different geographical areas of the European Union.

Crime statistics on extortion rackets in EU Member States

Administrative crime statistics provide only a limited description of extortion rackets in the EU Member States.

In general, the gathering of data is not specific to the offence of extortion racketeering. Usually such data are collected together with data on the general offence of extortion, which mainly includes offences which are not perpetrated by organised criminal groups, nor are they committed on a regular/professional basis. In some cases, data on extortion are grouped with other offences such as robbery, theft with violence or bribery. This applies to the majority of EU Member States, namely: Austria, Belgium, Denmark, Cyprus, Finland, France, Hungary, Ireland, Italy, Lithuania, Luxembourg, Malta, Poland, Portugal, Slovakia, Spain and the United Kingdom.

Only a few EU Member States appear to register extortion rackets separately. In these cases, data on the phenomenon are limited to small numbers. The following examples describe the data collected in Germany, Latvia, Slovenia and Greece.

According to the report on organised crime published by Germany's Federal Criminal Police Office (the Bundeskriminalamt), in 2007 nationwide there were 25 cases of organised crime in the field of violent crime. 11 of these 25 cases were cases of extortion, most of which involved protection rackets. Cases of protection rackets have only been specifically recorded in the general crime statistics since the beginning of 2008. There were 56 reported cases of protection rackets in 2008, but data acquisition is not yet completed (information has only been provided by eight of the 16 German Länder).

In Latvia, national statistics registered two extortion offences committed by organised criminals in 2007 and two in 2008. In Slovenia, data on extortion crimes committed by organised criminal groups amounted to 11 reported cases in 2006, 18 in 2007 and 11 in 2008. In Greece in 2004 (the latest information available) there were five criminal organisations subjected to extortion investigation (Hellenic Republic Ministry of Public Order, 2005).

These examples confirm the difficulties encountered by administrative crime statistics offices in recording extortion rackets. Most EU Member States collect data on extortion in general, while only a few Member States collect specific data on extortion racket. In these cases, the recorded cases showed a very low prevalence.

From this perspective, it is possible to envisage some possible alternatives to integrate data on extortion rackets (Gounev, 2006). Data on other criminal activities can provide additional information on extortion rackets. For example (see fig. 1), in 1993-1994, Bulgaria saw record levels of bombings and murders. However, registered cases of extortion rackets amounted to just a few hundred per year and saw less than a dozen individuals convicted. This draws attention to the large number of unreported racketeering incidents and the difficulties encountered in ensuring the conviction of suspects.[6] This situation can be explained by the fact that the National Statistical Institute (Republic of Bulgaria) only collects data on individuals who have been convicted of extortion. It does not collect crime data on extortion racket complaints as registration of such crimes can be difficult and the police frequently refrain from recording these activities or complaints. Never-

6 Information provided by the Bulgarian national expert Tihomir Bezlov, Center for the Study of Democracy, Sofia (Bulgaria).

theless, police recorded data on extortion cases show a peak of this type of crime in 1996. According to the national expert, 1996 was the 'golden' year for extortion rackets in Bulgaria

Figure 1.
Extortion racket and violence in Bulgaria, absolute values, 1991-2004

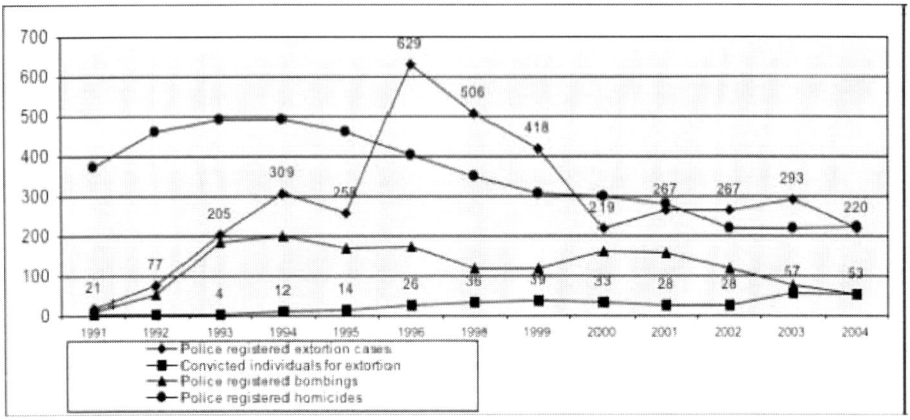

Source: Gounev (2006)

Additional data can provide a more integrated picture. Homicides, for example, show a lower dark figure. During the period between 1992-1996 bombings, homicides and police recordings of extortion saw an increase in rates and/or maintained significantly high levels. However, since 1997 the data gathered shows a decline in prevalence. This may be explained by attempts by the 'violent entrepreneurs' to curtail extreme forms of violence.

The Bulgarian experience suggests that data on other criminal activities could also be used as a proxy indicator for extortion rackets. However, this type of analysis requires great caution: it is very complex and requires detailed knowledge of national history, society and data collection methods. Furthermore, it is only possible to analyse the changing trends with unknown margins of error, rather than its magnitude.

In conclusion, administrative crime statistics on extortion racket are extremely limited and, most probably, display only the tip of the iceberg.

Victimisation surveys on extortion and protection rackets

As discussed earlier, victimisation surveys may provide additional information on extortion rackets, uncovering issues which are not recorded by police or judicial crime statistics. Consequently, it is important to consider data from victimisation surveys in order to complement the limited information provided by administrative crime statistics. However, in this case, as in all cases related to organised crime activities, omissions and incomplete answers may heavily affect the response rate. Particular attention was dedicated to business crime victimisation surveys. Since extortion rackets are likely to affect enterprises, business crime victimisation surveys may provide important information on this crime (Mugellini, 2010, p. 43).

The most relevant business crime victimisation surveys carried out so far may provide information on how extortion rackets are rarely tackled by law enforcement agencies. Unfortunately, these surveys cannot be compared as they were administered at different times, they examined different samples and they followed different methodologies.

Germany (1995/1996)

A victimisation survey of restaurateurs carried out in the mid-1990s (Ohlemacher, 1999, 2002) showed that direct experience of extortion was reported – varying by ethnic origin – by 4–13% of respondents and, within that figure, cases of extortion of protection money were reported by 2–6% of the respondents (N = 3.489). Additionally, results from telephone interviews showed that between 15% and 28% of the respondents reported cases of extortion amongst their *acquaintances*. The highest percentage in this range of vicarious victimisation (28%) was reported by Turkish respondents: about 40% of these cases (N=151) were claimed to be ones of 'asking for donations', e.g. for exiled political groups. For the Greek (N=204), German (N=2.755) and Italian (N=379) respondents the estimates of victimisation rates varied from 8–13%; only the Turkish respondents (N=151), with an average estimate of 27%, saw their fellow countrymen as being more likely to experience extortion. The estimates in the biggest cities (over 500.000 inhabitants) did not result in the high percentages commonly cited in the public discourse – the highest perceived victimisation was that of Turkish business-people in big cities, which amounted to some 31%.

International crime business survey (ICBS, 2000).

The ICBS carried out by UNICRI in nine central-eastern European capital cities (among the current EU Member States: Vilnius (Latvia, N=525), Sofia (Bulgaria, N=532) Bucharest (Romania, N=480) and Budapest (Hungary, N=517)) reported findings on extortion rackets. The percentage of respondents who experienced intimidation/extortion – defined in the survey as extorting money from a company, threatening and intimidating managers and/or employees, and threatening product contamination (such as poisoning of food, altering of colours, damaging of external packages, etc.) – were 8% in Sofia, 7% in Vilnius, 6% in Budapest and 10% in Bucharest. Requests for protection money – defined in the survey as somebody who requested money in exchange for his/their services to protect a company from robbery, extortion, acts of vandalism or further requests of bribes – had a lower prevalence, except for Bulgaria (steady at 8%): Vilnius 3%, Budapest 2%, Bucharest 1%. (See: Alvazzi del Frate, 2008). Unfortunately, the study was carried out in 2000 and has not yet been replicated. Consequently, the data collected are not likely to represent a reliable measure of the current situation.

Bulgaria (2000 and 2005)

The ICBS, conducted in 2000 for the United Nations Interregional Institute on Crime and Justice, provided a snapshot of protection rackets (Gounev, 2006). The survey findings indicate that 11,4% of Bulgarian businesses stated that extortion racket was either common or very common in their line of business. When asked if they had been subject to racketeering, 7,9% of businesses responded positively. For 78,9% of these respondents, this happened less than five times during 1999, but for the remaining 21,1% it had become a monthly experience. The respondents pointed to 'organised criminal groups' (79%) and rival businesses (21%) as the main perpetrators. The United Nations Interregional Crime and Justice Research Institute (UNICRI) study shows that, at that time, the phenomenon of protection racketeering was still much more widespread in Bulgaria than in most other Eastern European countries which had not been part of the former Soviet Union. Reliable figures remain scarce or as Gounev pointed out (2006: 115)

> "*the great majority of racketeering[. . .] remained unreported . . . . The main reason for the lack of reporting was fear of reprisals (63%). Two other reasons mentioned were that the police were not interested (40%) and were unlikely to be able to help (23%). It is probable that at the height of the racketeering boom (1993–1995) an even greater number of these crimes remained unreported*".

In the 2005 business crime victims survey (N=308), only 1,3% of the respondents indicated that they had been asked for *protection money* during 2005 – a significant reduction from the 2000 level of 7,3% (Gounev, 2006).

Overall, however, 9% of the companies had been victims of a range of threats and extortion (protection money being only one aspect). Generally, small companies with fewer than ten employees were up to five times more likely to fall victim to such crimes than companies with over one hundred employees. In only 7% of cases, though, were private security companies directly blamed as the perpetrators of such threats and extortion. In the other cases, local organised criminal groups (33%) and competition (26%) were named as the main culprits. Nevertheless, the data suggest that some private security companies remain involved in criminal activities. The levels of reporting threats and racketeering to the police were still low – 70% were not reported – although 22% had reported this type of crime, which is a clear increase from the earlier figure of 8%. However, this percentage is significantly lower than other types of crimes, which generally have reporting rates of over 50%. In 2005 the key reasons given for not reporting these incidents to the police were the perception that the police could not do anything about it (31%), and that this was a problem that had nothing to do with the police (31%). One key difference concerning the reasons for not reporting the crime to the police can be found in the survey administered in 2000. With regard to the possible reasons for not reporting the crime, one could have opted for the answer "fear of reprisals"; in 2005 only 21% mentioned this as a reason for not reporting, while in the survey administered in 2000 a staggering 63% mentioned it as a reason.

United Kingdom (2006/2007)

With reference to businesses as victims of extortion rackets, a study examined the impact of organised crime against businesses located in three high crime residential neighbourhoods. It was based on a survey of businesses in the three areas (420 interviews with owners and/or managers between November 2006 and January 2007). Police intelligence and local community contacts (Tilley *et al.*, 2008) indicated that only 1% of all respondents believed they had been victims of organised extortion. The same study showed that, within the London sample area, while businesses with Turkish/Kurdish/Cypriot (TKC) owners tended to have lower prevalence levels for external crimes committed against them, they tended to be victims of extortions perpetrated by their countrymen (Tilley *et al.*, 2008). However, as Tilley *et al.* remarked, "*the survey findings and police intelligence provide rather different impressions of organised crime and its dynamics in London, particularly in relation to the extent that businesses were being targeted for extortion*" (26). According to the authors there are several reasons which may explain the difference: businesses may have omitted to report incidents in the survey, business victims of extortion decided to not take part in the survey, the recall period selected in the survey (extortion victim within last 12-month) may have been too short, the police incident-focused approach tends to overestimate the magnitude of the phenomenon, there is a different perception of what is extortion and what is not inside and outside communities.

Italy (2008)

In 2008 the first Italian business victimisation survey was carried out by the Italian Ministry of Interior in collaboration with Transcrime, Joint Research Centre on Transnational Crime. The survey involved a representative sample of 11.477 Italian businesses.[7] Among the various topics covered by the survey, particular emphasis was given to the collection of data on criminal phenomena closely related to the presence of organised crime such as bribery, extortion and usury. Questions on the phenomenon of the extortion racket had the same structure as those used for the collection of data on common criminality.

The survey collected data on victimisation over two time periods, namely in the last three years and in the last twelve months. If the respondent declared that his or her business had been a victim during at least one episode in the last twelve months, further details on the last episode were gathered.

Key findings from a preliminary analysis of the data collected show that 10,9% of businesses in Italy were *concerned* about being victims of extortion (Fig. 2). This value is higher (20%) for businesses located in the Southern regions of the country (8,3% in the North). Independently of geographical position, the economic sectors more concerned about the possibility of being victims of an extortion racket were hotels and catering, along with the commercial and retail sector.

1,9 % of the businesses reported that extortion was very common in their line of business, and 7,4% that it was quite common. Data disaggregated in the southern provinces of Italy and the rest of the country confirmed the distribution of perceived concern: the phenomenon affects businesses in the Southern regions more frequently than those in the rest of the country.

Over the three years prior to the survey 1,7% of the Italian businesses had been victims of extortion, and 29,1% of these had been victims of protection rackets, which is when threats and intimidations are made in order to impose protection services. This rate is higher (43,2%) for businesses located in the south of the country.

During the twelve months prior to the Italian business victimisation survey 0,4% of Italian businesses had experienced at least one extortion episode. This figure actually varies considerably according to the geographical area. 1,4% of businesses from southern provinces reported being victimized, while this concerned only 0,1% of businesses in northern provinces. Businesses subject to extortion rackets mostly operated in the construction sector (0,7% of them were af-

---

[7] The survey covered the following crimes: theft, fraud, robbery, vandalism, counterfeiting, cybercrime, threats and intimidation, bribery, extortion, loansharking.The results are representative for all the Italian Businesses with more than one employee (N= approximately 2 million).

fected by the criminal practice) and in public and personal services (0,6%). Remarkably, 77,5% of the businesses victims of an extortion racket reported that the racketeers were members of local organised criminal groups.

Figure 2.
Italian businesses <u>worried</u> about being victim of extortion in 2008. Geographical distribution

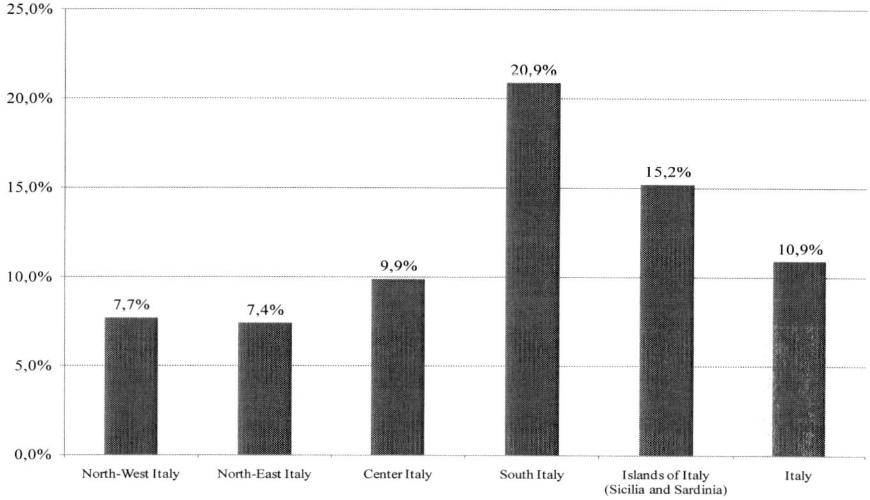

Source: Italian Ministry of Interior - Transcrime

Among the Italian businesses subject to extortion rackets only 6,6% declared that they had reported an extortion racket to the police, while 19,8% replied that they had informed the police without formal reporting and 73,6% of the victimised businesses had not reported to the police. It is to be noted that 92,5% of the businesses that declared they had reported a racket to the police had been subject to reprisals.

Combining existing data with national expert judgement

In the absence of reliable data on extortion rackets, additional information was collected through a network of national experts. The information obtained from 27 national expert judgment has been compared with national data on extortion rackets and with data from national technical reports dealing with organised crime in general. This approach allowed us to integrate the expert judgment with other sources in order to get a more comprehensive interpretation of extortion rackets. The main results have been framed by geographical areas.

Northern Europe

Consisting of Denmark, Estonia, Finland, Latvia, Lithuania, Sweden. These countries can be divided into two sub-groups: the Scandinavian region and the Baltic region. In the Scandinavian region (Denmark, Finland, Sweden) extortion rackets, when present, depended mainly on motorbike gangs. According to the Danish National Police, rival motorbike clubs are in competition for domination of the area of crime, extortion and protection money (Danish National Police, 2006). The same applies to Sweden (where, according to the most recent study carried out by the National Council for Crime Prevention against motorbike gangs, there were about 300 such gangs, 20 of which were involved in criminal activities) and in Finland, where extortion rackets seem to be committed by local motorbike gangs (Hells Angels, Banditos etc). It should be noted that currently the level of these activities appears to be very low in all three of these countries, although there are some forewarnings of future increases in such activities. Of particular concern are some juvenile gangs in Denmark where "*larger groups of youth and young adults . . . are now becoming increasingly involved in violent crimes such as extortion, protection money (. . .)*" (Cornilis and Greve, 2004), along with an increasing trend in the professionalisation of extortion rackets in Sweden.

In the Baltic region things seem to be different. Extortion rackets have changed since the beginning of the 1990s. They have switched from extortion of businesses through 'protection' to extortion activities performed through legal channels in the context of the privatisation of state-owned companies (BNS, 1999). Although there is a lack of updated information on the phenomenon, the impression is that extortion racket has become a more concealed practice (even harder to detect) in which physical violence is less used than in the past.

Western Europe

Comprising Austria, Belgium, France, Germany, Ireland, Luxemburg, the Netherlands, the United Kingdom. In these countries extortion rackets do not seem to represent a major problem, although the phenomenon exists in some regions. Separatist movements/paramilitary organisations perpetrate extortion racket in France and in the UK. In France the Corsican separatist movement *FNLC Union des Combattants* practices "*extortion racket on the island to the detriment of shopkeepers and civil engineering contractors.*" (Colombi, 2007). With reference to separatist organisations, Basque separatists also use France as a base for racketeers. The region bordering Ireland with Northern Ireland finds itself in the same conditions.

As well as being a means of raising finance for terrorist operations, extortion in North Ireland (UK) has also been used effectively since the early 1970s to exercise paramilitary control over the community. Extortion probably generates millions of pounds per annum for paramilitary organisations. The true extent of Northern Ireland's extortion problem is not reflected in the number of cases successfully prosecuted; it is likely that less than 10% of extortion is reported to police although the number of businesses coming forward to ask for police assistance is increasing. The building trade is affected even more so, while fast food outlets, restaurants and licensed premises, car dealerships and other retail outlets have also been affected.

Some hints of extortion racket practices inside ethnic communities have been indicated in Austria, Belgium, France, Germany, The Netherlands and UK. Unfortunately, it is hard to collect satisfactory pieces of information on such indications. In France foreign organisations – especially Turkish and Chinese – tend to engage in extortion against co-nationals living in large urban areas. The Turkish community records the largest number of blackmail and racket offences (680 implicated persons over two years in France). Moreover, these cases concern both extortion and the levying of the 'revolutionary tax' for the far left "TKP-ML". The Turkish community is followed by the Chinese one (91 implicated persons over the same period of time) (Colombi, 2007). In Paris, Chinese merchants make periodic payments of $500 to $2.500 in 'tea money' to buy protection from gangs (Faligot, 2001). Some gangs engaged in this form of extortion are known to be operated by higher-level mafia officials with impeccable credentials as legitimate businessmen.[8] In Belgium Chechen and Chinese groups raise some concerns of extortion racket practices but investigative evidence is poor. The same is happening in Austria where protection rackets in legal and illegal entertainment sectors being operated by foreign criminal groups (Russian, Turkish, Israeli, ex-Yugoslavian, Georgian) is anticipated to grow in the future due to the increase in the amount of foreigners becoming bar and restaurant owners. In Germany a

---

8 "Wenzhou gangs are active in extorting money from Chinese merchants from the same group in the Belleville section of northeast Paris, where gangs have waged violent turf battles. Similar protection rackets operate in Paris' Chinatown, in the 13th Arondissement (where the dominant group is the Teochew, from southeastern Guangdong Province), and in the suburbs of Paris, but gang competition in those areas is not as violent. (. . .) After the murder of two Chinese godfathers by rival gangs in Belleville in 1997, control of the local extortion business and the trafficking of illegal migrants went through a chaotic period. By 2000, the main activities of organised Chinese criminal groups in Paris were illegal labour and the traffic in illegal workers, illegal gambling and prostitution, kidnapping for ransom, armed robbery, and extortion. All these crimes often are accompanied by violence" (Curtis et al, 2002: 18- 57).

study delineated extortion racketeering practices against illegal cigarettes street vendors within the Vietnamese community (Von Lampe, 2002: 154). Nevertheless, it is still extremely difficult to find updated and complete information concerning extortion rackets both from police data or other sources.

Central and Eastern Europe

Comprising Bulgaria, the Czech Republic, Hungary, Poland, Slovakia, Slovenia, Romania. The main characteristic of this region is that it is made up of countries which have recently passed from a communist regime to a democratic state and consequently from a state-driven economy to the free market economy. This means that this region passed through some political instability. Several elements which may cause a situation of social, political and economic instability and uncertainty are also elements which facilitate organised criminal activities. Of course, even if these countries exhibit the above similarities, this does not mean that organised crime has evolved and continues to evolve in them in similar ways. In fact, these countries differ in terms of their crime situation.

Of particular interest, from a point of view of extortion racketeering, is Bulgaria where the model of entrepreneurship by violence (also 'dubbed' selling protection) has been well-documented in its evolution since just after the fall of the communist regime, when private security companies sprung up (Gounev, 2006; Tzvetkova, 2008). In this country private security companies (which usually practice protection racketeering) have been fuelled by three different sources, each of which can be considered direct or indirect consequences of the political transition. Group members were initially recruited *among athletes*, hence the popular name 'wrestler groups' or 'wrestlers'. Similarly to the former Soviet Union and the German Democratic Republic, Bulgaria had a well developed system for training professional athletes in Olympic sports. A network of sports schools was already in place, where a high number of children were trained to become professional athletes. At that time, the state ensured lifelong support for the elite athletes. With the demise of communist rule, the system was deprived of financial support, leaving tens of thousands of athletes practically out on the street. Some of them, in particular the heavy weight athletes, joined the violent entrepreneur groups, which guaranteed them a new identity, good incomes, and prospects for rapid prosperity amid the chaos of the transition. The members recruited by these organisations had thus unique psychological and physical experience in using violence, winning fights, enduring pain, etc. Structurally, the sports schools themselves formed the backbone of the future organised crime groups.

The second pool which provided recruits for the violent entrepreneur groups consisted of former *officers from the police and special services*. In the period between

1990-1992, twelve to seventeen thousand employees were discharged from this system for ideological reasons. It is generally believed that the representatives of this group, whose names rarely become public, have played a key role in the choice of activities undertaken by the violent entrepreneur structures. They also perform the critical function of mediators in the event of problems encountered with law enforcement authorities.

A third pool of recruits consisted of *criminals*, a great many of whom were given amnesty in the early 1990s.

Today the phenomenon, which registered its maximum visible violence in 1995/1996 (when Bulgaria regulated the private security companies system) and 2000/2001, still exits, although it has since evolved into a more subtle and invisible form. As Tzvekova suggested (2008: 23), "*some groups managed to adapt to the changing conditions by assuming new identities, others collapsed. In addition, some mobsters were pushed to criminal markets and activities while others managed to invest in a wide range of legitimate businesses*".

Bulgaria is not the only country which experienced the phenomenon of private security companies. This phenomenon can also be found in Poland, Romania and Slovakia. In recent years, Romania has had to deal ever more with criminal elements originating from the Republic of Moldova and the Ukraine. These elements are organised into different forms of association (usually criminal, but also disguised as private companies) and are usually involved in extortion racket practices (Carp *et al.*, 2007).

Some evidence of extortion rackets among ethnic communities (Ukrainian, Albanian, Russian and Chinese) has been namely witnessed in Hungary, Bulgaria, Slovakia, Slovenia even if the phenomenon plausibly seems to exist in all Europe.

Furthermore, in Poland organisations belonging to the so-called 'Polish mafia' are still involved in extortion rackets and protection rackets. They are generally made up of Polish citizens and are organised on a hierarchical basis.

Southern Europe

Comprising Cyprus, Greece, Italy, Malta, Portugal, Spain. This region is highly heterogeneous with reference to the conditions of both organised crime and extortion rackets. Differences outweigh the similarities in the structure of organised crime groups operating in these countries, and this is also reflected in the different ways in which extortion rackets are conducted. However, the areas most at risk of extortion rackets in Southern Europe seem to be the Basque region in Spain, where terrorist groups belonging to ETA perpetrate extortion rackets, and Southern Italy where mafia-type organised crime practices involve extortion racketeering. These groups use extortion in order to control the territory and to finance their criminal groups. Extortion racket in Italy is one of the most complex, due to the types of actors involved and the relationships they create with the victims they extort. The national criminal organisations (mafia-type groups) are involved in extortion rackets against both legitimate and illegitimate actors (Gambetta, 1996; SOS Impresa 2007; SOS Impresa 2008).

When committed by national mafia-type groups, extortion is both an instrument of territorial control and an expression of it. These groups infiltrate legitimate markets and restrict the activities of criminal actors (such as drug dealers) that do not belong to the organisation. The organisations involved in such criminal activities have hierarchical structures (La Spina, 2005; Filocamo, 2007) and tend to create parasitic and symbiotic relationships with their victims (SOS Impresa, 2008). In 2000 a new extortion strategy was detected (Grasso, 2002). In fact, the amount of protection money requested from victims had changed: it had been decreased, although a higher number of victims were obliged to pay the requested fee. The mafia's motto seems to be "*pagare meno, pagare tutti*" (pay less, everybody pays) which basically means that everybody should pay in order to decrease the demanded amount. Thus, reducing the requested fee means reducing business willingness to report. In this way the mafia not only decreases its risk of being detected but also gains increased control over the territory because businesses prefer to pay when the amount of money demanded is not excessive. This also means that the mafia continues to enrich itself, but at a lower risk of detection (violence is less visible) and of reporting (people who pay less are less likely to report crime to the police). Moreover, and this is the most dangerous aspect of this new strategy, the mafia can extend its power and control over a larger numbers of victims. This means that the groups' reputation and economic power are strengthened. Although it is to be noted that in recent years there have been rather strong reactions by civil society in this area, which subsequently lead to the establishment of several NGOs whose objectives are to assist and protect victims of racketeering.

Locally organised groups also operate in Greece. These criminal groups are known as the 'godfathers of the night'. They "*are ex-henchmen of nightclubs who have been released by their bosses. They formed their own gangs and they started to sell protection . . . It has been estimated that there are about seven gangs operating in Greece . . . These gangs co-operate with each other and have connections with the police. . . . The supremacy of Greek nationals controlling this area is almost absolute*" (Lambropoulou, 2003: 69-87).

Foreign criminal groups also operate extortion rackets in Italy, Spain and Portugal and usually exert violence against commercial activities owned by their fellow-nationals. The major foreign criminal groups involved in extortion come from Eastern Europe (Russian, Ukrainian, Romanian, Polish mafia in Spain), the Far East (mainly Chinese) and – as signalled in Spain – South America (Colombian groups).

According to the collected information there is no evidence of the phenomenon in Malta, while in Cyprus there is some evidence of extortion rackets.

Considerations

This explorative study analysed data on extortion rackets across twenty-seven EU Member States. Given the scarcity of information on the topic, the research proved to be extremely challenging. Indeed, the difficulties highlighted in the introduction are significant. Extortion rackets vary considerably across European countries. In general, administrative crime data and business crime victimisation surveys are unable to provide reliable information on extortion rackets. The very concept of extortion rackets shows a number of different nuances, ranging from regular one-shot extortion to criminal partnerships (amenable to the concept of criminal protection).

The general impression coming from experts and from some specific cases (e.g. Northern Ireland, Bulgaria and Italy) is that the phenomenon is progressively becoming more and more 'invisible'. Two possible explanations exist (or maybe coexist): reduction of extortion practices and/or transformation in their *modus operandi*. Both are plausible in different European areas. For example in Northern Ireland extortion rackets seem to be decreasing. This decrease may be due to the change in social and political conditions in the area which have almost completely eradicated the Irish Republican Army movement. In Italy the pressure applied by law enforcement agencies through arrests and seizures has had an impact on the *modus operandi* of mafia-type groups. As a result, violent intimidation has been substituted with more subtle and less evident practices.[9] There are further signs of

[9] In Italy, judicial investigations confirm the existence of a clear "strategy of submersion" of the activities mafia-type groups. As stated by the National Antimafia Direction (a body coordinating the prosecution of mafia-type groups and performing strategic analyses) Bernardo Provenzano, leader of Cosa Nostra, decided to minimize violent criminal activity such as murders and extortions and to focus on direct enterpreneurial activity, with a particular attention on public procurements. Several collaborators of justice (pentiti) confirmed this trend. Among them, Francesco Campanella, former politician and member of Cosa Nostra, stated that "Provenzano wants to bring Cosa Nostra to do business directly, that is he prefers to enter in the capital of enterprises rather than using the traditional activity of extortion of enterprises" (DNA 2006, 597).

transformation within Eastern Europe. The 'professionalisation' of extortion racketeers has evolved into a legal business in some Eastern countries. Consequently, visible violence against people was transformed into covert violence/corruption in commercial relations or within legal institutions as, for example, clearly happened in Bulgaria. Today, the rapid increase of immigration in Europe renewed the public opinion attention on closed communities of immigrants as a category of protection racketeers. This comes as no surprise as a very similar phenomenon occurred when Italians migrated from the Old Continent to the United States over a century ago (Dash, 2009).

Administrative crime statistics are generally not able to help in interpreting extortion rackets. This is because the crime is probably largely underestimated for different reasons. First, data may refer to extortion in general, not allowing to focus on extortion *rackets* as a distinctive and more dangerous type of extortion. Further, victims are less likely to report an extortion racket for fear of retaliation (higher dark figures than normal extortion can be assumed). This is nothing new in this field. However, as intelligence-led policing is a recurrent theme in the current law enforcement policy discourse, it is appropriate to wonder what kind of intelligence may be produced from incomplete and unsatisfactory data. Additional sources of information, such as business crime victimisation surveys, do not appear as a full credible option yet, either for the costs of these procedures and the general reliability of results.

This study represents a first phase in exploratory comparison among EU countries with regards extortion rackets. In view of the methodological caveats the analyses show that the path to a clear comparative picture of activities which involve extortion rackets is still extremely long and complex. As the manifestations of protection and extortion racketeering also evolve – given changing policing and cross-border mobility – it is important to monitor such developments for research as well as for policy making while improving the methodology of data collection.

References

Aebi, M., Measuring the Influence of Statistical Counting Rules on Cross-National Differences in Recorded Crime, In: K. Aromaa and M. Heiskanen (eds.), *Crime and criminal justice systems in Europe and North America 1995-2004*, Heuni Reports 55. (pp. 196-214) Helsinki: HEUNI, 2008

Albanese, J. S., *Organised Crime in Our Times*. 5th ed. Newark, NJ, Anderson Publishing, 2007

Albini, J. L., *The American Mafia; genesis of a legend*. Sociology series. New York, NY, Appleton-Century-Crofts, 1971

Alvazzi del Frate, A., Trends and Methodological Aspects in the International Collection of Crime and Criminal Justice Statistics, In: K. Aromaa and M. Heiskanen (eds), *Crime and criminal justice systems in Europe and North America 1995-2004*, Heuni Reports 55. (pp.215-230), Helsinki, HEUNI, 2008

Andrienko, Y., *Crime, wealth and inequality: evidence from international crime victim surveys*. Economics Education and Research Consortium – Russia and CIS, November, 2002

Armao, F., *Il Sistema Mafia: Dall'economia-Mondo Al Dominio Locale*. Torino, Bollati Boringhieri, 2000

Aromaa, K. andJoutsen, M., Introduction, In: K. Aromaa, S. Leppä, S. Nevala, and N. Ollus (eds), *Crime and criminal justice in Europe and North America, 1995-1997*, Helsinki, HEUNI, 2003

Baltic News Service (BNS). 27 October 1999. "Baltic Legal Officials Consult on Organized Crime."(NEXIS)

Bell, D., Crime as an American Way of Life. *The Antioch Review*, 1953, 13(2): 131-154.

Block, A. A., *East side, west side: Organizing Crime in New York 1930-1950*. New Brunswick, NJ, Transaction Publishers, 1983

Calderoni, F., *Organized crime legislation in the European Union*. Heidelberg, Springer, 2010

Carp, B., Gomeaja, M., Grosu, D., Criminal Organisations in Romania: *Seminar on Counteraction of Extortion Racketeering*, Frascati, Italy, March 8-10, 2007

Catanzaro, R., La mafia tra mercato e stato. In: G. Fiandaca and S. Costantino (eds.), *La Mafia, Le Mafie: Tra Vecchi E Nuovi Paradigmi*, (pp. 177-193). Roma, Laterza, 1994

Cohen, A.W., The Racketeer's Progress: Commerce, Crime, and the Law in Chicago, 1900-1940. *Journal of Urban History*, 2003, 29(5): 575-596

Colombi, J.J., Contribution to the Seminar on Extortion Racket. *Seminar on Counteraction of Extortion Racketeering*, Frascati, Italy, March 8-10, 2007

Cornilis, K. and Greve, V., Denmark on the road to organised crime, In: C. Fijnaut, L. Paoli (eds.), *Organised crime in Europe. Concepts, patterns and control policies in the European Union and beyond*, Dordrecht: Springer, 2004

Curtis, G.E., S.L. Elan, R.A., Hudson and N.A. Kollars, Transnational activities of Chinese crime organisations. *Trends in Organised Crime*, 2002, 7(3): 19-57

Danish National Police, *Organised crime in Denmark in 2005*. Copenhagen: Danish National Police, Civil and Police Department, 2006

Dash, M., *The First Family. Terror, Extortion and The Birth of The American Mafia*. London, Simon & Schuster, 2009.

Deflem, M., Surveillance and criminal statistics: Historical foundations of governmentality. In: A. Sarat and S. Silbey (eds.), *Studies in Law, Politics and Society*, 17, (pp.149-184). Greenwich, CT, JAI Press: 1997

Dijk, J. van, Mafia markers: Assessing organized crime and its impact upon societies. *Trends in Organized Crime*, 2007, 10(4): 39-56

Dijk, J. van, *The World of Crime*. Thousands Oaks, CA, Sage Publications, 2008.

Dijk, J. van, R. Manchin, J. van Kesteren, S. Nevala and G. Hideg, *The burden of crime in the EU - research report: A comparative analysis of the European crime and safety survey (EU ICS) 2005*: 2005
http://www.europeansafetyobservatory.eu/downloads/EUICS%20-%20The%20Burden%20of%20Crime%20in%20the%20EU.pdf.

DNA, Direzione Nazionale Antimafia, *Relazione annuale sulle attività svolte dal Procuratore nazionale antimafia e dalla Direzione nazionale antimafia nonché sulle dinamiche e strategie detta criminalità organizzata di tipo mafioso nel periodo 1 ° Luglio 2005 - 30giugno 2006*, Roma, December 2006

Duyne, P.C. van, Medieval thinking and organized crime economy. In: E. C. Viano, J. Magallanes, and L. Bridel (eds.), *Transnational organized crime: Myth, power, and profit*, (pp.23-44), Carolina Academic Press, 2003

Duyne, P.C. van and T. Vander Beken, The incantations of the EU organised crime policy making. *Crime, Law & Social Change*, 2009, 51: 261-281

Duyne, P.C. van and M. van Dijck, Assessing organised crime: the sad state of an impossible art. In: F. Bovenkerk and M. Levi (eds.), *The organised crime economy. Essays in honor of Alan Block*. New York, Springer, 2007

Elvins, M., Europe's response to transnational organised crime. In A. Edwards and P. Gill (eds.), *Transnational organised crime: Perspectives on global security*, (pp.28-41). New York, Routledge, 2003

Eurostat, *Annex A : Statistics on crime and the criminal justice system: Offence definitions and explanatory notes for countries unable to meet the standard definition*, 2009, epp.eurostat.ec.europa.eu/cache/ITY_SDDS/.../crim_esms_an1.pdf

Faligot, R., *La Mafia Chinoise en Europe*. Paris, Calmann-Lèvy, 2001

Felson, M., *The ecosystem for organized crime*. Vol. 26. HEUNI Papers. Helsinki, HEUNI, 2006

Filocamo, F., Il contrasto al racket delle estorsioni a Napoli: *Seminar on Counteraction of Extortion Racketeering*, Frascati, Italy, March 8-10, 2007

Finckenauer, J., *Mafia and organized crime: A beginner's guide.* Oxford, Oneworld Publications, 2007

Gambetta, D., *The Sicilian Mafia: The business of private protection.* Cambridge, Harvard University Press, 1996

Gounev, P., Bulgaria's private security industry. In: A. Bryden and M. Caparini (eds.), *Private actors and security governance.* Bulgaria, LIT & DCAF, 2006

Grasso, T. and A. Varano, *U Pizzu. L'Italia del racket e dell'usura.* Milano, Baldini e Castoldi, 2002

Hellenic Republic Ministry of Public Order, , *Annual report on organised crime in Greece for the year 2004.* Athens, Hellenic Republic Ministry of Public Order, 2005

Hagan, F.E., 'Organized Crime' and 'organized crime': Indeterminate problems of definition. *Trends in Organized Crime*, 2006, 9(4): 127-137

Ianni, F.A.J. and E. Reuss-Ianni, *A family business; kinship and social control in organized crime.* New York, NY, Russell Sage Foundation, 1972

Konrad, K.I. and S. Skaperdas, Extortion. *Economica*, 1998, 65(260): 461-477

Lambropoulou, E., Criminal 'organisations' in Greece and public policy: from non-real to hyper-real?. *International Journal of the Sociology of Law*, 2003, 31(1): 69-87

La Spina, A., *Mafia, legalità debole e sviluppo del Mezzogiorno.* Bologna, Il Mulino, 2005

Millis, H.A. and R.E. Montgomery, *Organized labour. Half-title: Business and economics publications.* New York, London, McGraw-Hill, 1945

Mugellini, G., *Measuring crime against business in the EU: the problem of comparability.* Ph.D. thesis, Milan, Università Cattolica del Sacro Cuore, 2010

Neuman, W.L. and R.J. Berger, Competing perspectives on cross-national crime: An evaluation of theory and evidence. *The Sociological Quarterly*, 1988, 29(2): 281-313

Ohlemacher, T., Viewing the crime wave from the inside: Perceived rates of extortion among restaurants in Germany. *European Journal on Criminal Policy and Research*, 1999, 7(1): 43-61

Ohlemacher, T., Racketeering and restaurants in Germany. Perceived deficiencies in crime control and effects on confidence in democracy. *British Journal of Criminology*, 2002, 42(1): 60-76

Oxford English Dictionnary, "extortion", 2008. oed.com (July 20, 2010). http://dictionary.oed.com/cgi/entry/50080978?query_type=word&queryword=extortion&first=1&max_to_show=10&sort_type=alpha&result_place=1&search_id=7C62-iO89Ye-3960&hilite=50080978

Oxford English Dictionnary, "racket", 2008. oed.com (July 20, 2010). http://dictionary.oed.com/cgi/entry/50195948?query_type=word&queryword=racket&first=1&max_to_show=10&sort_type=alpha&result_place=2&search_id=7C62-Qhsna6-4002&hilite=50195948

Paoli, L. and C. Fijnaut, Introduction to Part I: The history of the concept. In C. Fijnaut and L. Paoli (eds.), *Organised crime in Europe: concepts, patterns and control policies in the European Union and beyond*, (pp.21-46). Dordrecht, Springer, 2004a

Paoli, L. and C. Fijnaut, General Introduction. In C. Fijnaut and L. Paoli (eds.), *Organised crime in Europe: concepts, patterns and control policies in the European Union and beyond*, (pp.1-18). Dordrecht, Springer, 2004b

Reuter, P, *Disorganized crime: the economics of the visible hand.* Cambridge, MA, MIT Press, 1983

Santino, U., *Dalla Mafia Alle Mafie: Scienze Sociali E Crimine Organizzato.* Soveria Mannelli: Rubbettino, 2006

Schelling, T.C., Economics and criminal enterprise. *The Public Interest*, 1967, no. 7 (Spring): 61-78.

Shavell, S., An economic analysis of threats and their illegality: Blackmail, extortion and robbery, *University of Pennsylvania Law Review*, 1992, Vol. 141: 1877-1904

Smith, D. C., *The Mafia mystique.* New York, NY: Basic Books, 1975. http://openlibrary.org/b/OL5440589M/Mafia_mystique.

Soares, R. R., Development, crime and punishment: accounting for the international differences in crime rates, 2004, Vol. 73: 155-174 http://www.sciencedirect.com/science/article/B6VBV-49S80CF-2/2/0e538328ca411b70bc7392a2825078d0.

SOS Impresa, *Decimo Rapporto. Le mani della criminalità sulle imprese.* Roma, Confesercenti, 2007

SOS impresa, *Le mani della criminalità sulle imprese – XI rapporto.* Roma, Confesercenti, 2008

Tilley, N., M. Hopkins with the assistance of A. Edwards and J. Burrows, *Business views of organised crime: Key implications* (Second Edition). Research Report 10, London, Home Office, 2008

Tzvetkova, M., Aspects of the Evolution of Extra--legal Protection in Bulgaria (1989--1999). *Trends in Organized Crime*, 2008, 11:326-351.

Varese, F., How mafias migrate: The case of the 'Ndrangheta in Northern Italy. *Law & Society Review*, 2006, 40(2): 411-444.

Von Lampe, K., M. van Dijck, R. Hornsby, A. Markina, and K. Verpoest, Organised Crime Is . . . Findings from a Cross-National Review of Literature. In

P. C. van Duyne, A. Maljevic, M. van Dijck, K. von Lampe, J, L. Newell (eds.), *The organisation of crime for profit: Conduct, law and measurement.* Wolf Legal Publishers, 2006

Von Lampe, K. The trafficking in untaxed cigarette in Germany. A case study of the social embeddedness of illegal markets. In: P.C. van Duyne, K. von Lampe and N. Passas (eds.), *Upperworld and underworld in cross-border crime.* Nijmegen, Wolf Legal Publishers, 2002

Woodiwiss, M., Transnational organized crime: The strange career of an American concept. In: M.E. Beare (ed.), *Critical reflections on transnational organized crime, money laundering and corruption*, (pp.3-34). Toronto, University of Toronto Press, 2003

Situational Prevention of 'Organised Crime' Preventing phantom conceptions with phantom means?

Klaus von Lampe[1]

Introduction

There is a growing notion that traditional repressive measures against 'organised crime', to the extent they show the intended effects at all, provide only partial, temporary solutions. Tools such as electronic surveillance, undercover agents, confidential informants, asset forfeiture, conspiracy laws and newly defined offences criminalising membership in 'criminal groups' may selectively increase the pressure on criminals, but they seem to address symptoms more than causes. A more comprehensive strategy is called for which includes proactive measures that reduce the likelihood of the occurrence of the phenomena commonly labelled 'organised crime''.

One line of thought that has gradually emerged over the past 15-20 years is to transfer the framework of Situational Crime Prevention to the area of 'organised crime' (Van der Schoot, 2006). This pragmatic approach to dealing with crime problems has been successfully applied in dealing with a number of more ordinary, less 'organised' crimes, giving rise to the question to what extent similar successes could be claimed against 'organised crime'. The purpose of this paper is to provide some tentative answers to this question largely at the theoretical level. Following a brief description of Situational Crime Prevention and a clarification of what 'organised crime' means for the purpose of this chapter, the merits of a situational approach to the prevention of 'organised crime' will be discussed, drawing on an eclectic set of examples primarily from the trafficking in stolen motor vehicles.

---

1 Klaus von Lampe is assistant professor at John Jay College of Criminal Justice, New York, Department of Law, Police Science and Criminal Justice Administration. The author would like to thank Petrus C. van Duyne and two anonymous reviewers for their helpful comments on an earlier draft of this paper.

Situational Crime Prevention

Crime prevention is a very broad notion encompassing "*any activity, by an individual or group, public or private, that precludes the incidence of one or more criminal acts*" (Brantingham and Faust, 1976, p 284), and including long-term strategies to remove 'root causes' of crime as well as short-term, pragmatic approaches such as Situational Crime Prevention. Situational Crime Prevention, according to Marcus Felson (2006a, p 301) "*is the intermediate approach between reforming individuals and redesigning society*". It belongs to a school of thought in criminology which seeks to set itself apart from traditional one-dimensional explanations of crime that are usually focussed on either individual or social factors. Instead, crime is viewed in a more holistic way in terms of a multitude of criminal events each constituting "*an opportune cross-product of law, offender motivation, and target characteristic arrayed on an environmental backcloth at a particular point in space-time*" (Brantingham and Brantingham, 1993, p 259). Situational Crime Prevention is perhaps the most radical variant of this philosophy. While acknowledging that there are numerous factors on the societal and individual level conducive to crime, advocates of this approach argue that, from a theoretical and policy perspective, it is most important to look at the concrete circumstances under which the various influences intersect in a particular criminal event (Felson and Clarke, 1998).

Situational Crime Prevention aims at identifying points of intervention to reduce opportunities for crime. This requires focusing on highly specific forms of crime rather than broad categories commonly defined in criminology; and it entails considering a broad range of elements of the immediate context of a criminal event with a view to increasing the effort and risks of crime as well as to reducing the rewards from crime (Clarke, 1993, p 3; Cornish and Clarke, 1986, p: 2). Central to Situational Crime Prevention is the notion derived from Routine Activity Theory that crime results from the convergence in time and space of three key factors (see Figure 1), commonly referred to as the 'crime triangle', (1) motivated offenders, possibly aided by facilitating factors such as the availability of necessary tools, (2) suitable 'targets', and (3) the absence of capable 'guardians' or, more generally, the absence of individuals who are in a position to directly, or indirectly by alerting agencies of formal social control, intervene with a criminal event (Clarke, 1997, p 12; Clarke and Eck, 2005, p 13; Cohen and Felson, 1979, p: 589; Felson, 1995, pp 53-57; Felson and Clarke, 1998). Within this 'crime triangle', Marcus Felson (1995) distinguishes three types of what he calls "*discouragers of crime*" according to different types of responsibilities: 'guardians' who have responsibilities, in a broad sense, for a target, 'place managers' who are responsible for the premises where a crime may occur, and 'handlers' who are responsible for individuals that are potential offenders.

The offender according to this view is a 'reasoning criminal' (Cornish and Clarke, 1986) who, while encountering crime opportunities in the course of day-to-day ('routine') activities, takes into account the specifics of a given situation, and makes 'rational' decisions on whether or not to actually commit an offence based on a cost-benefit analysis. By changing the 'situation', i.e. the immediate circumstances of a potential crime, in a way that the costs of crime increase, and the benefits from crime decrease, it is possible, the assumption goes, to influence the criminal decision-making process and to prevent crime (Cornish and Clarke, 1986; Clarke, 1997).

Figure 1: The Crime 'situation'

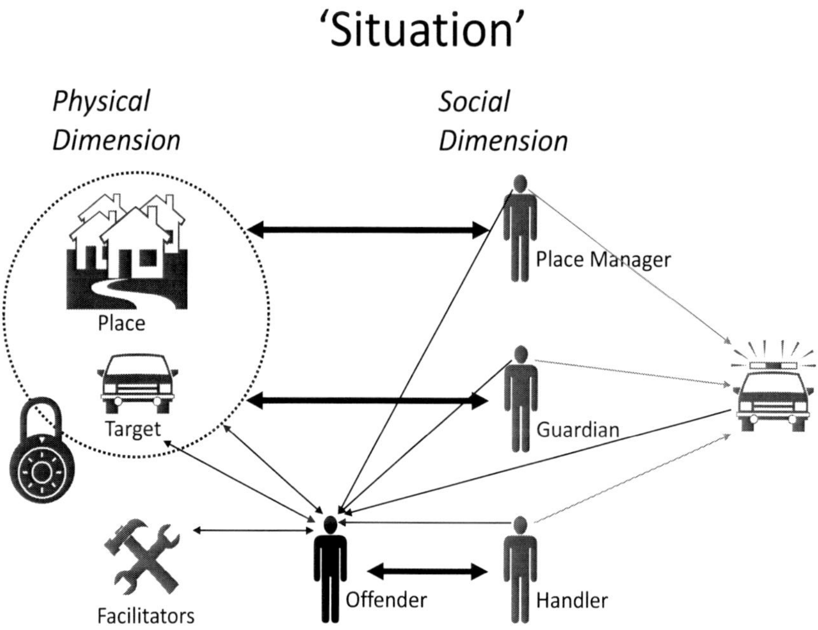

As highlighted in Figure 1, there are two dimensions that define a 'situation': the physical dimension of places, objects and tools, and the social dimension comprising individuals that potentially interfere with, or facilitate a criminal activity.

Clarke and Eck (2005) have systematised the diverse opportunity-reducing measures that have been developed so far, arriving at a classificatory scheme distinguishing 25 techniques. The essential ordering principle is the mechanism through which a technique achieves its preventive effect. The "Twenty Five Techniques" are grouped in five broad categories: increase the effort (or difficulties) of crime, increase the risks of being apprehended, reduce the rewards, reduce provocations, and remove excuses (Clarke and Eck, 2005, p 75).

'Organised crime'

Situational Crime Prevention has originally been developed with particular manifestations of crime in mind which are not immediately associated with 'organised crime': namely violent and property crimes committed by 'anti-social predators', or by occasional, 'mundane' or 'provoked' offenders (Cornish and Clarke, 2003). The question is to what extent the situational perspective can be applied in a meaningful way beyond the realm of what we may term 'normal' or 'non-organised crime' also in order to capture the various phenomena commonly labelled 'organised crime'. This question has been brought up in the past from two directions. While some have looked at Situational Crime Prevention for inspiration to more effectively address 'organised crime' (see *e.g.* Van de Bunt and Van der Schoot, 2003), others have sought to expand the framework of Situational Crime Prevention to a broader range of crime phenomena, including those labelled 'organised' (see *e.g.* Felson, 2006b). It is in reference to this literature as a whole that the topic of this chapter is framed as being about Situational Crime Prevention and 'organised crime'.

It cannot be stressed enough that the concept of 'organised crime'is an elusive construct of no analytical value (van Duyne, 2003) and one which is "*notoriously resistant to definition*" (Naylor, 2003, p 82). However, in its numerous interpretations it does refer to various phenomena which are real and not just 'phantoms'. These phenomena warrant the attention of researchers and policy makers irrespective of how closely they are connected and how, therefore, justifiable it is to apply to them one generic term such as 'organised crime'. There are two dimensions in particular along which a dividing line is commonly drawn between 'organised crime' and 'non-organised crime' and which appear relevant from the perspective of Situational Crime Prevention: (1) the qualities of criminal activities and (2) the qualities of offender structures.

'Organised crime' in terms of criminal activities is commonly associated with rational, planned and continuous criminal conduct in a business-like manner as opposed to impulsive, spontaneous, one-time-only criminal acts. This applies, specifically, to the provision of illegal goods and services for which there is a more or less constant demand. In one extreme, 'organised' crime occurs on a regular basis in short intervals of days or even hours following established rules and routines, such as in the case of illegal lotteries in the U.S. (Liddick, 1999). 'Organised' criminal activity can be fairly complex and sophisticated, for example in the case of the production of synthetic drugs, where even the simple 'cooking' of methamphetamine requires the careful and skilful execution of procedures extending over hours and days, not counting the efforts needed to procure the necessary precursor chemicals and laboratory equipment (Sexton, Carlson, Leukefeld and Booth, 2006, p 864).

'Organised crime' in terms of criminal organisation is commonly associated with the collective commission of crime and the existence of consistent structures linking numerous offenders independent from any particular criminal act. These kinds of patterns of cooperation and association are in stark contrast to lone, socially isolated offenders or sporadic co-offenders. Although it is often argued that under conditions of illegality organisations tend to be small and ephemeral (Reuter, 1983; Southerland and Potter, 1993), there are also large, complex criminal enterprises to be found, as exemplified by the legendary Colombian drug trafficking businesses of the 1980s and early 1990s with, allegedly, up to hundreds of full-time managers and staff (Zabludoff, 1997).

Of course, an even higher level of planning and offender organisation may be found in a corporate setting, for example in the cases of business fraud and illegal cartels (Van Duyne *et al.*, 2001; Van Duyne and Van Dijck, 2007).

Between the extremes outlined above: lone offenders acting upon impulse; and complex, stable illegal enterprises, there is great variation in the forms of organisation of crimes and criminals. For the purpose of this chapter it is not necessary to determine where a dividing line could or should meaningfully be drawn between 'organised crime' and 'non-organised crime'. What is important to note here is that there are forms of criminal behaviour that tend to differ from 'normal' crime with regard to the ways crimes are committed and in the way offenders are connected to co-offenders and co-conspirators. The term 'organised crime', therefore, is only used in a very loose sense to crudely delineate crime phenomena that, because of certain characteristics, may not easily lend themselves to a situational approach to crime prevention.

Situational Crime Prevention and 'organised crime': Existing approaches

Different attempts have been made in the scholarly literature to link Situational Crime Prevention and 'organised crime' with various degrees of conceptual adjustment in one direction or the other. Leaving aside some nuances, five different approaches can be distinguished, ordered by the degree to which they depart from the traditional situational model:

- applying the situational model to components of 'normal crime' within 'organised crime';
- reducing 'organised crime' phenomena to sets of interconnected crime 'situations';
- expanding the situational model to 'situations' of offender networking;
- including the dimension of power exerted by criminal groups in the equation of situational prevention;
- transferring the situational model to a higher level of observation from highly localized crime settings to 'niches of offending'.

All of these approaches rest on the notion –implicitly or explicitly– that Situational Crime Prevention is better applicable to 'organised crime' than to 'normal crime' because of the assumed rationality of 'organised' offenders (Bouloukos, Farrell and Laycock, 2003, p 178; Cornish & Clarke, 2002, p 41). However, transferring the situational model with the 'crime triangle' as its conceptual centrepiece, has proven to be more difficult.

Elements of 'normal crime' in 'organised crime'

One of the earliest contributions to the discussion has been made by David Hicks (1998) who, in a sense, established a connection between Situational Crime Prevention and 'organised crime' on the rhetorical level by arguing that 'organised crime' has an important 'normal'-crime component and that situational prevention can be applied against this component to successfully prevent 'organised crime'. According to Hicks there is an "instrumental fusion between organised and traditional criminal activity" (Hicks, 1998, p 331), further, he maintains that "*organised criminal associations [. . .] evolve and are supported through a process of individual or group engagement in less serious forms of crime before engaging in (directly or indirectly), or being recruited into, more serious forms of organised criminal activity*" (Hicks, 1998, p 332). In other words, 'non-organised crimes' are believed to provide fertile grounds for 'organised crime' and, therefore, looking at these 'non-organised crimes' through the 'situational lens' is all that is required to effectively apply the framework of Situational Crime Prevention to 'organised crime'.

Similarly, Bouloukos, Farrell and Laycock, in a paper on the prevention of 'transnational organised crime', noted that "*many measures directed at 'ordinary' crimes can have an effect on some forms of organised crime*" such as street lighting on reducing opportunities for car theft (Bouloukos *et al.*, 2003, p 187). They argued that Situational Crime Prevention "*from one perspective [. . .] already operates as an approach to the prevention of transnational organised crime, and has already demonstrated its efficacy*". However, they caution "*that it might be more effective if applied more formally and systematically*", namely by applying Clarke's 'opportunity reducing techniques' of Situational Crime Prevention (Bouloukos *et al.*, 2003, p 185; see also Korsell and Skinnari, 2010; Nelen, 2010; Savona, 2010; von Lampe, 2010).

Crime scripts and master-scripts

Other approaches, in contrast, are based on the notion that there are differences between 'traditional crime' and 'organised crime' which need to be reflected in the way the conceptual framework of Situational Crime Prevention is applied. Derek Cornish's (1994) concept of 'crime-commission scripts' represents perhaps the most cautious venture in this direction. The 'script' concept breaks down criminal events into specific component parts while at the same time highlighting their sequential interconnectedness. Scripts are 'hypothesised knowledge structures' by which individuals are guided in routinised, yet inherently flexible goal-oriented behaviour through a sequence of steps or sub-goals (Cornish, 1994, pp 157, 176). "*Scripts act as a device to tie people, places, props, and procedures into detailed accounts of purposeful and routinized activities at the right (micro-social) level for situational interventions*" (Cornish and Clarke, 2002, p 48).

To account for the complexities of 'organised crimes', Cornish and Clarke have introduced the concept of 'master-scripts' referring to "*an extended plan [. . .] that guides or, at least, makes sense of*" sub-sets of crime-commission scripts "*strung together to form a higher-order compound entity*" (Cornish and Clarke, 2002, p 50). They use professional car theft as an example to emphasize that complex crimes consist of different stages, each constituting separable offenses with their own script, carried out by different sets of actors at different locations (Cornish and Clarke, 2002, pp 50-51; see also Bullock, Clarke and Tilley, 2010).

Offender convergence settings

While the script concept proposed by Cornish refers to some of the operational complexities of 'organised crime', a different approach taken by Marcus Felson (2006b) focuses on the associational dimension of 'organised crime'. Felson argues that criminal activities involving more than one offender are not only contingent upon opportunity structures for crime commission but also depend on opportunity structures for the underlying processes of criminal networking (see also Cornish and Clarke, 2002; Hancock and Laycock, 2010). For 'situations' where offenders can find accomplices Felson has coined the term 'offender convergence settings'. These "*allow criminal cooperation to persist even when the particular persons vary*" (Felson, 2006b, p 9). The implication is that in light of the instability of criminal collectives, 'convergence settings' may be more important for the structure and continuity of crime than any group or network (Felson, 2006b, p 10).

Offender control over locations

In yet another modification of the situational framework, Felson (2006a) has incorporated the dimension of power in the form of territorial control. Referring primarily to gang-controlled neighbourhoods he points to the need to critically review basic assumptions about the social dynamics within a crime 'situation'. Situational Crime Prevention is based on the notion that third persons prevent crime by their presence alone or through offering assistance to ward off an attack (Miethe and Meier, 1994, p 90). Felson, however, argues that this is not true where offenders control a location. Then the mechanisms of supervision linked to the presence of others in a setting do not work against offenders but against 'crime's adversaries' who are discouraged from intervening in crime events (Felson, 2006a, p 91).

'Niches of offending'

The most profound modification of the situational model with reference to 'organised crime' has been proposed by Paul Ekblom (2003; but see also Levi and Maguire, 2004; Felson, 2006a, 2006b). Instead of a specific crime setting he looks more broadly at what he terms a 'niche for offending', defined as "*an identifiable concentration or flow of wealth from which offenders can make a living, using the resources at their disposal to exploit it whilst maintaining acceptable levels of effort and risk*" (Ekblom, 2003, p: 252). A 'niche' in Ekblom's understanding can encompass numerous settings (or 'scenes' in his terminology) which are connected through scripts, logistical structures and enterprise structures. According to Ekblom, the shift in focus from 'situation' to 'niche' is necessary because in the context of 'organised crime' offenders, through collaboration, are more resourceful (Ekblom, 2003, p 250). They do not simply encounter crime situations, they are able to seek or engineer opportunities and circumvent and neutralise obstacles, for example by corrupting officials (Ekblom, 2003, pp 248, 250 - 252, 257).

Another, more implicitly addressed aspect is the notion that the roles individuals in a crime setting play as offender, preventer and promoter are not necessarily fixed and may be subject to change in the course of a criminal event. As Ekblom's discussion suggests, roles may be negotiable in situational interaction processes. He argues that individuals present in a crime setting make "*decisions based on their diverse perceptions of risk, etc., including what each thinks the others will do*" and "*they may interact through move and countermove*" (Ekblom, 2003, p 251).

Theoretical and Practical Implications: The 'Situation' of Organised Criminal Activities

The existing literature on the situational prevention of 'organised crime' implies the need for a modification of the original model of the 'crime situation' in various respects, namely with regard to the situational contingencies of 'organised' criminal activities, and with regard to the mechanisms taking place within a given 'crime situation'.[2]

Dispersal of criminal activities across space and time

The first important difference, which is a difference in degree, between more or less 'organised' crimes is the spreading of activities across space and time. Instead of a convergence in one place at one point in time which characterises much of the overall crime picture, the criminal events associated with 'organised crime' tend to be detached from one such point. Two variations of this theme have to be distinguished. The first variation is Cornish's notion of crime scripts where a criminal venture is scattered across different places and different times. The second variation is Ekblom's notion of criminal 'niches' that transcend any given point in

2 For a more detailed discussion of the limits of the conceptual and theoretical framework of Situational Crime Prevention in the area of 'organised crime', see von Lampe (forthcoming).

time and space, within which resourceful offenders select and shape settings according to their respective needs.

The concept of crime scripts does not necessarily alter the basic assumptions about situational contingencies of crime to the extent that there is a convergence in space and time of offender and target at each and every step along the way. This can be illustrated using the trafficking in stolen motor vehicles as an example. Clarke and Brown (2005, p 319) have listed the following sequence of actions characterising this criminal activity:

- preferred vehicles are identified and stolen, either to order or "on spec";
- they may be moved to a safe place and their identities may be changed;
- they may be stored, awaiting pick-up for transfer across the border;
- depending on the method of transfer, they may be placed in sealed containers;
- at the destinations they may be handed over to a local contact or collected by such a person from the docks;
- they may be legally registered; and finally,
- they may be sold on the open market or to a private buyer.

Every step can be understood as a criminal event defined in time and space. In fact, from a Situational Crime Prevention perspective, targeting one such setting, such as the change of identity, or the storage prior to cross-border transport, may be sufficient to disrupt the entire chain of activity and prevent the criminal venture as a whole. However, there are important variations in the 'situation' from one step to the next. These variations have primarily to do with the 'target' that defines a crime setting (von Lampe, 2010). The 'target' is "*the central object of the crime (through attack, theft, counterfeiting, illegal transaction, possession or trafficking)*" (Ekblom, 2003, p 248). The 'target' defines to a large degree what kinds of skills and resources an offender needs for successfully committing a crime, and it determines who the stakeholders are that have the awareness and incentive to intervene in a criminal event as 'guardians'.

In a criminal endeavour which follows a sequential order such as the trafficking in stolen motor vehicles, the 'target' may be more or less clearly definable, more or less clearly discernible for outsiders, in greater or lesser proximity to the location of the actual criminal activity, and it may change from one setting (respectively 'scene') to the next. The 'target' of the original theft of a vehicle is, obviously, the vehicle itself. The same is true at the stage when the identity of the vehicle is changed by altering the appearance of the car and changing the vehicle identification number (VIN). But the same does not apply as regards the forgery of the accompanying vehicle documents. These documents, rather than the vehicle, become the 'target' proper which has to be protected, for example, through security features such as water marks and holograms. Storing and transporting the stolen vehicle once again has the vehicle itself as the 'target', but it becomes less obvious to onlookers that a crime is occurring in the first place. GPS tracking devices alerting stakeholders such as owners, insurance companies and the police to the whereabouts of the vehicle are one measure that helps overcome the lack of awareness of potential 'guardians' present at the crime location. The clandestine shipment of stolen vehicles abroad, the next step in a trafficking scheme, is directed less against the vehicle but at the integrity of the border regime. This type of 'target' presents itself to offenders in source, transit and destination countries, with customs services and transport businesses being closest to the criminal activity. The distribution of stolen vehicles in the country of destination, finally, involves yet other 'targets' and potential 'guardians', including the system of vehicle registration which may be manipulated using forged vehicle documents, and the buyer of the vehicle who, if unaware of the fact that the vehicle is stolen, is the victim of a fraud where the vehicle itself is being used as the instrument of a crime rather than being a 'target'.

The fact that the 'target' of the crime, and the prominence of that 'target' varies from one step in the crime script to the next means that each crime setting may have fundamentally different situational characteristics, requiring, respectively, specifically tailored preventive approaches. This is less important where the targeting of one neuralgic point is sufficient to achieve results. But normally one would expect the effective situational prevention of crimes such as the trafficking in stolen motor vehicles to be far more complex, facing many more uncertainties than the situational prevention of 'normal' crimes.

Resourceful offenders

The challenges are even greater where criminal activities are dispersed across space and time not only in a sequential order as dictated by the logic of a crime script but as the result of the flexibility of resourceful offenders. In fact, the notion of resourceful offenders undermines basic assumptions of Situational Crime Prevention. Rather than encountering crime opportunities in the course of 'routine' activities and making on-the-spot decisions with regard to a given, essentially unalterable 'situation', resourceful offenders seek out, change or even create the most favourable crime settings within a 'niche'. One key resource these offenders have in contrast to the offenders envisioned by the framework of Situational Crime Prevention is time. The offender decision-making process is not confined to one setting and one point in time. Instead of making 'quick choices' (Felson, 2002, p 37), there is preparation and planning which extends a criminal endeavour beyond the immediate 'situation' and allows for a more thorough analysis of the circumstances. The decision is less spontaneous and impulsive and more rational than the often only rudimentary rationality assumed by Rational Choice Theory (see Cornish and Clarke, 1986). Time as a resource also allows motivated offenders to wait for changes in a 'situation', for example the departure of 'guardians', or to look for more lucrative 'situations' elsewhere. Other resources may help bring about favourable changes within a crime setting. For example, financial assets or the use of violence may neutralize potential 'guardians' through corruption and intimidation. Similarly, the use of front companies may give the appearance of legitimate activity so that the intervention of potential 'guardians' becomes less likely. Finally, financial resources can help create favourable crime settings. Marc Bowden, in a book on drug traffickers (Bowden, 2001, p 165), provides one such example writing about Paco, a cocaine dealer residing in Florida, and the house where drug transactions would take place:

> *Paco's relatives and associates owned all the houses on his block, so that there was no worry about neighbours growing suspicious. There were armed guards to provide escort, and lookouts posted at either end of the block with walkie-talkies to sound the alarm if anything unusual was happening outside.*

In this case, substantial investments were made in real estate and manpower to create a safe environment for criminal activity.

In terms of Situational Crime Prevention, the notion of 'organised' criminals being more resourceful than 'normal' criminals means that two offender strategies to thwart preventive measures are more likely in the area of 'organised crime' compared to 'normal' crime: displacement and adaptation. Displacement means that motivated offenders postpone the commission of a criminal act or move to other places to commit crimes in response to unfavourable changes in a crime 'situation'. Adaptation means offenders learn how to cope with preventive measures in a given 'situation'. While displacement is believed not to occur under all circumstances and not to fully offset prevention benefits, adaptation is believed, in most cases, to diminish prevention benefits only over longer periods of time if at all (Clarke and Eck 2005).

While the likelihood of displacement and adaptation appears to be greater in cases of 'organised crime', it cannot be assumed that resourceful, 'organised' criminals are fully free to choose and shape settings. As Ekblom's concept of 'niche for offending' implies, opportunities for profitable criminal endeavours are contingent upon certain sets of circumstances which restrain the options resourceful offenders have. Going back to the example of the trafficking in stolen motor vehicles, there are only certain ways to steal a car, alter the appearance of a car, store and ship a car, and sell a stolen car with the appearance of a non-stolen car (Clarke and Brown, 2003, p 2005).

"Situational" mechanisms

So far, the focus of the discussion has been on the concept of 'situation' in terms of the convergence in space and time of offender and 'target' and to what extent this concept applies to 'organised' criminal activities. Two aspects have been highlighted that appear to limit the situational contingencies of 'organised crime': The variations in the composition of sequentially ordered crime settings, especially with regard to the shifting identity of the crime 'target', and the reduced dependency of resourceful offenders on any given crime 'situation'. There are, however, also implications for the mechanisms assumed to take effect within a 'situation' where an 'organised' criminal event does not necessarily transcend space and time. Situational Crime Prevention rests on the assumption that, all else being equal, the presence of individuals other than the motivated offender reduces the likelihood of crime. This notion can be called the 'dark alley assumption' which probably applies to most violent and property crimes with some notable exceptions where offenders seek the presence of others; namely pick pocketing (Felson, 2002). The underlying rationale is that others either discourage offenders by their mere presence, increasing the risk of detection and apprehension, or intervene with the actions of the offender to protect the 'target' (Miethe and Meier, 1994 p 51). One straightforward prevention strategy deriving from the 'dark alley assumption' is to populate potential crime settings, for example by trimming hedges so that passers-by and neighbours can spot burglars trying to enter a home (Felson and Clarke, 2010, p 115).

'Organised crime', in contrast, tends to be associated with crime committed by numerous offenders embedded in community and legitimate business contexts, providing illicit goods and services to a willing public (Hobbs 2001; Kleemans and Van de Bunt, 2002; Potter 1994). To the extent this imagery is accurate, a 'situation' typical of 'organised' crimes would be populated by a diverse set of individuals. Accordingly, strengthening 'guardianship' to situationally prevent 'organised crime' would have to rely less on increasing the number of individuals present in a 'situation' and more on changing the awareness and the attitudes of those already present, respectively on changing the composition of those present.

Another factor more often associated with 'organised' rather than 'normal' crime is the threat or use of violence to intimidate potential 'guardians'. Felson (2006a) has made this point, as mentioned, with regard to the control of criminals over a territory, but the intimidation of potential 'guardians' may well go beyond the phenomenon of territorial control to include all those who feel to be within the reach of revengeful 'organised' criminals. Anonymous or confidential hotlines to increase the willingness of the public to report on 'organised' criminal activities are one measure to increase the risk from bystanders (Levi and Maguire, 2004, pp 412-413), although one which is not necessarily successful, especially where criminal groups are strong and police are corrupt. In Mexico, for example, confidential phone lines together with rewards to encourage private persons to report criminal activity are said to have met with lingering resistance, "*especially when news reports circulate about threats made to those who do call in*" (Lacey, 2009, p A7).

Theoretical and Practical Implications: The 'Situation' of Criminal Networking

The existing literature on the situational prevention of 'organised crime' implies not only the need for a modification of the original model of the 'crime situation' with regard to the situational contingencies of 'organised' criminal *activities*, but also with regard to the situational contingencies of offender networking (Hancock and Laycock, 2010, p 176; Levi and Maguire, 2004, p 398). This aspect is not included in the traditional framework of Situational Crime Prevention. It has only been tentatively addressed by Felson with his concept of 'offender convergence settings' (Felson, 2006b, p 9). First and foremost, the concept of 'offender convergence settings' expands the focus of Situational Crime Prevention beyond 'situations' where crimes are committed to 'situations' where potential co-offenders meet. In light of the complexities of social networks linked to 'organised crime', however, the emphasis on the formation of (typically short lived) co-offending networks appears unnecessarily restrictive. There are other types of relationships offenders enter into for the commission of crime and which can also be considered with regard to situational contingencies, namely relations between suppliers and buyers of illicit goods and services, and relations between offenders and witting or unwitting facilitators and accomplices of crime (von Lampe, 2007). In addition, there are more or less formalized fraternal associations of criminals which only indirectly promote and support illegal (entrepreneurial) activities, for example by inducing a sense of solidarity and commitment (Haller, 1992). These associational networks may likewise be contingent upon situational factors; and while the link to the actual commission of crime is not always obvious, they may be an important target for crime prevention efforts.

There is, however, a problem with targeting offender convergence settings, broadly conceptualised, that does not arise with regard to crime settings: offender networking does not necessarily violate the law. Conspiracy statutes, laws against the formation of 'criminal associations' and injunctions against 'associating with known felons' notwithstanding; most of the social interaction between offenders seems to be non-criminal in nature and difficult to differentiate from any other form of social interaction. Intervention by 'guardians' in 'offender convergence settings', therefore, appears to be less likely, legally more problematic, and more prone to be fuelled by stereotyping than intervention by 'guardians' in a crime setting to protect a discernible crime 'target'.

Parameters of the Situational Prevention of 'organised crime'

Summing up the discussion so far, the question is to what extent Situational Crime Prevention presents a feasible approach to combating 'organised crime', taking 'organised crime' to be those crime phenomena which, compared to 'normal' crime, tend to be committed by more resourceful offenders and show greater complexity in how criminal activities are carried out and in how offenders take advantage of social networks in the commission of crimes.
Three main points can be made:

- 'organised crime' phenomena consist of a variety of components which appear to be situationally contingent, so that Situational Crime Prevention at first glance seems to be a useful approach;
- the complexity of the 'organised crime' phenomena calls for comprehensive, highly differentiated strategies of Situational Crime Prevention;
- in the context of 'organised crime', the social dimension of the 'crime situation' appears to be more relevant than in the context of 'normal' crime, because individuals present in an 'organised crime situation', for various reasons, are less likely to function as 'guardians'.

How, then, should situational prevention strategies against 'organised crime' be devised? First, it seems important to stress that Situational Crime Prevention needs to be highly crime specific and that any crime prevention strategy, therefore, needs to be tailor made to effectively address a concrete problem (Clarke, 1993). Second, Situational Crime Prevention requires careful analysis of the crime problem before preventive measures can be developed. This poses even more of a challenge in the case of 'organised crime' than in the case of 'normal' crime (Bullock *et al.*, 2010; Cornish and Clarke, 2002). It has been suggested that a project of situationally preventing crime needs to follow five steps (Clarke 1997, p15):

1. collection of data about the nature and dimensions of the specific crime problem;

2. analysis of the situational conditions that permit or facilitate the commission of the crimes in question;
3. systematic study of possible means of blocking opportunities for these particular crimes, including analysis of costs;
4. implementation of the most promising, feasible and economic measures;
5. monitoring of results and dissemination of experience.

For the purpose of this chapter the first three steps are of central importance. They provide the framework for a systematic analysis of the options that present themselves to tackle a particular 'organised crime' problem with a situational prevention approach.

The nature and dimension of a specific crime problem

Understanding the nature and dimension of a specific 'organised crime' problem, the first step, does not simply require an understanding of a single criminal event in a particular setting. It tends to require an understanding of diverse settings and the ways in which they are linked in the overall context of a criminal venture, respectively a class of criminal ventures. The focus has to be on the underlying 'logistical structure' (Cornish and Clarke, 2002, p 50; Ekblom, 2003, p 253; Kleemans, Soudijn and Weenink, 2010; Sieber and Bögel, 1993). In an 'organised' criminal venture there tends to comprise an interplay of a number of activities, each serving one or more logistical functions, including procurement, production, warehousing, transportation, marketing, camouflaging, protection, communication *etc.* (Sieber and Bögel, 1993, p 64; see also Cornish, 1994; Cornish and Clarke, 2002). Each component needs to be analysed with regard to interdependencies with other logistical components. Only when the logistics are analysed in a comprehensive way will it be possible to identify neuralgic points and to assess the potential outcomes of particular interventions. Of interest, for example, is the flexibility offenders demonstrate in completing a specific task, such as the procurement of cars in the trafficking in stolen motor vehicles. Targeting just one of several procurement schemes may have little impact on the procurement of stolen cars as such. At the same time, different procurement schemes may have different consequences for other components of the logistical structure. For instance, when cars are procured from rental companies, offenders obtain genuine keys and documents which otherwise would have to be forged, replaced or stolen, thereby greatly facilitating the production and transportation logistics of the trafficking in stolen motor vehicles, although other problems are likely to emerge resulting from the direct interaction with car rental companies. For example, offenders may need forged personal identification papers (Europol, 2006).

The patterns of social interaction and networking underlying the logistics of a criminal venture also need to be analysed systematically. Namely, it is important to determine which logistical components likely involve the establishing of new interpersonal contacts (see von Lampe, 2007).

The situational conditions that permit or facilitate the commission of a crime

For each type of criminal activity and offender networking in the overall logistical structure the question is which settings exist that would provide the situational conditions required for its completion, and what logistical efforts it would take offenders to purposefully create the necessary situational conditions if suitable settings are not available. This analysis provides an assessment of the overall situational contingencies of a criminal venture. It should also give an indication of the relative distribution of favourable settings for each logistical component. Those activities which are dependent on a limited number of available settings would create logistical bottlenecks for a criminal venture that could potentially be targeted by situational prevention measures with a higher degree of efficiency (Kleemans *et al.*, 2010). For example, in a scheme where car wrecks are rebuilt using parts from stolen motor vehicles, offenders are dependent on garages with fairly sophisticated equipment (von der Lage, 2003; see also Tremblay, Talon and Hurley, 2001).

Possible means of blocking opportunities

The third step in the analytical process is to determine which aspects of a 'situation' could be altered in order to block opportunities for criminal activities, respectively the underlying criminal networking. Clarke and Eck's "*Twenty Five Techniques of Situational Crime Prevention*" (2005, p 74) are a useful device to systematically consider the options theoretically available. Essentially what needs to be done is to go through the list of 25 techniques for each logistical element of a criminal venture and to ponder in what way these techniques could effectively be applied. In some instance more than one technique might be applicable while in other instances it may be difficult to implement any of the 25 techniques (Bouloukos *et al.*, 2008; Van der Schoot, 2006).

Discussing the merits of each of the 25 techniques with regard to a particular 'organised crime' problem is beyond the scope of this study (for an application to the illegal cigarette trade, see von Lampe, 2010). What should be mentioned, however, is that, taking the trafficking in stolen motor vehicles as an example, a number of prevention measures have shown effect, namely measures that make it more difficult for offenders to commit a crime. These measures include 'target hardening' in the form of steering wheel locks and ignition immobilisers and access control in facilities such as garages where lucrative cars are parked (Clarke and Eck, 2005). However, alternative procurement schemes such as carjacking, the theft of car keys, and the theft of rental cars have partly offset these opportunity reducing effects (Europol, 2006).

Measures to increase the risks of crime by increasing the likelihood of an offender getting caught have also been implemented to prevent car theft. The key element in this context is to strengthen the social dimension in a 'situation' (see Figure 1 above). Alarm systems that sound an alarm when a car is tempered with, for example, alert others to the fact that a car theft might be in progress which, in effect, increases the level of (formal and informal) surveillance over a car as a potential crime target (Clarke and Eck, 2005). In a broader sense, risks for 'organised' criminals can be increased by strengthening and extending guardianship through 'responsibilisation' of government and private agencies and the public at large (Nelen, 2010; Van der Schoot, 2006; Van de Bunt and Van der Schoot, 2003).

A major aspect is awareness about crime schemes so that observed behaviour embedded in legal social or business contexts can be identified as criminal activity (see *e.g.* Finckenauer and Chin, 2010, pp 76-77). Awareness of crime schemes also potentially reduces opportunities for offender networking to the extent that it prevents individuals from becoming unwitting accomplices or from being recruited into a criminal enterprise which otherwise could involve a slow process of realising the illegal nature of the activity.

Setting rules of conduct can also improve guardianship. As Huisman and Klerks have argued, "*(d)rawing up an explicit set of disciplinary rules setting out the responsibilities of those working in certain business domains can help maintain integrity and expose irregular or outright criminal practices*" (2003, p 38). For example, rules could be introduced requiring businesses in the transport sector to record and verify comprehensive sets of contact information of their customers. This would increase the risks (and costs) for smugglers who, pretending to represent an import-export company, outsource the transportation of contraband to a legitimate hauling business (see von Lampe, 2007, p 150).

In this context it should not be ignored that traditional repressive means to combat 'organised crime' can influence the situational opportunity structure. For example, the use of undercover agents and confidential informants generally increases the risks of offender networking, and in particular the risks of on-the-spot transactions.

The third major category of crime prevention techniques, apart from increasing efforts and increasing risks, is reducing the rewards from crime. For example, mandating car parts to be marked with the vehicle identification number (VIN) makes it easier to determine if a car has been stolen, thereby reducing the resale value of a stolen car (Clarke and Eck, 2005). Similarly, raising the awareness of common schemes to alter the VIN may help potential buyers to recognise a stolen car.

Summary and conclusion

This paper has discussed the possibilities and limits of applying the framework of Situational Crime Prevention to the prevention of 'organised crime'. A number of differences in degree between 'organised' and 'non-organised crime' have been highlighted, including:

- the assumed broader time horizon and geographical scope of 'organised' criminal ventures which tend to transcend any one spatio-temporal setting;
- the assumed greater resourcefulness of 'organised' criminals;
- the assumed importance of 'offender convergence settings';
- the assumed greater embeddedness of 'organised' criminal activity in legal social and economic contexts;
- the assumed importance of power and territorial control as factors minimising or neutralising situational prevention mechanisms, and
- the assumed absence, remoteness and variation of 'crime targets' in 'situations' that are part of a larger criminal event.

These differences between 'non-organised crime' and 'organised crime' notwithstanding, it appears that 'organised crime' phenomena have situational contingencies which can be targeted using the toolkit of Situational Crime Prevention. Given the need for a highly crime specific approach, spelling out in any detail a situational crime prevention strategy against 'organised crime' is beyond the scope of this paper. However, some parameters for such a strategy have been pointed out.

First, given the complexity of 'organised' crimes, situational contingencies need to be analysed with a view to the overarching logistical structure of a criminal venture.

Second, patterns of social interaction and networking have to be taken into consideration apart from criminal activities.

Third, given the embeddedness of 'organised crime' into legal social and economic contexts, a key component of any strategy of situational prevention in this area needs to be the 'responsibilisation' of public and private actors, for example in the form of awareness campaigns about criminal schemes in order to strengthen and expand 'guardianship'.

It is not certain how effective overall and in particular contexts the situational prevention of 'organised crime' can be. Displacement and adaptation are more likely to occur here than in the area of 'non-organised crime' while guardianship tends to be weaker, especially where crime and corruption take on systemic dimensions (Edwards and Levi, 2008). Still, once the elusive concept of 'organised crime' is broken down into clearly discernible and observable phenomena which can be analysed with respect to their situational contingencies, there is no reason not to try to change these 'situations' to make crime more difficult, more risky and less rewarding. It is not about applying phantom means against phantoms. It is about applying pragmatic, common sense approaches to down-to-earth crime problems.

References

Bouloukos, A.C., G. Farrell, and G. Laycock, Transnational organised crime in Europe and North America: the need for situational crime prevention efforts. In: K. Aromaa, S. Leppä, S. Nevala and N. Ollus (eds.), *Crime and Criminal Justice in Europe and North America 1995-1997: Report on the Sixth United Nations Survey on Crime Trends and Criminal Justice Systems.* Helsinki: HEUNI, pp. 176-192, 2003

Bowden, M., *Doctor dealer.* New York: Grove, 2001

Bunt, H.G. van de and C. van der Schoot, *Prevention of organised crime: A situational approach.* The Hague, NETH: WODC, 2003

Brantingham, P.J. and F.L. Faust, A conceptual model of crime prevention, *Crime and Delinquency*, 1976, *22*, 284-296

Brantingham, P.L. and P.J. Brantingham, Environment, routine, and situation: Toward a pattern theory of crime. In: R.V. Clarke, M. Felson (eds.), *Routine activity and rational choice, advances in criminological theory.* 1993, *vol. 5*, New Brunswick, NJ: Transaction, pp. 259-294

Bullock, K., R.V. Clarke and N. Tilley, Introduction. In: K. Bullock, R.V. Clarke, N. Tilley (eds.), *Situational Prevention of Organised Crimes*. Cullompton, UK: Willan Publishing, 2010, pp. 1-16

Clarke, R.V.. Editor's introduction. In: R. V. Clarke (ed.), *Crime prevention studies*, 1993, *vol. 1*. Monsey, NY: Criminal Justice Press, 1993, pp. 1-6

Clarke, R.V., Introduction. In: R.V. Clarke (ed.), *Situational crime prevention: Successful case studies*, 2nd ed., Guilderland, NY: Harrow and Heston, 1997, pp. 1-43

Clarke, R.V. and R. Brown, International trafficking in stolen vehicles. In: M. Tonry (ed.), *Crime and Justice: A Review of Research*. Chicago: The University of Chicago Press, 2003, pp. 197-227

Clarke, R.V. and R. Brown, International trafficking of stolen vehicles. In: M. Natarajan (ed.), *Introduction to international criminal justice*, Boston: McGrawHill, 2005, pp. 317-324

Clarke, R.V. and J.E. Eck, *Crime analysis for problem solvers: In 60 small steps*. Washington DC: U.S. Department of Justice, 2005

Cohen, L.E. and M. Felson, Social change and crime rate trends: A routine activity approach. *American Sociological Review 44*, 1979, 588-608

Cornish, D.B. (1994). The procedural analysis of offending and its relevance for situational prevention. In: Ronald V. Clarke (ed.), *Crime Prevention Studies*, 1994, *vol. 3*. Monsey, NY: Criminal Justice Press, pp. 151-196

Cornish, D.B. and R.V. Clarke, Introduction. In: D.B. Cornish, R.V. Clarke (eds.), *The reasoning criminal*. New York: Springer, 1986, pp. 2-16

Cornish, D.B. and R.V. Clarke, Analyzing Organized Crimes. In: A.R. Piquero and S.G. Tibbetts (eds.), *Rational choice and criminal behavior: Recent research and future challenges*. New York: Routledge, 2002, pp. 41–62

Duyne, P.C. van, Medieval thinking and organised crime economy. In: E.C. Viano, J. Magallanes, L. Bridel (eds.), *Transnational organised crime: Myth, power, and profit*. Durham, NC: Carolina Academic Press, 2003, pp. 23-44

Duyne, P.C. van and M. van Dijck, All in the Dutch construction family: cartel building and organised crime. In: L. Holmes (ed.), *Terrorism, organised crime and corruption: networks and linkages*. Cheltenham, Edward Elgar, 2007, pp. 112-134.

Duyne, P.C. van, M. Pheijffer, H.G. Kuijl and A.Th.H. van Dijk, *Financial investigation of crime: A tool of the integral law enforcement approach*, The Hague: Koninklijke Vermande, 2001

Edwards, A. and M. Levi, Researching the organization of serious crimes. *Criminology and Criminal Justice 8*, 2008, 363-388

Ekblom, P., Organised crime and the conjunction of criminal opportunity framework. In: A. Edwards, P. Gill (eds.), *Transnational organised crime*, London: Routledge, 2003, pp. 241-263

Europol, *An overview of motor vehicle crime from a European perspective*. The Hague: Europol, 2006

Felson, M., Those who discourage crime. In: J.E. Eckand and D. Weisburd (eds.), *Crime Prevention Studies*, 1995, vol. 4, Monsey, NY: Criminal Justice Press, pp. 53-66

Felson, M., *Crime and everyday life*. 3rd ed., Thousand Oaks, CA: Sage, 2002

Felson, M., *Crime and nature*. Thousand Oaks, CA: Sage, 2006a

Felson, M., *The ecosystem for organised crime*. Helsinki: HEUNI, HEUNI Paper No. 26, 2006b

Felson, M. and R.V. Clarke, *Opportunity makes the thief: Practical theory for crime prevention*. London: Home Office, 1998

Felson, M. and R.V. Clarke, Routine precautions, criminology, and crime prevention. In: H. Barlow and S.H. Decker (eds.), *Criminology and public policy: Putting theory to work*. Philadelphia: Temple University Press, 2010, 106-120

Finckenauer, J.O. and K.-L. Chin, Sex trafficking: a target for situational crime prevention? In: K. Bullock, R.V. Clarke, N. Tilley (eds.), *Situational prevention of organised crimes*. Cullompton, UK: Willan Publishing, 2010, pp. 58-80

Haller, M.H., Bureaucracy and the mafia: An alternative view. *Journal of Contemporary Criminal Justice 8*, 1992, 1-10

Hancock, G. and G. Laycock, Organised crime and crime scripts: prospects for disruption. In: K. Bullock, R.V. Clarke, N. Tilley (eds.), *Situational prevention of organised crimes*. Cullompton, UK: Willan Publishing, 2010, pp. 172-192

Hicks, D.C., Thinking about organised crime prevention. *Journal of Contemporary Criminal Justice 14*, 1998, 325-350

Hobbs, D., The firm: Organisational logic and criminal culture on a shifting terrain. *British Journal of Criminology*, 2001, *41*, 549-560

Kleemans, E.R., M.R.J. Soudijn and A.W. Weenink, Situational crime prevention and cross-border crime. In: K. Bullock, R.V. Clarke, N. Tilley (eds.), *Situational prevention of organised crimes*. Cullompton, UK: Willan Publishing, 2010, pp. 17-34

Kleemans, E.R. and H.G. van de Bunt, The social embeddedness of organised crime. *Transnational Organised Crime*, 2002, *5*, 19-36.

Klerks, P. and W. Huisman, The role of public administration and local businesses. In: H.G. van de Bunt and C. van der Schoot (eds.), *Prevention of organised crime: A situational approach*. The Hague, NETH: WODC, 2003, pp. 33-44.

Korsell, L. and J. Skinnari, Situational prevention against unlawful influence from organised crime. In: K. Bullock, R.V. Clarke, N. Tilley (eds.), *Situational prevention of organised crimes*. Cullompton, UK: Willan Publishing, 2010, pp. 151-171.

Lacey, M., Mexico lawmen outmatched by drug violence. *The New York Times*, A1, A7, (2009, 17 October)

Levi, M. and M. Maguire, Reducing and preventing organised crime: An evidence-based critique. *Crime, Law and Social Change*, 2004, *41*, 397-469

Liddick, D., *The Mob's daily number: organised crime and the numbers gambling industry*. Lanham, MD: University Press of America, 1999

Miethe, T.D. and R.F. Meier, *Crime and its social context: Toward an integrated theory of offenders, victims, and situations*. Albany, NY: State University of New York Press, 1994

Naylor, R.T., Towards a general theory of profit-driven crimes. *British Journal of Criminology*, 2003, *43*, 81-101

Nelen, H., Situational organised crime prevention in Amsterdam: the administrative approach. In: K. Bullock, R.V. Clarke, N. Tilley (eds.), *Situational prevention of organised crimes*. Cullompton, UK: Willan Publishing, 2010, pp. 93-110

Potter, G., *Criminal organisations: vice racketeering and politics in an American city*. Prospect Heights, IL: Waveland Press, 1994

Reuter, P., *Disorganised crime: the economics of the visible hand*. Cambridge, MA: MIT Press, 1983

Savona, E., Infiltration of the public construction industry by Italian organised crime. In: K. Bullock, R.V. Clarke, N. Tilley (eds.), *Situational prevention of organised crimes*. Cullompton, UK: Willan Publishing, 2010, pp. 130-150

Schoot, C.R.A. van der, *Organised crime prevention in the Netherlands: exposing the effectiveness of preventive measures*. Doctoral dissertation, Erasmus Universiteit Rotterdam, 2006

Sexton, R.L., R.G. Carlson, C.G. Leukefeld and B.M. Booth, Patterns of illicit methamphetamine production ('cooking') and associated risks in the rural south: An ethnographic exploration. *Journal of Drug Issues*, 2006, *36*, 853-876

Sieber, U. and M. Bögel, *Logistik der organisierten Kriminalität*. Wiesbaden, GER: Bundeskriminalamt, 1993

Southerland, M. and G. Potter, Applying organisation theory to organised crime. *Journal of Contemporary Criminal Justice*, 1993, *9*, 251-267

Tremblay, P., B. Talon and D. Hurley, Body switching and related adaptations in the resale of stolen vehicles: Script elaborations and aggregate crime learning curves. *British Journal of Criminology*, 2001, *41*, 561-579 von der Lage, R., Litauische Kfz-Banden in der Bundesrepublik Deutschland, *Kriminalistik*, 2003, *57*, 357-363

von Lampe, K., Criminals are not alone: Some observations on the social microcosm of illegal entrepreneurs. In: P.C. van Duyne, A. Maljevic, M. van Dijck, K. von Lampe and J. Harvey (eds.), *Crime business and crime money in Europe: The dirty linen of illicit enterprise*. Nijmegen, NETH: Wolf Legal Publishers, pp. 131-155, 2007

von Lampe, K., Preventing organised crime: The case of contraband cigarettes. In: K. Bullock, R.V. Clarke, N. Tilley (eds.), *Situational prevention of organised crimes*. Cullompton, UK: Willan Publishing, 2010, pp. 35-57

von Lampe, K., The Application of the framework of Situational Crime Prevention to 'organized crime'. *Criminology and Criminal Justice*, forthcoming

Zabludoff, S.J., Colombian narcotics organisations as business enterprises. *Transnational Organised Crime*, 1997, *3*, 20-49

Legal Protection against OLAF The European fraud watch dog

Severin Glaser[1]

Introduction: powers and protection

Fraud and corruption not only damage the finances of the EU but also its reputation. The efficient protection of the EU's financial interests is thus an important policy to instil confidence in the EU. In order to fight and prevent fraud, corruption and other illegal activities affecting the EU's financial interests the European Anti-Fraud Office (Office Européen de Lutte Anti-Fraude – OLAF) was established in 1999.[2] OLAF's most important task is carrying out administrative investigations of irregularities that may end up in an investigation report forwarded to competent authorities, such as the public prosecutor in a certain Member State or a certain EU institution functioning as disciplinary authority.

Although OLAF is a Directorate-General of the European Commission, its Director-General decides in paramount authority on the beginning, the process

1 Dr. Severin Glaser works as research assistant at the Institute for Austrian and European Economic Criminal Law, Vienna University of Economics and Business.

2 Commission Decision of 28 April 1999 establishing the European Anti-fraud Office (OLAF), 1999/352/EC, ECSC, Euratom, OJ 1999 L 136/20; Regulation (EC) No 1073/1999 of the European Parliament and of the Council of 25 May 1999 concerning investigations conducted by the European Anti-Fraud Office (OLAF), OJ 1999 L 136/1; Council Regulation (Euratom) No 1074/1999 of 25 May 1999 concerning investigations conducted by the European Anti-Fraud Office (OLAF), OJ 1999 L 136/8; Interinstitutional Agreement of 25 May 1999 between the European Parliament, the Council of the European Union and the Commission of the European Communities concerning internal investigations by the European Anti-fraud Office (OLAF), OJ 1999 L 136/15. OLAF succeeded the Task Force for the Co-ordination of fraud prevention (Unité de coordination et de Lutte Antifraude – UCLAF), a part of the Secreteriat-General of the European Commission that did not enjoy independence when conducting investigations. After a series of corruption scandals concerning the European Commission and the European Parliament in 1998/99, UCLAF was not seen capable of protecting the EU's financial interests sufficiently any more and replaced by OLAF. See for example *Quirke*, Economic Crime and Legal Competence in the EU, in: *van Duyne/Maljevic/van Dijck/von Lampe/Newell* (Eds.), The Organisation of Crime for Profit (2006) pp. 90-91; *Gleß*, Das Europäische Amt für Betrugsbekämpfung (OLAF), EuZW 1999, pp. 618-621; *Pétillon*, Réussites et Défis de l'Office Européen de Lutte Antifraude, eucrim 2008, pp. 154-156.

and the end of these administrative investigations. OLAF conducts external investigations in the Member States (for example in companies under suspicion of having abused their EU grants) as well as internal investigations inside EU institutions (for example in the office of a Member of the European Parliament under suspicion of having accepted a bribe).

Internal and external investigations have different legal grounds, giving OLAF's investigators different powers in regard to on-the-spot inspections in private premises and official EU buildings.[3] During both kinds of investigations, OLAF may forward information to national authorities or affected EU institutions.

All this implies that OLAF has been provided with considerable powers within the European Commission as well as towards third parties. From a law enforcement perspective these powers are highly significant and have attracted some scholarly interest. But what about the limitations of these powers in term of protection of investigated subjects? This has been far less addressed by legal scholars. Indeed, the literature is not rich on this subject of legal protection.[4] Therefore, this chapter aims to answer the questions whether there is a need for legal protection vis-à-vis acts of OLAF. And if there is such a need, what remedies exist and are these remedies sufficient?

The legal grounds of OLAF mention in their disposing parts the point of legal protection against OLAF, but only in regard to officials of the EU itself. If EU officials get a visit from OLAF and, for example, documents and computer hardware are seized, Article 14 Reg 1073/99 gives them the right to submit a complaint to OLAF's Director-General, challenging acts of OLAF's staff. As stated in this article, the Staff Regulations[5] ruling the conditions of service and employ-

---

3 External investigations: Council Regulation (Euratom, EC) No 2185/96 of 11 November 1996 concerning on-the-spot checks and inspections carried out by the Commission in order to protect the European Communities' financial interests against fraud and other irregularities, OJ 1996 L 292/2;
Internal investigations (examples for decisions of certain institutions implementing the Interinstitutional Agreement): Council Decision of 25 May 1999 concerning the terms and conditions for internal investigations in relation to the prevention of fraud, corruption and any illegal activity detrimental to the Communities' interests, 1999/394/EC, Euratom, OJ 1999 L 149/36; Commission Decision of 2 June 1999 concerning the terms and conditions for internal investigations in relation to the prevention of fraud, corruption and any illegal activity detrimental to the Communities' interests, 1999/396/EC, ECSC, Euratom, OJ 1999 L 149/57; Article 10 and Annex XI European Parliament - Rules of Procedure, 16th edition July 2004, OJ 2004 L 44/1.

4 Interesting articles concerning this question are the exception. See for example *Balogová*, The Developments in the Case Law of the Community Courts with Regard to OLAF Investigations, eucrim 2008, pp. 142-145; *White*, The Judgment of the Court of First Instance in the Case Franchet and Byk v European Commission, eucrim 2008, pp. 146-147.

5 Regulation (EEC, Euratom, ECSC) No 259/68 of the Council of 29 February 1968 laying down the Staff Regulations of Officials and the Conditions of Employment of Other Ser-

ment for persons working for the EU have been amended.[6] Meanwhile, the new Article 90a stipulates that every person falling under the rule of the Staff Regulations may request a legally binding decision (according to Article 288 Treaty on the Functioning of the European Union – TFEU) from OLAF's Director-General in regards to an investigation affecting him.[7] Likewise such a person may submit a complaint to OLAF's Director-General against any burdensome measure regarding an investigation.[8] If the latter rejects the complaint under Article 90a Staff Regulations/Article 14 Reg 1073/99, his decision can be subject to remedies, like an appeal, falling under the jurisdiction of the EU courts. Hence there is a regime of legal protection for civil servants working in the EU. But are they the only protected persons? And is that protection sufficient? Has the protection against this watchdog been sufficiently thought through? This chapter will show that on the one hand the EU legislator has theoretically provided sufficient possibilities for remedies against OLAF's acts. However, on the other hand, it will have to be concluded, that the competent judicial authorities do not fulfil their roles sufficiently, leaving a gap in the legal protection against OLAF.

The need for legal protection

What does 'legal protection' mean in this context? The term refers to any legal remedy a person has against OLAF. Legal remedy can come in different forms. First, there is the possibility of a compensation for (financial) damages under EU law as well as under national law. Second, an affected person can try to seek fundamental right protection, meaning to contest a specific measure taken by OLAF or a national authority because it violates an individual right laid down in a Constitution, the EU Primary Law or an international convention on Human Rights. The purpose of fundamental right protection is to stop the unlawful situation and to prevent the investigation, procedure or decision that is built upon a violation of fundamental rights.

For the correct understanding of the different systems of legal protection it is highly important to distinguish between investigative measures taken by OLAF itself and measures taken by national authorities following OLAF's recommenda-

vants of the European Communities and instituting special measures temporarily applicable to officials of the Commission, OJ 1968 L 56/1.

6 Council Regulation (EC, Euratom) No 723/2004 of 22 March 2004 amending the Staff Regulations of officials of the European Communities and the Conditions of Employment of other servants of the European Communities, OJ 2004 L 124/1.

7 In combination with Article 90 para 1 Staff Regulations.

8 In combination with Article 90 para 2 Staff Regulations.

tion. This distinction only applies to *on-the-spot inspections*. OLAF enjoys control rights in EU institutions and has the power to execute coercively its rights to control and seize vis-à-vis EU officials. But not only EU officials but also private persons and enterprises, called 'economic operators', can be controlled and thus affected in their individual rights by OLAF. Here OLAF depends on the help of the competent national authorities (for example the police) to execute coercively its right to enter offices and other premises. As regards economic operators, only national authorities and not OLAF have the right to seize information and pieces of evidence. As we will see later, this has consequences for the legal protection, which is totally different regarding indirect acts (committed by national authorities) and direct acts of OLAF.

However, unlike EU officials, OLAF's legal grounds do not stipulate a procedure of legal protection for economic operators affected by an OLAF investigation. This fact raises the questions what the reasons for this difference are and whether economic operators do not have a need for legal protection, as well. Since the provisions for a complaint to OLAF's Director-General would be useless otherwise, it must be concluded that OLAF's actions are in principle capable of violating individual rights. When is that the case? Apart from press releases, three situations in OLAF's investigation procedure can be determined in which OLAF sets external acts and therefore can affect individual rights. These are principally:

- on-the-spot inspections (including house searches, searches of offices, controls of enterprises etc.);
- the investigation report, and;
- the forwarding of information.

A fourth situation, the decision to open an investigation, cannot jeopardise the position of individuals.[9] On-the-spot inspections, the investigation report and the forwarding of information, in contrast, do affect for example the inviolability of the home (house searches), the right to property (seizure of items) as already mentioned, but also data protection (forwarding of information) or procedural rights (for example when the access to the records is denied).[10]

It must thus be examined whether and to what extent there is (fundamental) right protection vis-à-vis OLAF's on-the-spot inspections, investigation reports and forwarding of information. It is also important to learn the differences be-

9 This can be deduced a maiore ad minus from a judgement and a decision regarding the investigation report: ECJ decision of 8 April 2003 in case C-471/02(P) *Santiago Gómez-Reino v Commission*; ECFI case T-193/04 *Hans-Martin Tillack v Commission* [2006] ECR II-3995.

10 For example the right to a fair trial (Article 6 ECHR) or the right to an effective remedy (Article 13 ECHR).

tween EU officials and 'economic operators' in this regard. If any, they will be demonstrated and discussed and the demand for legal protection for economic operators will be clarified in detail.

Competent authorities controlling OLAF

OLAF does not stand alone and there are many institutions which have a controlling judiciary function concerning its activities. In the first place there are the EU courts:

- the European Court of Justice (ECJ);
- the European Court of First Instance (ECFI), and – hearing disputes between the EU and her officials –
- the European Union Civil Service Tribunal.[11]

These organs are exclusively competent to review the legality of the acts[12] of OLAF and to decide over compensation for damages.[13] As far as the EU is concerned, there is no law of procedure connecting national courts and the EU courts, but the question is whether fundamental right protection could also fall under the jurisdiction of national courts. After all national remedies have been exhausted one could then appeal to the European Court of Human Rights (ECtHR) in Strasbourg of the Council of Europe. But it is not certain whether all these courts mentioned above recognise a specific need for legal protection regarding OLAF's on-the-spot inspections, investigation reports and forwarding of information, and grant such a legal protection. In fact, this question will prove to be the problem for a well-functioning legal protection against OLAF. The following sections will focus on the competence of the EU courts, national courts and the European Court of Human Rights to grant legal protection against OLAF. Afterwards, it will be elaborated whether those courts that are competent to grant legal protection against OLAF are also willing to do so, regarding the investigation report, the forwarding of information and the on-the-spot-inspections one by one.

---

11 Established by: Council Decision of 2 November 2004 establishing the European Union Civil Service Tribunal, 2004/752/ EC, Euratom, OJ 2004 L 333/7.

12 Article 263 TFEU.

13 Article 268 TFEU in combination with Article 340 para 2 TFEU.

EU courts (ECJ, ECFI, Civil Service Tribunal)

a. Jurisdiction and stages of appeal

There are three types of actions a person who feels prejudiced may undertake.

First, if an EU *official* feels infringed in his individual rights by an act of OLAF he can address the Director-General with a complaint (Article 14/90a). If the Director-General comes to a decision that is detrimental to the complainant, the decision may be subjected to an action before the Civil Service Tribunal under Article 270 Treaty on the Functioning of the European Union. Article 270 TFEU provides the jurisdiction of the EU courts in disputes between the EU and its civil servants. All disputes following complaints submitted by EU officials to OLAF's Director-General under Article 14/90a fall under this category.

The decision of the Civil Service Tribunal may be subject to an appeal to the European Court of First Instance. However, this appeal is limited to questions of law and can only be based on (a) the lack of competence of the Civil Service Tribunal, (b) a breach of procedure in the process which adversely affects the interests of the appellant or (c) the infringement of EU law. Decisions of the European Court of First Instance may only be subject to review by the European Court of Justice if there is a serious risk of the unity or consistency of EU law being affected.[14] In other words only when landmark decisions are required.

Secondly, Article 340 para 2 Treaty on the Functioning of the European Union stipulates that in cases of non-contractual liability the EU must make good any damage caused by its institutions or by its civil servants in the performance of their duties in accordance with the general principles common to the laws of the Member States. For this purpose, Article 268 Treaty on the Functioning of the European Union provides the action for damages. If OLAF or its employees cause damage (not only due to investigative actions), everybody affected (not only EU officials) may bring an action for damages to the European Court of First Instance.[15] Decisions of the ECFI may be subject to review by the European Court of Justice, again limited to questions of law.[16] Evidence matters are excluded when the ECJ reviews a judgement of the ECFI.

A third type of action relevant to this field is the *action for annulment*. Acts of the European Commission[17] can be challenged under Article 263 Treaty on the Functioning of the European Union on grounds of lack of competence, in-

14 Article 256 para 2 TFEU.
15 Article 256 para 1 TFEU.
16 Article 268 TFEU.
17 Actions can only be brought against the European Commission and never against OLAF itself.

fringement on an essential procedural requirement, infringement on the Treaty on the European Union or the Treaty on the Functioning of the European Union or of any rule of law relating to their application, or misuse of powers by any EU institution.

Natural and legal persons must be concerned directly and individually to institute such a proceeding.[18] Just like the action for damages, the action for annulment falls in the jurisdiction of the European Court of First Instance whose decisions may be subject to review by the European Court of Justice.[19] This judicial review by the European Court of Justice is also limited to questions of law.

It follows that the EU courts are competent to grant (fundamental) right protection against OLAF. Three different actions are in theory capable of providing a successful remedy if a person feels violated in individual rights by one of OLAF's actions. Whether the EU courts are really willing to grant legal protection and fundamental right protection vis-à-vis specific acts mentioned will be answered later. The next section will highlight the catalogue of fundamental rights by which the actions of OLAF could be measured by the EU courts. Which fundamental rights are used in the case law of the EU courts?

b. Catalogue of fundamental rights applied

The protection of the fundamental rights in the EU experienced a late start compared to the development of other EU politics. Several sources of law for fundamental rights must be taken into account: fundamental rights enshrined in the constitutions of the EU Member States, the European Convention of Human Rights and Fundamental Freedoms (hereafter ECHR) and the Charter of Fundamental Rights of the European Union. Since the latter has entered into force, the EU has a fundamental rights catalogue that is legally binding for all EU institutions. With the help of the different types of actions mentioned above, the EU courts watch with the catalogue the compliance of the EU institutions.

Since 1969 the European Court of Justice dedicates itself in settled case law to the protection of the fundamental rights enshrined in the general principles of EU law.[20] In a couple of decisions made in the following years the European Court of Justice specified this unwritten primary law. It was stated, that the fundamental rights enshrined in the general principles of EU law derive from the constitutional

---

18 Article 263 subparagraph 4 TFEU.

19 Article 263 subparagraph 1 and 2 TFEU.

20 The landmark decision in regards to EU fundamental right protection was ECJ case 29/69 *Erich Stauder v City of Ulm – Sozialamt* [1969].

traditions common to the Member States[21], and that international treaties for the protection of human rights[22] and the ECHR[23] can supply guidelines which should be followed within the framework of EU law. Finally the European Court of Justice began to regard the ECHR not just as a source of insight in the constitutional traditions common to the Member States but as directly applicable law[24], in due consideration of the jurisprudence of the judicial authorities in Strasbourg.[25]

Until it was amended by the Lisbon Treaty, Article 6 para 2 Treaty of the European Union transferred this case law into written primary law. It declared explicitly that the EU respects the fundamental rights as guaranteed by the ECHR on the grounds that they result from the constitutional traditions common to the Member States. Since the entry into force of the Lisbon Treaty, the amended Article 6 para 2 Treaty of the European Union provides the accession of the EU to the ECHR. As soon as this accession has taken place, even the jurisprudence of the European Court of Human Rights will be formally binding for the European Court of Justice.[26]

Despite the fact that the fundamental rights enshrined in the constitutional traditions common to the Member States are respected, the European Court of Justice does not apply a fundamental rights catalogue from a particular Member State. In the judgement of 1970 in the case *Internationale Handelgesellschaft* it is stated that the fundamental right protection granted by the European Court of Justice must fit into the framework of structure and objectives of the EU.[27] Thus, infringements of fundamental rights by EU institutions could only be judged in the light of EU law itself and not by special criteria for assessment stemming from the legislation or constitutional law of a particular Member State.[28] With the legal position unchanged since then, it became clear over the years that the EU with its slow approach to the ECHR was at that time lacking of a fundamental rights charter.

---

21 ECJ case 11/70 *Internationale Handelsgesellschaft mbH v Einfuhr- und Vorratsstelle für Getreide und Futtermittel* [1970].

22 ECJ case 4/73 *J. Nold, Kohlen- und Baustoffgroßhandlung v Commission of the European Communities* [1974].

23 ECJ case 36/75 *Roland Rutili v Ministre de l'intérieur [1975]; ECJ case 44/79 Liselotte Hauer v Land Rheinland-Pfalz* [1979].

24 ECJ case 222/84 *Marguerite Johnston v Chief Constable of the Royal Ulster Constabulary* [1986].

25 ECJ joined cases 46/87 and 227/88 *Hoechst AG v Commission of the European Communities* [1989]; ECJ case 347/87 *Orkem v Commission of the European Communities* [1989]; ECJ case C-94/00 *Roquette Frères SA v Directeur général de la concurrence, de la consommation et de la répression des fraudes, and Commission of the European Communities* [2002].

26 This the danger of a possibly diverging interpretation of the ECHR, see *Philippi*, Divergenzen im Grundrechtsschutz zwischen EuGH und EGMR, ZEuS 2000 pp. 107 et seq.

27 ECJ *Internationale Handelsgesellschaft* at para 4.

28 ECJ *Hauer* at para 14.

On December 7, 2000 the Charter of Fundamental Rights of the European Union was signed and solemnly proclaimed. Since then, the Charter had been used by the EU courts as a source of insight for fundamental rights enshrined in other sources of law.[29] The Lisbon Treaty 2007 finally declared the Charter as a legally binding part of primary law.[30] Hence, the EU courts can now review whether OLAF's acting is in compliance with a written catalogue of fundamental rights that is considered clear and precise and without any doubt legally binding for OLAF.

It is now clear that the EU courts are competent to control OLAF as well as it has become clear by which fundamental right catalogue (in the first line, the Charter of Fundamental Rights of the European Union, as well as in future the ECHR) all acting of OLAF would have to be measured by the EU courts. Next, it must be checked whether national courts or the European Court of Human Rights are also in the position to grant fundamental right protection to persons affected by OLAF.

National courts using the example of Austria

Fundamental rights do not only have to be respected by EU institutions, but also by national authorities and national courts of the EU Member States. Therefore, judicial protection of fundamental rights against national authorities and the judicial system is an important task for national courts. The question arises whether they are able to protect fundamental rights also vis-à-vis acts of an EU authority such as OLAF. The answer is no and for the following reason: the European Court of Justice had assumed these rights in 1970s. And not just parallel to the Member States, but exclusively[31] even though the Member States, like the Italian

---

29 See for example ECFI case T-54/99 *max.mobil Telekommunikation Service GmbH v Commission of the European Communities* [2002]; ECFI case T-177/01 *Jégo-Quéré et Cie SA v Commission of the European Communities* [2002]; ECFI joined cases T-377/00, T-379/00, T-380/00, T-260/01 and T-272/01 *Philip Morris International Inc. and Others v Commission of the European Communities* [2003]; ECFI case T-242/02 *The Sunrider Corp. v Office for Harmonisation in the Internal Market (Trade Marks and Designs) (OHIM)* [2007]; ECJ Order of the President of the Court of First Instance of 4 April 2002 in case C-232/02P(R) *Technische Glaswerke Ilmenau GmbH v Commission of the European Communities*; ECJ case C-263/02P *Commission of the European Communities v Jégo-Quéré et Cie SA* [2004].

30 Article 6 para 1 TEU.

31 ECJ case 6/64 *Flaminio Costa v E.N.E.L.* [1964]; ECJ *Internationale Handelsgesellschaft*; ECJ case 106/77 *Amministrazione delle Finanze dello Stato v Simmenthal SpA* [1978]; ECJ case C-213/89 *The Queen v Secretary of State for Transport, ex parte: Factortame Ltd and others* [1990]; ECJ case C-217/88 *Commission of the European Communities v Federal Republic of Germany* [1990].

and German Constitutional Courts tried to state their rights.[32] Since Austria became a Member State of the EU in 1995, it has inherited the legal position based on this case law of the EU courts. It must therefore be concluded that under EU law Austrian courts cannot grant any legal protection against OLAF, not even when OLAF is acting in Austria or vis-à-vis Austrian citizens.

It is important to remember that OLAF depends on the assistance of national authorities to enforce coercively its control rights vis-à-vis economic operators. The fact, that national courts are unable to grant fundamental right protection against OLAF directly does not preclude them to review the acting of the assisting national authorities. As will be discussed in greater detail below, national remedies are supposed to offer sufficient legal protection in that regard.

Example 1:

The Austrian journalist A writes an article on corruption inside the European Union Agency for Fundamental Rights (FRA) which is located in Vienna. Since A quotes confidential reports, it is suspected that he bribed the EU official B working for FRA himself in order to get a copy of the quoted reports. OLAF conducts a search in the office of the EU official B and seizes his notebook. OLAF further asks the Austrian Public Prosecutor to conduct a dawn raid in the office and the private apartment of A. Since bribery of EU officials is a crime under Austrian law, the Austrian Public Prosecutor orders the house searches and conducts them together with Austrian policemen and OLAF officials. Both A and B feel violated in their fundamental rights. A considers his right to respect for private and family life (Article 8 ECHR) violated by the house search which is based upon a suspicion he considers vague and unsubstantiated. He further complains of a violation of his freedom of expression (Article 10 ECHR) which also includes the freedom of press. B complains a violation of his right to a fair trial (Article 6 ECHR) since he can not make use of the files on the seized notebook to prepare his defence. The economic operator A and the EU official B have no possibility to contest OLAF's acts before Austrian courts or authorities. However, since the Austrian police and the Austrian Public Prosecutor have been involved in the case of A, he could challenge their acting with a legal remedy during the Austrian criminal procedure itself.

32 See for example the *Frontini* judgement of the Italian constitutional court or case law of the German constitutional court based upon its *Solange I* judgement: Corte Costituzionale, 27.12.1973, n. 183, Giurisprudenza Italiana. Serie 7a. Volume CXXVI 1974, 519 („*Frontini*“);BVerfG 2 BvL 52/71 = 1/2 EuGRZ 1974/1975, pp. 5 et seq. („*Solange I*“); BVerfG 2 BvL 6/77, BverfGE 52, 187 („*Vielleicht*“); BVerfG 2 BvR 1107, 1124/77 und 195/79, BverfGE 58, pp. 1 et seq. („*Eurocontrol I*“); BVerfG 2 BvR 197/83 = 14 EuGRZ 1987, pp. 10 et seq. („*Solange II*“); BVerfG 2 BvO 3/89 = EuR 1989 („*Tabak-Etikettierungsrichtlinie*“); BVerfG 2 BvR 2134/92, 2159/92, BverfGE 89, pp. 155 et seq. („*Maastricht*“).

This means that as far as OLAF's very own conduct is concerned and a violation of somebody's fundamental rights directly by OLAF is alleged (irrespective if the affected person is an EU official or an economic operator), the affected person, in theory, has the possibility of asking the EU courts only for judicial review, but not an Austrian court. Another possibility could be fundamental right protection by the European Court of Human Rights in Strasbourg.

ECtHR: The European Court of Human Rights

The European Court of Human Rights of the Council of Europe ensures the compliance with the ECHR by its High Contracting Parties.[33] Any person, non-governmental organisation or group of individuals claiming to be the victim of a violation by one of the High Contracting Parties of the rights set forth in the ECHR and its protocols may submit an individual application to the European Court of Human Rights.[34] Until the entry into force of the Protocol No. 11 to the Convention for the Protection of Human Rights and Fundamental Freedoms in November 1998, the European Commission of Human Rights (EComHR) decided as "first instance" over the admissibility of applications. This body drafted reports on possible violations of the Convention, which were the basis for an admission to the European Court of Human Rights. The European Commission of Human Rights had thus the function of a preparatory filter for the European Court of Human Rights. The case law of the European Commission of Human Rights is still important to questions relevant to this chapter. However, the 11th Protocol restructured the control machinery of the ECHR as the Council of Europe abolished the European Commission of Human Rights (1998). Since then the European Court of Human Rights itself decides over the admissibility of applications.

As soon as the EU has accessed the ECHR, infringements of the fundamental rights as provided in the ECHR committed by EU institutions, including OLAF, will fall under the jurisdiction of the European Court of Human Rights. As shown above, the European Court of Justice already regards the fundamental rights provided by the ECHR as binding to the EU institutions. However, the issue of a directly binding of these EU institutions to the jurisprudence of the European Court of Human Rights can only be answered fully with a view to the European Court of Human Rights case law as regards to this question.

This case law has provided an interesting development. It started from the thesis that the Strasbourg institutions were not competent to judge over the com-

33 Article 19 ECHR.
34 Article 34 ECHR.

pliance of legal acts of the EU with the ECHR because the EU is not a High Contracting Party of the ECHR. After a phase of less than coherent decisions, the European Court of Human Rights ended up disclaiming its jurisdiction over EU authorities, expressing confidence that the EU would grant sufficient fundamental right protection itself.

a. ECtHR not competent

In 1978 the Strasbourg authorities have been confronted first with the questions of the admissibility of actions against the EU and the responsibility of the EU Member States (severally or jointly) for fundamental right violations committed by EU institutions. This happened in the case *Confédération Francaise Démocratique du Travail (C.F.D.T.).*[35] The applicant, a French trade union had not been appointed by the Council to become a member of the Consultative Committee of the European Coal and Steel Community (former part of the EU). The trade union considered this a violation of the prohibition of discrimination (Article 14 ECHR) and violation of the freedom of assembly and association (Article 11 ECHR). After unsuccessful remedies before the European Court of Justice and the French Administrative court (Conseil d'Etat), the trade union further claimed to be violated in its right to an effective remedy (Article 13 ECHR). All three applications (against the European Union and their Member States jointly as well as severally) were declared inadmissible *rationae personae*, meaning they were inadmissible because the EU was not a High Contracting Party of the ECHR. For a long time, Strasbourg did not change its case law in regards to the jurisdiction over the EU[36], although the European Commission of Human Rights slightly adapted its case law in so far as Member States which make use of their right to assign their sovereign powers to the EU[37] must continue to guarantee the fundamental right protection for sovereign powers transferred.[38]

In *Melchers* (1990) the applicant, a German enterprise importing Hi-fi products from Japan, had been fined by the European Commission for forming a cartel

35 EComHR Application No 8030/77, *Confédération Francaise Démocratique du Travail versus the European Communities, alternatively: their member states a) jointly and b) severally*, Decision of 10 July 1978 on the admissibility of the application, Council of Europe. European Commission of Human Rights, Decisions and Reports. 13, 240.

36 EComHR Application No 13539/88, *Christiane Dufay v/ the European Communities, alternatively the Community of their member states and the member states severally*, Decision of 19 January 1989 on the admissibility of the application.

37 EComHR Application No 8364/78, *Kennedy Lindsay and others versus the United Kingdom*, Decision of 8 March 1979 on the admissibility of the application, Council of Europe. European Commission of Human Rights, Decisions and Reports. 15, pp. 247 et seq.

38 EComHR Application No 11123/84, *Etienne Tete v/ France*, Decision of 9 December 1987 on the admissibility of the application, Council of Europe. European Commission of Human Rights, Decisions and Reports. 54, p. 52 et seq.

with other European importers of Japanese Hi-fi products. The European Court of Justice had just reduced applicant's fine but dismissed the remainder of its action. Before national courts, Melchers unsuccessfully tried to prevent the German judicial authorities from issuing a writ of execution and also failed with a subsequent action for damages against Germany. Then Melchers turned to the European Commission of Human Rights, claiming violations of its right to a fair trial. In its decision, the European Commission of Human Rights refers to its decisions in earlier cases, declaring itself not competent to control procedural methods and decisions of EU institutions because the EU was not a High Contracting Party of the ECHR .[39] More important is that the European Commission of Human Rights goes beyond this, stating that the transfer of sovereign powers to an international organisation is compatible with the ECHR if fundamental rights receive equivalent protection within this organisation as it is the case with the EU.

Therefore, applications against a Member State based on a violation of fundamental rights by EU law, are inadmissible *ratione materiae*, meaning that the Strasbourg institutions declare themselves not competent to judge over the compliance of legal acts of the EU with the ECHR because (and as long as) fundamental rights are protected effectively within the EU. The *Melchers* decision is thus not so interesting because of his result (still no possibility to appeal to Strasbourg in EU matters), but because of the changed reasons for this decision: 'Strasbourg' does test the fundamental right protection within the EU. This argumentation was extended in subsequent decisions, such as in the *Heinz* case.

In the decision *Heinz* of 1994 the applicant had filed a European Patent application at the European Patent Office, an international organisation located in Munich. When Mr. Heinz could not pay the renewal fee immediately and the European Patent Office refused to give him an extension of time for payment, he considered this a violation of the protection of property (Article 1 1st Protocol to the ECHR). He turned to the European Commission of Human Rights considering the Member States of the European Patent Convention being jointly responsible for the breach of fundamental rights by the international organisation. In this case that can be applied by analogy to the EU, the European Commission of Human Rights made clear that the EU Member States can be sued jointly for EU acts.[40] Moreover, the European Commission of Human Rights underlined the

---

39 EComHR Application No 13258/87, *M. & Co. v/ the Federal Republic of Germany*, Decision of 9 February 1990 on the admissibility of the application, Council of Europe. European Commission of Human Rights, Decisions and Reports. 64, 138 et seq.

40 EComHR Application No 21090/92, *Karl Eckart Heinz versus contracting states also parties to the European Patent Convention*, Decision of 10 January 1994 on the admissibility of the application, Council of Europe. European Commission of Human Rights, Decisions and Reports. pp. 125 et seq.

Melchers decision and went beyond it by stating that any possible legal protection within an international organisation (here: the European Patent Convention) is regarded as equivalent to the ECHR even without any further proof. This means that the European Commission of Human Rights did not only regard the fundamental right protection of the EU as equivalent to the ECHR, it also regarded the – probably simpler – systems of remedy within other international organisations (that have nothing to do with the EU, such as the European Patent Convention) as equivalent to the ECHR as well.

b. ECtHR competent?

In the mid-nineties, Strasbourg's case law regarding the judicial control over EU acts began to become inconsistent. While in two judgements[41] the European Court of Human Rights regarded itself competent to control EU law and to be a supreme instance in relation to the European Court of Justice, the European Commission of Human Rights emphasized a short time later that vis-à-vis EU acts there is not only no possibility to sue the EU itself but also that no action is admissible against Member States, be it jointly or severally.[42] In some judgements the European Court of Human Rights avoided to decide on the responsibility of EU Member States for EU acts.[43]

However, some judgements of the European Court of Human Rights (which decides on the admissibility of applications itself since the 11th Protocol to the ECHR entered into force in 1999) evolved the case law of the *Melchers* decision, in which the European Commission of Human Rights declared the Strasbourg institutions not competent to judge over the compliance of legal acts of the EU with the ECHR because (and as long as) fundamental rights are protected effectively within the EU. The landmark decisions on the way to the present legal position were the cases *Matthews*[44], *Waite and Kennedy*[45] and *Beer and Regan*[46], all decided on 18 February 1999.

41 ECtHR Application No 14570/89, *Procola v. Luxembourg*, Judgment of 28 September 1995, Registry of the Court. Council of Europe. Publications of the European Court of Human Rights. Series A. Judgments and Decisions. Vol. 326; ECtHR Application No 17862/91, *Michel Cantoni gegen Frankreich*, Urteil vom 15. November 1996, 26 EuGRZ 1999, p. 193.

42 EComHR Application No 32384/96, *Bruno Garzilli v/ member states of the EU*, Decision of 22 October 1998 on the admissibility of the application.

43 ECtHR Application 51616/99, *Société Guérin Automobiles v. 15 member states of the EU*, Decision of 4 July 2000 on the admissibility of the application, RUDH 2000, pp.199 et seq.; ECtHR Application 56672/00, *Senator Lines GmbH v. Austria, Belgium, Denmark, France, Finland, Germany, Greece, Ireland, Italy, Luxembourg, the Netherlands, Portugal, Spain, Sweden and the United Kingdom*, Decision as to the admissibility of the application, 10 March 2004.

44 ECtHR Application No 24833/94, *Denise Matthews v. the United Kingdom*, Judgment of 18 February 1999, European Court of Human Rights. Registry of the Court. Council of

In *Matthews*, the plaintiff was a British Dependent Territories' citizen from Gibraltar that considered her right to free elections (Article 3 1st Protocol to the ECHR) and the prohibition of discrimination violated by the fact that Gibraltar was excluded from the elections to the European Parliament.[47] The judgement in the *Matthews* case decided that a Member State (here: the United Kingdom) is responsible not because of implementing acts of EU law into national law, but because of its participation in acts of international law (here: the Maastricht Treaty) forming the basis of the national law: In this case, the responsibility of the United Kingdom for the consequences of the Maastricht Treaty was a result of the argumentation in the *Melchers* case. The European Commission of Human Rights stated in *Melchers* that actions against Member States because of EU acts are inadmissible because the European Court of Justice grants fundamental right protection equivalent to the ECHR. As far as the European Court of Justice cannot protect the fundamental rights (for example when EU Primary Law is concerned), the fundamental law protection must thus fall in the competence of the European Court of Human Rights.

While the *Matthews* case is about the responsibility of Members for EU acts, the cases *Waite and Kennedy* and *Beer and Regan* address the question whether the Strasbourg has jurisdiction over international organisations and which role the fundamental right protection within the international organisation plays. The European Court of Human Rights stated that although the foundation of international organisations does not release the High Contracting Parties of their obligations flowing from the ECHR, it is possible to give international organisations immunity in national judicial procedures if there is equivalent legal protection within the international organisation itself. But unlike in *Melchers* and *Heinz* the equivalent legal protection in the international organisation (here: the European Space Agency) did not lead to the immediate inadmissibility of an action but to a substantive examination through the European Court of Human Rights. Strasbourg thus started to check the fundamental right protection of other international organisations and refrained from unfolding judicial control over their acts as long as the fundamental right protection inside these international organisations is sufficient. This implies on the other hand, that the European Court of Human

---

Europe. Reports of Judgments and Decisions 1999-I, pp. 251 et seq. = 26 EuGRZ 1999, pp. 200 et seq.

45 ECtHR Application No 26083/94, *Richard Waite and Terry Kennedy v. Germany*, Judgment of 18 February 1999, European Court of Human Rights. Registry of the Court.Council of Europe. Reports of Judgments and Decisions 1999-I, pp. 393 et seq. = 26 EuGRZ 1999, pp. 207 et seq.

46 ECtHR Application 28934/95, *Karlheinz Beer and Philip Regan v. Germany*, Judgment of 18 February 1999.

47 ECtHR *Matthews* p. 266.

Rights was now presuming to have judicial control over acts of other international organisations in principle.

c. ECtHR waives its judicial control rights

The assumption of theoretical judicial control rights (that had not been used in reality until then) was the precondition to the landmark decision shaping the current legal situation: The European Court of Human Rights waives its control rights regarding the EU.

The newest judgement regarding the questions relevant to this work is *Bosphorus* of 2005.[48] Bosphorus Hava Yollari Turizm, a Turkish airline charter company, had leased two aircrafts from Yugoslav Airlines in 1992. During maintenance works in Ireland, one of the aircrafts was impounded by the Irish authorities executing an EU regulation which implemented UN sanctions against Yugoslavia. During the subsequent procedure, the European Court of Justice which was asked for a preliminary reference decided that the disputed EU regulation was applicable for leased aircrafts, with the result that the aircraft was kept impounded by the Irish authorities. The applicant company then turned to the European Court of Human Rights, complaining that the protection of property had been violated by Ireland.

In *Bosphorus*, the European Court of Human Rights quoted many principles of the previous case law, examining once again whether the EU still guarantees an equivalent fundamental right protection. This examination was even more detailed than in *Melchers*, but again led to the same result: The EU guarantees fundamental right protection equivalent to the ECHR. However, the European Court of Human Rights did not declare the application inadmissible *ratione materiae* as he had done in *Melchers*. The European Court of Human Rights concluded that since the fundamental right protection by the EU itself is sufficient, it can always be presumed that the implementation of EU law (including administrative acts!) is no violation of the ECHR. According to the European Court of Human Rights it must just be examined whether the granted fundamental right protection has been insufficient in the particular case, which is done through a superficial control of procedural and substantive conditions of fundamental right protection, not of the facts themselves. The European Court of Human Rights thus set up a blanket clause in favour of the EU and presumes that the fundamental rights granted by the ECHR are not violated by EU acts because of the fundamental

48 ECtHR Application 45036/98, *Bosphorus Hava Yolları Turizm ve Ticaret Anonim Şirketi v. Ireland*, Judgement of 30 June 2005.

right protection within the EU. The European Court of Human Rights thus seems to back out of the judicial control of EU acts.

The judgement stands in line with *Melchers*, *Heinz* and *Matthews* but goes beyond these decisions. Just like in these earlier decisions, the Strasbourg authorities acknowledge that in the EU fundamental rights are protected by the European Court of Justice in an equivalent way to the European Court of Human Rights. However, in *Bosphorus* this result leads the European Court of Human Rights to the presumption that EU acts cannot violate fundamental rights at all unless in exceptional cases the EU fundamental right protection has been insufficient. The European Court of Human Rights does not consider itself incapable to unfold judicial control over EU authorities or even the European Court of Justice in principle, but disclaims to execute this fundamental right protection in future because of its confidence to the European Court of Justice.

The judgement was opposed by some judges of the European Court of Human Rights, warning of possible double standards in the fundamental right protection. The concurring opinion of Judge *Ress* reveals concerns that violations of the fundamental right protection in the EU could possibly not be visible on the first sight while still not being in accordance with the guarantees of the ECHR.[49] The danger of possible double standards in the fundamental right protection is also criticised in the joint concurring opinion of Judges *Rozakis*, *Tulkens*, *Traja*, *Botoucharova*, *Zagrebelsky* and *Garlicki*.[50]

d. Conclusions

The case law of the European Commission of Human Rights and the European Court of Human Rights leaves no coherent impression. While Strasbourg rejected any judicial control over the EU as well as responsibility of the Member States for EU acts in the first years, it made incoherent decisions and judgements in a second phase, partly claiming the right of judicial control over the EU, partly rejecting even the responsibility of the Member States for acts of the EU. Finally, the European Court of Human Rights came to the conclusion that the implementation of EU acts cannot violate fundamental rights at all, since the fundamental right protection within the EU is equivalent to the system of the ECHR. It is clear that the EU itself and its institutions cannot be sued in Strasbourg. This is going to change with the accession of the EU to the ECHR. The precondition to this accession has been made by the entry into force of the Lisbon Treaty.

---

49 Concurring opinion of Judge *Ress* in ECtHR *Bosphorus*.

50 Joint concurring opinion of Judges *Rozakis*, *Tulkens*, *Traja*, *Botoucharova*, *Zagrebelsky* and *Garlicki* in ECtHR *Bosphorus*.

The question of a direct judicial control over the EU itself has to be distinguished from the question whether the Member States can be sued separately or jointly for acts of the EU and its institutions. The latter question cannot be answered so clearly. The acknowledgement of equivalent fundamental right protection within the EU led to different conclusions, but finally the European Court of Human Rights decided in *Bosphorus* that EU acts and their implementation cannot violate fundamental rights at all and the European Court of Human Rights had just to examine whether the system of legal protection of the EU was not available for the applicant in the particular case.

The responsibility of the Member States for EU acts therefore seems to be limited to exceptional cases. Moreover, as seen in the *Matthews* case, the Member States just remain responsible for EU acts as far as the legal protection by the European Court of Justice is legally excluded like in the field of the Founding Treaties of the EU (such as the Treaty on the Functioning of the European Union).

The author of this chapter is convinced that this responsibility of the Member States for EU acts (and therefore the fundamental right protection by the European Court of Human Rights) cannot be extended to cases where the European Court of Justice grants no legal protection voluntarily because it sees no need for such a legal protection as it is the case vis-à-vis acts of OLAF when the European Court of Justice dismisses actions for annulment.[51] The *Bosphorus* case shows that the European Court of Human Rights accepts all the European Court of Justice case law on fundamental right protection, including the case law regarding OLAF. If the European Court of Justice thus theoretically could grant legal protection but refrains to do so with the argument that OLAF could not violate fundamental rights, it follows that the European Court of Human Rights does not grant fundamental right protection vis-à-vis OLAF's on-the-spot inspections, investigation reports and forwarding of information.[52] If a person feels violated in his rights by an act of OLAF, neither national courts nor the European Court of Human Rights can provide legal protection.

Example 2:

The Austrian farmer C receives EU grants for buying and planting a specific type of wheat. Having received an anonymous call, OLAF (accompanied by the Austrian police) conducts a search on the premises of C's farm and finds out that C plants another type of wheat which is not supported by EU grants. As C has received EU grants for many years, OLAF asks the Austrian public prosecutor to seize C's accounting records

51 See the section below.

52 However, this does not mean that the European Court of Human Rights would not grant fundamental right protection vis-à-vis acts of national authorities during or as a consequence of an OLAF investigation. See below.

and computer and interviews C's workers. C is kept from making business as usual for almost one week and claims to be violated in the protection of property. As seen in example 1, C cannot contest OLAF's acts before national courts. If he submits an application to the European Court of Human Rights in Strasbourg contesting OLAF's acts directly, it will be dismissed. However, instead of OLAF C may contest the acts of the Austrian police or the Austrian Public Prosecutor before Austrian courts. If he stays without success there, he may – after all national remedies have been expired – turn to the European Court of Human Rights. In doing so, his only chance is to turn against the acts of Austrian law enforcement authorities. If he submits an application against OLAF's acts, suing Austria, all 27 EU Member States or the EU itself, the application will be dismissed, since the European Court of Human Rights presumes that the EU protects fundamental rights sufficiently.

The result could be a glaring gap in the fundamental right protection against acts of OLAF, since neither national courts nor the European Court of Human Rights are offering help (the first due to a lack of legal competence, the latter due to a lack of will). However, it is too early yet for such a final conclusion: as seen above, the EU courts in principle are able to protect the fundamental rights vis-à-vis OLAF. If their system of fundamental right protection vis-à-vis OLAF were flawless, the European Court of Human Rights would be right in its opinion that no additional judicial review was necessary.

Legal protection vis-à-vis direct acts of OLAF

It is now time to remember the difference between acts committed by OLAF itself (investigations reports, forwarding of information, on-the spot inspections in EU institutions) and acts recommended by OLAF, but committed by national authorities (on-the-spot inspections at economic operators). First, we will focus on the direct acts of OLAF.

As a result of the above elaboration, neither national courts nor the European Court of Human Rights but only the EU courts could in principal provide legal protection vis-à-vis on-the-spot-inspections, investigations reports and forwarding of information by OLAF. The need for legal protection must, therefore, be examined from the point of view of the EU courts. In this section the case law of the EU courts concerning legal protection vis-à-vis OLAF's on-the-spot inspections, investigation reports and forwarding of information is examined. It will be shown whether the use of different actions before the EU courts can be successful for the legal protection vis-à-vis the different acts of OLAF. While the positions of EU officials and economic operators affected by investigation reports and forwarding of information are similar, they have to be distinguished during on-the-spot inspections. Since economic operators may be affected by acts of national authorities conducting an on-the-spot inspection on request of OLAF, the next section will be dedicated to the legal protection vis-à-vis these acts.

Vis-à-vis the investigation report

The EU courts have made it clear that the investigation report is not regarded as a binding decision as defined in Article 288 Treaty on the Functioning of the European Union.[53] It is "*merely a recommendation or opinion without binding legal effects*"[54] that "*does not bring about a distinct change in the legal position of those persons who are referred to in it by name*".[55] The investigation report can thus not be contested with an action for annulment under Article 263 Treaty on the Functioning of the European Union. In this context it is of no relevance if the investigation report is submitted to national (judicial) authorities[56] or EU institutions because it has no binding legal effects for these authorities or institutions.[57] However, serious breaches of law by OLAF which lead to a wrong description of facts in the investigation report causing damage to a person do not need to be accepted. Reports of that nature may lead to a non-contractual liability (Article 340 para 2 Treaty on the Functioning of the European Union) that can be asserted by an action for damages under Article 268 Treaty on the Functioning of the European Union.[58] In these cases, a person that feels violated in his rights by an investigation report submitted by OLAF has no chance to contest the investigation report itself. But damages caused by a wrong description of facts in an investigation report may lead to compensation if breaches of law by OLAF led to the wrong description.
Example 3:

> *The French enterprise D receives financial aids of the EU for its ecological innovations. OLAF suspects the chief executive officer E to have committed fraud damaging the EU by submitting falsified invoices and balance sheets to the competent French authorities and the European Commission. After having finished the investigation that has supported the initial suspicion, OLAF drafts an investigation report including its observations, conclusions and a recommendation to open criminal proceedings against D and E.*

53 ECFI decision of 13 July 2004 in case T-29/03 *Comunidad Autónoma de Andalucía v Commission*; ECFI case T-309/03 *Manel Camós Grau v Commission* [2006].

54 ECFI case *Andalucía* at para 2.

55 ECFI case *Camós Grau* at para 1.

56 ECFI case *Tillack* at para 1.

57 ECFI case *Camós Grau* at para 1.

58 ECFI case *Camós Grau* at para 4.

The investigation report is sent to the competent French Public Prosecutor. E thinks that he should have had the possibility to make a statement on the charges before the report was sent. He considers his right to defend himself and thus his right to a fair trial being violated. He tries to contest OLAF's submission of the investigation report before the European Court of First Instance with an action for annulment. The action is dismissed, because the investigation report can not bring a distinct change in the legal position of persons referred to in it by name. However, an action for damages would be more promising: E could be successful in obtaining compensation for any material damage he suffered from a wrong description of facts in the investigation report (for example depressions) caused by OLAF's procedural error of not interviewing E.

Vis-à-vis the forwarding of information

Just like the investigation report, the forwarding of information to national authorities under Article 10 para 1 and 2 Reg 1073/99 is not considered a measure that has binding legal effects which could bring about a distinct change in the legal position of persons referred to in it.[59] Therefore, it can not be challenged by an action for annulment either. The statement of grounds is almost the same as in the case of the investigation report: The national judicial authorities can assess the content and significance freely within their competences.[60] The possible initiation of legal proceedings and subsequent legal acts remain in their sole responsibility. This freedom of the national authorities is not called into question by the duty to cooperate under Article 4 para 3 Treaty on European Union when OLAF forwards them information, because this duty only obliges the national authorities to examine the information carefully and draw appropriate consequences from it in order to comply with EU law.

The situation as regards to the forwarding of information to the EU institution concerned under Article 10 para 3 Reg 1073/99 is alike the hitherto existing case law regarding the forwarding of information to national authorities.[61] The forwarding of information to the institution concerned has no binding legal effects for this institution and cannot be challenged by an Article 14/90a complaint and a subsequent action.[62]

However, the forwarding of information can cause damage. In the case of *Franchet and Byk* the European Court of Justice states that the fact that OLAF forwarded files on the applicants to national authorities *without giving the applicants*

59 ECFI case *Tillack* at para 1.

60 See for the following ECFI case *Tillack* at para 1.

61 ECFI decision of 18 December 2003 in case T-215/02 *Santiago Gómez-Reino v Commission* at para 50-51.

62 ECFI case T-261/09P *Commission v Antonello Violetti and others and Nadine Schmit* [2010].

a chance to express their views on the facts directly concerning them and to defend themselves (under breach of Article 4 of Decision 1999/369) "*necessarily produced feelings of injustice and frustration in the applicants. It should be noted that that damage was the direct result of the unlawful conduct of OLAF (forwarding of information without hearing the affected persons) and that there is thus a causal link between that conduct and the damage.*"[63] The European Commission was ordered to pay compensation for non-material damage.

Example 4:

> *OLAF suspects the Italian Member of the European Parliament F to have accepted bribes and his brother G, who owns a restaurant in Italy, of having committed money laundering in order to help F hiding the illegal origin of the money. OLAF summarizes its observations and forwards the information regarding F to the President of the European Parliament and the information regarding G to the competent Italian Public Prosecutor. Neither F nor G will be successful in contesting the forwarding of information with an action for annulment before the European Court of First Instance. However, if OLAF should have committed a procedural error (such as unnecessarily not informing them about the investigation) that caused them any material damage both stand a chance to obtain compensation by the help of an action for damages.*

We have seen that the European Court of Justice and the European Court of First Instance unfold a very restrictive case law in regards to legal protection vis-à-vis forwarding of information as well as investigation reports. They are open to grant compensation for damages, but always refuse fundamental right protection with the argument that these measures have no binding legal effects which could bring about a distinct change in the legal position of persons referred to in it. However, although compensation for damages might be sufficient in these cases, the next section will show that the same argumentation of the EU courts regarding on-the-spot inspections is partly problematic.

Vis-à-vis on-the-spot inspections

Since on-the-spot inspections within EU institutions and concerning economic operators have different legal grounds[64], there are different systems of legal protection as well. Conducting an on-the-spot inspection within an EU institution, OLAF enjoys extensive permissions of control that can even affect fundamental

63 ECFI case T-48/05 *Yves Franchet and Daniel Byk v Commission* [2008]. See also *Niestedt/Boeckmann*, Verteidigungsrechte bei internen Untersuchungen des OLAF – das Urteil Franchet und Byk des Gerichts erster Instanz und die Reform der Verordnung (EG) Nr. 1073/1999, EuZW (2009) pp. 70 et seq.

64 Commission decision establishing the European Anti-fraud Office, Interinstitutional Agreement and the Model Decision, Reg 1073/99, Reg 1074/99, Reg 2185/96.

rights, as in the case of a seizure of documents.[65] Albeit Article 14 Reg 1073/99 stipulates the control of the legality of OLAF's acts as part of an internal investigation, the EU courts seem to be of the opinion that indirect legal control would be sufficient. In *Gómez-Reino* the European Court of Justice states that in cases concerning EU officials, measures in preparation of a final decision cannot burden their legal positions. Therefore, these measures can only be challenged indirectly with an action against the final decision made upon the affected EU official.[66] This broad denial of a right to appeal directly seems to include all investigative acts done by OLAF. This legal opinion restricts the scope of the complaint right very much[67] and has led to criticism.[68] It is the opinion of the author that this case law is against the spirit and purpose of Article 14 Reg 1073/99 and negates a need for fundamental right protection that cannot be properly addressed by indirect legal control.

Notwithstanding this jurisprudence as regards to fundamental rights the EU courts permit actions for damages if OLAF or its officials cause damages during an internal investigation.[69] Just as it is the case with the investigation report and the forwarding of information, this compensation for damage can also include non-material damage caused by an on-the-spot inspection within EU institutions[70], for example compensation for damages of honour.

As regards to on-the-spot inspections concerning economic operators OLAF's employees, as indicated above, depend on assistance of national authorities to execute their control rights coercively. OLAF itself has no coercive powers vis-à-vis economic operators. The only case law regarding economic operators concerns the forwarding of information, where the European Court of First Instance states that such an act cannot entail gravamen and therefore not be challenged.[71] Since OLAF is dependent on external assistance conducting an on-the-spot inspection concerning an economic operator, it can be concluded in the light of the

65 See for example *Tittor*, OLAF und die Europäisierung des Strafverfahrens (2006) pp. 165-166.

66 ECJ decision of 8 April 2003 in case C-471/02(P) *Santiago Gómez-Reino v Commission* at para 62 and 65.

67 Art 14 Reg 1073/99 and a subsequent action still serve as a legal basis for fundamental right protection vis-à-vis press releases. See ECFI *Franchet and Byk*.

68 See for example *Tittor* pp. 165-166; European Parliament resolution of 24 April 2009 on the protection of the Communities' financial interests and the fight against fraud – Annual report 2007 (2008/2242(INI)), OJ 2004 C 103/435; *Theato*, Contribution to a public hearing of the Committee on Budgetary Control of the European Parliament on 12 and 13 July 2005.

69 ECFI case *Camós Grau* at para 2-4.

70 Civil Service Tribunal case F-23/05 *Jean-Louis Giraudy v Commision* [2007]; ECFI *Franchet and Byk*.

71 ECFI case *Tillack* at para 1.

Gómez-Reino case that legal control vis-à-vis the executing national authorities is regarded as sufficient. OLAF cannot set an act that would burden an economic operator.[72] As has been noted before, in the light of the *Tillack* case in which the Belgian police searched a journalist's office accompanied by OLAF and seized *inter alia* documents, procedural acts by national authorities cannot be ascribed to OLAF.[73] National remedies are supposed to offer sufficient legal protection against acts set by national authorities during an investigation conducted by OLAF. Apart from fundamental right protection, the action for damages should be open for economic operators that suffered damage from OLAF's employees conducting an on-the-spot inspection.

Example 5:

> *OLAF receives information that the lobbyist H has bribed the EU official I. OLAF opens an investigation on the case and conducts a search in I's office in a building of the European Commission. OLAF further asks the Belgian police to conduct search in H's office in Brussels. The Belgian police does so accompanied by OLAF investigators. Both on-the-spot inspections lead to several long-term seizures, which is regarded by both affected persons as a violation of the protection of property. Both H and I try to contest the seizures with actions for annulment. The EU Civil Service Court dismisses I's action for the same reason the European Court of First Instance dismisses H's action: because OLAF's acts are regarded as measures in preparation of a final decision that cannot burden the legal situation of the affected person. While the economic operator H still can contest the measures of the Belgian authorities (in his case not OLAF, but the Belgian police has conducted the search coercively and seized his property) with national remedies and an application to the European Court of Human Rights, the EU official has no further remedy. However, both H and I have a chance to succeed before the EU courts with an action for damages in receiving compensation for their material damage if OLAF made a procedural error.*

The EU courts do not grant fundamental right protection vis-à-vis on-the-spot inspections conducted by OLAF, arguing that indirect legal control (remedies against final decisions) would be sufficient. This leaves EU officials affected by seizures *etc* without protection until a final decision is made (often long time) later. Economic operators have on the other hand still the possibility to challenge all acts committed by national authorities conducting an on-the-spot inspection together with OLAF. This will be shown in the next section.

---

72 There is no possibility of bringing an action against purely factual acts, see *Grabitz/Hilf* (eds.), Das Recht der Europäischen Union. Teil I, Primärrecht (1999) Article 173 note in margin 5.

73 In *Tillack*, a complaint against an act set by OLAF (the forwarding of information), which led to a domiciliary visit and the seizure of documents, is rejected.

Legal protection vis-à-vis acts of indirect enforcement

The section above examined the question whether there is sufficient legal protection vis-à-vis acts set by OLAF and revealed a gap as regards to on-the-spot inspections within the EU institutions concerning EU officials. This leaves open the question of legal protection vis-à-vis acts of national authorities obliged to assist OLAF as in the execution of OLAF's control rights vis-à-vis economic operators. Procedural acts of national authorities during or as a consequence of an OLAF investigation cannot be ascribed to OLAF. Nevertheless, the national authorities do not act exclusively within the realm of their national laws. Article 4 para 3 Treaty on European Union obliges the Member States to "*take any appropriate measures, general or particular, to ensure fulfilment of the obligations arising out of the Treaties or resulting from the acts taken of the institutions of the Union.*" Furthermore, they have to facilitate the achievement of the EU's tasks. This duty to act and the obligation to tolerate regarding OLAF investigations could be seen as indirect enforcement of EU law by the Member States, so that the national authorities (including judicial authorities) have to comply with their national law only in accordance with the judgement of the European Court of Justice in the case *Deutsche Milchkontor.*[74]

In this case, the European Court of Justice had made a preliminary decision in a dispute between several German dairies and the competent German authority for paying support for the processing of skimmed-milk powder. One of the questions the European Court of Justice had to answer concerned the possible application of national law by national authorities enforcing EU law in case the latter does not include (substantive or procedural) rules for a specific situation or question. Although the question came from a different context, the answer is still highly relevant for national authorities assisting OLAF to execute its control rights. The European Court of Justice stated that national authorities have to apply their national law if there are no common rules in EU law (including the general principles) regarding the same question. If national law is applied it must be restricted as far as it is necessary for a uniform application of EU law and an equal treatment of economic operators. In this respect, the case *Hauer* is of interest. In this case, the European Court of Justice had to adopt a preliminary ruling in a dispute about a German wine-grower, Liselotte Hauer, who was prohibited

---

74 ECJ joined cases 205 to 215/82 *Deutsche Milchkontor GmbH and others v Federal Republic of Germany* [1983] at para 17.

to plant new vines on the basis of a provision stipulated in an EU regulation. The competent German Administrative court asked the European Court of Justice for an interpretation of this provision of the EU regulation in order to answer the question whether the EU regulation must be applied in a way taking regard to a certain German law on wine-growing. Ms. Hauer considered her fundamental right to freely pursue a trade, stipulated in the German Constitution being violated if the EU regulation was fully applicable in her case. In the judgment, the European Court of Justice made clear that possible infringement of fundamental rights by measures of EU institutions can only be judged in the light of EU law itself and not with "special criteria for assessment stemming from the legislation or constitutional law of a particular Member State"[75], because otherwise it would damage the substantive unity and efficacy of EU law. This applies also to national authorities assisting OLAF to execute its control rights: In the light of the *Hauer* judgement, national law applied in order to enforce EU law must not lead to special criteria for assessment stemming from the legislation or constitutional law of a particular Member State.

The judgments *Deutsche Milchkontor* and *Hauer* have special consequences for the application of the ECHR by national authorities enforcing EU law, because the ECHR forms part of the general principles of EU law as well as of the legal systems of all EU Member States. EU law supersedes for example Austrian law, including Article 18 Austrian Federal Constitution which obliges all Austrian administrative and judicial authorities to stick to the Austrian laws and constitutional laws, which also includes the fundamental rights. When an Austrian (judicial) authority enforces EU law, it is bound to Austrian fundamental rights only within the framework specified by the judgements *Deutsche Milchkontor* (meaning national law can only be applied if the EU law does not provide rules for a certain situation, and only to the extent uniformity of EU law is not jeopardised) and *Hauer*: the compliance with fundamental rights can only be assessed in the light of the EU law itself. The ECHR, forming part of the Austrian constitutional law[76] as well as the general principles of EU law, cannot lead to special criteria for assessment stemming from the Austrian legislation or constitutional law and therefore must be applied.

The compliance of Austrian authorities with fundamental rights during and in the aftermath of an OLAF investigation thus falls under the judicial control of the competent criminal courts or the Austrian Constitutional court. After all national remedies have been exhausted, the fundamental right protection then falls under

75 ECJ *Hauer* at para 14.

76 The ECHR has been declared to Austrian constitutional law by a federal constitutional act in 1964. See Austrian federal law gazette 1964/59.

the judicial control of the European Court of Human Rights in Strasbourg. The European Court of Human Rights also watches over the application of the fundamental rights at the indirect enforcement of EU law.[77] In its judgement of 2007 in the *Tillack* case, the European Court of Human Rights proved its will to grant fundamental right protection also in regards to an OLAF investigation.[78]

Mr. Tillack, a journalist working as a correspondence clerk for a German magazine in Brussels had written an article on corruption within the European Commission, quoting an internal EU paper. OLAF suspected him of having bribed an EU official in order to obtain the document and asked the Belgian police to conduct a house search in Mr. Tillack's apartment and office in Brussels. The Belgian police did so in attendance of OLAF controllers and seized two computers, four mobile phones, virtually all documents they detected and even some furniture. Mr. Tillack submitted an action to the European Court of First Instance which was dismissed because the police's acts cannot be ascribed to OLAF. After having exhausted all national remedies under Belgian law, Mr. Tillack turned to the European Court of Human Rights, claiming that the seizures of a journalist's documents would violate the freedom of expression. The European Court of Human Rights convicted Belgium for infringements of the Convention committed by the Belgian police during an OLAF investigation and acting on a suggestion by OLAF.

It can thus be concluded that the fundamental right protection vis-à-vis acts of national authorities acting during or in consequence of an investigation of OLAF is sufficient. National judicial authorities and the European Court of Human Rights grant judicial control and fundamental right protection in those cases.

Example 6:

> *OLAF investigates against the Austrian entrepreneur J who is suspected of having committed transnational value added tax fraud. OLAF asks the competent Austrian tax authority to conduct a house search in J's warehouse. OLAF investigators participate in the house search. Since neither J nor his employees are attendant while the house search takes place, J considers his rights under the Austrian criminal procedure violated. He contests the measure of the tax authority with national remedies. After having exhausted his last remedy under Austrian law, he can turn to the European Court of Human Rights, claiming a violation of his right to a fair trial.*

---

77 EComHR *Procola*; EComHR *Cantoni*.

78 ECtHR Application 20477/05, *Tillack v. Belgium*, 27 November 2007.

Conclusions

OLAF's different powers in regards to internal and external investigations have an impact on the issue of legal protection against it. Neither the investigation report nor the forwarding of information are regarded as decisions under Article 288 Treaty on the Functioning of the European Union. There is thus no direct remedy against these acts. However, since the EU courts began to grant compensation for damages as regards to the investigation report and the forwarding of information the possible lack of legal protection is confined to the fundamental rights. The fundamental right protection does not fall in the jurisprudence of the national courts. The European Court of Human Rights does not provide fundamental right protection vis-à-vis acts of OLAF and its officials directly (only indirectly vis-à-vis acts of national authorities assisting OLAF), presuming that EU acts do not violate fundamental rights.

The author cannot agree completely with the legal opinion of the EU courts that there was no need for legal protection vis-à-vis OLAF's on-the-spot investigations because no act could entail gravamen. It is true that OLAF has no coercive powers concerning economic operators and thus cannot infringe their fundamental rights. In regards to economic operators, OLAF needs the assistance of national authorities which are bound to the fundamental rights and fall under the judicial review of national instances of appeal and the European Court of Human Rights. The latter basically confirmed this case law of the EU courts by convicting Belgium in the *Tillack* case for violations of the freedom of speech when they conducted a house search in a journalist's office and home on behalf of OLAF and seized documents and other items. Thus, regarding economic operators there is really no further need for legal protection against OLAF.

Things have to be seen differently in regard of on-the-spot inspections within EU institutions where OLAF needs no help of other authorities. Nobody could be sued for violations of fundamental rights but OLAF. However, to an EU official concerned the seizure of documents by OLAF is just the same as a confiscation by the police. Aware of this, the EU legislator has given EU officials the possibility for a complaint under Article 14/90a. But the case law of the EU courts has dismissed all actions for annulment against negative decisions of OLAF's Director-General on these complaints as inadmissible. These rulings ignore a need for legal protection and lead to a lack of fundamental right protection.

The lack of fundamental right protection for EU officials vis-à-vis OLAF's on-the-spot inspections within EU institutions observed in this article is at first glance not a problem of legislation, since all legislative possibilities for an effective remedy already exist on paper (Article 14/90a). The issue could be resolved solely by a change in the case law, either of the EU courts or the European Court of Human Rights. The EU courts would have to change their approach to actions for annulments against negative decisions on Article 14/90a complaints, enabling the purpose of these complaints. In recent years, the EU courts have already begun to open their case law for actions for damages when OLAF caused material damage during its investigations. Maybe one day the EU courts acknowledge that OLAF's acts during on-the-spot inspections within EU institutions can be burdensome and stop dismissing on principle actions for annulment against these acts.

A second pathway to closing the gap in the fundamental right protection would be a fundamental change in the case law of the European Court of Human Rights in Strasbourg. If the European Court of Human Rights would start to unfold direct jurisdiction over EU acts including decisions and judgments of the European Court of Justice, it could protect EU officials against violations of fundamental rights committed by OLAF. Although in some judgments the European Court of Human Rights left the impression that such a jurisdiction over EU authorities could be possible, the European Court of Human Rights has not yet departed from the notion that EU acts and their implementation do not violate fundamental rights at all because all EU acts were subject to an effective fundamental right control system of the EU courts. Maybe the future accession of the EU to the ECHR will motivate the European Court of Human Rights to rethink this case law. Either way, one can only hope that the fundamental right protection vis-à-vis OLAF will become accessible for everyone soon.

Abbreviations, location and role of European bodies

European Union Institutions:

European Court of Justice (ECJ); location: Luxemburg; task: ensure that in the interpretation and the application of Founding Treaties of the European Union (such as the TFEU) the law is observed; different types of actions; appellate court for the ECFI; it's case-law is highly important for the interpretation of EU law.

European Court of First Instance (ECFI); location: Luxemburg; task: in most cases court of first instance to ensure that in the interpretation and the application of Founding Treaties of the European Union the law is observed; appellate court for the European Union Civil Service Tribunal.

European Union Civil Service Tribunal; location: Luxemburg; task: court of first instance for disputes between the EU and its officials.

European Commission; location: Brussels; task: propose legal acts of the EU, ensure the application of EU law, execute the EU budget, take initiatives to promote the general interest of the EU, further coordinating, executing and managing functions.

European Anti-Fraud Office (Office de Lutte Anti-Fraude – OLAF); Directorate-General of the European Commission with a special status; location: Brussels; task: the protection of the EU's financial interests by investigation and prevention of fraud, corruption and any other illegal activity affecting the financial interests of the EU.

Council of Europe Institutions:

European Court of Human Rights (ECtHR); location: Strasbourg; task: ensure the observance of the engagements undertaken by the Member States of the ECHR; individuals considering their fundamental rights violated may submit an application to the ECtHR after all domestic remedies have been exhausted.

European Commission of Human Rights (EComHR); former location: Strasbourg; former task: serving as first instance for applications of individuals complaining the violation of their fundamental rights in order to proof their admissibility; admissible applications were brought before the ECtHR by the EComHR; abolished by the 11th Protocol to the ECHR (entered into force 1998).

Conventions, treaties and other important EU legal acts:

Convention for the Protection of Human Rights and Fundamental Freedoms (ECHR); 1953.

Protocol to the Convention for the Protection of Human Rights and Fundamental Freedoms (1st Protocol to the ECHR); 1954.

Regulation (EEC, Euratom, ECSC) No 259/68 of the Council of 29 February 1968 laying down the Staff Regulations of Officials and the Conditions of Employment of Other Servants of the European Communities and instituting special measures temporarily applicable to officials of the Commission, OJ 1968 L 56/1 (Staff Regulations), 1968.

Treaty on European Union (TEU, Maastricht Treaty); 1993.

Protocol No. 11 to the Convention for the Protection of Human Rights and Fundamental Freedoms (11th Protocol to the ECHR); 1998.

Regulation (EC) No 1073/1999 of the European Parliament and of the Council of 25 May 1999 concerning investigations conducted by the European Anti-Fraud Office (OLAF), OJ 1999 L 136/1 (Reg 1073/99); 1999.

Treaty of Lisbon amending the Treaty on European Union and the Treaty establishing the European Community (Lisbon Treaty); 2009.

Charter of Fundamental Rights of the European Union; 2009.

Treaty on the Functioning of the European Union (TFEU); 2009.